D0203657

Mexican Banking and Investment in Transition

Mexican Banking and Investment in Transition

John A. Adams, Jr.

Q

QUORUM BOOKS
Westport, Connecticut • London

332.109
A21m

Library of Congress Cataloging-in-Publication Data

Adams, John A., 1951–
    Mexican banking and investment in transition / John A. Adams, Jr.
      p. cm.
    Includes bibliographical references and index.
    ISBN 1–56720–054–0 (alk. paper)
    1. Mexico—Economic conditions—20th century. 2. Banks and
banking—Mexico. 3. Investments, Foreign—Mexico. 4. Mexico—
Commerce. 5. Devaluation of currency—Mexico. I. Title.
HC135.A64   1997
332.1'0972—dc20   96–38333

British Library Cataloguing in Publication Data is available.

Copyright © 1997 by John A. Adams, Jr.

All rights reserved. No portion of this book may be
reproduced, by any process or technique, without
the express written consent of the publisher.

Library of Congress Catalog Card Number: 96–38333
ISBN: 1–56720–054–0

First published in 1997

Quorum Books, 88 Post Road West, Westport, CT 06881
An imprint of Greenwood Publishing Group, Inc.

Printed in the United States of America

The paper used in this book complies with the
Permanent Paper Standard issued by the National
Information Standards Organization (Z39.48–1984).

10 9 8 7 6 5 4 3 2 1

To my dad

Col. John A. Adams
Director
First Security National Bank

University Libraries
Carnegie Mellon University
Pittsburgh PA 15213-3890

Contents

Figures   ix

Glossary of Terms and Acronyms   xi

Acknowledgments   xvii

Introduction   xxi

1. Mexico on the Brink: Turmoil and Change   1

2. Banking and Debt in Mexico   13

3. U.S.-Mexican Border: Crossroads of Trade and Finance   32

4. Regional Trade and Cooperation   51

5. Investment in Mexico   67

6. The Christmas Surprise: Devaluation 1994   87

7. Crisis of Confidence: 1995   112

8. Tequila Hangover: Impact of the Peso Crisis on Argentina   135

9. Back from the Abyss   153

Appendixes   177

A. Mexican Banking and Financial Milestones, 1935–97   179

B. Foreign Investment Law, December 27, 1993   181

C. Foreign Ownership Allowed in 1993 Investment Law   194

Bibliography   199

Index   233

Figures

1-1	Mexican Economy: 1984–97	8
2-1	Economic Indicators: 1972–83	17
2-2	Mexican Bank Privatization: 1991–92	25
2-3	Population per Bank Branch	26
3-1	In-Bond Maquilas: 1970–96	37
3-2	Twin-Cities Border Population: 1950–2000	38
3-3	U.S.-Mexico Trade: 1989–95	44
4-1	Risk Classification by Region: 1994	56
5-1	Cumulative Flow of Direct Foreign Investment as Measured by the National Foreign Investment Commission	71
5-2	Foreign Investment in Mexico: 1988–95	72
5-3	Foreign Investment in Mexican Stocks: 1993	74
5-4	Securities and Investments Offered for Sale in Mexico	75
5-5	Foreign Investment by Major Economic Blocs	80
5-6	Direct Foreign Investment by Sector	82
5-7	Cumulative Direct Foreign Investment in Mexico	82
5-8	Authorized Foreign Investment	83
6-1	International Average Savings Rates	91
6-2	Cost of Funds, Banco de Mexico: 1994–95	92
6-3	U.S. Fed-Funds Interest Rates: 1991–96	94
6-4	Key Monetary and Economic Indicators: 1993–95	96
6-5	U.S. Interest Rates: Effect on Mexico	101

6-6   Foreign Investment in Mexican Equity: August 1994 and 1995 and
      December 1994   102
7-1   Mexico: Then and Now   114
7-2   The Old and the New: A Comparison of the Mexico Plans   118
7-3   Petroleum Production: 1980–94   121
7-4   Mexico: Ratio of Past-Due Loans to Total Loans: 1979–96   124
7-5   Average Nominal Annual Interest Rates   126
8-1   Latin America Inflation Profile   137
8-2   Net Capital Flows to Latin America   138
9-1   Mexico Stabilization Funds: 1995   154
9-2   Mexico: Peso Value, 1900–97   161

Glossary of Terms and Acronyms

AD	Antidumping
ADE	Agreement for Immediate Support of Bank Deposits
ADRs	American Drawing Rights
AFORE	Administracion de Fondos de Retiro (Retirement Fund Manager)
ALADI	Association for Latin American Integration
AJUSTABONOS	Fixed rate 3- or 5-year Mexican bonds
APC	Alliance for Agriculture
APEC	Asian Pacific Economic Cooperation
ARE	Alliance for Economic Recovery
AUSEE	Agreement of Unity to Overcome the Economic Emergency
BA	Bankers Acceptances
BANAMEX	Banco Nacional de Mexico
BANCOMEXT	Banco Nacional de Comercio Exterior
BANXICO	Banco de Mexico (the central bank)
BECC	Border Environmental Cooperation Commission
BEMs	Big emerging markets: A group of target countries identified by the U.S. Department of Commerce as fast-growing economies of the next decade
BIP	Border Industrialization Program
BIS	Bank of International Settlements
BIT	Bilateral Investment Treaty

BONDES	Floating rate 1- or 2-year Mexican bonds
BTA	Border Trade Alliance
CANACINTRA	Camara Nacional de la Industria de Transformacion (National Chamber for Manufacturing Industries)
CBI	Caribbean Basin Initiative
CETES	Mexican treasury notes: zero coupon, peso-denominated
CEMAI	Consejo Empresarial Mexicano para Asuntos Internacionales (Mexican Entrepreneurial Council for International Affairs)
CFE	Comision Federal de Electricidad
CGPE	Criterios Generales de Politica Economica (General Criteria for Economic Policy)
CISEN	Center for National Security Investigations
CITEL	Inter-American Commission on Telecommunications
CME	Chicago Mercantile Exchange
CNB	Comision Nacional Bancaria
CNBV	Comision Nacional Bancaria Valores
CNIE	National Commission of Foreign Investment (Mexico)
CNIME	Consejo Nacional de la Industria Maquiladora de Exportacíon (National Council of the In-Bond Export Industry)
CONASUPO	National Popular Subsistence Company
CTM	Confederacion de Trabajadores Mexicanos (Confederation of Mexican Workers)
Current Account	The broad measure of trade, service, and investment flows with other countries.
CVD	Countervailing Duty
DF	Distrito Federal (Federal District: Mexico City or Mexico, D.F.)
DFI	Direct Foreign Investment
Dumping	The sale of goods into a market at prices below which comparable goods are sold in the exporter's home market; could involve foreign products that have been subsidized by the government.
EAI	Enterprise for the Americas Initiative
EC	European Economic Community
ECLAC	Economic Commission for Latin America and the Caribbean
"ejidos"	Community-owned farms set aside in the land redistribution after the Mexican Revolution of 1910
EPA	Environmental Protection Agency
ESF	Exchange Stabilization Fund
EXIM	Export-Import Bank

EZLN	Ejercito Zapatista de Liberacion Nacional (Zapatista Army of National Liberation)
FAMEVAL	Stockbroker insurance fund
FDI	Foreign Direct Investment
FICORCA	Fideicomiso para la Cobertura de Riesgos Cambiarios (Trust Fund for Converting Foreign Exchange Risk)
FOBAPROA	Fondo Bancario de Proteccion al Ahorro (Mexico's deposit insurance agency)
FOMC	Federal Open Market Committee
FTA	Free Trade Agreement
G-3	Free trade group: Mexico, Colombia, Venezuela (est. June 1994)
GAO	U.S. General Accounting Office
GATS	General Agreement on Trade in Services
GATT	General Agreement on Tariffs and Trade
GDP	Gross Domestic Product
GDSs	Global Depositary Shares
GNP	Gross National Product
GSP	Generalized System of Preferences
IBC	International Boundary Commission
IBS	International Bank of Settlements
IBWC	International Boundary and Water Commission
ICRAS	Interagency County Risk Assessment System
IDB	Inter-American Development Bank
IFC	International Finance Corporation
IMF	International Monetary Fund (est. 1945)
IMSS	Mexican Social Security Institute
In-bond	Offshore production of component parts for re-export; known as the ''maquila'' industry in Mexico
INEGI	Instituto Nacional de Estadistica, Geografica, e Informatica (National Institute of Statistics, Geography, and Information)
INFONAVIT	Workers' Housing National Institute
IPC	Indice de Precios y Cotizaciones (Mexican Stock Index)
IPR	Intellectual Property Rights
ISAC	Industry Sectory Advisory Committee
ISI	Import-substitution industrial
ISSFAM	Social Security for Mexican Armed Forces Institute
ISSSTE	Government Workers' Social Security and Services Institute
ITC	International Trade Commission
ITO	International Trade Organization

IVA	Impuesto al Valor Agregado (VAT)
JIT	Just-in-time
LAFTA	Latin American Free Trade Association
LDC	Less developed country
LIBOR	London Inter-bank Offer Rate
MAI	Multilateral Agreement in Investment
Maquila	Manufacturing company located in Mexico that imports components duty-free and exports finished goods, paying duty only on the value added in Mexico
MERCOSUR	Southern cone common market of Argentina, Brazil, Paraguay, Uruguay, and Chile
MFN	Most-Favored-Nation treatment
MIB	Mexican Investment Board
MITI	Ministry of International Trade and Industry (Japan)
MOU	Memorandum of Understanding
MTN	Multilateral Trade Negotiations
NADBank	North American Development Bank
NAFINSA	Nacional Financiera, S.A. (National Financing Institution)
NAFTA	North American Free Trade Agreement
NIC	newly industrialized country
NTB	Non-tariff barrier
OAS	Organization of American States
OECD	Organization for Economic Cooperation and Development (est. 1961—membership 25 industrialized nations)
OPEC	Organization of Petroleum Exporting Countries
PACTO	Pacto de Solidaridad Economica (wage and price control policy to bring down inflation)
PAN	Partido Accion Nacional (National Action Party)
Par Bond	Collateralized fixed-rate bond set up with Brady Package to mature in the year 2019
PARAUSEE	Action Program to Reinforce the Agreement of Unity to Overcome the Economic Emergency
PARM	Partido Autentico de la Revolucion Mexicana
PDM	Partido Democrata Mexicano
PEA	Poblacion Economicamente Activa (Economically-active population)
PECE	Pacto para la Estabilidad y el Crecimiento Economico, also known as the ''Pacto''
Pemex	Petroleos Mexicanos (state-owned Mexican oil company)

PIB	Producto Interno Bruto (GDP)
PPICE	Program for Industrial Policy and Foreign Trade
PRD	Partido de la Revolucion Democratica (Party of the Democratic Revolution)
PRI	Partido Revolucionario Institucional (est. January 1946); formerly know as the PRM—Party of the Mexican Revolution (est. 1929)
PROAFI	Programa de Apoyo a Deudores del Fisco (Program for Tax-Debtor Support)
PROCAPTE	Programa de Capitalizacion Temporal de las Instituciones de Credito (Temporary Capitalization Program for Credit Institutions)
PRODUCE	Direct and Productive Assistance to Agriculture Program
PROMIN	Programa Unico de Financiamiento a la Modernizacion Industrial (Sole Financing Program for Industrial Modernization)
PRONAFICE	Programa Nacional de Fomento Industrial y Comercio Exterior (National Program of Industrial Development and Foreign Trade)
RNIE	National Registry of Foreign Investment (Mexico)
SAGAR	Ministry of Agriculture, Livestock and Rural Development
SAR	Sistema de Ahorro para el Retiro (Retirement Savings Fund)
SECOFI	Secretaria de Comercio y Fomento Industrial (Mexico Department of Commerce and Industrial Promotion)
Section 301	In the 1974 Trade Act, a statutory tool to help open foreign markets when another country is violating a trade agreement or is engaged in unfair trade practices
SEDESOL	Mexican environmental agency similar to U.S. EPA
SEDUE	Secretaria de Desarrollo Urbano y Ecologia: Merged with other departments in 1992 to form SEDESOL
SELA	Latin American Economic System
SHCP	Secretaria de Hacienda y Credito Publico (Ministry of Finance and Public Credit)
SIC	standard industrial classification
SMEs	Small- and medium-sized enterprises
TDA	Tasa de Desempleo Abierto (Open Unemployment Rate)
TelMex	Telefonos de Mexico: state-owned phone company privatized in 1990
Tesobonos	Short-term dollar-denominated bonds
TIIE	Tasa de Interes Interbancaria de Equilibrio (Average Balance Interest Rate)
TIIP	Tasa de Interes Interbancaria Promedio (Average Interbank Interest Rate)
UDI	Unidades de Inversion (Loan Restructuring Program)

Glossary of Terms and Acronyms

UNCTAD	United Nations Conference on Trade and Development
USDA	U.S. Department of Agriculture
USITC	U.S. International Trade Commission
USTR	U.S. Trade Representative
VAT	Value-added tax
VRA	Voluntary Restraint Agreement
VRR	Value Recovery Rights
WTO	World Trade Organization (est. January 1, 1995 as successor to GATT)

Acknowledgments

The conclusion of the North American Free Trade Agreement (NAFTA) in late 1993 between the United States, Mexico, and Canada was a pivotal event resulting in a major impact on U.S.-Mexican financial services and banking. The evolution of the cross-border banking and financial services during the past decade was impacted by a number of key events in Mexico that were influenced and shaped by the nationalization of the Mexican banks in 1982 as well as the advent of the debt crisis in the mid-1980's. The devaluation of the peso in late 1994 raised many questions about the future of Mexico's economic stability and investment environment. These events, along with the development of the U.S.-Mexican border commercial and financial operations, had a tremendous influence on the financial services and investment portions of NAFTA. It was in this environment of the pre-NAFTA debate that I began this project.

With the implementation of NAFTA on January 1, 1994, significant changes were needed in the Mexican banking and investment laws, and there was the need to update and modernize the financial services sector. Fair market access and the "transparency" of Mexican rules and procedures are paramount to the expansion of U.S. banking subsidiaries into Mexico, as well as the future stability of the Mexican banking sector. At the same time, Mexico, while functionally and technologically underbanked, did not desire to be overwhelmed by foreign banking operations. This was neither prudent nor politically acceptable given the historical relationship of the two nations. By early 1994, the procedural framework had been established between Mexico and the United States to review foreign banking applications. An understanding of these tremendously significant events was facilitated by a large number of people in both Mexico and the United States.

The research and capture of these events has taken me to a broad cross-section of experts, financial institutions, and data sources in both the United States and Mexico. During the course of this project the Mexican banking and investment sectors underwent extensive changes, and I am indebted to those who gave freely of their time, knowledge, and resources. I am deeply grateful to the staff at the Southwestern Graduate School of Banking (SWGSB) at SMU in Dallas for their assistance and counsel during the early stages of this project. Special thanks is extended to Dr. William E. Pinney for his encouragement and professional expertise, as well as Dr. George Hemple and Kay McKee for their unwavering support and dedication to the banking profession.

The staff at the Union National Bank of Texas, with locations in Laredo and San Antonio, provided timely assistance and encouragement at all stages of this project. I have gained a vast amount of knowledge on the banking industry, international trade, banking in Mexico, and trade finance as well as an appreciation of the U.S.–Mexican border region from Ray M. Keck, Jr., UNB Chairman, and John H. Keck, UNB President and CEO. Their advice and contributions proved timely.

Governor Lawrence Lindsey at the Federal Reserve Board in Washington, D.C., along with Charles Siegman, Senior Associate Director, Division of International Finance, provided tremendous insight into the changing banking and regulatory environment as well as the Fed's interaction with Mexico during and after the debt crisis. The U.S. Treasury Department was very helpful with updates and background materials on NAFTA, the Mexican devaluation of 1994, and the North American Development Bank—NADBank. At the Federal Reserve of Dallas, Harvey Rosenblum, Senior Vice President and Director of Research, Senior Economist William Gruben, Skip Edmonds, and Susan Tetley gave of their time to review and discuss a number of key areas of this study. I received additional assistance in Washington from the members and staff of ISAC-14, as well as Regina K. Vargo, Deputy Assistant Secretary for the Western Hemisphere, and Sarah Kent in the Office of NAFTA at the U.S. Department of Commerce; from Stephen Ruhlen, Chief of Staff for Congressman Henry Bonilla; from the staff of Congressman Kika de la Garza; and from the Embassy of Mexico. The staff at the Federal Reserve research library in Dallas and Eugene Ferguson, Director of the Exim Bank library in Washington, were very helpful in locating key documents, data, and publications.

In Mexico I extend thanks to Antonio Berentsen, Gary Crump, Victor Bujanda, and Emil Courtney of Probrusa; the research department at the Banco de Mexico; Fausto Garcia, President of Garcia Associates; Dawn Cooper Bahar, Commercial Attache at the U.S. Embassy; Kevin Hall with the *Journal of Commerce* in Mexico City; Raul Cardenas Heraldez, Consul de Mexico in Laredo; and the American Chamber of Commerce of Mexico. At various stages of this project Jeff Smith in Roswell, Don Michie of El Paso, James Arthur, Dan Hastings, Jr., and Jeff Pryor of Laredo, Blair Krueger of San Diego, Santos Flores in Ft. Worth, Phil Lane and John Logan at Texas A&M International University in Laredo, Barnard Thompson and Mike Collins at Ford in Detroit, Michigan,

Troy Genzer and Mont Hoyt in Houston, Don Nibbe publisher, and Mike Pattan, editor of *Twin Plant News* in El Paso, and Larry Johnson with Baker and McKenzie in Dallas were all a tremendous help. James Crisp, Director, Texas Center for Border Economic and Enterprise Development, and Dr. Michael Patrick, Chair, Department of Economics and Finance, and Baldomero Garcia, Director, Office for the Study of U.S.-Mexico Trade Relations at Texas A&M International University, were very helpful with sourcing current data and materials. At Texas A&M University in College Station I am indebted to noted banking and finance experts Pete Rose, Jim Kolari, and Kerry Cooper for providing timely and substantive comments and suggestions for the improvement of the technical aspect of this book.

A special word of thanks to Erwin von Allmen, Adalberto Nava, Calvin John Green, Greg Zepeda, Anita Doncaster, John Adams III, Jim Herrick, Wanda Hale Gonzales, Dwane Burdorf, Annie Turner, and David Perez, who offered assistance and valuable comments along the way. Dr. Linda Homco provided timely insight and corrections of the final draft.

My wife, Sherry, has been my most constant and supportive companion throughout this undertaking. Her patience and calm encouragement—while tolerating my hectic schedule—has allowed me to pursue such projects. I hope she knows how grateful I am.

Introduction

Of all that extensive empire which once acknowledged the authority of Spain in the New World, no portion, for interest and importance, can be compared with Mexico.

—William H. Prescott, October 1, 1843

The evolution and emergence of the Mexican economy over the past decade has been a bittersweet mix of tragedy and immense success. Since the mid-1970's, Mexico has worked to throw off an initial layer of historical, old-line, nationalistic, inward-looking economic and political policies, to allow a new generation to reshape the nation into a growing global economy. These progressive efforts in Mexico have resulted in varied consequences. To understand present-day banking and investment in Mexico and to provide a window to the future, it is imperative to have a focus on the events, policies, and conclusions of the recent economic and financial restructuring.

The economic and commercial events both in Mexico and in the dual U.S.-Mexico relationship have significant relevance. Mexico, both the government and the private sector, took bold initiatives (1) to open a once-closed and restrictive economy, (2) to reshape and reprivatize the banking and financial sector, (3) to attract much-needed foreign direct investment, (4) to gain respect not only regionally but worldwide, (5) to fight and reduce inflation, and (6) to reach a political consensus to pass the North American Free Trade Agreement—only to suffer a series of political setbacks and economic disruptions as seen in the devaluation of the peso in December 1994. These incidents halted the euphoria of what many have called the "Mexican Miracle."

Years of research and planning, restructuring, and economic and gradual political reform by a new generation of Mexican leaders, referred to as the "techn-ocrats" during the late 1980's and early 1990's, resulted in Mexico's being hailed as a model of economic success among emerging nations. Yet, such praise was suddenly dashed by early 1995 as the Mexican nation was on the brink of total insolvency following the crushing devaluation. There are those skeptics, as well as realists, both in and out of Mexico who would respond that these events should come as no great surprise. However, the major international financial markets and government economists failed to signal a warning—or, if there was advance knowledge, no plan was set forth to avert the resulting economic crisis that plagued Mexico during 1995–96.

More significantly, the momentous impact of these events is that the Mexico of the mid- and late 1990's is not the Mexico of old. While Mexico carries with it much of the economic baggage of the past, it clearly has endeavored to emerge as a more democratic, financially solid, and diversified industrial nation. Fur-thermore, as Sidney Weintraub observed in 1990, in *A Marriage of Convenience*, "Mexico is now going through a profound change in its economic structure involving opening of the market . . . this is a transformation of historic propor-tions . . . the longer the economic opening endures, the more irreversible it be-comes." Thus, the specter of the political intrigue and the devaluation shocked world financial markets and threatened the economic stability not only in Mex-ico, but also in financial markets worldwide. The resulting impact along with the crisis recovery policies and actions are crucial to an understanding of the Mexican economy and commercial environment as we enter the next century. The shock of the so-called "Tequila Effect"—the hangover after the 1994–95 economic calamity—had and will continue to have broader ramifications for Mexico, the United States, and Latin American and world markets than any previous economic crisis in an emerging nation. In this regard, a specific section of this book is dedicated to an initial look at the consequences of the 1994 devaluation and the effect of the Mexican crisis on the Argentine economy in 1995.

Structural changes in the internal Mexican economy, banking and financial sector, central bank, and private industrial arena not already addressed during the administration of Carlos Salinas were tremendously jolted during the post-1994 devaluation period. The incoming Ernesto Zedillo government inherited a significant political challenge and the most severe economic slump since the 1930's. Furthermore, Mexico had worked to be a respected player in world commercial and financial markets, thus rasing its profile and exposure to eco-nomic pressures and dynamics it often did not and could not control. Mexico by its actions (or lack thereof) is today a vastly different nation than a decade ago, given its decision to be a player on a more global scale. This broadened activity brings both reward and risk. The management of such risk and economic fluctuation is the challenge faced not only by Mexico, but by any rapidly emerg-ing industrial economy.

The advent of increased U.S. and worldwide direct investment in Mexico during the early 1990's, the windfall created by the reprivatization of over 1,000 government-owned enterprises, the reprivatization of the banking and financial sector, the political and social challenges of a viable multiparty political system, and the pressure to pass and implement the North American Free Trade Agreement (NAFTA) all have and will continue to dramatically influence how Mexico will prosper as well as project to the world its image and stability. Foreign investors and money managers, primarily from the United States, were quick to rush to the ''Mexico Miracle'' to invest, and just as eager to withdraw, primarily because of a crisis of confidence in the Mexican nation and its leadership. Furthermore, a cycle of boom-bust-recession-inflation has taken its toll not only on investors and the Mexican economy, but also on Mexico's citizens.

Modern Mexico is further challenged by the need to keep pace with a wave of technological and global interaction that has always been weighted against its historical and cultural past. While dedicated to an open, diversified economy, Mexico would hope to avoid the domestic foreign intrigue that has dotted its history since the arrival of Hernán Cortés in the halls of Moctezuma. The past decade of adjustment and economic turbulence will be weathered by Mexico and its people, and the problems experienced and lessons learned will provide a valuable backdrop to an otherwise promising and prosperous future.

The fate of both Mexico and the United States is that the two countries are forever tied by geography. The historical evolution of the dual interaction between the peoples of these two nations is and will be significant for the futures of both countries. With this in mind, this book is divided into chapters reviewing such themes as the interaction and historical financial events that transpired during the advent of the North American Free Trade Agreement (NAFTA), the expansion of cross-border financial and investment services, as well as a framework and background review of the events leading up to and resulting from the devaluations of the 1970's and 1980's, and more recently the evolution of the peso crisis of 1994–95. The imperceptible, yet gradual economic integration of the two economies has required time in developing, while not always being seamless in its implementation and transition. American macroeconomic policy has long had a direct impact on the economy of Mexico, as is evident by the impact of U.S. interest rates on the financial underpinnings of the Mexican treasury and the banking system to assist with the overall economic growth of the nation. An appreciation of the historically sensitive issues and perspectives, be they nationalization of the oil industry, immigration, or market access for foreign financial services, is paramount to a fuller understanding of doing business on both sides of the border.

Quotations at the beginning of each chapter are intended to set the framework of the subject matter. The Mexican economy and its positioning in world markets is in rapid transition. As U.S. firms look to broaden market access and services in Mexico, a clear disparity often emerges due to structural and procedural issues that have their bases in differences of cultures, time lines, and overall desired objectives. My approach has been one of addressing the key economic issues that have impacted the cross-border interaction between the United States and Mexico over the past few decades. To do this, I have drawn on observations of significant milestones that occurred prior to this time period in order to provide a framework and understanding of how issues and priorities have evolved.

The intertwining of economic activity between Mexico and the United States at an unprecedented rate has clearly accelerated during the early 1990's. More-over, there are two very significant evolutionary trends—also major themes of this book—that will for years to come impact the dual U.S.-Mexico interests and relationship: first, demands and actions in world markets and by interna-tional monetary agencies, far removed from the U.S.-Mexico relationship, have and will continue to have a tremendous impact on the economies, investment, banking, and competitiveness of both nations. Second, and probably more piv-otal for future considerations, given the reaction to the Mexican crisis of 1994–95, economic policies and political events that occur in Mexico have reached a level of tremendous significance on both the financial markets of developed nations and those of emerging markets worldwide, if for no other reason than the very demands that are exerted in the first trend.

In the process of drafting these thoughts over the past couple of years, the economy of Mexico has experienced a number of momentous events and chal-lenges. Having often been asked, ''Where do you end such an assessment given the dynamics of the Mexican economy?'', I have come to a fairly firm conclu-sion that any such contemporary attempt will always be more a work-in-progress than a definitive study. Thus, the trends and events highlighted in this book are important to students of the subject as well as investors, financial advisors, and bankers looking to expand their understanding of Mexico. Changes, for example, in the Mexican investment and banking laws, foreign banking access, and an assessment of the future potential of the Mexican financial markets is paramount for those positioning investors and business decisions for the balance of the decade and the century ahead. With this in mind I have endeavored to include rather detailed notes as well as an extensive bibliography of key source material, much of which has never before appeared in such a book. The data in the supporting figures are as presented by the cited sources.

The financial and investment framework established in the post-1994 deval-uation period by the parties to the Mexican financial support package and the restructuring of the financial sector, both public and private, are essential to an understanding of the challenges, benefits, and problems for the reemergence of the Mexican economy. These observations and the conclusions are mine alone.

Mexican Banking and Investment in Transition

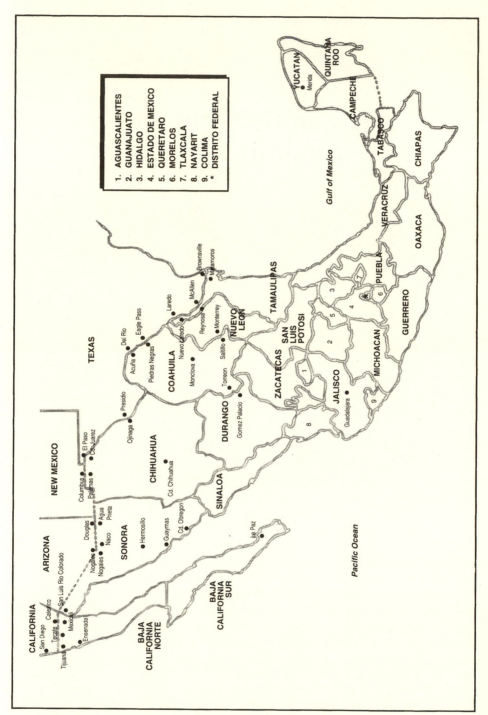

Legend:
1. AGUASCALIENTES
2. GUANAJUATO
3. HIDALGO
4. ESTADO DE MEXICO
5. QUERETARO
6. MORELOS
7. TLAXCALA
8. NAYARIT
9. COLIMA
* DISTRITO FEDERAL

Source: Twin Plant News.

Chapter 1

Mexico on the Brink: Turmoil and Change

Mexico cannot grow in solitude. Nothing of what occurs beyond our borders is foreign to us. In times of a growing international interdependence isolation becomes an impossible task. . . . we should be conscious that our destiny is bound to the transformations that are taking place beyond our borders. A decision not to participate in such transformations would only mean the transfer to the foreign realm of our possibility to determine the future of our nation.

—Luis Echeverria A., 1973

During the past decade there has been a major change in transborder financial interactions and services between the United States and Mexico. While the two have been trading partners for over two centuries, their financial dealings have not always been transparent or jovial. In recent years, there has been a major effort on the part of both nations to harmonize relations and expand financial services across a common border. This presentation reviews the evolution of the U.S.-Mexican banking and financial relationship. Events in Mexico, at one time viewed as distant domestic internal concerns, have, since the early 1980's, had a relevant impact on the political and economic policy of the United States. Reaction to an economic crisis in Mexico is and will be of major concern to the United States. Nationalization of the Mexican banks in 1982, the restructuring of the foreign debt crisis of the mid-1980's, the role of the U.S.-Mexican border economy on commercial and financial operations, and the enhancement of a more open and transparent investment environment in Mexico have shaped the basis of today's policies. Mexico, in the 1980's, consciously moved from a closed economy to a more open investment regime marked by the introduction of diversified financial services. These bold initiatives were not without repercussions. Most importantly, the role and impact of the North American Free Trade Agreement (NAFTA) during its initial period of implementation, as well as the causes and jolt of the December 1994 devaluation of the peso are critical to an understanding of the ongoing Mexican economic restructuring and the prospects for stability and future growth.

MEXICO: MIRACLE OR MIRAGE

Hardly a case can be found in modern economic history that mirrors the seemingly dramatic economic transformation of the Mexican economy during the period from 1980 to 1994.[1] Alan Greenspan, Chairman, Board of Governors of the Federal Reserve, noted in testimony to Congress during the early days following the December 1994 devaluation, that ''Mexico, which had been hobbled for a number of years after the debt crisis of 1982, has more recently gone through a major economic metamorphosis toward significant improvement in its economic and financial structure. . . . Mexico has made major strides.''[2] The return of optimism and economic stability were central to Mexico's becoming what it had hoped to be—a world class nation. However, hampered by uneven growth, capital flight, overregulation by the government, the fall of the price of crude oil, a poor financial services base, and the ever-present potential for devaluation and hyperinflation—Mexico faced a series of turning points of major significance. Politically and commercially, a theme of ultranationalism, long a Mexican tradition reaffirmed by the administrations of Luis Echeverria (1970–76) and Jose Lopez Portillo (1976–82), advocated the rejection of foreign interaction in most sectors of the Mexican economy including banking and direct investment in the industrial area. While generally viewed as a popular and independent domestic move in Mexico, the protectionist economy and the highly regulated decade of the 1970's planted false hopes on the magnitude of Mexican oil reserves and the relative strength of world oil prices. In the process, Mexico embarked on a series of policies that crippled the economy—most particularly the aging industrial base and the fragile financial underpinnings. The hallmark of this ''economic nationalism'' was the fact that the Mexican banking sector was both isolated and protected from virtually all foreign competition. Such limitations on foreign banks operating on an equal footing in Mexico both predated and stimulated the rise of the concept of national treatment so pivotal in the evolution of cross-border trade in financial services.[3]

The investment policies of the Mexican government during the 1970's and early 1980's, along with the tightly regulated guidelines of the Banco de Mexico, moved to further constrict the viability of the banking system.[4] During the administration of Luis Echeverria, inflation accelerated causing a critical problem of disintermediation—the movement of funds out of Mexican banks and into quasi-financial groups known as ''financieros.'' Furthermore, out-country capital flight was also a serious problem.[5] The introduction of new financial sector laws, intended as controls and prudent measures, actually served to further confuse attempted reforms and undermine the banking sector. The Law on Credit Institutions (1974) attempted to address the capital flight from Mexican banks by allowing the formation of multitiered financial groups that offered brokerage services, insurance products, trust services, and "stock" positions in a select group of Mexican industries. The Securities Market Law (1975) gave added powers to the brokerage houses, a plan by the government to help create a quasi-government-controlled conduit to raise money domestically in the "open market," much like the offering of Treasury Bills by the U.S. government. In 1978, Mexican government treasury notes, Certificados de la Tesoreria or "CETES," were introduced.[6]

During the 1970's the number of Mexican commercial banks dropped dramatically as the larger institutions fostered and encouraged an atmosphere for mergers. Although hampered by persistent inflation, the economy seemed solid. By 1975 the Mexican economy had experienced a post–World War II real rate of growth that averaged over 6 percent annually. Thus, the wave of bank consolidation demonstrated no cause for concern. From 1975 to 1982 the number of banks dropped from 139 to 60. Although the government budget began to decline after 1988, the downward trend in the financial markets would continue until the early 1990's, when reprivatization of the Mexican banking sector once again encouraged the creation of new institutions and an increase in capital via foreign direct investment in Mexico.[7]

To further compound problems in the banking sector, the Mexican economy suffered a series of dramatic peso devaluations and unchecked inflation that stretched from 1976 to the present. The economic signals were mixed. During the 1970's, Mexico averaged an annual growth rate of real per capita GDP of a positive 3.5 percent, while the average in the 1980's was a minus 1.01 percent. Capital flight and increasing dependence on the U.S. dollar (to shore up the government and the economy) predated the problems of the mid-1990's, further undermining confidence in both the peso and the banking system. The impact of the devaluations overshadowed a brief feeling of prosperity in the mid-1970's. The oil boom and price controls by the Organization of Petroleum Exporting Countries (OPEC) had given the Mexican government the false sense of security and the hope that they could drill for petroleum and "buy" (via export revenues) their way out of an economic disaster. The dramatic rise in the price of a barrel of oil, from $4.00 in 1970 to over $15.00 per barrel by 1979, disrupted the international monetary system. This had its greatest impact on nations like Mexico that could ill afford to absorb radical economic changes. During the 1973–74 oil shock, the international market was disrupted as the price of oil increased 77 percent. Thus, the gamble on the petroleum reserves and reliance on the dynamics of the world oil pricing left Mexico with few controllable options. The oil shock was followed by a drastic rise in interest rates worldwide, in the late 1970's and early 1980's; this coupled with a rapid fall in world oil prices undermined the Mexican miracle and proved to be the near fatal blow to the

Mexican economy that ultimately diminished both the domestic and foreign confidence in the banking and financial sectors.[8]

IT IS NOW OR NEVER

Shortly after the collapse of world oil prices in 1981, Mexico began to experience a number of aftershocks and setbacks that hampered its ability to be either regionally or globally competitive.[9] The banking industry, both in Mexico and along the U.S.-Mexican border, experienced a tremendous number of disruptions associated with the stability of the peso. Despite pledging a public oath to defend the Mexican peso "like a dog," Lopez Portillo devalued the currency in February 1982. Falling from 26 to 45 pesos to the dollar, this was the first of numerous devaluations of the peso during 1982. The resulting impact, both financially and psychologically, was a blow to the once prosperous Mexican economy and signaled a major loss of confidence by foreign investors in Mexico. The Mexican economy has gradually "dollarized" in an attempt to stabilize the overvalued peso. Capital flight in 1982 and 1983 reached an all-time high as Mexican citizens, private investors, banks, and multinational companies moved deposits and investment funds out of Mexico. The capital flight, estimated at over $100 billion dollars, thwarted growth of the Mexican banking sector as interest rates skyrocketed, exchange controls were imposed, and bank deposits fell. Capital flight in both Mexico and throughout Latin America impacted the foreign debt of most debtor nations, undermining not only the banking system but also hampering industrial growth. Mexico's capital flight from 1976 to 1985 represented 71 percent of its national debt growth. The deteriorating nature and underlying instability of the financial system, both public and private, reached a breaking point. Faced with a declining capital base, a loss of confidence, and a growing apprehension on the part of foreign lenders to limit and/or recover loans made to Mexico, 58 out of the 60 banks in Mexico were nationalized by the Mexican government on September 1, 1982.[10]

In an effort to justify government intervention in the banking and finance sector, President Lopez Portillo concluded his sixth and last address to the nation, know as the "Informe":

I can assert that in a few, recent years, a group of Mexicans . . . headed, counseled and aided by the private banks, have withdrawn more money from this country than all of the empires that have exploited us from the beginnings of our history.

We cannot continue to risk that those resources be channeled through the same conduits that have contributed in such a dynamic fashion to generate the severe situation we are going through. We have to organize ourselves to save our productive structure, in order to provide it with sufficient financial resources to go forth; we have to stop the injustice of this perverse process: capital flight, devaluation, inflation, which affects us all, especially the workers, employment, and the companies that generate it. These are our critical priorities.

In order to respond to these, I have issued in consequence two decrees: one that nationalizes the private banks of the country; and another one that establishes the generalized foreign exchange control, not as a policy that has survived "better late than never," but rather because today the critical conditions that have developed require it and justify it. *It is now or never.* They have already plundered us. But Mexico has not ended. And they shall not plunder us again.

Many have attributed the present-day problems and inconsistencies of the Mexican economy during the 1980's and 1990's to the bank nationalization of 1982. The signal to foreign investors was unmistakable—in times of economic turmoil you could stand to lose your investment in Mexico. This last-ditch effort to take domestic action in the hope of correcting extensive systematic economic difficulties that went beyond the border of Mexico was a benchmark event. This corrective action set in motion a wave of devaluation-inflation-recession-devaluation that exists to the present day.

The 1982 situation became as critical a concern to foreign investors—part of the "they" referred to by Lopez Portillo—as to the Mexican government. Reflecting on the plight of the sinking financial and commercial sector, the Mexican government declared it would be unable to service the massive foreign debt on its numerous international loans. In short order, Mexican businesses followed suit and all but ceased debt service to foreign banks.[11] Who was to blame? The untimely collapse of oil prices was viewed by those in Mexico as partially the fault and responsibility of international lending organizations and commercial banks worldwide. The foreign banks, eager to lend growing reserves of petro-dollars, had unwittingly encouraged borrowing based on poor collateral considerations, little or no risk assessment, and faulty repayment assumptions. Nevertheless, by 1986, the magnitude of the debt problems in Mexico would necessitate a worldwide effort by over 1,000 banks, supported by the U.S. Federal Reserve, the International Monetary Fund (IMF), the World Bank, and the U.S. Treasury Department, to restructure a debt repayment plan to address both the Mexican government loans and private sector debt service.

One solution was to discount the face value of outstanding obligations and create an avenue to collateralize the discounted value. In early 1988 J. P. Morgan introduced the Aztec Bonds, consisting of $3.7 billion of Mexican sovereign loan debt restructured into $2.6 billion worth of 20-year securities at a floating coupon of LIBOR plus 1.625 percent, with the principal fully collateralized by zero-coupon U.S. Treasury bonds. Thus, Mexico unwittingly became the pilot case for less developed countries' (LDC) foreign debt restructuring worldwide. Mexico's cumulative public and private external debt totaled nearly $100 billion and required over $14 billion in debt service payments by 1986. The Aztec Bonds proved to be only a temporary solution. Swift action was imperative to avert a financial crisis that could spread beyond Mexico. Spearheaded by Citibank of New York (the only U.S. bank in Mexico allowed to retain its operation since 1923) and U.S. Treasury secretaries James Baker and Nicholas Brady, a multiyear plan was developed to prevent the complete failure of the Mexican financial system, both governmental and private sector.[12] By 1988–89 the debt restructuring initiative provided an initial crucial boost of confidence in Mexico's credit worthiness and allowed Mexico to begin a slow process of stabilization of its economy by addressing the external debt and fiscal structural problems that had brought about the financial crisis.[13]

The results of the 1989–90 Mexican debt restructuring then and now proved to be a pivotal financial event, yet it fell short of its promise to stimulate sustainable growth, an essential element to prevent a recurrence. Not only was Mexico the first nation to sign a sweeping debt agreement involving banks worldwide, but it also set a precedent for debt-crisis management and restructuring worldwide. To address the crisis, a new agreement was concluded on February 4, 1990 between Mexico and its worldwide creditors on $48.5 billion in outstanding debt. The essence of the bailout package was threefold: (1) reduce the value of the outstanding debt (while lowering the interest burden), (2) extend the repayment time frame, and (3) provide fresh capital to stimulate the growth of the economy in anticipation of receiving repayment over a long period of time. Creditor banks were allowed to swap their bad loan portfolios for 30-year debt-reduction bonds at a 35 percent discount of the face value. The bonds, most of which will mature in the year 2019, have an interest margin of 13/16 percentage points over the London Interbank Offer Rate (LIBOR). Over time, Mexican-style debt-reduction packages were structured and signed by twelve countries: Venezuela, Uruguay, the Dominican Republic, Costa Rica, the Philippines, Nigeria, Brazil, Argentina, Ecuador, Jordan, Bulgaria, and Poland. However, the impact of the Mexican agreement had its greatest influence on nations in Latin America. Of additional significance is the resulting enhanced involvement of world banking and international monetary agencies in the Mexican crisis. The IMF, the World Bank, and the Japanese Export-Import Bank for the first time all became full partners in the resolution of the late 1980's Mexican debt crisis and more importantly, all future economic crises.[14]

The road to a stable economy and lower inflation, the attraction of more direct foreign investment, and the revitalization of the Mexican banking industry would require critical decisions and sacrifice. Critics of the Mexican economy and government did not think it possible to reform such an age-old system of neglect, political intrigue, and economic negligence.[15] The political monopoly of the Partido Revolucionario Institucional (PRI) is often cited as part of the problem. The destabilizing policies of the government and central bank are not uniquely a Mexican phenomenon, as structural, banking, inflation, and economic problems exist in other single-party countries, namely Italy, Japan, and Korea. In the case of Mexico, the economic ''crisis'' of the 1980's occurred at a time when the country and its leaders had hoped to shed the tag of an LDC and begin to gain a broader respect, thus emulating a ''newly industrial country'' or NIC. The recovery process would be slow and painful.[16]

A combination of structural and economic forces rather than a single factor had to be addressed to reverse the declining economic cycle. Foreign investment and support of Mexican capital demands began to dry up. During the late 1980's, U.S. banks (soon followed by banks in Asia and Europe) had lost all interest in loans to Mexico. Institutions were presented the outcome of the Baker and Brady plans to reschedule the debt payment, and in the case of private sector loans, were left on their own to collect unpaid debts. The Brady package would represent the master restructuring plan combining a number of earlier debt plans such as the 1983 FICORCA (Fideicomisio para la Cobertura de Riesgos Cambiarios) facility agreement under the direction of a young, Yale-trained economist Ernesto Zedillo Ponce de Leon, the current president of Mexico.[17] Reaction to the Mexican Brady bailout was mixed:

Multinational banks were supposed to come forward with additional lending to help countries such as Mexico overcome their debt repayment difficulties. The predictable problem soon became apparent: the major international banks thought this was a great idea—for someone else. Each bank understood that its own loans would be more secure if supplemented with additional funds. With loans selling on the secondary market for a fraction of their face value, few banks were willing to take the plunge aimed at making all banks better off.[18]

As the Mexican banking system struggled to recover, nonbank financial groups sought opportunity and grew tremendously. To become more competitive, the Mexican banks needed both a major injection of capital and the ability to do business in a more deregulated environment. While foreign banks began to absorb their loan losses, increasing their reserves to unprecedented levels, few if any new loans were forthcoming, which created uncertainty about the final outcome of the debt restructuring.[19] The return of substantial foreign capital to Mexico required an assessment of outdated investment policies. To assist with the economic recovery, sweeping changes were made in the investment regulations in 1989 and 1993 to open up the economy to more foreign investment. However, these efforts were undermined in Mexico by a combination of high reserve requirements, interest rate controls, low GDP, and hyperinflation (see Figure 1-1).[20]

THE "TECHNOCRATS"

In a little-noticed move, the Director of Planning for the Miguel De La Madrid administration (1982–88), Carlos Salinas de Gortari and a team of economists and planners—known collectively as the "technocrats"—began in 1985–86 to restructure the external debt, privatize government-owned enterprises, and fashion a long-range plan to position the Mexican economy on a solid footing.[21] Salinas, Harvard-trained, helped secure a renewed interest for membership of Mexico in the General Agreement on Tariffs and Trade (GATT) by mid-1986. Under the GATT provisions, duties on imports were reduced from an average

Figure 1-1
Mexican Economy: 1984–97

	GDP	Inflation*	Population in Millions
1984	3.6	59.2	77
1985	2.6	63.7	78
1986	-3.8	105.7	79
1987	1.7	159.2	81
1988	1.4	51.7	84
1989	3.1	19.7	86
1990	3.9	29.9	88
1991	3.6	18.8	89
1992	2.6	11.9	90
1993	0.4	8.0	91
1994	3.0	6.9	92
1995	-7.1	50.4	93
1996f	3.2	28.5	95
1997f	4.0	19.5	97

*CPI; f = forecast.

Source: Banco de Mexico.

of 100 percent to under 20 percent, thus opening the Mexican economy to increased world trade. The reduction of the inflation rate along with the attraction of more direct investment became top priorities. As an added benefit, GATT set the stage for a broader base of respect on world markets, the negotiation and passage of the North American Free Trade Agreement (NAFTA), as well as membership in the elite Organization for Economic Cooperation and Development (OECD). Notwithstanding the economic and political turbulence of the past years, membership in GATT will prove to be the most significant single catalyst to the expansion and opening of the Mexican economy in the past five decades.[22]

The efforts of the eager technocrats were carried over into the Salinas presidency (1988–94), based almost exclusively on the revitalization of the Mexican economy, the privatization of the banking and financial sector, and the completion of NAFTA by early 1994. These efforts to address the political and economic structure in Mexico would prove vital to the growth of the Mexican economy. Pedro Aspe, one of the leading Salinas-era technocrats chronicled ten lessons or keys that shaped the approach to the structural changes and progress in Mexico between 1983 and 1993:

1. The worst thing is [was] to do nothing.
2. Vital to the success of the reform program is the quality and commitment of key public servants.
3. There is no macroeconomic stability without a deep and permanent reform of public finances.
4. Stabilization and structural change have to be viewed as integral elements of a single strategy.
5. The worst defect of an economic program is negligence.

6. Start at the beginning.

7. Consistency plus credibility equals confidence.

8. The government cannot go it alone.

9. Be fair.

10. It is easier to lower inflation from 200 percent to 20 percent than it is to take it from 20 percent to international levels.[23]

The challenge for the technocrats was formidable. Of the original 58 Mexican banks nationalized in 1982, only 18 banks (holding 98% of the banking capital) remained in operation under government control in 1990. In a period of one year (1991–92) all 18 banks were reprivatized, selling at 14.7 times earnings with an average price-to-book ratio of 3.49 (the average ratio in the United States and Europe is around 2.2).[24] Optimism was high for the long-awaited recovery of the Mexican banking sector. Privatization of the banks raised over $12 billion for the national treasury. This success would prove premature with the rise of banking problems after the implementation of NAFTA in January 1994. These events and the post–December 1994 devaluation are crucial to an understanding of financial and economic trends and activity in Mexico.

Today Mexico has a population of over 95 million, of which one-half are under the age of 20 and 80 percent are under 40. Only 4 percent are over 65![25] Population estimates exceed 100 million by the year 2000. As a result of the broad policy of privatization, Mexico has attracted the attention of new direct capital investment. While general political stability has been the hallmark of PRI rule since 1929, the Mexican nation—in light of the political turmoil, devaluation, and presidential transition of 1994—will face a new set of social, political, and economic challenges by the year 2000. To foster the industrialization of Mexico, the social and political fabric must be kept intact. Furthermore, the message was clear—notwithstanding inflation, devaluations, and debt programs—the Mexican government in concert with assistance from the United States, foreign lenders, and other world trading partners viewed domestic tranquility and the stability of the Mexican banking and financial sector as well as measured economic reforms to be paramount.

The reprivatization of the Mexican full-service, one-stop banking sector, offering banking, brokerage, insurance, and factoring services, has vastly contributed to a stable economy that has shown steady growth up until January 1995. With inflation in check through 1994, the private sector had begun to make its most dramatic growth in over 30 years. The total net public sector debt as a percentage of GDP between 1988 and 1992 dropped from 62.4 percent to 28.4 percent.[26] Growth of the economy brought on an increasing demand for interdependent banking services and financial expertise. With the passage of NAFTA, tremendous opportunities were expected for both the Mexican and U.S. financial sectors to expand their markets and services. Moreover, the U.S.-Mexican transborder region has played and will play a major role in the interface of trade and financial services. The three-country NAFTA region has shaped and will influence the future of transborder commerce and banking well into the next century. To understand the opportunities requires a closer look at the trends and events of the past decade with a look at the structural changes in banking, investment, monetary policy, and financial services on both sides of the border.

NOTES

1. Robert R. Moore, "The Government Budget Deficit and the Banking System: The Case of Mexico," *Financial Industry Studies*, October 1993, p. 27; John M. Hennessy, "Lessons from Mexico," *New York Times*, November 15, 1993; Daniel Levy and Gabriel Szekely, *Mexico: Paradoxes of Stability and Change* (Boulder: 1987), pp. 151–71, 265–66; Jorge G. Castaneda, "Mexico at the Brink," *Foreign Affairs*, Winter 1985–86, pp. 287–303. Note: Paul Kennedy, *The Rise and Fall of the Great Powers* (New York: 1987), pp. 516–17, states a pessimistic view that "Mexico is on the verge of economic bankruptcy and default."

2. Statement by Alan Greenspan before Committee on Foreign Relations, U.S. Senate, January 26, 1995, as seen in the *Federal Reserve Bulletin* (Washington, D.C.), Vol. 81, No. 3, March 1995, p. 261.

3. Banco de Mexico, "Mexico: A Political Overview," *Mexico-U.S. Trade Advisory*, July 1991, pp. 2–4; John H. Welch and William C. Gruben, "A Brief Modern History of the Mexican Financial System," *Financial Industry Studies*, Dallas Federal Reserve Bank (FRBD), October 1993, pp. 1–9. For statistics on Mexico see U.S. Department of Commerce, Office of Mexico, "Mexico-Vital Statistics," 1993, pp. 3–8; see also David M. Gould, Graeme L. Woodbridge, and Roy J. Ruffin, "The Theory and Practice of Free Trade," *Economic Review* (FRBD), Fourth Quarter 1993, pp. 1–14. See also George J. Clark, "Foreign Banks in the Domestic Markets of Developing Countries," seen in Richard E. Feinberg and Valeriana Kallab (eds.), *Uncertain Future: Commercial Banks and the Third World* (New Brunswick: 1984), pp. 79–86; and U.S. Department of the Treasury, *Report to Congress on Foreign Government Treatment of U.S. Commercial Banking Operations* (Washington, D.C.: 1979).

4. Daniel Whitaker, *Mexico 1993: Annual Report with Forecasts through End-1994* (London: June 1993), pp. 102–5. For an overview of the political structure in Mexico, see "Mexico: A Political Overview," *Mexico-U.S. Trade Advisory*, July 1991, pp. 2–4.

5. Welch and Gruben, "A Brief Modern History of the Mexican Financial System," p. 3.

6. Ibid., pp. 4–5. For a brief overview of Mexican banking and investment law, see Mont P. Hoyt, "The Legal Framework of the Mexican Financial System," *Texas Banking*, May 1993, pp. 5, 10.

7. Jose Blanco, "El Desarrollo de la Crisis en Mexico, 1970–1976," in Rolando Cordera (ed.), *Desarrollo y Crisis de la Economia Mexicana* (Mexico, D.F.: 1995), pp. 279–335; Robert R. Moore, "The Government Budget Deficit and the Banking System: The Case of Mexico," *Financial Industry Studies* (FRBD), October 1993, pp. 31–35.

8. Susan Kaufman Purcell, "Mexico-U.S. Relations: Big Initiative Can Cause Big Problems," *Foreign Affairs*, Winter 1981–82, pp. 79–392; Alan Riding, *Mexico: Inside the Volcano* (London: 1985), pp. 165–87; John H. Welch and Daryl McLeod, "The Cost and Benefits of Fixed Dollar Exchange Rates in Latin America," *Economic Review*

(FRBD), First Quarter 1993, pp. 38, 41; John S. Gruppo, "Banking in Mexico," presentation to the American Bar Association, Adolphus Hotel, Dallas, Texas, June 8, 1993. Note: The oil industry in Mexico was nationalized by President Lazaro Cardenas in 1938.

9. George W. Grayson, "Oil and Gas Policy under Lopez Portillo," in *The United States and Mexico: Patterns of Influence* (New York: 1984) pp. 57–90, 175–79; Alan Riding, "The Oil Is Ours," in *Distant Neighbors: A Portrait of the Mexicans* (New York: 1985) pp. 227–59; Hector A. Camin and Lorenzo Meyer, *In the Shadow of the Mexican Revolution 1910–1989* (Austin: 1993), pp. 177–78.

10. Levy and Szekely, *Mexico*, pp. 35–36, 64; Ramon E. Ruiz, *Triumphs and Tragedy: A History of the Mexican People* (New York: 1992), pp. 455–57. Note: Two banks escaped nationalization by the government, U.S.-owned Citibank-Mexico and labor union–owned Banco Obrero.

11. Camin and Meyer, *In the Shadow*, pp. 213–16.

12. Richard B. Miller, *Citicorp: Story of a Bank in Crisis* (New York: 1993) pp. 4, 34, 111–15; Camin and Meyer, *In the Shadow*, pp. 197–78; Luis Rubio, "Mexico Once Again at the Brink?" *Journal of Commerce*, October 24, 1988, p. 10A; Nova Lustig, *Mexico: The Remaking of an Economy* (Washington, D.C.: 1992), pp. 46–47. Also see William R. Cline, *Mobilizing Bank Lending to Debtor Countries*, Institute for International Economics (Washington, D.C.: 1987), pp. 1–90.

13. George Junge, "Towards More Active Management at Developing Country Debt," *Economic and Financial Prospect*, June 1993, pp. 4–7; William Greider, *Secrets of the Temple: How the Federal Reserve Runs the Country* (New York: 1987), pp. 436–67, 484–87, 502–3, 516–23; Business Monitor International (BMI), *Mexico 1994* (London: 1994), p. 97; Carol Palombo, "Brady Bonds: Past, Present & Future," *Latin Finance*, September 1996, pp. 46–51.

14. The United Mexican States, *Discount and Par Bond Exchange Agreement: Implementing Part I of the 1989–90 Financing Package for Mexico* [Citibank, N.A. as Closing Agent] (Mexico, D.F., and Washington, D.C., February 4, 1990); Haluk Unal, Asli Demirguc-Kunt, and Kwoc-Wai Leung, "The Brady Plan, 1989 Mexican Debt-Reduction Agreement, and Bank Stock Returns in United States and Japan," *Journal of Money, Credit, and Banking*, Vol. 25, No. 3, August 1993, pp. 410–29.

15. Lawrence Kootnikoff, "Salinas Stumped Critics by Achieving Major Reforms," *San Antonio Express-News*, December 28, 1993; Riding, *Distant Neighbors*, pp. 194–226; Kennedy, *The Rise and Fall of the Great Powers*, p. 517; Jerry R. Ladman (ed.), *Mexico: A Country in Crisis* (El Paso: 1986) pp. 1–23, 144–69.

16. William H. Bolin and Jorge Del Canto, "LDC Debt: Beyond Crisis Management," *Foreign Affairs*, Summer 1983, pp. 1099–12; John Adams et al., "If You Were President of Mexico, What Would You Do?" *The International Economy*, January-February 1996, pp. 28–32; James M. Lutz, "Shifting Comparative Advantage, the NICs, and the Developing Countries," *International Trade Journal*, Vol. 1, No. 4, Summer 1987, pp. 339–58.

17. Ernesto Zedillo, Director, FICORCA: Banco de Mexico to The International Banking Community, "FICORCA Facility Agreement," Mexico City, August 6, 1987; The United Mexican States, *Discount and Par Bond Exchange Agreement: Implementing Part I of the 1989–90 Financing Package for Mexico*, February 4, 1990.

18. "Japan Ups Ante in Mexico," *JEI Report*, No. 25B, June 30, 1989, p. 9.

19. Paul A. Griffin and Somoa J. R. Wallach, "Latin American Lending by Major U.S. Banks: The Effects of Disclosures about Nonaccrual Loans and Loan Loss Provi-

sions," *The Accounting Review*, Vol. 66, No. 4, October 1991, pp. 832–33; Myron B. Slovin and Subbarao V. Jayanti, "Bank Capital Regulation and Valuation Effects of Latin American Debt Moratoriums," *Journal of Banking and Finance*, Vol. 17, 1993, pp. 159–71.

20. Miguel de la Madrid H., "Mexico: The New Challenges," *Foreign Affairs*, Fall 1984, pp. 72–74; Peter Korner et al., *The IMF and the Debt Crisis* (London: 1986), pp. 69–71; Catherine M. Carstens, *Las Finanzas Populares en Mexico* (Mexico, D.F.: 1995), pp. 17–35; Jeffrey Sachs, "Making the Brady Plan Work," *Foreign Affairs*, Summer 1989, pp. 87–104; SECOFI, "Mexico Liberalizes Foreign Investment Regulations to Stimulate Domestic Economic Growth," press release, Mexico, D.F., March 15, 1989.

21. "President Salinas Adjusts Policies to Avoid Disappointment and Disaster," *Mexico and NAFTA Report*, September 23, 1993, pp. 1–4, 7; "Moctezuma's Revenge," *The Economist*, April 3, 1993, p. 65; "Central Bank Details Deficits, Surpluses," *El Financiero International*, May 3, 1992, p. 3; "Mexican Economy," *Mexico-U.S. Trade Advisory*, Vol. 3, No. 1, 1993, p. 2; "Latin American Outlook: 1994," *Latin American Watch*, December 15, 1993, p. 7; December 31, 1993, p. 4; and January 10, 1994, p. 4; David Goldman and Evan Kalimtgis, "Risk Analysis of the Cost of Capital in Mexico," *Mexico 2000 Council*, June 10, 1993, pp. 7–9; U.S. Embassy (Mexico), *Mexico: Economic and Financial Report*, Summer 1994, p. 3.

22. Pedro Aspe, *Economic Transformation the Mexican Way* (Cambridge: 1993), pp. 1–122 (published in 1994 in Mexico, D.F. under the title *El Camino Mexicano de la Transformacion Economica*); John A. Adams, Jr., "Without GATT, There'd Be No NAFTA," *Laredo Morning Times*, December 17, 1993; Riding, *Distant Neighbors*, p. 226; Marario Schettina, *El Costo Del Miedo: El Costo del Miedo* (Mexico, D.F.: 1995), pp. 5–6. Note: Mexico rejected GATT in 1980 after a heated domestic debate on the impact to the Mexican economy, see Grayson, *The United States and Mexico*, pp. 121–38; Levy and Szekely, *Mexico*, p. 168; and Camin and Meyer, *In the Shadow*, p. 198.

23. Aspe, *Economic Transformation*, pp. 54–60. See also Arturo Huerta, *La Politica Neoliberal de Estabilizacion Economica en Mexico: Limites y Alternativas* (Mexico, D.F.: 1994), pp. 17–62.

24. Aspe, *Economic Transformation the Mexican Way*, pp. 209–21; John M. Hennessy, "Lessons From Mexico," *New York Times*, November 15, 1992.

25. Joel Russell, "How Countries Compete," *Business Mexico*, 1994, pp. 35–36; BMI, *Mexico 1994*, p. 14.

26. The President of Mexico, Press Office, *Mexico: On the Record*, October/November 1992, p. 6; Lustig, *Mexico: The Remaking of an Economy*, pp. 125–40.

Chapter 2

Banking and Debt
in Mexico

By 1982, in spite of massive oil finds and a superb international credit rating, high levels of economic growth could no longer be sustained, the mistaken ways of previous years caught up with the system.
                                                              —Jorge G. Castaneda

The evolution and growth of the banking and financial sector in Mexico are clearly a result of both the political and the economic environments over the past four decades. At the end of World War II, Mexico, with a population of about 20 million, began a process that stressed an inward-looking, "protectionist" industrial policy based on the concept that domestic growth was best stimulated by the government. This policy emphasized a restriction on the importation of foreign goods and services. The exception was the attraction of direct capital investment, primarily in infrastructure and construction; however, foreign ownership was limited. A federally mandated policy of import-substitution (ISI) resulted in only $450 million in "cumulative" direct foreign investment in the early 1940's.[1]

POSTWAR CHANGES

During the post–World War II years Mexico, like many emerging less developed countries, began to shift from a traditional, agricultural-oriented economy—ever mindful of the agrarian mandate of the 1910 Mexican Revolution that stressed land reform—to a more urban, industrial base. The primary market was domestic consumption. The roots of these changes date from the post-Revolution land reform of the "ejido" land system—small family farms created for the peasant farmers by the government from the seizure of large landed estates—that gradually gave way to demands for a more diversified economy. The process was both painful and slow. From 1940 to 1970, the share of the economy dedicated to agriculture dropped from 20 to 11 percent of GDP and the industrial sector grew from 25 to 34 percent of GDP during the same period.[2] By the early 1990's, over 60 percent of Mexico's ejidos were under 12.5 acres in size—generally not sufficient to support a family given the quality of the land, productivity, and access to markets. The efforts to shift an industrial economy reinforced the ever-present pressures on the social role of the government, industry, and the banking sector.[3]

Beginning in the early 1950's, the government began to gradually exercise more control over the private sector. A policy rooted in protectionism and "import substitution," also popular in other emerging Latin America countries, was pursued.[4] The hallmark of this concept was to foster domestic production of goods previously imported. To appease and stimulate industry, Mexican officials allowed for a virtual blanket policy to "favor particular sectors believed to warrant priority financing" as well as to protect domestic companies from foreign competition.[5] This was accomplished by a rise in import tariffs and fees, quotas, exchange controls, and the creation of a maze of nontariff barriers that dissuaded and "insulated" even the most aggressive foreign advances from doing business in Mexico. Furthermore, the government provided an array of incentives such as lower taxes, subsidies, and indirect investment in the commercial infrastructure that was intended to foster internal industrial growth.

This intense control by the government over the economy, however, failed to keep pace with the changing social demands. The ruling Partido Revolucionario Institucional or PRI had, for decades, neutralized political opposition and maintained domestic tranquility with a mix of social services and jobs doled out via a network of public works projects, social health programs, and farm subsidies. This strategy of political control, social services, and patronage worked effectively until the late 1960's. However, balancing the transition from a historically rural society controlled by centralized authority in Mexico City to a more industrial-urban scheme proved difficult, and hopes for a gentle transition were dashed in 1968. As Mexico prepared to be the first "developing" nation ever to host the Olympics, pent-up demands and the need for more social programs resulted in riots that erupted over the high degree of government authoritarianism.[6] The violent student demonstrations and confrontations with police and soldiers in the Plaza of the Three Cultures in the Tlatelolco section of Mexico City became worldwide news on October 2–3, 1968, shattering the image of a tranquil, newly industrializing Latin American nation. The rapid shift by Mexico to a newly industrialized country (progressively more urban-focused than rural) had failed to fully account for the impact of globalization and rapid change on Mexican society. Such adjustments will impact and influence Mexico well into the next century.[7]

BANK RESTRUCTURING: THE 1960'S

For Mexican banking, the 1960's was a watershed period as institutions worked to keep pace with the economy that had an annual average GDP growth of 7 percent. Per capita income rose 40.7 percent during the decade and inflation averaged a modest 3.5 percent per annum. While bank deposits, as a percent of GDP, grew from 13.3 to 29.4 percent, income from lending was problematic due to the ever-present concern over inflation and exchange rate risk. Most lending, even to the best of corporate accounts, was short term. Long-term funding was provided by a number of government agencies, the most prominent being Nacional Financiera (NAFIN). The Banco de Mexico, established in 1925 and operating as the government's central bank, controlled the money supply via flexible marginal reserve requirements and set interest rates on deposits and loans. At the end of the decade the total external debt was under $4 billion and the peso remained stable and strong. While the 1920's was a boom decade, industry leaders silently knew they could not sustain growth at this pace due to inefficient processes that precluded profitable competition in world markets. Mexican banks were lulled into loans that often refinanced outdated equipment, projected to produce an unrealistic level of products, based on erroneous economic and market data.[8]

During this period, banks were subject to wide swings of reserve requirements and laws governing operations from the Banco de Mexico that proved both confusing and costly. An excellent example was the continual change in the cash reserve requirements for demand and savings deposits that ranged from 50 to 100 percent. Such swings of policy, intended to protect depositors and increase the national savings rate, undermined the extension of credit, which shut off the flow of funding for industrial expansion. Another factor that placed commercial banks at a competitive disadvantage was the activity of nonbank intermediaries that vied for the same deposits and financial opportunities yet were treated differently by government regulation.[9]

The greatest challenge came from the "financieras." Financieras were financial groups that resembled banks, but with a more limited scope of operation. Backed by time deposits, with a minimum duration of one year, they concentrated on providing long-term loans to the industrial sector. Financieras were permitted to issue long-term certificates of obligation, termed "bonos financieros." With the ability to offer high-yielding liquid paper, financieros were able to concentrate loans to prime industrial clients to provide working capital, trade financing, equipment loans, and the acquisition of fixed-term obligations. Meeting the capital demand of a rapidly industrializing country, the financieras, though a latent contribution to disintermediation, proved to be a critical source of capital. Mortgage companies and a growing insurance sector played a less significant role. Economists at the Federal Reserve Bank of Dallas categorized the significance of the postwar period of thin financial markets and the interface of the regulated bank with the nonbank sector as follows:

The trading of fixed-interest instruments on the stock and securities exchange was limited because market makers were banks, financieras, mortgage banks, capitalization banks and, ultimately the Banco de Mexico and the Nacional Financiera. Moreover, the market for long-term obligations was particularly thin. Market thinness and market-inhibiting financial regulations had resulted in costly intermediation during the 1940s, 1950s, and 1960s. These high credit costs and the scarcity of long-term credit, in turn, inhibited the development of Mexican industry.[10]

After a relatively stable period of economic growth, the early 1970's demonstrated the first hint of fiscal pressure both on the economy to grow and sustain itself, and on the banks' ability to meet capital requests. Francisco Suarez Davila, a former deputy minister of finance in Mexico, identified the pending crisis. "From the early 1970's Mexico began relying more and more on bank credit. The money was there, the market was there. We had great needs, so we took it."[11] Very quickly the country lost its internal ability to finance sustained growth, thus undermining a key element to sustainability of an import-substitution program. The administration of President Luis Echeverria (1970–76), in an effort to stimulate government-sponsored growth, launched an intensive mini-New Deal–styled program to build public works and roads to generate jobs. Contrary to his boast that "Mexico cannot grow in solitude," he restated his policy to increase domestic-only production and reduce the dependence on imported foreign products. Increasingly, the private sector began to be uneasy about the continued meddling of the government in private business. To reassure the domestic private sector, the government imposed the "49 percent" ownership rule, stipulating that foreign investment in Mexican industry and joint ventures (under the Foreign Investment Law of 1973) limit all non-Mexican ownership. Laws calling for foreign investment controls proved counterproductive as new foreign direct investment came to a halt, which was followed by a new wave of capital flight.[12]

As a defense to the deteriorating economy, Echeverria tightened control over the banks, further laid blame on the private sector, and introduced inefficient, costly social programs that were an additional drain on the treasury. Disintermediation of bank funds to the domestic financieras as well as out-country capital flight went unchecked. The strict and unpredictable bank reserve requirements coupled with the inability to attract deposits at rates offered by the financieras made the institutions less competitive. Inflation increased from 4.9 percent in 1972 to 12 percent in 1973 and to 23.8 percent by 1974 (see Figure 2-1).[13] Capital flight, inflation, higher oil prices (strangely, Mexico was a net importer of oil in 1973), and declining direct foreign investment depressed the Mexican economy. Furthermore, a major contributing and damaging long-range action was the reluctance or negligence of the government to assist the banks with regulatory relief. Additionally, the government failed to effectively raise and collect taxes to fund expanded social services and federal projects. Alan Riding, in *Distant Neighbors*, points out, "instead of financing [growth] through

Figure 2-1
Economic Indicators: 1972–83

	GDP	Inflation	Number of Commercial Banks	Pesos/ $Dollar
1972	8.38	4.9	155	12.5
1973	8.16	12.0	x	12.5
1974	5.98	23.8	x	12.5
1975	5.53	15.2	136	12.5
1976	4.15	15.8	x	12.5
1977	3.29	29.0	x	21.6
1978	8.15	17.5	x	22.7
1979	9.20	18.2	100	22.8
1980	8.22	26.4	x	23.2
1981	8.77	27.9	x	26.2
1982*	-.63	58.9	60	96.4
1983	-4.20	101.8	31	143.9

*Nationalization of Mexican Banking.

Source: James W. Wilkie (ed.), *Statistical Abstract of Latin America*, Vol. 30, Part 2, pp. 1182, 1242–43.

higher taxes . . . the government had begun covering its budget deficit with foreign credits.''[14] The slide into the stagnant 1980's had begun.

REFORMS OF THE 1970'S

It became clear that the commercial banking sector could not long withstand a future deterioration of its capital base. A substantive review of government banking and investment regulations was conducted by Finance Minister Jose Lopez Portillo in 1972–73 to develop a regulatory scheme that would allow the banks to compete with nonbank operations. The results were the sweeping reforms embodied in the 1974 Law of Credit Institutions. These reforms reflect a turning away from the U.S.-style (Anglo-Saxon model) banking system that stressed a strict division and specialization of financial institutions toward a Germanic system of multiple bank services or "universal banking."[15] Financial institutions were now able to offer insurance, mortgage products, factoring, brokerage (to include holding stock positions in industrial companies), and trust activities under a holding company umbrella. These new financial groups were primarily the result of mergers that began a bank concentration wave that would shrink the number of banks from over 200 to 18 by 1993. To further stimulate the financial sector, the Securities Market Law of 1975 reorganized the securities exchanges originally set up in 1946 and permitted the creation of brokerage houses. The securities sector experienced a tremendous growth, which is reflected in the dramatic rise of the Bolsa to record levels at the beginning of the 1992–94 period.[16]

The initial indications of reforms during the mid-1970's seemed promising. During the late 1970's, the inflation rate marginally improved, dropping below 20 percent. Additionally, bank reforms in 1976 allowed financial institutions to offer a multitude of services. These modifications were an effort to broaden the banking system away from the pre-1975 system of single-purpose, specialized banks. As the securities sector grew, it became imperative to broaden the market offerings beyond dependence on U.S. and European instruments. Petrobonds, introduced in 1977, were the first step. These bonds represented a share in the federal oil reserve at Nacional Financiera. In time, these would become very volatile due to the fact that they were pegged to the world price of oil. Treasury notes or CETES, introduced in the late 1970's, were followed in 1980 by the government approval of tradable commercial paper and bankers' acceptances.[17]

The surge of inflation during the Echeverría administration resulted in a dramatic peso devaluation in 1976 from the over two-decade-old rate of 12.5 pesos to the U.S. dollar and eventually floating to over 21 pesos/$. U.S. commercial banks were very concerned with the devaluation, but panic was avoided in April by a secret emergency stabilization bridge loan or currency swap of $600 million (a dollar "swap" or exchange for pesos redeemable at a future date in U.S. dollars) arranged by the U.S. Department of the Treasury and the Federal Reserve. The incoming presidential administration of Jose Lopez Portillo (1976–82) was faced with not only a loss of confidence in the ruling PRI party but also a wave of capital flight of much-needed deposits. The flight to dollar-denominated accounts and loans (at times at the rate of $100 million a day) created tremendous instability in the Mexican financial markets. By 1981, over 25 percent of all Mexican domestic deposits were dollar-denominated.[18] Faced with a dilemma, Lopez Portillo decided to forego the liberalization of trade and monetary policy; instead, his administration maintained and reendorsed the functionally "bankrupt" import-substitution policies of his predecessors.[19]

Lopez Portillo was lured to this decision out of a fear of initiating new reforms so early in his administration and, more importantly, in the hope that there would be a full economic recovery based on income from the gradual liberalization of trade and the rising oil revenues. Petroleum was viewed as a panacea by many Mexicans. Mexican oil reserves, managed exclusively by Petroleos Mexicanos (PEMEX), were estimated at 200 billion barrels, ranking sixth in world oil reserves.[20] It was at this moment, some time in late 1976 or early 1977, that Mexico hung its fate and destiny on the world price of oil. Unchecked borrowing, based on the expectation that loans would be paid with future oil income, ballooned Mexico's foreign debt.[21] A feature article in *Fortune* magazine ran a cover story entitled, "Mexico Becomes an Oil Power." Optimism was high:

Because of Pemex's hand-to-mouth past the country is still virtually unexplored. Optimists on Mexican oil say that the total potential reserves are in the billions of barrels . . . whatever the true figure, there is certainly plenty to sustain production well into the twenty-first century at rates far higher than anything Pemex now plans. That is certainly good news for Mexico, for bankers holding Mexican debt, and for Mexico's oil-hungry neighbor to the north.[22]

Much has been said and written about the Organization of Petroleum Exporting Countries (OPEC), the embargo and oil crisis of 1973–74, and world reaction to oil pricing in the 1970's. For Mexico, the situation was even more critical due to the fact that the fragile, closed domestic economy could not easily afford to chance economic disaster. Although bold measures were taken to increase exports, Mexico was caught in a vicious backlash it could neither control nor pull away from. Real growth of the Mexican economy dropped from an annual rate of 6.1 percent in the early 1970's to 1.7 percent in 1976. The Mexican commercial banks were caught in a web that demanded ready capital for industrial output and growth yet were hampered by government controls. In spite of an acceleration in sovereign risk lending (lending to foreign governments) after the oil shock of 1973, the global recession in 1974–75, an increase in world interest rates in 1979–81, and the meteoric drop of oil prices in 1980–81 began to spell economic disaster for Mexico. These factors, along with mounting foreign debt, caused inflation to jump from 27.9 percent in 1981 to over 100 percent in 1983.[23]

1980'S—NATIONALIZATION AND DEBT

As a result of banking reform, the more than 230 financial institutions in Mexico were merged into less than 100 banking institutions by early 1980. Mexico can trace its current state of "underbanked" operations to 1980.[24] The protectionist domestic industrial policy of Mexico began to further break down as the government bought or controlled 1,000 private sector businesses. The "domestic only" policy that in reality turned its back on world markets also caused Mexico to reject membership in the General Agreement on Tariff and Trade (GATT) in 1980.[25]

While no bank since 1941 has been allowed to fail in Mexico, the banking system would not fully attain its previous potential. In the calm before the bank nationalization of 1982, over 1,000 foreign financial entities were registered to offer financial services in Mexico. Of this number, 160 foreign institutions operated offices in Mexico, and of this number, only a few made loans in Mexico. The foreign banks in Mexico served primarily as agents for the parent institutions in their individual countries. What loans were made were limited to domestic bank financing, trade/commercial transactions, and government loans. Nevertheless, numerous foreign banks continued to grant new loans to Mexico, despite their high debt-service ratios, until the middle of 1982. The exception to this foreign bank profile is Citibank, S.A., which has been in Mexico since the early 1920's and offers full-service banking.[26]

In 1982, the simmering conditions of the past decade came to a dramatic economic conclusion. An increasing external debt and a loss of confidence in the government resulted in peso devaluations in February and March. In August 1982, there was another devaluation and Mexico was forced to announce a "moratorium," stating it could no longer service its foreign debt, which had ballooned from $82 billion to in excess of $100 billion.[27] In a last-minute effort to curb the crisis, Lopez Portillo selected Carlos Tello to direct the Central Bank of Mexico. To salvage the economy, Tello announced an economic program that called for swift action, yet fell short of both timeliness and execution:

- a hard line against the IMF concerning bridge loans
- strict controls on foreign imports
- the suspension of the convertibility of the peso
- foreign exchange controls
- government intervention in Mexican banks[28]

Tello's solution was the classic Mexican response to economic crisis—direct all efforts for the recovery of the domestic economy by alienating foreign investors and closing the borders to outside assistance. During August and September, the government could not control the economic chain of events that followed the major peso devaluation and the resulting capital flight.[29] As noted earlier, on September 1, 1982, President Lopez Portillo presented drastic exchange control regulations, eliminated dollar accounts, and announced the nationalization of the commercial banks. The bank nationalization, fashioned after the French Socialist Party program of 1981, was a symbolic move in an effort to buy time and much-needed political capital for the government. In both France and Mexico, nationalization ''fell far short of their goals.''[30]

Trade in dollars was halted and all dollar accounts were converted to pesos at an exchange ratio of 70 pesos to the dollar. The immediate result was a dramatic loss in bank liquidity nationwide.[31] The economic impact on Mexico was dramatic:

Mexico reaped $55 billion from oil exports from 1980 to 1983, economic growth in 1982 was negative for the first time in more than 50 years. The annual growth rate from 1940 to 1982 averaged 6.3 per cent. Inflation, which rarely had crept above 20 per cent, jumped from the onset of the oil boom in the late 1970's to above 150 per cent in 1987. The price of tortillas, a staple food of poor Mexicans, skyrocketed by 416 per cent between 1982 and mid-1986; bread increased 1,800 per cent; and beans went up 776 per cent. Between 1982 and 1987, real wages fell to 1960's levels. Real gross domestic product fell 5.3 per cent in 1983 and has seen only modest gains since. In 1982, the fiscal deficit reached 18 per cent of the gross domestic product, and the peso soared from 25 to the U.S. dollar in January 1982 to more than 1,500 per dollar in 1987.[32]

The debt crisis of the late 1970's and early 1980's had a profound impact on U.S. banking and American investment in Mexico. Aggressive lending, not only to Mexico but to a number of LDCs, continued unchecked as the major commercial banks, flush with Mid-east petrodollars, paid little or no attention to their own in-house, country-by-country risk assessments. During this period, U.S. inflation was high, and thus it made sense to lend on the basis of steadily depreciating dollars. The U.S. Federal Reserve unwittingly fueled the LDC debt crisis by its efforts to overmanage inflation concerns. Nine of the largest U.S. money-center banks had an exposure in Mexican loans equal to 44.4 percent of their capital.[33] Thus, a default by Mexico would send shock waves and possibly even a collapse throughout the American banking system. The Federal Reserve authorized a number of secret overnight currency swaps (i.e., bridge loans) of dollars for potentially worthless pesos to prop up the Mexican financial system. At the height of the debt crisis in late August 1982, Federal Reserve Chairman Paul Volcker and Treasury Secretary Donald Regan, in a three-day marathon session, worked out (what was at that time) an incredible $7.5 billion package of loans, letters of credit, and swaps that included the Department of Energy buying Mexican oil, the Department of Agriculture extending future loans for grains, as well as a network of credits from the central banks of industrial nations in Europe and Asia.[34] Once the August 1982 plan was completed the Fed waited five days before informing U.S. banks on *the full extent* of the bailout package. When briefed, the Fed advised the banks to allow Mexico a 90-day moratorium. While many banks "wanted out" of the deal, they had no recourse until a detailed debt restructuring plan could be worked out. Looking back on the situation in both Mexico and the United States, one observer noted, "the survival of the largest banks in America literally depended on keeping Mexico afloat."[35]

The debt crisis and the nationalization of the banks in 1982 "highlighted" a decade-long period of stagnation, high inflation, and a steady pattern of capital flight. In all, 58 banks were nationalized. In addition to converting dollar-denominated accounts to pesos, a highly favorable exchange rate of 40 pesos per dollar was used to convert dollar-denominated loans. To obtain stability in the banking system the government fostered the consolidation of institutions. The Miguel de la Madrid administration (1982–88) took office as the country struggled with a profound economic and political crisis, yet maintained the nationalization of the banks and did not attempt to undermine the system with additional controls. Jesus Silva Herzog replaced Tello as foreign minister and immediately reversed the policies of the Lopez Portillo administration:

- closer cooperation with the IMF in order to renew loans
- foreign exchange controls were relaxed
- the peso was allowed to float
- a commitment by the government to reduce spending
- increase in prices for government-provided goods/services
- reduce imports and increase exports[36]

The nonbank financial sector, in contrast to the weakened banks, had tremendous growth in the 1980's as assets increased from 9.1 percent to 32.1 percent of the total Mexican financial sector. A rapid rise in the securities market indirectly resulted in the government's decision to allow limited deregulation of the banks in 1989 to increased bank competitiveness. Restrictions on interest rates were slowly removed, money market accounts (cuentas maestras) were authorized, and multibancos or "universal" banking (which means they can sell a broad range of financial products—investment banking, securities brokerage, commercial lending and leasing, insurance, trust) were expanded under the Financial Groups Law of 1990. Nevertheless, inflation soared due to the high public debt and loss of confidence by foreign investors during the mid-1980's.[37]

With inflation steadily out of control, it became distinctly apparent to both the government and private sector in Mexico that a radical reversal was needed to restore confidence in the country. Restoring confidence in the banking system was imperative. During the late 1980's transition from the de la Madrid administration to the presidency of Carlos Salinas de Gortari, the main objectives were to "restructure" the external debt via the Brady Plan, lower inflation, attract new foreign direct investment, join GATT and OECD, and ensure a solid environment for banking. Major obstacles were lack of confidence and the objections of the foreign commercial banks, who were still reluctant to reduce their claims. Such bold action would require planning as well as changes within the Mexican financial and political framework—all of which could be hard to achieve within a Mexico striving to be a first-world nation but burdened with a volatile past.[38]

To recapitalize the banks weakened via devaluations and inflation, the government created a capital infusion program in 1987 called CAPS, or Certificates of Claim on Net Worth. CAPS allowed for trading of one-third of a bank's holdings in private markets. No dividends were paid, as the banks retained all earnings to enhance the capital base of the bank. CAPS were to be convertible at a future date. Beginning in 1988, there was further liberalization on the issuance of bankers' acceptances to ease and lower reserve requirements. Subject to a low 30 percent liquidity requirement, bankers' acceptances were competitive with certificates of deposit and other deposit accounts, which were subject to approximately 60 percent reserve or liquidity coefficients.[39] Recapitalization of the banks was stymied as public sector borrowing drastically dropped in 1982 from 17 percent of GDP to −1 percent in 1992. One response was to permit interest payments on checking accounts in 1989, resulting in a tremendous increase in the use of such consumer accounts.[40]

One of the greatest challenges during the early years of the Salinas administration was the restructuring of the country's debt and a strategy for repayment, thus restoring confidence for direct as well as portfolio investment by foreign capital providers. The Mexican Minister of Finance and the "debt negotiating team" adopted a regime under the Brady plan that was the first country-specific approach to a debt crisis that influenced not only Mexico but all emerging nations worldwide.[41] The extensive debt crisis forced many LDC governments to begin painful austerity programs, often at the risk of losing domestic political support. During intensive hearings before the Banking, Finance and Urban Affairs Committee of the U.S. House of Representatives, it was concluded that "rightly or wrongly, the results of the Mexican debt negotiations provided a litmus test of the effectiveness of the Brady proposals."[42] To achieve a resolution to the debt crisis in Mexico, a payment schedule and criteria were required. Political opposition parties in Mexico, as well as labor groups, voiced concern that the new bailout package would not get Mexico out of its short-term economic crisis nor forestall future crises. Salinas, in office only six months, responded:

With work, order and discipline, Mexico can now leave the crisis behind. This is a great moment for our country, the product of an unparalleled effort by all Mexicans. You can now, my compatriots, tell your children that the world in which they will live will not be easy . . . but it will be better, because no longer will they bear the burden of excessive indebtedness.[43]

To reverse the economic downtown, Mexico would have to stabilize its economy by reducing the private sector debt, reducing inflation, and working with the World Bank and IMF to reduce the deficit in the current account of its balance of payments. Second, a market-oriented economy needed to be implemented that stressed privatization of all sectors of the economy, trade liberalization, and deregulation. Third, the government, as well as the private sector, would need to fully cooperate with major multilateral institutions, such as the World Bank, IMF, and foreign commercial bank creditors to stabilize the situation. And fourth, outdated concepts concerning protectionism and a closed economy would have to be marked by improvements in the climate for foreign and domestic investments. In no way was the sovereignty of Mexico to be compromised or diminished. The road to recovery lay in a cooperative approach to enhance the economic underpinnings of the nation.[44]

THE 1990'S—PRIVATIZATION

As the open economy concept was gradually endorsed by all sectors within Mexico, the most dramatic impact on the economy of Mexico was the projected privatization of nearly 1,000 government-owned and -managed entities. In addition to providing much-needed revenue for the treasury, it also served to stimulate the economy by attracting back to Mexico a substantial portion of the flight capital of the 1980's, as well as new direct foreign capital investment. Cumulative direct foreign investment in Mexico tripled from $10 billion in 1980 to over $30 billion by 1990. Two Mexican banks, Bancomer and Banamex, were ranked in the top 20 financial institutions in emerging countries.[45]

At the heart of the crisis of the 1980's had been the need to modernize the financial and regulatory systems, as well as governmental fiscal reform. To this end, the Mexican Congress, in July 1990, amended the Constitution to allow for the privatization of commercial banks. The result was the approval of the Credit Institutions Law that fully restructured and restored the multiple bank system.[46] The privatization of the 18 remaining banks began in June 1991. To insure an orderly transition to bank privatization, the Bank Divestiture Committee was established to review proposals by interested bidders. The committee interviewed each prospective buyer or buying group, from which a list of qualified buyers was drafted. Total foreign investment in a Mexican financial group or bank was limited to 30 percent of equity capital. Each bidder had to deposit a $10 million downpayment prior to bidding. The process took 13 months, raised $12.4 billion (37.8 trillion pesos) for the government, and increased the number of shareholders in Mexican banks from 8,000 to more than 130,000.[47] A sealed bidding process was used to select buyers. The average weighted price of the bank sold was 14.7 times earnings and 3.49 times book value. Four banks were bought by private investment groups and 14 of the 18 banks were purchased by financial group/brokerage houses (see Figure 2-2).[48]

The new legislation created three types of multibank financial groups:

a. a bank with leasing, factoring, foreign exchange, mutual fund management and origination, and warehousing activities.

b. a brokerage firm with leasing, factoring, foreign exchange, mutual fund management and origination, and warehousing activities, and

c. a holding company that must have at least three of the following institutions, with no more than one of each type:

    1. bank

    2. insurance company

    3. brokerage house

    4. leasing company

    5. factoring company

    6. bonding company

    7. mutual funds management company

    8. currency exchange broker and

    9. warehousing company[49]

Under the Credit Institutions Law, three types of stock were approved as a framework for bank capitalization and to assist the transition to privatization. Common stock was designated as ''A'' shares (held only by Mexican nationals), to comprise the controlling interest up to 51 percent of the total outstanding shares. The second class of stock was ''B'' shares (held by Mexican nationals and institutional investors), which could comprise 19–49 percent of the total shares outstanding. To attract foreign investment, ''C'' class shares could be owned by foreigners but could represent no more than 30 percent of the outstanding ownership. To limit concentrations of ownership, no individual could own more than 10 percent of shares outstanding.[50]

In addition to a tremendous boost to the treasury of Mexico, privatization of

Figure 2-2
Mexican Bank Privatization: 1991–92

Bank	Purchase*	Date Sold	Price US Dollar Millions**	Price Times Book Value
MERCANTILE	G.F. Probursa	6/10/91	201	2.66
BANPAIS	G.F. Mexival	6/17/91	179	3.03
CREMI	Private Investors	6/24/91	246	3.40
CONFIA	G.F. Abaco	8/05/91	293	3.73
BANORIENTE	G.F. Margen	8/12/91	73	4.04
BANCRESER	Private Investors	8/19/91	139	2.60
BANAMEX	G.F. Banacci	8/26/91	3,197	2.62
BANCOMER	G.F. Varnsa	10/28/91	2,808	2.99
BCH	Private Investors	11/11/91	288	2.67
SERFIN	G.F. Obsa	1/27/92	916	2.69
COMERMEX	G.F. Inverlat	2/10/92	876	3.73
SOMEX***	G.F. Invermexico	3/02/92	608	3.31
ATLANTICO	G.F. Bursatil Mexicano	3/30/92	476	5.33
PROMEX	G.F. Val. Finamex	4/06/92	348	4.25
BANORO	G.F. Estrategia Bur.	4/13/92	368	3.95
BANORTE	G.F. Maseca	6/15/92	575	4.25
INTERNACIONAL	G.F. Privado Mexicano	6/29/92	482	2.95
BANCEN	Private Investors	7/06/92	282	4.65
TOTAL			**12,355**	**3.07******

*G.F. stands for Grupo Financiero (Financial Group).
**Exchange rate used to convert 1991 bank sales was 3,048 pesos/dollars, e.g. the average peso/
  dollar exchange rate between 6/91 and 11/91. The rate used for sales made in 1992 was 3,088
  pesos/dollars.
***Somex was renamed "Banco Mexicano."
****Average weighted price-book value ratio.

Source: El Diario Oficial and the Mexican Finance Ministry, *El Nuevo* "Perfil de la Economia
  Mexicana," September 1992 and January 1993 as seen in Mexico: Economic and Financial
  Report (U.S. Embassy, Mexico), April 1993, p. 33–34.

the Mexican banking system during the early years of the Salinas administration
resulted in an initial increase in investor confidence in the country's economic
recovery. This resulting stability was viewed as critical to bringing inflation
under control as well as attracting large sums of new direct investment to Mexico's infrastructure projects, industrial expansion, and stock market. Notwithstanding these changes, the Mexican economy has been underbanked and in
need of technology, as well as trained managers to staff continued industrial and
financial services growth (see Figure 2-3). GATT membership in 1986 paved
the way for the emergence of a more stable and competitive Mexican economy
as well as the initial framework for drafting and passage of NAFTA. Furthermore, trade liberalization in the banking sector proved pivotal to the general

Figure 2-3
Population per Bank Branch (December 1991)

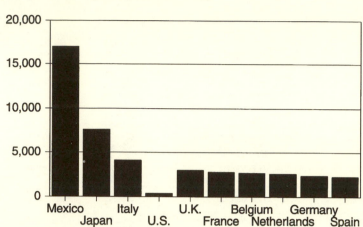

Source: Banco de Mexico.

framework of the financial services section of the North American Free Trade Agreement.

The rush to export to Mexico and the thin capital base of both the government and the Mexican banking system went unreported and/or undetected for much of the early 1990's. The "Mexican Miracle" of growth and low inflation, touted by the Salinas administration, was both the envy and model of other emerging nations. The historically well-documented fragile nature of the Mexican economy seemed a distant memory, yet was seldom forgotten. One reason for the euphoria during the early years of the Salinas administration was the tremendous growth and trade flows that were accented by the level of urban growth, industrial expansion, and commercial activity on the U.S.-Mexican border.

NOTES

1. Miguel de la Madrid, "Mexico: The New Challenge," *Foreign Affairs*, Fall 1984, pp. 62–76; Adolfo A. Zinser, "Mexico: The Presidential Problem,"*Foreign Policy* No. 69, Winter 1987–88, pp. 43–46; T. R. Fehrenbach, *Fire and Blood: A Bold and Definitive Modern Chronicle of Mexico* (New York: 1973), pp. 602–32; Camin and Meyer, *In the Shadow*, pp. 161, 165, 174. Also see Roger Hansen, *The Politics of Mexican Development* (Baltimore: 1971), pp. 1–56. Note: Import-substitution is also referred to as import-substitution-industrial or ISI.

2. Tom Barry, *Zapata's Revenge: Free Trade and the Farm Crisis in Mexico* (Boston: 1995), pp. 117–28. Note: Governmental controls of Mexican banks during this period required restrictions on interest rates, high reserve requirements, forced lending programs to select sections of the economy, and overwhelming barriers to market entry. See Raymond Vernon, *The Dilemma of Mexico's Development* (Cambridge, Mass.: 1963).

3. Barry, *Zapata's Revenge*, p. 119; Virgil M. Cummins (ed.), *The Evolution of Banking in Mexico: A History of Banca Serfin* (Mexico City: 1981), pp. 32–58; Welch and Gruben, "A Brief Modern History of the Mexican Financial System," *Financial Industry Studies* (FRBD), October 1993, pp. 1–3; Riding, *Distant Neighbors*, pp. 194–226; Alex M. Saragoza, *The Monterrey Elite and the Mexican State, 1800–1940* (Austin: 1988), pp. 96–209; see Levy and Szekely, *Mexico*, pp. 132–37, 144–46 and Judith Adler Hellman, *Mexico in Crisis* (New York: 1983), pp. 84–102 for a review of Mexican agricultural policy.

4. Rene Villarreal, "The Latin American Strategy of Import Substitution: Failure or Paradigm for the Region?" as seen in Gary Gereffi and Donald L. Wyman (eds.), *Manufacturing Miracles: Paths of Industrialization in Latin America and East Asia* (Princeton: 1990), pp. 292–320; William Diebold, Jr. (ed.), *Bilateralism, Multilateralism and Canada in U.S. Trade Policy* (New York: 1988), pp. 72, 109–12.

5. U.S. Congress, House, Committee on Banking and Finance, *International Monetary Fund*, Serial 102–8, 102nd Cong., 1st sess., 1991, p. 80.

6. James N. Goodsell, "Mexico: Why the Students Rioted," *Current History*, January 1969, pp. 31–35; David J. Mabry, *The Mexican University and the State: Student Conflict, 1910–1971* (College Station: 1982), pp. 246–94. Note: Mexico was the first Spanish-speaking country, even surpassing Spain, to host the Olympic Games.

7. Susan K. Purcell, "Mexico-U.S. Relations: Big Initiations Can Cause Big Problems," *Foreign Affairs*, Winter 1981–82, pp. 384–85; Welch and Gruben, "A Brief Modern History of the Mexican Financial System," pp. 1–3; Hellman, *Mexico in Crisis*, pp. 173–86; Riding, *Distant Neighbors*, pp. 83–85; Ladman (ed.), *Mexico: A Country in Crisis*, pp. 12–13; Castaneda, "Mexico at the Brink," *Foreign Affairs*, p. 297; Levy and Szekely, *Mexico*, p. 136; Goodsell, "Mexico: Why the Students Rioted," *Current History*, pp. 31–35. For an excellent overview of this period see A. B. Barrera, *A Study of the Economic and Financial Development of Mexico and Its Impact on Laredo, Texas and Its Financial Institutions*, unpublished thesis, March 1968, Southwestern Graduate School of Banking, SMU Dallas, Texas.

8. Ladman (ed.), *Mexico: A Country in Crisis*, pp. 12–13, 19–20, 26; Welch and Gruben, "A Brief Modern History of the Mexican Financial System," pp. 1–4 [see Brother and Solis (1966), pp. 59–64.]; Pedro Aspe, *Economic Transformation: The Mexican Way* (Mexico, D.F.: 1993), pp. 65–76; Catherine M. Carstens, *Las Finanzas Populares en Mexico* (Mexico, D.F.: 1995), pp. 9–35. Note: The Banco de Mexico was established in 1925 as the central bank with a capital stock of 50 million gold pesos.

9. Jaime Suchlicki, *Mexico: From Montezuma to NAFTA, Chiapas, and Beyond* (Washington, D.C.: 1996), pp. 141–42.

10. Welch and Gruben, "A Brief Modern History of the Mexican Financial System," p. 6.

11. As seen in Karen Lissakers, *Banks, Borrowers, and the Establishment* (New York: 1981), p. 46.

12. *Diario Oficial*, May 5, 1973.

13. Ladman (ed.), *Mexico*, pp. 13–15; Grayson, *The United States and Mexico*, pp. 37–42.

14. Riding, *Distant Neighbors*, pp. 203–4. Also see Lissakers, *Banks, Borrowers, and the Establishment* pp. 108–10.

15. Sylvia Maxfield, "The International Political Economy of Bank Nationalization: Mexico in Comparative Perspective," *Latin American Research Review*, Vol. 25, No. 3,

1991, p. 79; Welch and Gruben, "A Brief Modern History of the Mexican Financial System," pp. 4–5.

16. Tim Heyman, *Investing in Mexico* (Mexico City: 1989), pp. 13–17; Aureliano Gonzalez-Baz, "A Survey of Mexican Laws Affecting Foreign Businessmen," *Denver Journal of International Law and Policy*, Spring 1974, pp. 37–50; Camin and Meyer, *In the Shadow*, pp. 170–71.

17. Charles E. Butler, "Mexico's Foreign Trade and Balance of Payments," *Texas Business Review*, Vol. 56, November-December 1982, pp. 297–302.

18. Carlos Tello, *La Nacionalizacion de la Banca en Mexico* (Mexico City: 1984), pp. 7–8, 48–49; Hellman, *Mexico in Crisis*, pp. 209–15.

19. Greider, *Secrets of the Temple*, pp. 119, 485–86; James H. Street, "Prospects for Mexico's Industrial Development Plan in the 1980's," *Texas Business Review*, May-June 1980, pp. 125–26.

20. "Oil Potential of Mexico Barely Tapped," *Journal of Commerce*, September 27, 1976; Camin and Meyer, *In the Shadow*, pp. 197–98. Note: For an excellent overview of the role of Mexican oil and NAFTA, see Richard D. English, "Energy in the NAFTA: Free Trade Confronts Mexico's Constitution," *Tulsa Journal of Comparative & International Law*, Fall 1993, pp. 1–32.

21. Grayson, *The United States and Mexico*, pp. 65–90; Purcell "Mexico-U.S. Relations: Big Initiatives Can Cause Big Problems," *Foreign Affairs*, pp. 379–92; Lissakers, *Banks, Borrowers and the Establishment*, pp. 30–33.

22. Hugh Sandeman, "Mexico Becomes an Oil Power: Pemex Comes Out of Its Shell," *Fortune*, April 10, 1978, pp. 44–48.

23. Korner et al., *The IMF and the Debt Crisis*, pp. 6–7; Grayson, *The United States and Mexico*, pp. 65–70; Greider, *Secrets of the Temple*, p. 435; Street, "Prospect for Mexico's Industrial Plan in the 1980's," pp. 126–27.

24. Ladman (ed.), *Mexico*, pp. 24–27.

25. Levy and Szekely, *Mexico*, pp. 142–43, Mexico, Secretaria de Programacion y Presupresto, *Segundo informe de gobierno, anexo I* (Mexico City: 1978), pp. 295–300.

26. Levy and Szekely, *Mexico*, pp. 151–157; Korner et al., *The IMF and the Debt Crisis*, p. 9; Alan Riding, "World Push by Mexican Banks Irks Rivals," *New York Times*, April 18, 1981; Alan Robinson, "Mexico Urged to Cool Economic Engine," *Journal of Commerce*, April 24, 1981; George Getschow, "Foreign Investment in Mexico Swells," *Wall Street Journal*, May 12, 1981; James R. Kraus, "Citicorp Rules the U.S. Banking Roost in Mexico," *American Banker*, February 27, 1992, p. 7A. Note: The Citibank office in Mexico City is a branch, not a subsidiary.

27. William E. Brock, "Trade and Debt: The Vital Linkage," *Foreign Affairs*, Summer 1984, p. 1045; Roy C. Smith, *The Global Bankers* (New York: 1990) pp. 114–16; Greider, *Secrets of the Temple*, pp. 517–18. Note: The exact total of the external debt varies from source to source, but was in the range from $80 to $110 billion. Myron B. Slovin and Subbarao V. Jaganti, "Bank Capital Regulations and the Valuation Effects of Latin America [Mexico and Bolivia] Debt Moratoriums," *Journal of Banking and Finance*, Vol. 17, 1993, pp. 159–71.

28. Hellman, *Mexico in Crisis*, pp. 217–28.

29. Note: Capital flight from Mexico in 1981 and 1982 totalled $12.3 and $13.15 billion as compared to $4.4 billion in 1979. *Financial Times*, December 1, 1983, and *Business Week*, October 3, 1983, p. 132. See also Lissakers, *Banks, Borrowers, and the*

Establishment, pp. 76–82; Greider, *Secrets*, pp. 486–87, 517–19; Camin and Meyer, *In the Shadow*, pp. 197–98.

30. Maxfield, "The International Political Economy of Bank Nationalization," pp. 75–82; interview with Charles J. Siegman, Senior Associate Director, Division of International Finance, Board of Governors, Federal Reserve, Washington, D.C., March 15, 1994.

31. *Diario Oficial*, September 1, 1982; Robert R. Moore, "The Government Budget Deficit and the Banking System: The Case of Mexico," *Financial Industry Studies*, Summer 1992, pp. 27–35; Castaneda, "Mexico at the Brink," *Foreign Affairs*, pp. 282–92. For details of the 1982 nationalization see Jeff Brannon, "The Nationalization of Mexico's Private Bank System," in Ladman (ed.), *Mexico*, pp. 24–44.

32. Aguilar Zinser, "Mexico: The Presidential Problem," *Foreign Policy*, Winter 1987–88, p. 44.

33. Feinberg and Kallab (eds.), *Uncertain Future*, p. 53. Note: The nine money-center banks cited were Bank of America, Citibank, Chase, Morgan Guaranty, Manufacturer's Hanover, Continental Illinois, Bankers Trust, Chemical, and First National Bank of Chicago.

34. Greider, *Secrets of the Temple*, pp. 435–37, 484–87, 502–3, 516–22; "Japan Ups Ante In Mexico," *JEI Report*, No. 25B, June 30, 1989, pp. 9–11. Note: Within a year after the August 1982 debt crisis in Mexico, 14 other countries were experiencing the same type of fiscal and foreign debt crisis.

35. Greider, *Secrets*, pp. 484–87; Miller, *Citicorp*, pp. 34, 111–15. Note: Mexico has had a cycle of debt and monetary crisis dating back over a century which has involved multinational banks and corporations. See Frank G. Dawson, *The First Latin American Debt Crisis* (New Haven: 1990), pp. 1–281; "The Mexican Crisis," *The Chronicle*, Vol. XL, June 27, 1885, pp. 752–53; "Growth of Mexican National Revenues," Ibid., Vol. LXVI, April 2, 1898, pp. 642–43; "Mexico's Adoption of Gold Standard," Ibid., Vol. LXXX, April 22, 1905, pp. 1446–49.

36. Greider, *Secrets*, p. 519; Hellman, *Mexico in Crisis*, pp. 228–31. Note: Jesus Silva Herzog was named ambassador to the United States during the Zedillo administration.

37. Donald C. Shuffstall, "Economic Crisis and Recovery—The Maquiladora: A True National Priority," *Crisis and Response: A Roundtable on Mexico* (San Diego: March 1986), pp. 79–88; Welch and Gruben, "A Brief History," p. 47; Heyman, *Investing in Mexico*, pp. 49–160; Hobart Rowen, "Back to Third World Debt," *Washington Post*, December 28, 1987. See also William R. Cline, *Mobilizing Bank Lending to Debtor Countries* (Washington, D.C.: 1987), pp. 1–90.

38. Jack Egan, "The Onset of Big-Debt Blues," *U.S. News and World Report*, July 24, 1989, pp. 20–22; "Bush Pleased with Plan to Reduce Mexican Debt," *The Eagle*, July 25, 1989; John A. Adams, Jr., "Mexican Debt Review: The Background and Possible Solution," *Infonational Review*, July 5, 1989, pp. 1–5; Jeffrey T. Bannon, James H. Holcombs, and Richard L. Sprinkle, "An Evaluation of Mexican Policy Toward Foreign Direct Investment," *Southwest Journal of Business and Economics*, Spring 1990, pp. 20–26; Robert Taylor (ed.), "Mexican Finance Reform and Prospects," *International Reports*, IBC (New York: 1990), pp. 29–35: Philip L. Russell, *Mexico under Salinas* (Austin: 1994), pp. 160–229; Peter Truell, "Mexico, Creditor Nations Reach Accord on Debt," *Wall Street Journal*, June 1, 1989, p. A4. Note: The creditor banks held $70 billion of Mexico's $100 billion in foreign debt. Of the $70 billion, about $54 billion was medium-term and long-term debt owed by the Mexican government. Mexico wanted

a reduction of 50 percent in the government debt, but banks only offered cuts between 10 and 20 percent.

39. As noted by Welch and Gruben, "liquidity coefficient" refers to required reserves that can be held in liquid interest-bearing assets such as CETES. This is different from "required reserve coefficient," which typically refers to the percentage of liabilities that must be held in cash reserves or non-interest-bearing (or low-interest-bearing) deposits at the central bank.

40. Eugene L. Stewart et al., "Statement of PPG Industries, Inc., Regarding the Accession of Mexico to the General Agreement on Tariffs and Trade (GATT)." Before the Trade Policy Staff Committee of the Office of the United States Trade Representative, February 18, 1986, pp. 1–61; Welch and Gruben, "A Brief Modern History," pp. 6–9. See also John A. Haslem, Carl A. Scheraga, and James P. Bedingfield, "An Analysis of the Impact of International Activity on the Domestic Balance Sheet of U.S. Banks," *Management International Review*, Vol. 35, No. 1, 1995, pp. 45–68.

41. Jonathan Fuerbringer, "Mexico Debt Pact Welcomed," *New York Times*, July 25, 1989, p. 25.

42. Korner et al., *The IMF and the Debt Crisis*, pp. 1–82; Russell, *Mexico under Salinas*, pp. 160–76; John Clark, "Debt Reduction and Market Reentry under the Brady Plan," Federal Reserve Bank of New York, *Quarterly Review*, Vol. 18, No. 4, Winter 1993–94, pp. 38–62; U.S. Congress, House, *Impact of Accounting and Regulation Procedures on the Third World Debt*, Committee on Banking and Finance, Serial No. 101–29, 101st Cong., 1st sess., 1989, pp. 1–20; Ibid., *International Monetary Fund*, Committee on Banking and Finance, Serial No. 102–48, 102nd Cong., 1st sess., 1991, pp. 42–47; BMI, *Mexico 1994*, p. 97. Note: During 1983, the rescheduling of Mexico debt involved over 500 banks.

43. Larry Rohter, "Salinas and Business Hail Debt Agreement," *New York Times*, July 25, 1989, p. 43. See also Rohter, "Mexico Feels Squeeze of Years of Austerity," Ibid., July 25, 1989, p. 1.

44. James S. Gruppo, "Banking in Mexico," presentation to the American Bar Association, Dallas, Texas, June 8, 1993; "Moctezuma's Revenge," *The Economist*, April 3, 1993, p. 65; Haluk Unal, Asli Demirgvc-kunt, and Kwok-Wai Leung, "The Brady Plan, 1989 Mexican Debt-Reduction Agreement, and Bank Stock Returns in the United States and Japan," *Journal of Money, Credit, and Banking*, Vol. 25, No. 3, August 1993, pp. 410–29.

45. Camin and Meyer, *In the Shadow*, pp. 165–66; "Top 50 [Banks] in Emerging Countries," *Euromoney*, June 1992, p. 106. Note: The only other Latin American banks mentioned were in Brazil.

46. Catherine Mansell Carstens, *The Social and Economic Impact of the Mexican Bank Reprivatization* (La Jolla: 1993), pp. 1–39; Eduardo Andere and Georgina Kessel (eds.), *Mexico y el Tratado Trilateral de Libre Comercio* (Mexico: 1992), pp. 215–46.

47. John Hennessy, "Lessons from Mexico," *New York Times*, November 15, 1993; Adams, "Overview of Banking and Financial Services in Mexico: Prospects in the NAFTA Environment," presentation made in Dallas, Texas, June 8, 1993. Note: Total revenues are actually greater due to the fact that the Mexican government holds approximately 8.8 percent of the total capital in the banking systems.

48. Adams, "Overview of Banking and Financial Services in Mexico: Prospects in the NAFTA Environment," June 8, 1993; Jeffrey W. Gunther, "Mexico Offers Banking Opportunities," *Financial Industry Issues* (FRBD), Fourth Quarter 1992, pp. 1–2. Note:

Each bidder had to place a U.S. $10 million downpayment and it is reported that the highest bidder for each bank won in each sale; as of March 1993 the first 11 banks have completed all postpurchase audits and on the average the government has refunded to the new owners 3 percent of the bank's purchase price.

49. Welch and Gruben, ''A Brief Modern History,'' p. 8.

50. Banco de Mexico, *The Mexican Economy* (Mexico City: 1992).

Chapter 3

U.S.-Mexican Border: Crossroads of Trade and Finance

The globe is fast becoming a single marketplace. Goods are being made wherever they can be made the cheapest, regardless of national boundaries. And the most effective places for much mass productions are coming to be third world countries.

—Robert B. Reich
(U.S. Secretary of Labor 1993–1996), 1983

Our southern frontier is not simply American on one side and Mexican on the other. It is a third country with its own identity . . . born of necessity.
—Tom Miller, *On the Border*, 1981

The United States–Mexican border is like no other region in the world. Reaching from the Gulf of Mexico westward along the Rio Grande and across the desert from El Paso, Texas, to Tijuana and the Pacific Ocean, the 2,000–mile boundary has been one of the fastest growing areas in the Western Hemisphere during the past decade. Historically, the United States and Mexico have had a love–hate relationship over the border region. For decades in the United States, the South-west border region represented the remotest section of the continent, and for Mexico it has remained far from the mainstream of Mexican growth and politics. The term for the northern border area of Mexico, "la frontera norte," has long had a unique meaning and importance for Mexico. The border is a distinct region, compressed between two nations, two cultures, two economies, and two histories. It is, as one author noted, "Where the United States blends into Mexico."[1] More than a boundary, the border region has experienced dramatic changes over the past decade. However, with the passage of the North American Free Trade Agreement, the border region is expected to experience a further transformation in both urbanization and industrialization expansion well into the next century.[2]

Over the past three decades, cross-border banking, trade, manufacturing, and commerce have driven the growth and importance of the border region. The U.S.-Mexican border is unique. Nowhere else is there a major industrial country bordering an emerging industrialized nation. The boundary is the most crossed border in the world—both legally and illegally. Commercially, the border is a very diverse region. For example, the inland port at Laredo/Nuevo Laredo is the number one border crossing between any two nations worldwide. While a strict protectionist policy has historically been adopted for the Mexican national economy, a fairly liberal commercial cross-border policy was established for the border region, thus increasing two-way trade and interdependency with cross-border communities of the United States. An always present circumstance was the political and social questions involving immigration. The Bracero Program (migrant agricultural workers), the north-south flow of goods and services, the rise of the twin-plant ''maquiladora'' industry, and the role of border commercial banks have been paramount to the economic growth of the border region. The banks of the border region have played a profound role. Their ability to deal in a dual culture and currency is pivotal to border commerce and growth. Banking on the border reflects the meshing of cultures, a tremendous awareness and expertise in global trade, and a regional commercial vitality seldom seen.[3]

THE BRACERO PROGRAM AND BIP

Today's image of the border and its most recent commercialization and urban transformation can trace its historical and economic roots from the mid-1960's. In an effort to address immigration, agricultural issues and regional industrial operations, the emphasis and priorities have shifted over the past few decades. At the heart of any discussion on the border is the status, role, and impact of immigration. Thus, the assessment and dialogue on immigration issues has formed one of the cornerstones of the trade debate. In his book *Mexico Shock* (1995), Jorge G. Castañeda argues the case for Mexico. His thesis centers on the debate that the roots of immigration boil down to a need for cheap, plentiful labor first for the agriculture sector, and second for border industrial support. Castañeda stresses, ''The single most important reason why Mexico should matter to Americans: immigration.''[4]

North-south flow of migrant agricultural labor has been common since the early 1900's. The random crossing of workers was not styled into a formal program until the advent of the Bracero Program.[5] Often overlooked, there was a tremendous demand not only in the Southwest but also in the upper Midwest for labor from Mexico to work the sugar beet fields as well as harvest blueberries and grain. There was such a large concentration of Mexican workers in Michigan that some braceros referred to the state as the ''Michoacan del norte''—Michoacan of the north. Many of these workers were employed by the canneries and packers that dotted the Midwest during the 1950's and 1960's. The origins of the Bracero Program date back to two-way talks during the early part of World War II, dealing with the severe wartime U.S. labor shortage. The program was formalized in the early 1950's to allow for cheap, plentiful "braceros" (hired hands, or in Spanish, "arms") on both sides of the U.S.-Mexican border. In spite of its relative success in employing over 12.5 million Mexicans between 1942 and 1964 as seasonal agricultural workers, the Kennedy administration (reacting to pressure from American labor unions) terminated the Bracero Program in 1963 on grounds that it was detrimental to American workers. This action had a direct nationwide impact on agricultural growers and packers that needed and depended on Mexican labor. Furthermore, the ending of the formal migrant labor program cut off a safety valve deemed advantageous to social stability in Mexico.[6]

Although Mexico touted its "domestic only" policy geared to exclude what many hard-liners in Mexico deemed "foreign intrigue," an option was needed to directly or indirectly maintain an immigration safety net while at the same time holding true to the "protectionist" policy. Historically, northern Mexico and its close proximity to the United States made American products easily available and negated the impact of the import-substitution policy along the border. The solution to excess Mexican labor was developed by the Diaz Ordaz (1964–70) administration. After a delegation from the Ministry of Industry and Commerce toured U.S.-owned assembly plants in the Far East in 1964, the idea developed to create an atmosphere on the Mexican side of the border that would attract foreign investment and create jobs, yet not compromise the government's quasi–closed-door policy. The answer came in 1965–66 when the Mexican government approved the Border Industrialization Program or BIP. Over time this led directly to the rejuvenation of the border region.[7]

The Border Industrialization Program was formalized in 1966 with these objectives:

1. provide jobs for the severe unemployment in the border region,
2. encourage a means to obtain much-needed foreign exchange[8]
3. expand the industrial base of the border cities and northern Mexico
4. shift the labor base from agriculture to modern industrial production
5. allow a means for effective technology transfer.[9]

This industrial development focus was envisioned to attract direct foreign investment into Mexico and to build production facilities and infrastructure that would provide both commercialization and jobs. The BIP was truly an anomaly in the prevailing import-substitution strategy of Mexico. Foreign-owned production plants under the BIP would obtain preferable tariff treatment in order to allow foreign companies, primarily from the United States, to assemble component parts free of increased duties or tariffs—"in-bond"—in Mexico and to return the completed assembled components back to the United States to be placed in final production. While Mexico (not the United States) created the BIP, one of its primary aims was to take advantage of specific tariff schedules concerning offshore production and reimportation outlined in Items 806.30 and 807.00 of the U.S. Customs Code. Item 806.30 allowed metal products manufactured in the United States, assembled abroad, and returned to the U.S. manufacturer for final production to be imported duty free except on the value added during the foreign processing. Item 807 allowed fabricated components made in the United States to be reimported duty free if they were assembled abroad into either intermediate or final goods. Variations of the BIP sprang up worldwide as emerging countries vied for hard currency investments from the industrialized nations. Projecting as much as a 50 percent reduction in total manufacturing cost, the governments of Taiwan, Singapore, Malaysia, and Korea also established or expanded what some called "export platforms" (assembly operations) to encourage foreign direct investment.[10]

The concept of this tariff clarification on offshore manufacturing was to apply duties only on the "value added" to assembled components. The new manufacturing facilities in Mexico were also able to take advantage of the tax break and duty-free status (if certain conditions were met) created by the U.S government under the Generalized System of Preferences (GSP) in 1976. Initially, the in-bond duty preference applied only to factories located within a 20 kilometer band along the U.S.-Mexican border.[11] This two-country exchange of materials assemble-and-reexport became known as the twin-plants concept (production sharing) or "maquiladoras." For Mexico it was envisioned that the piecework nature required by these foreign subsidiaries in Mexico would provide a tremendous job base. Few, either in the Mexican government or private industry during the late 1960's, could envision the eventual impact and growth of the maquila concept on both the border region and the overall Mexican economy. Though routinely covered in the mass media, the maquila concept of offshore production went virtually unnoticed among the general public in the United States until the 1992–93 NAFTA debate.[12]

MAQUILAS

Real growth of the border maquila industries under the BIP did not begin to expand until the early 1970's.[13] Numbering only a few dozen at the start of the decade, the total number of maquiladora plants in Mexico increased from 160 in 1970 to 625 by 1980. Employment at these plants during this period grew sixfold, from 20,000 to over 120,000. The early maquila period prior to 1982 is marked by the stereotyping of these new foreign-owned plants as unsafe sweatshops. While much of the pre-1980 labor was unskilled and dominated by women—work force wages tripled and health benefits were expanded in comparison to the Mexican norm.[14]

The prime stimulus for maquila growth by the 1980's in Mexico, fresh from the crash of the oil market and recession of the late 1970's, benefitted from an export-oriented strategy. The de la Madrid administration reduced protective tariffs and boldly declared the maquila sector a priority for the revitalization of the Mexican economy. While jobs were always the underlying focal point for Mexico, the maquila sector would provide a much-needed source of hard currency foreign exchange. The development of private industrial "parques" (parks) and the expansion of infrastructure to move goods and services accelerated the growth of both the maquilas and border urban areas. Except for an economic downturn during the high interest rate period of 1980–81 and the peso devaluations of 1982, the number of plants, employees, value-added goods processed, and salaries have steadily increased yearly since 1980.[15]

Although a modification in the law allowed establishment of production facilities in the interior of Mexico in 1972, most maquilas were located on the border. "By the early 1980's about one-half of all duty-free imports assembled in all nations worldwide by U.S.-owned companies were those from Mexican maquiladoras," generating an "export credit" of over $2 billion annually.[16] Mexico slowly realized that the maquila sector generated a significant amount of much-needed hard currency and served as a multiplier effect to create secondary jobs in support of the offshore manufacturing. In August 1983, the government of Mexico issued revised BIP guidelines expanding the scope of the in-bond industry, enhancing the foreign exchange capability, and further encouraging in-bond plants in the less developed areas of the interior. New maquila plant locations were excluded from the congested industrial centers of Mexico City and Monterrey. By 1985, the maquiladora sector was the largest source of foreign exchange after petroleum exports and before tourism (see Figure 3-1).[17]

By the early 1980's, approximately 10 percent of maquilas were located in the interior away from the U.S.-Mexican border. The growth of global production and the emphasis on state-of-the-art technology, technology transfer, and more sophisticated plants have gradually changed and improved the industrial base in Mexico. The maquilas began a shift away from unskilled, labor-intensive assembly job shops to more specialized, capital-intensive manufacturing. After 1980 labor cost as a percentage of total operating cost dropped dramatically. This is reflected in increased worker productivity due in large measure to the increased use of new technology requiring skilled workers. Skilled workers command higher wages, thus Mexico over time will become less competitive in easily transportable, low-wage maquila jobs. Growth of the maquila sector continued through the decade and totaled nearly 2,000 maquila plants, employing over 460,000 by 1990. Furthermore, assembly plants during this period grew in both size and sophistication as the major automotive makers, telecommunication firms, and defense contractors increased investments in Mexican operations. By the mid-1990's, the products produced and/or assembled by maquilas fell into the following general categories: electronic/electric materials 34 percent, transportation equipment 13 percent, electrical equipment 9 percent, petroleum, plas-

Figure 3-1
In-Bond Maquilas: 1970–96

| | Number | Employees | Plant Location | |
			Border	Interior
1970	160	20,327	160	0
1971	251	29,214	339	0
1972	339	48,060	339	0
1973	400	64,330	390	10
1974	455	75,977	429	26
1975	444	67,213	418	26
1976	448	74,496	406	42
1977	443	78,433	398	45
1978	457	90,204	420	37
1979	540	111,365	500	40
1980	620	123,879	576	44
1981	605	130,973	565	40
1982	588	127,048	550	38
1983	629	173,128	592	37
1984	722	202,078	678	44
1985	789	217,544	742	47
1986	987	268,388	915	72
1987	1,129	322,743	1,139	120
1988	1,490	389,245	1,334	156
1989	1,795	437,064	1,572	223
1990	1,789	460,293	1,523	266
1991	2,013	486,723	1,682	331
1992	2,129	511,339	1,789	340
1993	2,143	546,588	1,773	370
1994	2,064	600,585	1,689	375
1995	2,241	680,209	1,786	455
1996f	2,400	750,000	1,850	550

f = forecast.

Source: SECOFI; INEGI.

tics, and chemicals 6 percent, services 6 percent, metal industries 6 percent, food/agricultural 5 percent, medical supplies 5 percent, clothing and textiles 2 percent, and other manufactured products 14 percent. In 1996 maquila employment at over 2,300 plants exceeded 700,000 workers.[18]

URBANIZATION

While much attention has been given to the production aspects of the maquila sector, relatively little attention has been directed to explore the dynamics of urbanization in the border region. Urbanization and industrial growth will continue to have a major impact on the Southwest border region. Over two-thirds of the border population is centered in six of the fourteen primary twin-city locations on the border: Tijuana-San Diego, Ciudad Juarez-El Paso, Nuevo Laredo-Laredo, Reynosa-McAllen-Pharr, Matamoros-Brownsville, and Mexicali-Calexico. Between 1975 and 1995, maquila employment annual growth rate has

Figure 3-2
Twin-Cities Border Population: 1950–2000 (in Thousands)

	1950	1960	1970	1980	1990	2000 *
San Diego	334.3	573.2	1358	1618	2348	2,900
Tijuana	59.9	152.4	277.3	429.5	742.6	1,200
El Paso	130.4	276.7	360.0	477.0	571.0	690
Ciudad Juarez	122.6	262.0	414.9	544.5	797.7	910
Laredo	51.9	60.7	72.9	99.1	130.0	180
Nuevo Laredo	57.6	92.6	148.9	201.7	405.0	615
McAllen-Pharr	51.9	79.6	181.5	263.1	279.9	360
Reynosa	34.1	74.1	137.4	194.7	281.6	390
Brownsville, Harlingen	59.3	89.2	140.4	196	208.2	265
Matamoros	45.8	92.3	140.7	188.7	303.4	395
U.S.	151M	179M	203M	227M	249M	273M
Mexico	25.5M	34.6M	48.3M	66.8M	90M	106M

*forecast.

Sources: U.S. Department of Commerce, Bureau of the Census; INEGI.

been 12.7 percent, while the number of plants increased by only 5.3 percent. The population growth as well as the ability of the maquila sector to create a steady source of jobs in these twin-border communities has outpaced the national average in both Mexico and the United States.[19] One exception to this trend is the mid-1990's hypergrowth in the Asian-owned multinational companies located in the Tijuana area, resulting in unemployment levels near zero. Furthermore, there has been an annual trend for more plants to locate in the interior of Mexico. It is perceived that wages are lower and there is a trend toward a lower turnover of the work force. Besides injecting massive amounts of capital and technology into Mexico, the maquila sector also served as a catalyst for social change and higher incomes. The companies that have located in Mexico chose their sites as a means to be more competitive in the global marketplace.[20] For example, in 1994–95, General Motors, one of the largest U.S. manufacturers in Mexico, had over 30 plants in Mexico, followed by Ford with over 24 sites. Sourcing of competitive parts and assembled components, along with such production schemes as "just-in-time" and inventory-delivery-production, have proved critical to the ongoing industrial revolution in global manufacturing (see Figure 3-2).[21]

Due to the significant role and publicity of the border maquilas by 1993, there has been a tendency to attribute all the region's industrial accomplishments, environmental problems, and social ills to the twin-plant concept. To be sure, maquilas have had an impact, yet as the record will demonstrate, this impact has been on a smaller scale than first reported. Contrary to conventional wisdom and anti-NAFTA rhetoric, manufacturing in Mexico and the attraction of Mexican migrants to the U.S. border predates the maquila program by many decades.[22] Maquila factory workers make up less than 5 percent of the total U.S.-Mexican border population of over 10 million in 1996. Thus, the dynamics of the border urbanization and growth far exceed the overall impact of the maquilas. The conclusions of a 1984 report on the Texas-Mexican border, predating the maquila growth of the 1990s, have largely been sustained:

The BIP does generate increases in trade—but not through wages paid to workers. Rather, it is more likely that employment and sales are generated through service industries [multipliers] such as transportation, communication, construction, customs brokerage, and warehousing.[23]

ASIAN TIGERS IN MEXICO

While most maquilas operations are primarily owned and operated by U.S. firms, an effort was initiated from the Pacific Rim in the mid-1980's (primarily by the Japanese) to obtain a substantial foothold in Mexico. Most Japanese maquilas are in the electronic industry, and over 60 percent of these operations are located in the Tijuana area of Northern Baja California. Location of Japanese manufacturing plants, prior to the passage of NAFTA, was a means to backdoor or "slip into" the expansive U.S. market. The Japanese Economic Institute in Washington, D.C. concluded that Japanese corporate interest in Mexico was directed overwhelmingly toward its proximity to the United States. Also appealing are the low labor costs and Mexico's eligibility for the U.S. Generalized System of Preference, a benefit most newly industrialized countries ("NICs") lost at the end of 1988.[24] Japanese, as well as other foreign-owned operations in Mexico, will clearly receive modified treatment under the NAFTA rules of origin section that, for example, place an obstruction to Japanese auto exports due to the requirements that 62.5 percent of finished automobiles have North American (U.S., Mexican, or Canadian) content to qualify for duty-free status under NAFTA.[25]

While the maquiladora sector in Mexico had gone almost unnoticed in the United States, partly due to the perception that this activity was only a small component of U.S. offshore manufacturing, the issue of American jobs and their potential loss, so hotly contested during the NAFTA debate, failed to fully appreciate the evolution and globalization of manufacturing. Due in large part to the rise of technological innovations and worldwide sourcing, multinational manufacturing on a global scale (not the Mexican maquilas) accounts for two key trends: (1) reduced production cost and (2) a shift in demand for manufacturing labor (due primarily to technology) away from the United States and to less developed countries.[26] As the maquila concept gradually changes under NAFTA, it will be less profitable for outside multinationals to assemble foreign component products in Mexico. Nevertheless, Japan's investment in Mexico exceeded $3 billion during 1987–91 and was targeted in antipollution projects, telecommunications, petrochemicals, and tourism infrastructure, that is, toll roads, airport improvements, seaports, and hotels. Additionally, the Japanese have had a keen interest in the Mexican banking and financial sector in order to support their production and investment activities.[27]

The Asian "tigers" were very anxious during the debate about the impact of the NAFTA. One senior Japanese official implied that NAFTA was a form of "sneak protectionism." The fear that Mexico can duplicate or even better the experience of offshore production on the Pacific Rim in the 1990's was and is significant.[28] Virtually unnoticed in the national media, the Japanese lobbied heavily in Washington, D.C. during late 1993 to defeat the three-nation accord. Japanese planners and industrialists fear a growing, progressive Mexico will draw investment away from the Asian market due to abundant labor, improved infrastructure, and competitive transportation costs. To add to Japan's concerns, a United Nations outlook report concluded that the production of capital goods as a share of total value added in the manufacturing sector of developing countries is expected to increase from 28 percent on average in 1981–85 to 33 percent in the year 2000, thus reflecting increased production capacity and competition, in spite of the fact that over 30 Japanese banks, including Dai-Ichi Kangyo Bank, Ltd. and Sumitomo Bank, Ltd., have billions of dollars in outstanding loans and direct investment in Mexico. At issue are the fundamental changes agreed to in NAFTA concerning market access and rules of origin.[29]

MAQUILADORAS AND NAFTA

Under NAFTA there will be a gradual elimination of tariffs that created the primary incentive for maquiladoras. GATT and NAFTA have reduced import permits and tariffed items from 8,459 in 1983 to less than 100 tariff items in 1995. This phased elimination of import duties is valid provided such products meet the NAFTA rules of origin. Mexico further eliminated or reduced maximum tariff levels from over 100 percent in 1983, to the 20 percent range by 1987 and to an average duty of less than 6 percent in 1994.[30] As the "in-bond" industry opens to market access in Mexico, the significance of the in-bond production will change with time. In January 1995, maquilas were allowed to sell up to 60 percent of their production in the Mexican domestic market with a 5 percent yearly increase until a 100 percent penetration in the year 2001. Additionally, new foreign investment laws have been liberalized with the passage of an extensive modification of the Foreign Investment Law on December 27, 1993, thus allowing for 100 percent foreign ownership in most industrial sectors. Additionally, duty-drawback programs will be eliminated by January 1, 2001.[31]

In the wake of new NAFTA trade rules, GATT, and the peso devaluation in December 1994, many predicted the demise of the maquila sector. However, in the three-decade history of in-bond production, 1995 hallmarked the highest percentage growth of new maquila incorporations, totaling over 500. An estimated 30 percent of this new growth was in automotives, textiles, and electronics. Total maquila employment rose 10 percent to exceed 660,000 workers in 1995 and an estimated 740,000 workers in 1996. More than 50 percent of the aggregate value of the maquiladora industry is generated in salaries.[32] The new maquila operations and growth strategies in Mexico are looking beyond the U.S. market. By the turn of the century, the ''maquiladora'' industry will no longer be a unique and separate industrial sector. While still a vital business sector, production facilities under new Mexican tax laws will shift their emphasis from a cost center to a profit center.[33] Furthermore, U.S. exports to Mexico for consumption or reexport to other markets was foretold shortly after the beginning of NAFTA in a report by the United States International Trade Commission that concluded:

The benefits that currently attract companies to the border for assembly, however, will continue to exist: low cost, trainable labor and proximity to the U.S. market. The phased-in access to the Mexican market for the maquiladora industry production occurring under NAFTA will likely encourage companies with existing facilities to expand production in their border assembly plants, further increasing the level of exports to Mexico of U.S. components used in assembly operations.[34]

Thus, the maquiladora industry has been a tremendously important component of the emerging Mexican economy, accounting for $7 billion in foreign exchange to Mexico in 1995. Furthermore, the maquila sector—competing with other nations—has given Mexico the advantage to source state-of-the-art foreign technology, tremendous direct foreign investment, access to foreign markets, as well as new products and services at competitive prices for the domestic Mexican market.[35] All 31 states in Mexico have at least one maquila operation. However, the long-range impact of such change has great significance, ''By virtue of its membership in GATT and NAFTA, Mexico moves beyond the developing-nation image which often can be seen only as protective, restrictive and demanding of maquila-type manufacturing.''[36]

BORDER BANKING

While both border and Mexican banks have played a pivotal role in developing the industrial parks and financing maquiladora construction, the true significance to the commercial sector as well as the banks is the pattern of urbanization in the border region that has allowed it to grow into a shipping, distribution, and retail-service center.[37] Some concern was voiced prior to the conclusion of NAFTA that the trade agreement would open Mexico, under the national treatment clause, to an overbearing influx of U.S.–owned banks, thus possibly causing an outflow of deposits from border banks. The trend has been just the opposite, as banking services have been expanded on the border, due in large part to the slow pace of U.S. banks opening commercial and retail banking in Mexico. The initial wave of new foreign banks in Mexico were joint ventures by the large multinationals that targeted loans and services to the large corporate and government-related customers. Although Mexico is vastly under-banked, it will be a number of years before U.S.-owned retail banking expands in volume across the border.[38]

Retail merchants, warehousing, and commercial growth along the border over the past three decades have been nothing less than spectacular. The growth of the retail-service sector has been fueled by a customer base that is not exclusive to the border towns. Buyers from as deep as 250 miles inside Mexico routinely shop and bank on the border. Bank deposits of Mexican clients represent over 50 percent of many border banks. Borderwide, over $30 billion in assets are deposited in U.S. border banks. Correspondingly, banking services of border banks include a full range of retail as well as commercial services to include letters of credit, trust services, trade finance, and investment services. Due to the daily presence of the dual currencies, border banks are well versed in foreign exchange services and country risk analysis.[39]

As the population on the border grew, so did the retail sector. This urban growth during the 1960's and 1970's was steady, paralleling the growth in manufacturing (maquilas contributed $1.1 billion in foreign exchange earnings to Mexico in 1982), transportation, construction, and services.[40] With the new-found wealth initiated by the reviews in oil production in Mexico and an over-valued peso, large numbers of Mexicans shopped on the U.S. side of the border and as far north as San Antonio, Phoenix, Los Angeles, Tucson, and Houston. For example, retail sales in the six largest border counties in Texas—Cameron, El Paso, Hidalgo, Val Verde, Maverick, and Webb—posted an average annual growth of 20 percent between 1978 and 1981. The surge in sales came at a time when the U.S. economy was slipping into the recession of 1980–81.[41]

The euphoria of the retail-distribution sector on the border in the late 1970's and early 1980's was dashed in February 1982 when the peso value to the dollar nearly doubled from 27 to 46 pesos and by December climbed 148 pesos/$.[42] Between February and mid-summer 1982, retail sales dropped drastically, as most downtown border areas depended on a large percentage of their sales to Mexicans. Business fell into three primary categories: (1) consumer sales to cross-border customers buying for personal consumption, (2) "chiveros"—usu-ally small export buyers who bought in volume at distributor prices from downtown retailers (for resale in Mexico), and (3) true distributors that pur-chased in the United States to target buyers in the larger, interior Mexican market.[43]

Historically, the border had been insulated from the rest of the national econ-omy due to strong localized cross-border trade. Some economists estimate that prior to 1982, over 70 percent of goods purchased and consumed in Mexican border towns came from stores in the United States. The devaluations during the 1980's additionally impacted employment patterns, distribution, city serv-ices, and the financial services sector. Laredo, located at the prime crossing point between Mexico and the United States, had (during the 1982–83 period) the greatest disruption of the retail sector and the highest unemployment rate when compared to other border cities such as El Paso, McAllen, and Brownsville.[44] During congressional hearings into the impact of the 1982 devaluation of the border, Senator Lloyd Bentsen of Texas noted: "not long ago I was in Laredo on a Saturday and you could have fired a cannon down the streets without hitting anyone . . . in the past you would have found these streets jam packed with Mexican nationals coming across to buy . . . the buying power along the border just collapsed."[45]

The reaction to and impact on U.S. border banking during the 1982 devaluation was dramatic. The banks' main concerns were the exposure to peso transactions and the need to assist individuals, commercial clients, and retail merchants with a means to have an orderly conversion. As the deposits from retail business dropped due to the slowdown in sales, there was a corresponding increase in deposits of flight capital from Mexico. One Laredo banker noted that "The main concern was to limit exposure while at the same time helping customers to make the adjustments . . . due to the many currency fluctuations in 1982 we had to constantly monitor the situation."[46] Although hard hit, border banks weathered the devaluation better than those institutions that did not understand the dynamics of the border and the economic shifts within Mexico. Banking on the U.S. side of the border during the balance of the 1980's and early 1990's proved to be a major challenge, as institutions became acutely aware of economic swings and urban growth in both nations. While most border banks grew in deposit size due to capital flight from Mexico, bankers became more concerned with credit quality of their loan portfolios due to the rapid expansion. The economic downturn—hallmarked by past due loans, overbuilt real estate, and falling energy portfolios—in the Southwest United States during the mid-1980's also created additional concerns. During the early 1990's, Mexican banking and investment groups either acquired or substantially expanded their stake in border banks in Brownsville MacAllen, Laredo, El Paso, and San Diego, California. On the U.S. side of the border the leading banks in growth and investment during the mid-1990's included Laredo National Bank, International Bank of Commerce, and Mercantile. Norwest Bank gained a significant portion of the Laredo and El Paso markets as part of its overall Texas expansion.[47]

As the border communities grew into "twin-city" urban and commercial areas, bank lending activity moved away from agricultural and oil and gas loans, and steadily became more concentrated in commercial, home mortgage, and consumer credits. As the maquila industry moved inland in Mexico, border banks during the late 1980's and early 1990's tempered their domestic lending practices for industrial park development and factory construction by expanding into more retail (mortgage, construction, as well as account receivables loans) and real estate development.[48] Laredo, McAllen, Brownsville, El Paso (all in Texas), and San Diego, California and Phoenix, Arizona became major retail centers. Warehousing, freight forwarding, and transportation services (land and

Figure 3-3
U.S.-Mexico Trade: 1989–95 (Billions of U.S. Dollars)

	1989	1990	1991	1992	1993	1994	1995
Exports (to Mexico)	25.0	29.0	33.3	40.6	41.6	50.8	45.4
Imports (from Mexico)	27.0	31.0	31.2	35.2	39.9	49.5	61.7
Total	**52.0**	**60.0**	**64.5**	**75.8**	**81.5**	**100.3**	**107.1**

Source: U.S. Department of Commerce.

rail) showed major growth beginning in late 1986 following Mexican member-ship in GATT. Additionally, a major public-private review of infrastructure needs, highlighted by private sector trade organizations such as the Border Trade Alliance (BTA), was organized to inform both the U.S. and Mexican govern-ments of border needs and problems. In sum, the trade between the United States and Mexico expanded and grew steadily over the six-year period of 1989–94. With the passage of NAFTA, trade volumes between the United States and Mexico are expected to exceed U.S.-Japanese trade interaction by 1997–98 (see Figure 3-3).[49]

Increased trade was directly related to the opening of the Mexican economy after the 1986 membership in GATT. With the reduction of tariffs on imports and exports between the United States and Mexico, trade volumes doubled from 1987 to 1994. It was during this period that strong consideration was given to a bilateral agreement with the United States as well as a broader hemispheric role. As the border region grew during the late 1980's and early 1990's, so, too, did the demand for broader market access, a harmonized dual trade policy, and better access to financial markets.[50] By the mid-1990's only 2 percent of input materials in the maquila sector were sourced in Mexico. This trend will change as the basic framework of the maquila industry becomes gradually more liber-alized. In 2001, for example, maquiladoras will be able to sell 100 percent of the value of their export production to the domestic Mexican market, up from 50 percent in 1993. These changes will require more local sourcing, the en-hancement of local research and development and design work, as well as a steady increase in technology transfer to meet the demands of the expanding export markets. Furthermore, to keep pace with the growth will require an on-going assessment of border needs in order to enhance the regional infrastructure and insure that a balanced industrial plan, urban development, and transportation network is in place to facilitate north-south commerce. This industrialization and commerce in a growing urban-border region must be ever mindful of the en-vironmental concerns associated with growth and trade. The North American Development Bank (NADBank) and the El Paso-based Border Environmental Cooperation Commission (BECC), both mandated by NAFTA, will in time be significant sources of support to local, state, and federal environmental planning along the border. Initial border projects under the BECC have targeted waste water treatment and water quality.[51]

Thus, the dialogue resulting in the North American Free Trade Agreement provides the means to open broad trading relations as well as market access to transborder financial services and foreign direct investment. The role of the financial services and investment portions of the NAFTA accord (chapters 11 and 14, along with Annex XII, passed in late 1993 and placed into force on January 1, 1994) hallmarks the potential for major changes in banking and finance. The impact of NAFTA, along with the resulting banking regulatory changes, will be the focus of the next chapter.

NOTES

1. Frank Leach, "The Border: What It Is; What It Isn't," *San Antonio Business Journal*, March 31, 1995.

2. Paul Horgan, *Great River: The Rio Grande* (New York: 1954), 2 vols.; John M. Crewdson, "Border Region Is Almost a Country Unto Itself, Neither Mexican Nor American," *New York Times*, February 14, 1979; Niles Hansen, "Interdependence along the U.S.-Mexico Border," *Texas Business Review*, November-December 1983, pp. 249–54; Mark Kramer, "U.S.-Mexican Border: Life on the Line," *National Geographic*, June 1985, pp. 720–49; William Langewiesche, "The Border," *Atlantic Monthly*, May 1992, pp. 53–92; Francisco Alba, "Mexico's Northern Border: A Framework of Reference," as seen in Cesar Sepulveda and Albert E. Utton (eds.), *The U.S.-Mexico Border Region* (El Paso: 1982), pp. 21–35; *Border Business Indicators* (Laredo: March 1994), Vol. 19, No. 5, p. 1.

3. Ellwyn R. Stoddard, *Maquila: Assembly Plants in Northern Mexico* (El Paso: 1987), pp. 16–18; W. Dirk Raat, *Mexico and the United States: Ambivalent Visitors* (Athens: 1992), pp. 184–95; J. Michael Patrick and James E. Crisp, "The Texas Border with Mexico: Opportunities and Challenges," Texas A&M International University (Laredo: 1994), pp. 1–40. Also see Hollis E. Brown, *The Mexican Border Industrial Program: Its Meaning to the El Paso–Juarez Banking Community*, unpublished thesis, July 1971, Southwestern Graduate School of Banking, SMU Dallas, Texas. Note: Laredo in 1993 and 1994 was ranked the second fastest-growing city in the United States; Las Vegas, Nevada was first.

4. Jorge G. Castaneda, *The Mexican Shock: Its Meaning for the United States* (New York: 1995), pp. 1–61; Hellman, *Mexico in Crisis*, pp. 109–18; Richard S. Belous and Jonathan Lemco (eds.), *NAFTA as a Model of Development* (Albany: 1995), pp. 137–39.

5. Dennis Nodin Valdes, *Al Norte: Agricultural Workers in the Great Lakes Region, 1917–1970* (Austin: 1991), pp. 1–164.

6. Craig J. Jenkins and Charles Perrow, "Insurgency of the Powerless: Farm Workers Movement, 1946–1972," *American Sociological Review*, Vol. 42, April 1977, pp. 249–67; Donald W. Baerresen, *The Border Industrialization Program of Mexico* (Lexington: 1971), pp. 2–3; Instituto Mexicano de Comercio Exterior, *Mexico 1982 In-Bond Industry*, Publication No. 629 (Mexico, D.F.: 1983), pp. 8–12; Camin and Meyer, *In the Shadow*, pp. 190–94.

7. Patricia A. Wilson, *Exports and Local Development: Mexico's New Maquiladoras*

(Austin: 1992), pp. 36–42; Sally Wyeth, "Mexico's Maquiladoras: In-Bond Assembly Attracts Foreign Investment," *Site Selection Handbook*, 1985, pp. 54–59. Also see Niles Hansen, *The Border Economy: Regional Development in the Southwest* (Austin: 1981), pp. 82–86; Scott M. Schwartz, "The Border Industrialization Program of Mexico," *Southwest Journal of Business and Economics*, Summer 1987, pp. 1–51; and Leslie Sklair, *Assembling for Development: The Maquila Industry in Mexico and the United States* (Boston: 1989).

8. Roger Turner, "Mexico Turns to Its In-Bond Industry As a Means of Generating Exchange," *Business America*, November 28, 1983, pp. 27–32.

9. Secretaria de Comercio y Fomento Industrial, "Imagen de la Industria Maquiladora," 1977 as seen in Edward Y. George and Robert D. Tollen, "The Economic Impact of the Mexican Border Industrialization Program," No. 20, Center for Inter-American and Border Studies (El Paso: 1985), p. 6. Also see Stoddard, *Maquila*, pp. 16–26, and Hellman, *Mexico in Crisis*, pp. 112–15.

10. United States International Trade Commission, *Production Sharing: U.S. Subheadings 9802.00.60 and 9802.0080, 1985–1988: Formerly Imports under Items 806.30 and 807.00 of the Tariff Schedules of the United States* (Washington, D.C.: December 1989), pp. 1–1 to E–7; Laura D. Tyson, *Who's Bashing Whom? Trade Conflict in High-Technology Industries* (Washington, D.C.: 1992), pp. 90–93.

11. U.S. Congress, House, Subcommittee on Trade of the Committee on Ways and Means, *Background Information and Compilation of Materials on Items 807.00 and 806.30 of the Tariff Schedules of the U.S.* (Washington, D.C., July 12, 1976), pp. 1–14. See also C. Daniel Dillman, "Assemble Industries in Mexico," *Journal of Inter-American Studies and World Affairs*, Vol. 25, No. 1, February 1983, pp. 31–58.

12. William Stockton, "Mexico's Grand 'Maquiladora' Plan," *New York Times*, January 19, 1986; Joseph Grunwald, "Restructuring Industry Offshore: The U.S.-Mexico Connection," *The Brookings Review*, Spring 1983, pp. 24–27; Martin E. Rosenfeldt, "U.S.-Mexico Borderland Industrialization Policies Revisited: The Need for Binational Strategies," *Akron Business and Economic Review*, Winter 1985, pp. 12–19. Note: The term "maquila" (mah-kee-lah) is the Spanish word for the toll, usually in product, the miller takes for grinding corn; corn-measure, the 24th part of a "fanega" or bushel. The terms "maquila" and "maquiladora" are used interchangeably.

13. Anna-Stina Ericson, "An Analysis of Mexico's Border Industrialization Program," *Monthly Labor Review*, May 1970, pp. 33–40; John H. Christman, "Border Industries Foster New Jobs, More Exports," *Mexican-American Review*, February 1968, pp. 9–15; Lawrence E. Koslow and Rodney R. Jones, "The Mexican-American Border Industrialization Program," *Public Affairs Bulletin*, Vol. 9, No. 2 (Tempe: 1970), pp. 1–5. For a view from organized labor see David T. Lopez, "Low Wages Lures South of the Border," *AFL-CIO American Federationist*, June 1969, pp. 1–7.

14. Wilson, *Exports and Local Development*, pp. 37–42; Sklair, *Assembling for Development*, pp. 55–67.

15. Donald W. Baerresen, "Mexico's Assembly Program: Implications for the United States," *Texas Business Review*, November-December 1981, pp. 253–57; In-Bond and Industrial Regional Development Committee, "Mexico's Maquiladora Industry," *Business America* (Mexico, D.F.: December 1987), pp. 14–16, 18.

16. Stoddard, *Maquila*, pp. 18, 33; William Stockton, "Mexico's Grand 'Maquiladora' Plan," *New York Times*, January 19, 1986, p. 4F. See also Peter F. Drucker, "The Rise in Production Sharing," *Wall Street Journal*, March 15, 1977, p. 1.

17. Hansen, *The Border Economy*, pp. 97–100; Philip N. Diehl, "The Effects of the Peso Devaluation on the Texas Border Cities," *Texas Business Review*, 57, No. 3, May-June 1983, pp. 120–25; Roger Turner, "Mexico Turns to Its In-Bond Industry As a Means of Generating Exchange," *Business America*, November 1983, pp. 1–8; Wilson, *Exports*, pp. 40–41. See also Donald W. Baerresen, "Unemployment and Mexico's Border Industrialization Program," *Inter-American Economic Studies*, September 1975, pp. 79–90; C. D. Dillman, "Maquiladoras in Mexico's Northern Border Communities and the Border Industrialization Program," *Tijdschrift voor Econ. en Soc. Geografie* (Nr. 3: 1976), pp. 138–50; and Khosrow Fatemi (ed.), *The Maquiladora Industry: Economic Solution or Problem* (New York: 1990).

18. "Maquila Scoreboard," *Twin Plant News*, July 1995, pp. 41; Joshua A. Cohen, "The Rise of the Maquiladoras," *Business Mexico*, 1994, pp. 52–55; *EPA and Texas Environmental News*, February 1994, p. 1; Wilson, *Exports*, p. 44; Belous and Lemco (eds.), *NAFTA*, p. 52.

19. Lawrence A. Herzog, "The U.S.-Mexico Transfrontier Metropolis," *Business Mexico* (Mexico, D.C.: March 1992), pp. 14–18; Marco A. Valenzuela and Francisco Lara Valencia, "Border Cities: Their Evolution and Future Development," *In-Bond Industry*, National Maquila Association (Mexico, D.F.: 1995), pp. 26–32; Texas Comptroller of Public Accounts, "Growing Pains: Texas-Mexican Border Absorbing Pressure of Increased Trade and Traffic," *Fiscal Notes* (Austin: April 1993), pp. 5–7, 12.

20. U.S. Congress, NAFTA Congressional Fact Finding Mission to Laredo, Texas; comments by Tommy Tomko, plant manager of Packard Electric, October 17, 1993; Tyson, *Who's Bashing Whom?*, p. 91; Allen R. Myerson, "The Booming, Bulging Tex-Mex Border," *New York Times*, August 7, 1994.

21. Peter F. Drucker, "Trade Lessons from the World Economy," *Foreign Affairs*, January-February 1994, pp. 99–108; Stoddard, *Maquila*, pp. 27–41; "Manufacturing in Mexico: On Uncle Sam's Coat Tails," *The Economist*, September 16, 1989, pp. 82; interview with Mike Collins, Project Manager Ford Motor Co., 23 March 1994. Note: Ford opened its first production plant in the 1920's and GM and Chrysler followed in the early 1930's [Camin and Meyer, *In the Shadow*, p. 138]. A report in the January 7, 1994 *San Antonio Business Journal* noted a 4.9 percent growth in the maquila industry from 2,071 to 2,178.

22. Stoddard, *Maquila*, p. 10; Clark W. Reynolds and Carlos Tello (eds.), *U.S.-Mexico Relations: Economic and Social Aspects* (Stanford: 1983), pp. 3–34; Peter Andreas, "U.S.-Mexico: Open Markets, Closed Borders," *Foreign Policy*, Summer 1996, pp. 68–69.

23. Richard J. Holder, *Maquiladoras along the Texas/Mexico Border: An Economic Evaluation of Employment and Retail Sales Effects on Our Texas Border Cities* (Austin: 1984), pp. 1–95.

24. "In the United States' Back Yard . . . ," *JEI Report*, No. 31A, August 11, 1989, pp. 16–18; John J. Lawrence and Ryh-song Yehm, "The Influence of Mexican Culture on the Use of Japanese Manufacturing Techniques in Mexico," *Management International Review*, Vol. 34, 1994, pp. 49–66.

25. U.S. Government, *North American Free Trade Agreement* Part I, Section 4–6 to 4–26 (Washington, D.C.: 1993).

26. William C. Gruben, "Mexican Maquiladora Growth: Does It Cost U.S. Jobs," *Economic Review* (FRBD), January 1990, pp. 15–29; Peter F. Drucker, "Mexico's Ugly

Duckling—the Maquiladora,'' *Wall Street Journal*, October 4, 1990; Tyson, *Who's Bashing Whom*, p. 91.

27. Gruben, ''Mexican Maquiladora Growth,'' Ibid. p. 17; Embassy of Mexico, Nobutoshi Akao (Washington, D.C.) to John A. Adams, Jr., January 11, 1989; Matt Moffett, ''Mexico Tries to Please Japanese Investors,'' *Wall Street Journal*, November 1, 1989; Eugene Carlson, ''Japanese Companies Increase Presence Near Mexican Border,'' Ibid., December 22, 1987; Jeffrey T. Brannon and Dilmus D. James, ''Cometh the NAFTA, Whither the Maquiladora? Reflections on the Future of Industrialization in Northern Mexico,'' *Journal of Borderlands Studies*, Vol. IX, Fall 1994, pp. 1–22; Ira Magaziner and Mark Patinkin, *The Silent War: Inside the Global Business Battle Shaping America's Future* (New York: 1990), pp. 320–22. Also see ''Kaifu Announces Aid to Mexico,'' *JEI Report*, No. 35B, September 15, 1989, pp. 3–4.

28. Terry McDermott, ''TQM: The Total Quality Maquiladora,'' *Business Mexico*, Vol. 4, November 1994, pp. 42–45; Kerry Pechter, ''Mexico Beats China,'' *International Business*, Vol. 7, January 1994, pp. 22–25; ''Electronics: Mexico Against Asia,'' Ibid., Vol. 7, March 1994, p. 102.

29. ''Last NAFTA Obstacle Removed,'' *Latin American Monitor*, January 1994, p. 4; ''Japan Ups Ante In Mexico,'' *JEI Report*, No. 25B June 30, 1989, pp. 9–11; ''Asia Fears a Latin 'Dragon','' *Far Eastern Economic Review*, as seen in *World Press Review*, October 1991, p. 44; David Goldman, ''A Revolution You Can Invest In,'' *Forbes*, July 9, 1990, pp. 48–51; United Nations, *Global Outlook 2000: An Economic, Social and Environmental Perspective* (New York: 1990), p. 183; Sam Quinones, ''Maquila Economic,'' *Mexico Business*, October 1995, pp. 55–56.

30. *Diario Oficial*, August 27, 1983; December 22, 1989; and December 24, 1993.

31. *Diario Oficial*, December 27, 1993; Brannon and James, ''NAFTA and Maquiladoras,'' *Journal of Borderland Studies*, Fall 1994, p. 27; Scott Morrison, ''The Maquila Miracle,'' *U.S.-Latin Trade*, July 1995, pp. 24–25; Gary C. Hufbauer and Jeffrey J. Schott, *NAFTA: An Assessment*, Institute for International Economics (Washington, D.C.: 1993), pp. 2, 3, 144–45. See also Carlos Angulo, Edmundo Elias Fernandez, and Carol Osmond (Baker and McKenzie), *Maquiladoras in the New Environment* (El Paso: 1996), pp. 1–51; Jim Giermanski, ''The Potential Effect of a North American Free-Trade Agreement on the United States Maguila Industry in Mexico,'' Office for the Study of U.S.-Mexico Relations (Laredo: March 1991), pp. 1–19.

32. Christopher Palmeri, ''The Flip Side of Devaluation,'' *Forbes*, February 13, 1995; Candace Siegle, ''Maqs Are Back,'' *World Trade*, August 1995, pp. 22–26; John A. Adams, Jr., ''Window on the Future,'' *Twin Plant News*, January 1996; ''Maquiladoras Booming from NAFTA, Peso,'' *San Antonio Express-News*, June 13, 1995; Tim Coone, ''Mexico: On the Borderline,'' *Business Latin America*, December 18, 1995, pp. 6–7.

33. Border Trade Alliance, ''BTA: Maquiladora Investment Activity Report'' (El Paso: 1994), pp. 1–11.

34. U.S. International Trade Commission, *Production Sharing: U.S. Imports under Harmonized Tariff Schedule Provisions 9802.00.60 and 9802.00.80, 1989–1992* (Washington, D.C.: February 1994), p. xii.

35. John F. Pfaff et al., ''Technology Transfer in Mexico: Past Patterns and New Problems Related to the North American Free Trade Agreement,'' *The International Executive*, Vol. 35, March-April 1993, pp. 125–46; Gary C. Hufbauer and Jeffery Schott, ''Prescription for Growth,'' *Foreign Policy*, No. 93, Winter 1993–94, pp. 104–14; Sandra Medellin, ''Suben Maquiladoras un 90% sus ventas,'' *El Norte*, February 16, 1996.

36. Jim Giermanski, "Old Maquilas Don't Die, They Just Fade Away," *Mexico Insight: Excelsior* (Mexico City: March 6, 1994), p. 33; Lucinda Vargas, "The Changing Dynamics of the Maquiladora Industry," *Business Frontier* (FRBD) El Paso Branch, September/October 1994, pp. 1–4. Also see Joshua A. Cohen, "The Rise of the Maquiladoras," *Business Mexico* (1994), pp. 52–55; Chandler Stolp, "Texas under Free Trade: Some Sectoral Regional, and Modeling Considerations," in *North America Free Trade: Proceeding, Federal Reserve Bank of Dallas* (Dallas: June 14, 1991), pp. 53–62.

37. Mitchell A. Seligson and Edward J. Williams, *Maquiladoras and Migration: Workers in the Mexico-United States Border Industrial Program* (Austin: 1981), pp. 71–81; C. Daniel Dillman, "Urban Growth along Mexico's Northern Border and the Mexican National Border Program," *Journal of Developing Areas*, July 1970, pp. 487–508.

38. Khosrow Fatemi, "Mexico Free Trade Agreement: An Overview," *Free Trade and the United States Borderlands*, Joint Economic Committee, 102nd Cong., 1st sess. (Washington, D.C.: July 1991) p. 4; James W. Kolari, "FTA Negotiations and Banking Services," Texas Consortium on Free Trade, Financial Services Subcommittee-Banking Area Report, June 28, 1991, pp. 1–79.

39. U.S. International Trade Commission, *The Impact of Increased U.S.-Mexican Trade on Southwest-Border Development Investigation No. 332–223* (McAllen: 1986), pp. 1–284.

40. Richard J. Holden, "Maquiladoras' Employment and Retail Sales Effects on Four Texas Border Communities, 1978–1983: An Econometric Analysis," *Southwest Journal of Business and Economics*, 1984, pp. 16–26; Sally Wyeth, "Mexico's Maquiladoras: In-Bond Assembly Attracts Foreign Investment," *Site Selection Handbook*, 1985, pp. 54–56, 59; Herzog, "The U.S.-Mexico Transfrontier Metropolis," *Business Mexico*, pp. 14–19.

41. Donald W. Baerresen, "Devaluation and Merchandising in Texas Border Cities," *Texas Business Review*, September-October 1982, pp. 229–31; Philip N. Diehl, "The Effects of the Peso Devaluation on Texas Border Cities," *Texas Business Review*, May-June 1983, pp. 120–25. Note: For an excellent overview of the border, see William A. Orme, Jr., "The Tex-Mex Axis," in *Continental Shift: Free Trade & The New North America* (Washington, D.C.: 1993), pp. 151–58.

42. Richard Castro, "Oil: Mexico's Social Solution," *Rocky Mountain News*, May 1, 1981; Reynaldo Baca and Dexter Bryan, "The 'Mexican Dream': Al Norte, and Home Again," *Los Angeles Times*, April 12, 1981.

43. Baerresen, "Devaluation and Merchandising in Texas Border Cities," *Texas Business Review*, pp. 229–31. Also see U.S. Congress, House, Committee on Government Operations, *The Federal Response to the Impact of Mexican Peso Devaluation on U.S. Border Business*, 98th Cong., 1st sess., House Report No. 98–579 (Washington, D.C.: November 18, 1983), pp. 1–88.

44. Louis Harrell and Dale Fischer, "The 1982 Mexican Peso Devaluation and Border Area Employment," *Monthly Labor Review*, October 1985, pp. 25–32, also printed in *Southwest Journal of Business and Economics*, Winter 1989, pp. 19–27; Alberto E. Davila, Ronald H. Schmidt, and Gary M. Ziegler, "Industrial Diversification, Exchange Rate Shock, and the Texas-Mexico Border," *Economic Review* (FRBD), May 1984, p. 6; Ken U. Black and William A. Staples, "The Impact of Peso Devaluations on Retailers along the U.S.-Mexico Border," *Southwest Journal of Business and Economics*, 1985, pp. 1–11, see Table 2.

45. U.S. Congress, House, Subcommittee on Economic Goals and Intergovernmental

Policy, *The United States-Mexico Border Economic Situation*, 98th Cong., 1st sess. (Washington, D.C.: August 1983), pp. 1–2.

46. Interview with John H. Keck, Laredo, Texas, February 24, 1994.

47. Dianna Solis and Mary W. Walsh, "U.S. Business Near Mexican Border Move Fast to Cope With Changing Peso," *Wall Street Journal*, January 27, 1986.

48. John B. McNeece III, Alfredo Andere-Mendiola, and Jerome A. Grossman, "Issues in Maquiladora Lending" (San Diego: 1991), pp. 1–28; Derek Fromsom, "Mushrooming Malls: Developers Search for the Perfect Lure," *Business Mexico*, October 1992, pp. 14–19, 43.

49. U.S. Congress, House, Committee on Banking and Finance, *Export-Import Bank*, Serial 102–16, 102nd Cong., 1st sess., 1991, p. 204–5; U.S. Trade Representative, *Testimony of John H. Keck, President and CEO Union National Bank, Laredo, Texas*, Washington, D.C., September 4, 1991, pp. 1–6; Border Trade Alliance, "BTA: Southwest Border Infrastructure Initiative—Final Report" (Laredo: February 1993); John A. Adams, Jr., "Laredo Bank: On the Front Line of Financing U.S.-Mexican Trade," *International World Trade*, Spring 1993, p. 7; Caleb Solomon, "At Last, Hint of Recovery along the Mexican Border," *Wall Street Journal*, June 5, 1996.

50. Lucinda Vargas, "U.S.-Mexican Trade Revisited," *Business Frontier* (FRBD), Vol. 2, No. 2, March 1995, pp. 1–4; Laura Johannes, "Cities Fight for Freeway to Mexico," *Wall Street Journal*, March 29, 1995; Cindy Houser and Tom Fullerton, "Attempts to Discredit NAFTA Are Premature," *NAFTA Digest*, Vol. 5, No. 2, p. 1; "Border Bonanza: Clean-up Crusade Spurs Construction," *Mexico Service*, July 28, 1995, pp. 1–2.

51. Lucinda Vargas, "Beyond the Borders: Maquiladora Mexico's Bright Spot," *The Southwest Economy* (FRBD), Vol. 5, 1995, pp. 9–10; Verne G. Kopytoff, "NAFTA Ignites a Tijuana Realty Boom," *New York Times*, December 24, 1995, p. 22; Jeff D. Opdyke, "In Border Towns, the Peso's Plunge Fails to Damp the Bustle of Business," *Wall Street Journal*, March 29, 1995, pp. T1, 4; Quinones, "Maquila Economic," *Mexico Business*, p. 56. See also EPA, *Environmental Plan for the Mexican-U.S. Border Area* (Washington, D.C.: 1992), pp. 2–33; U.S. Department of Commerce, ITA, *U.S.-Mexico Border Economic Development Task Force* (Washington, D.C.: October 1994); and Ibid., *Financing the Border of Tomorrow: Progress Report on the U.S.-Mexico Border Infrastructure Finance Conference* (San Antonio: October 1994).

Chapter 4

Regional Trade and Cooperation

Mexico has gone from a closed to an open economy with its sights set on the economic challenges of the future: productivity and competitiveness. Modernization is a complex task, that requires competitive companies in healthy financial condition.
—Carlos Salinas de Gortari, November 1, 1993

Beginning in the early 1980's it became apparent to Mexico that to attract more direct investment, to lower inflation, and to be more globally competitive, major change was needed. The staunch protectionist attitude and outdated import-substitution policies failed to grow the Mexican economy. Over time, a series of structural and fiscal changes were implemented to slowly open the Mexican economy. A successful economic revitalization *initiative* required *bold* measures on the part of both the public and private sectors in Mexico. Furthermore, for the first time in its history, Mexico "formally" aligned its economic recovery, market expansion, and future with the United States, as embodied in the North American Free Trade Agreement (NAFTA). Prior to NAFTA there had long been an implied north-south relationship between Mexico and the United States, yet nationalist and protectionist pressures had prevented Mexico from "seeming" to be too cooperative with or dependent on the United States for commerce, trade, and financial services.[1] The debt crisis and bailout programs during the late 1970's and 1980's gradually drew the two nations and economies closer together. However, as previously noted, the border region had long ago shunned the closed-market, protectionist attitudes and official policies of the central government in Mexico City. The border communities were dependent on the cross-border trade, thus the region prospered, intertwining banking, industrial, and commercial, as well as cultural activities.[2]

ECONOMIC REALITY

A number of political and economic events allowed Mexico to redirect the nation's efforts and begin modernization of the economy during the late 1980's and early 1990's. These efforts can be divided into two areas: internal domestic Mexican factors; and external diplomatic, financial, and trade initiatives to bring the economic potential of the country more in line with regional and global financial and commercial markets. Given the gradual transformation of the nation from an agrarian base to a more diversified, industrial-urban economy, the economic development process would take time. Furthermore, the process would require a very delicate internal political evolution to insure acceptance among old-line nationalists in both the dominant PRI party and in a number of lesser opposition parties that feared being overwhelmed by the United States. A close review of U.S.-Mexican relations shows clear historical bases for this concern. Although Mexico is emerging as a formidable industrial nation, the fact remains that the political, cultural, historical, and constitutional roots of the Mexican nation are shaped in terms of its agrarian heritage.[3] Notwithstanding the fact that today a majority of the Mexican population resides in urban areas, the tradition and importance of the cultural-rural bedrock of Mexico survives in all phases of Mexican life. Of Mexico's more than 90 million people in 1995, 30 percent work the land, yet produce less than 9 percent of the country's GDP. In excess of 60 percent of Mexican farms are small and inefficient, under 12.5 acres in size. Thus, Mexico has been a net importer of nearly all its primary foodstuffs (beans, rice, floor, corn) for nearly a decade. A means to adequately feed the country, while at the same time expand its industrial base, is a priority of both the public and private sectors that will be an ongoing challenge well into the next century.[4]

In the mid-1980's it was realized that a strategy was needed to insure that the shift in the economy would be orderly. Mexico is a dynamic nation of many parts, meaning the changes would have to take place in the mainstream of Mexican politics, public opinion, and economic progress. Furthermore, demographic changes have been significant. Annually, over the past decade, the average age of the population of Mexico has tended to be younger and more urban. For example, the metropolitan area of Mexico City has more residents than the entire country of Canada; on the border, the twin cities of Laredo/Nuevo Laredo, "Los Dos Laredos" will have a combined population of over one million by the year 1999; and in northern Mexico, Monterrey, a major industrial hub (150 miles from the border) and regional leader in the production of steel, glass, and cement products, has become (with a population over 4 million) one of the leading urban and commercial centers in the hemisphere. The growth of the Mexico-California border town of Tijuana, with an unemployment rate near zero through most of 1995–96, rivals industrial cities anywhere in the world. Thus, the challenge to feed, house, employ, educate, and clothe the population while adjusting to the rise in urbanization over the next decade will prove tremendous. In this transition, economic and political stability in Mexico is paramount.[5]

During the period prior to the passage of NAFTA, the *internal measures* to open Mexico to "freer" trade can be traced to a number of political and economic initiatives designed to maintain stable relationships with the United States, while at the same time insuring that Mexico is not being overpowered by influences from the U.S. economy. A series of joint, government-to-government meetings and minor trade agreements over the past decade, as well as ongoing efforts by U.S. multinationals to invest and market in Mexico, set the stage. U.S. investment has been generally welcomed in Mexico as long as it did not dominate any particular industrial or financial sector. Laws regarding foreign exchange, dollar-denominated accounts, property ownership, and an ownership limit of 49 percent by foreigners comprised a means for internal domestic control. A pattern to gradually modify and ease such requirements has been developed over the past decade.[6] Stability and the political will to effect such change, like those introduced during the early years of the Salinas administration, have slowly taken their course.[7]

All politics are local, and there is no better example of this fact than the changes underway in Mexico. Except for the U.S.-Mexican border, the centralized government in Mexico City has ruled with the tight hand of a "patron"— encouraging domestic industry (that, in many cases, fell further behind technologically with each passing year); doling out funding for infrastructure projects in select regions to create short-term jobs, and always heeding the "spirit" of the 1910 Revolution that embodied the symbolism of the small land owners, the "ejido," revered as the backbone of the economy (though agricultural production levels have dropped and the land usage has become less efficient and profitable).[8] The PRI, which has been in power since 1929, has in recent years begun to receive more organized opposition and has demonstrated greater efforts to focus on strong domestic ideals and social programs. The assassination of PRI presidential candidate Luis Donaldo Colosio in March 1994, in part a backlash on the course and speed of economic change in Mexico, sent momentary shock waves not only through Mexico, but also through the financial markets in Latin America and the United States, as well as on the European exchanges.[9] The act of violence against the PRI candidate, the most likely winner of the fall 1994 election, undercut the fabric of seemingly orderly presidential transition within Mexico. The significance and tragedy of the Colosio assassination has yet to be fully realized and will take years to unfold. Thus, from a political standpoint, Mexico has long been aware of the structural and economic changes that impact jobs, the trade unions, education, rural issues, urban and industrial growth, as well as abundant social services, the essence of which is the fundamental protection of the "national" integrity.[10]

DOMESTIC GROWTH

The overriding internal factor, embodying immense political overtones, has been the stabilization of the domestic economy. This process has been a rocky road. The large governmental budget deficits of the 1980's had a tremendous impact on the stability of Mexico's financial system. Internal fiscal improvements, to insure a stable business environment, helped influence investor attitudes. Foreign investment in Mexico exceeded $7 billion in 1993, 10 percent higher than 1992. From 1989 to 1993 foreign investment totaled $35 billion, 40 percent higher than the 1989 goal set by the Salinas administration. The current account deficit estimated at between $21 and $24 billion in 1993 increased to $26 billion or 6.5 percent of the projected GDP in early 1994.[11] Unrest, as a result of rebel activity in southern Mexico and the assassination of Colosio, was blamed for capital flight of between $5 and $6 billion during the first quarter of 1994. By mid-1994, as a wave of U.S. imports entered Mexico and Mexican exports remained stable, the current account began to diminish as hard currency went to pay the bills and support still thinly capitalized Mexican banks, all out of sight of the public review both in Mexico and the United States. Since the "reported" current account deficit during the first half of 1994 did not change substantially during this period, and ignoring the fact that the peso was over-valued against major currencies, it was assumed that adequate amounts of new capital investments were entering Mexico to replace that which had left. Increasingly, more investors were investing in what appeared to be the never-ending "Mexican Miracle." A majority of the capital movement, approximately 8 out of 10 dollars, was invested in the Mexican Bolsa.[12]

In addition to new, direct foreign investment and privatization, exports increased, the government deficit was reduced, and inflation was lowered to the single-digit range by late 1993. The austere fiscal policy and the prudent handling of monetary policy were crucial to economic progress. However, overall economic activity stalled in 1993, due in large part to uncertainty surrounding the NAFTA vote and the impact of the high domestic interest rates on consumer and small business loans.[13] The 1994 budget projections reported by the government were consistent with the Pact for Stability, Competitiveness and Employment (PECE), or "Pacto," which indicate that preestablished agreements on prices, wages, and inflation are within the targeted range in order to stimulate growth and insure stability. The hard decisions by the Salinas administration appeared, at least on the surface, to have created economic stability and growth seldom seen in either Mexico or most of Latin America.[14]

Yet, by the third quarter of 1994, the continued effort to hold the line on the value of the peso and delay a much-needed adjustment of its value until after the August presidential election and November inaugural began to erode the financial stability of government's ability to meet its obligations. (Chapter 6 will detail the events of 1994 prior to the devaluation.) High consumer consumption, low inflation, and optimism overshadowed the reality of a pending peso crisis.

Jaime Serra-Puche, Secretary of Trade and Industry during the Salinas administration, highlighted the predevaluation direction of Mexico's economic development:

Our country has taken great strides in a relatively brief period to create a positive and progressive business climate for the benefit of both domestic and international entrepreneurs. Mexico's new philosophy toward foreign investment is clearly evidenced in the sweeping liberalization of the regulations governing foreign investment as well as the deregulation and privatization of major economic sectors and other profoundly important policy initiatives. All of these actions have been taken with the investor in mind and are intended to accelerate the process of economic development through the attraction of capital and technology.[15]

TOWARD "FREER" TRADE: GATT AND OECD

The external measures underpinning the groundwork for NAFTA began over two decades ago as a group of planners, business leaders, and economists began to assess the competitive position of Mexico in the world economy. The Korean success model was carefully studied by Mexican officials, as well as comparative economies, export policies, and industrialization trends in New Zealand and in the European Community (EC).[16] Latin America as a whole had been left out of the global boom of the 1980's, as each country fought inflation, gradually shifted its government away from authoritarian to more democratic institutions, privatized inefficient government-owned enterprises, and realized it was time to focus more on the broader global market and less on the existing protectionist scheme that only insulated each nation from new investment, technology, open markets, and progress.[17]

In the case of Mexico, fiscal and economic reality was faced when the Mexican economy was, on numerous occasions, brought to its knees by high inflation, devaluation, and overregulation by the government. Mexican domestic industries needed to be opened and a diversified import-export policy developed to increase nonpetroleum exports, while at the same time attracting both foreign exchange and new direct investment in Mexico. Although rejected in 1980, the membership of Mexico in the General Agreement on Trade and Tariffs (GATT) in July 1986 is, to date, the most significant event in Mexico's efforts to improve and open its economy. In addition to gaining a broader entry into over 100 national markets, and dropping import duties in Mexico from over 120 percent to an average of about 20 percent, GATT opened the thinking of both the government and the private sector to consider a broader North American trading pact. Without the 1986 membership by Mexico in GATT, there would have never been the successful conclusion of the North American Free Trade Agreement.[18]

As duties under GATT were dropped, the Mexican government also began an extensive program to privatize government-owned or -managed businesses,

Figure 4-1
Risk Classification by Region: 1994

Area	Moody's	Standard & Poor's	Perspectives
ASIA			
China	A3	BBB	positive
India	Ba3	BB+	stable
Indonesia	Baa3	BBB-	positive
Malaysia	A2	A	stable
Philippines	Ba3	BB-	stable
Thailand	A2	A-	stable
LATIN AMERICA			
Argentina	B1	BB-	positive
Chile	Baa2	BBB-	stable
Colombia	Ba1	BBB-	stable
Mexico	Ba2	BB+	positive
Venezuela	Ba2	BB-	uncertain

Source: Department of Economic Research; Banamex.

many of which were undercapitalized, technologically backward, and operated at a loss to the government. Companies and enterprises included airlines, mines, ports, and hotels. The Mexican government during the 1970's and 1980's also acquired a number of operations that stretched the meaning of "strategic and primary activities" to include horse stables, sweater factories, a soccer club, and nightclubs. The sale of these businesses brought in much-needed funds to insure the country could meet all its domestic obligations as well as payments under the Brady Debt Plan. This action, in addition to turning away from sole dependence on an oil-based export economy, was crucial in reestablishing confidence both at home and abroad with Mexico's trading partners. The drop in the inflation rate from 1990 to 1994 also corresponded with the drop in interest rates.[19]

On April 14, 1994, Mexico was admitted to the Organization for Economic Cooperation and Development (OECD), making it the newest member since New Zealand was admitted in 1973.[20] OECD membership was significant and symbolic of Mexico's participation in the "club of industrialized countries," and a key measure of consideration for potential investors. Composed of 25 developed nations in 1994, the OECD represents 16 percent of the world population, contributes 80 percent of the economic aid to developing countries, and accounts for over 65 percent of the world's goods and services. Mexico's credit rating stabilized at Ba2 by Moody's and BB+ by Standard and Poor's in mid-1994 (see Figure 4-1). It was expected that both these credit rating organizations would raise their credit rating closer to investment grade after the December 1994 inauguration of incoming President Ernesto Zedillo. However, even though substantial investment continued into late 1994, the ratings were not raised. Mexico's progress to improve the economy had been swift and to some extent mirrored the emergence of new NIC economies worldwide. Over a dozen investment firms in Europe, the United States, and Mexico predicted that Mexico should and would be rated investment grade by early 1995.[21]

The political and diplomatic path to closer economic ties and the successful conclusion of NAFTA were lengthy. Mexico had been left out of the world scene far too long. Throughout the late 1980's a tremendous amount of attention was placed on the economic unification of Western Europe into the European Common Market (EC). The EC process had begun in the mid-1950's and addressed many of the challenges the Mexican economy would have to face in the late 1980's and early 1990's. The prime question for Mexico was how to bring about more regional economic harmonization and cooperation without appearing to abrogate national traditions and mandates to the United States. Politically, Mexico could not appear to weaken its sovereignty, and some suggested that Mexico could look south to Central America and not feel violated. However, there was a great deal of concern fueled by political opposition parties in Mexico regarding "freer" trade with the United States. Notwithstanding the lament of opposition PAN leader Cuauhtemoc Cardenas that "No past Mexican regime has ever gambled its fate so completely on political and economic support of the United States," times were changing.[22]

In addition to the rise of globalization—hallmarked by in-bond maquila industries, just-in-time production, and global sourcing—the initial steps of the process that would allow Mexico to politically and psychologically merge into a broad trading relation were the negotiation and passage of the U.S.-Canadian Free Trade Agreement. While Mexico was not a direct part of this broad, binational trade accord, the U.S.-Canadian FTA proved to be the model and framework which the Salinas administration could style and package as an approach to a Mexican-U.S. free trade agreement that would make good business sense as well as be politically acceptable at home.[23]

MEXICO AND NAFTA

The Salinas administration, shortly after taking office in 1988, began informal talks with the Reagan administration on ways to streamline trade and cross-border commerce. The two countries had for some time been reviewing tariff and nontariff barriers to trade (i.e., import-export licenses, fees, permits, work requirements; as well as dispute settlement, cross-border transportation concerns, intellectual property rights, and the opening of the financial services sector in banking, insurance, and brokerage). Internal Mexican laws and policies were periodically being updated to meet the changes, yet no formal binational effort was yet developed. Two-way trade between the United States and Mexico had steadily increased each year from 1986 to 1993. Twin-plant "maquila" operations had steadily increased locations in Mexico during this period and were a leading source of hard currency and new technology for the economy. Shortly after the conclusion of the U.S.-Canada FTA, a memo of understanding was signed between the United States and Mexico to pursue, for the first time in the history of the two nations, a broad and formal regional trade arrangement that would protect the national integrity of all involved while opening a common market–type scheme that would give broader market access, and equitable "national treatment" for both nations. Fast track legislation was drafted in early 1990 and approved by the U.S. Congress in a close vote, after extensive negotiations.[24]

In June 1990, direct talks were started, initially between the United States and Mexico, and shortly thereafter (February 1991) with Canada, to address a long list of trade-related and market access issues first highlighted by GATT and later by the U.S.-Canadian Free Trade Agreement.[25] While multifaceted, the treatment and assessment of NAFTA for the purpose of this discussion focuses primarily on the financial services section and to a lesser degree on the investment treatment. After four years of negotiations, countless drafts and compromises, and the broad involvement of both the public and private sectors, the three-way accord was initialed by presidents George Bush and Carlos Salinas, and Prime Minister Brian Mulroney in San Antonio, Texas on October 7, 1992; ratified by Congress in late 1993; and placed into force on January 1, 1994. The basic thread of the NAFTA agreement in all its chapters and annexes was to address globally recognized, basic principles including "national treatment, most-favored-nation (MFN) treatment, and transparency"—terms that in essence recognize the sovereign rights of each nation while substantially eliminating barriers to trade.[26]

The specific objectives and goals of the accord were, in a broad set of industries and services, to diminish or eliminate impediments to trade, facilitate cross-border activities, promote fair competition, substantially increase investment opportunities, provide adequate enforcement of intellectual property rights, and promote multilateral regional cooperation. While advocating and addressing "freer" trade, "free" trade should not be misjudged to mean trade which is completely void of an organized regime of "fair" trade, and, where required, restraint, review, and regulation. Cross-border movement of goods and services under NAFTA in no way implies the surrender of national sovereignty nor the abrogation of basic laws of each of the party nations. In no sector is this more important and crucial than in the area of financial services and banking.[27]

While NAFTA is a three-way treaty between the United States, Mexico, and Canada, only those sections applicable to the U.S.-Mexico portion of the financial services and investment chapters will be reviewed in this overview. Chapter 14, embodied in the North American Free Trade Agreement on Finance: "Financial Services," and Annex XII set forth a comprehensive framework to, over time, redirect each NAFTA country's statutes and laws toward the reduction of barriers in financial services. Such services include banking, insurance, brokerage, as well as factoring and bonding. Time-line commitments, transition periods, and market access principles are key to this process, which in most sectors will be phased in over a six- to fifteen-year period.[28]

MARKET ACCESS

In Mexico, laws and application procedures were under review to expand the current 33 banks to over 50 institutions by 1995–96. These plans meet with major delays after the December 1994 devaluation. Nevertheless, except where exempted, no country can impose new regulations to hamper cross-border financial services unless specifically outlined under NAFTA. Mexico reserved the right to review and approve on a case-by-case basis ownership of Mexican banks or securities firms. Most importantly, Mexico insisted that "national treatment" be the overriding theme, as outlined in the agreement to mean no less favorable treatment than that accorded by a NAFTA country to its own investors, financial services providers, and financial institutions in like circumstances. This theme was vital to the explanation of the accord in Mexico to those who questioned the status of the nation's sovereignty. Equal treatment is to be given the conduct of business related to acquisition, management, operation, expansion, joint ventures, or sales related to investments in financial institutions in each country. While each signatory country reserved the right to both define (or redefine) and regulate solicitation of financial service providers, differences in market share, profitability or institution size do not determine a refusal of equal competitive opportunities.[29]

Financial service providers in each of the NAFTA countries may establish banking operations in the other member countries. Market presence in Mexico can be obtained either through acquisition of existing Mexican banks, joint ventures, or by the establishment and capitalization of Mexican banking subsidiaries. Foreign banks in Mexico must establish themselves as separately capitalized subsidiaries, without the ability to base loan decisions on the parent bank's capital. This aspect was intended to reduce the size of loans by foreign banks in Mexico. Guidelines released on April 21, 1994 set the minimum of 30 million dollars of capital to operate in Mexico. Foreign banks had until mid-1994 to officially apply for approval to operate as subsidiaries. Upon release of the requirements, the Finance Ministry, mindful of the underbanked consumer sector of the Mexican economy, noted: "The increase in competition will bring an opening which will permit service to segments of the population currently ignored by the system."[30]

Market access and the application process for direct investment and location in each NAFTA country was a paramount concern to all parties. To reduce the notion of nontariff or purely procedural barriers and/or delays, extensive attention was given to the "transparency" approach for applications and entry into each market. Under NAFTA, application requirements to open a new financial institution were published within 90 days; information provided in a timely manner; an administrative determination on a completed application was to be made within 120 days. An office was established to answer questions on procedures and provide status updates.[31] In contrast, under U.S. banking law there

is a well-documented broad base of regulation on international banking operations and examinations.[32] To meet the letter and spirit of the transparency concept in financial services, Mexico has both revised its investment laws and
released the framework for application, capitalization, and establishment of financial institutions. Annex VII to the NAFTA accord notes the following about
aggregate authorized capital in the Mexican financial sector:

The aggregate of the authorized capital of all foreign financial affiliates of the same type,
measured as a percentage of the aggregate capital of all financial institutions of such type
in Mexico, shall not exceed the percentage . . . for that type of institution. Beginning one
year after the date of entry into force of this Agreement, these initial limits shall increase
annually in equal increments so as to reach the final limits specified in the chart in this
paragraph at the beginning of the last year of the transition period:

Type of Financial Institution	Percentage of Total Capital	
	Initial Limit	Final Limit
Commercial banks	8%	15%
Securities firms	10%	20%
Factoring companies	10%	20%
Leasing companies	10%	20%

Any capital in existence as of the date of signature of this Agreement of a foreign
bank branch [i.e., Citibank] established in Mexico prior to such date shall be excluded
from each of the aggregate capital limits referred to in this schedule.[33]

Over 40 U.S. banking groups submitted application to the Hacienda by mid-
1994. Within the process, each NAFTA country reserved the option to prevent
or limit market access based on national laws related to the ''safety, soundness,
integrity or financial responsibility'' of each financial entity. This safety net was
intended for Mexico, due to the fact there was a concern that the country could
be put in jeopardy if uncontrolled investing attempted to dominate the financial
markets. Weakness in the Mexican banking sector by early 1995 would change
the interpretation of capital investment in Mexican banks. Thus, more specifically, a country can take measures for certain balance-of-payment purposes under limited or special circumstances and the member nations are to ''consult''
each other in time of potential crisis.[34] An example of such action was the joint
agreement between the Banco de Mexico and the U.S. Federal Reserve to have
available a $6 billion line of credit in the event of market instability shortly
after the assassination of PRI presidential candidate Luis Colosio. More significantly, these agreements and framework to ''consult'' and assist in time of
crisis were in place well before the late 1994 peso devaluation.[35]

The initial transition period in the financial services sector is scheduled to
conclude by the year 2000 in all three NAFTA countries. A gradual market
access and/or percentage ownership in banks, insurance companies, and brokerage will follow set procedures. The prime consideration in the 1993–94 period

during the organization of new financial institutions in Mexico was the market share limits. During the transition period, the aggregate market share limit was established to gradually increase from 8 percent to 15 percent. The initial 8 percent market share rule allowed for a maximum capitalization by foreign banks as a group to be about $1.3 billion in 1994. U.S. banks and subsidiaries, under the application and capitalization guidelines, will have practically unlimited access to the Mexican market. The aggregate foreign investment in holding companies and in commercial banks is limited to 30 percent of common stock capital—"capital ordinario."[36] Initial competition in 1994 to enter the underbanked Mexican market was fierce. It is interesting to note that a last minute addition to the NAFTA treaty allowed "foreign bank" subsidiaries of non-U.S. institutions that currently hold U.S. bank charters to also gain equal access to the Mexican financial market. This additional clarification within NAFTA was apparently included to avoid the possibility of retaliation by the European Community. The intent was to conform with the "market access" sections of the Uruguay Round of GATT that were being negotiated at the same time as NAFTA to insure harmony.[37]

One of the principal trade negotiating objectives of the United States called for equal market access for "all services," and also agreed to by Mexico to include financial services such as banking, securities, insurance, and financial intermediaries. Known as GATS, the General Agreement on Trade in Services, this portion of NAFTA is the first multilateral, legally enforceable agreement covering trade and investment in the services sector. The objectives were:

a. to reduce or eliminate barriers to, or other distortions of, international trade in services, including barriers that deny national treatment and restrictions on establishment and operation in such markets;

b. to develop internationally agreed rules, including dispute settlement procedures, which will reduce or eliminate such barriers or distortions, and help insure fair, equitable opportunities for foreign markets; and

c. to pursue these objectives while taking into account legitimate U.S. domestic objectives including, but not limited to, the protection of legitimate health or safety, essential security, environmental, consumer or employment opportunity interest and the law and regulations in these areas.[38]

Within the financial service section of NAFTA, two additional sets of market access and investment rules are paramount to cross-border banking. On December 27, 1993, the Mexican legislature released extensive new investment laws which modified and expanded the context of rules and ownership qualifications. These new guidelines further opened the Mexican economy to direct investment and brought the legal requirements in line with the details in NAFTA. These new investment rules, along with the March/April 1994 announcement of procedures for bank investment, have set the stage for significant changes in all future dealings in the cross-border financial services sector.[39] These three foundation documents—NAFTA Chapter 14, the new Mexican Investment law of December 1993, and the April 1994 application procedures set of guidelines formed the foundation for cross-border banking until the turn of the century.[40]

In early 1995 the National Securities and National Banking Commissions were merged into one entity, called the National Banking and Securities Commission, in order to streamline and resolve differences in accounting and regulatory standards. The improved supervision of the numerous types of financial institutions was determined necessary in the wake of the 1994–95 currency crisis. The Mexican government has continued to promote both diversification and competition in all financial sectors as well as the attraction of new joint venture partners with the ailing banks. In February 1995 the first of a number of financial sector investment laws was modified in order to attract more capital into the banking system. By October 1995 the government had agreed to a broad group of financial intermediaries under the NAFTA investment guidelines. Over 90 foreign financial institutions—commercial banks, financial groups, factoring companies, insurance groups, leasing companies, brokerage houses—have been authorized or received favorable opinions to establish offices in Mexico. Two-thirds are U.S. companies or subsidiaries. The expectation is that these financial groups will expand services and products to an already underserviced market in need of not only new capital but also new technology and training to reach a broader market.[41]

The magnitude of these cross-border changes in financial services is expected to require a period of time and refinement to be fully implemented. The net result will be a broader financial base in Mexico and more opportunity for direct investment by corporations, individual investors, and the U.S. banks. The Mexican financial market during the past decade has been very underbanked—in terms of population per branch, availability of consumer credit, adequacy of home loans, as well as small business and agricultural loans—at a time when direct investment and commercial expansion are vital to the growth of the country. The evolution of an investment regime in Mexico, establishment of full-service consumer and commercial credit reporting agencies, and the fine-tuning of the capital markets will in the long run provide a critical underpinning that will, it is hoped, streamline the peaks and valleys in the Mexican economy.

NOTES

1. The United States and Mexico have negotiated a number of trade and commercial agreements over the past 100 years. The prime base of all trade accords, both in fact and implied, have been on the level of tariffs imposed by each country. U.S. tariffs dating back to 1897, 1913 (Underwood), and 1930 (Hawley-Swoot) imposed high import duties. While nearly all Mexican tariffs were specific, U.S. duties were *ad valorem*. During the 1930's the United States and Mexico cooperated on a number of border projects, primarily flood control along the Rio Grande. During World War II a formal trade accord was signed in 1942 to allow imports of strategic materials. See also Raat and Beezley

(eds.), *Twentieth-Century Mexico*, pp. 61–65, 287–91; Canela Santoro, "United States and Mexican Relations during World War II," unpublished dissertation, Syracuse University, April 1967, pp. 16–56, and L. M. Lawson, "Mexico and United States Join in Border Flood Control," *Engineering News-Record*, October 4, 1934, pp. 419–23.

2. Tommie Sue Montgomery (ed.), *Mexico Today* (Philadelphia: 1982), pp. 109–26; Jonathan Kandell, *La Capital: The Biography of Mexico City* (New York: 1988), pp. 478–79; Raat, *Mexico and the United States*, pp. 148–99.

3. William H. Prescott, *History of the Conquest of Mexico* (New York: 1886), vol. 1, pp. 109–11; Barry, *Zapata's Revenge*, pp. 1–64.

4. U.S. Bureau of the Census (CIR), Frank B. Hobbs, *Mexico's Total, Employed, and Excess Labor Force: Future Prospects, 1985–2000*, CIR Staff Report No. 47 (Washington, D.C.: March 1989), pp. 1–68; Barry, *Zapata's Revenge*, pp. 49–51, 73; Walter Mead, "The Consequences of NAFTA," *Worth*, March 1994, pp. 43, 45–46; Philip True, "Peasants Warned of Bank Invasions," *San Antonio Express-News*, February 26, 1994; "Farmers Take over 2 banks in protest," *Laredo Morning Times*, February 26, 1994, p. 2; "1993 Inflation Hits 21 Year Low," *Mexletter*, February 1994, pp. 1–4. Note: By comparison in 1900, 39.2 percent of the U.S. population lived on the land compared to 1.9 percent today.

5. Larry Rohter, "Mexico Feels Squeeze of Years of Austerity," *New York Times*, July 25, 1991; John Naisbitt, *Global Paradox* (New York: 1994), pp. 259–60, 267–68; Frank Leach, "Laredo Development Foundation: The Charts on Laredo" (Laredo: 1994), pp. 1–12. Also see Lorenzo Moreno, "The Linkage between Population and Economic Growth in Mexico: A New Policy Proposal," *Latin American Research Review*, Vol. 26, No. 3, 1991, pp. 159–70.

6. Rogelio Ramirez de la O, "The North American Free Trade Agreement from a Mexican Perspective," as seen in Steven Globerman and Michael Walker (eds.), *Assessing NAFTA: A Trinational Analysis* (Vancouver: 1992), pp. 60–86; Donald L. Wyman, *The United States Congress and the Making of U.S. Policy Toward Mexico* (San Diego: 1981), pp. 1–74.

7. Philip L. Russell, *Mexico under Salinas* (Austin: 1994), pp. 134–36, 194–229.

8. John Womack, Jr., *Zapata and the Mexican Revolution* (New York: 1968), pp. 371–87; Frank Tannenbaum, *The Mexican Agrarian Revolution* (New York: 1929), pp. 185–330; Riding, *Distant Neighbors*, pp. 59–68; Kenneth Shwedel, "A Game of Wait and See," *Business Mexico*, December 1992, pp. 4–7.

9. Anthony De Palma, "Mexico's Market Rebounds with Help," *San Antonio Express-News*, March 26, 1994; De Palma, "Mexico Facing Sternest Test," Ibid., March 25, 1994; David Bennett, "Slaying Jolts Financial Markets," Ibid, March 25, 1994; Anthony Ramirez, "Fears Send Markets Plunging," *New York Times*, March 25, 1994, p. 1.

10. Kandell, *La Capital*, pp. 478–79; Laura Carlsen, "Ejido Reforms Spark Debate," *Business Mexico*, December 1991, pp. 32, 34. Also see Santiago Levy and Sweder van Wijnberger, "Maize and the Free Trade Agreement between Mexico and the United States," *World Bank Economic Review*, Vol. 6, No. 3, September 1992, pp. 481–502, and Peter Singelmann, "The Sugar Industry in Postrevolutionary Mexico: State Intervention and Private Capital," *Latin American Research Review*, Vol. 28, No. 2, 1993, pp. 63–65.

11. "Central Bank Releases 1993 Report," *El Financiero, International*, April 11, 1994, p. 3.

12. Judith A. Hellman, "The Riddle of New Social Movement: Who They Are and What They Do," as seen in Sandor Halebsky and Richard L. Harris (eds.), *Capital, Power, and Inequality in Latin America* (Boulder: 1995) pp. 169–75; David Hendricks, "Mexican CETES Yield Soars," *San Antonio Express-News*, April 15, 1994; Associated Press, "Foreign Investments Fleeing Instability," *Laredo Morning Times*, April 19, 1994; Bear, Stearns & Co., "Mexican Interest Rates, Economy and Politics," *Latin America Watch*, April 20, 1994, pp. 6–7.

13. Alan Greenspan, "Statement to the Congress," *Federal Reserve Board* (Washington, D.C., March 1994), p. 231. Note: The Federal Reserve has worked closely with the Mexican government and central bank to insure smooth binational operations in the financial markets. In this effort, the Dallas Fed has taken the lead in data accumulation and analysis of trends impacting cross-border banking.

14. Banamex, "Economic Policy: Results," *Review of the Economic Situation of Mexico*, Vol. LXIX, No. 811, June 1993, pp. 226–36; Robert R. Moore, "The Government Budget Deficit and the Banking System: The Case of Mexico," *Financial Industry Studies* (FRBD), October 1993, pp. 27–36; Bear Stearns, "Action on Capital Gains Should Lift Markets," *Economic Outlook*, October 1993, p. 18; Solomon Brothers, *Emerging Markets Research: Latin America*, March 30, 1994, pp. 2–7; Business International, *Business Latin America*, November 9, 1992, pp. 385–96. Note: Foreign investment in Mexico in 1993 was divided into $3.7 billion in the equity market, $1.9 billion in existing investment projects, and $1.4 billion in new investment projects.

15. Comite para la Promocion de la Inversion en Mexico, *Economic and Business Overview* (Mexico, D.F.: June 1990), p. 3. Note: According to an April 18, 1994 Knight-Ridder report on the analysis of the conclusion of the current GATT Round, Serra-Puche, not Salinas, was the first person under consideration for the top job at the World Trade Organization, the body set up to replace GATT.

16. Darryl McLeod and John Welch, "The Problem with the Peso," *Business Mexico* (Mexico City: November 1991), pp. 22–23; "Europe's Horn of Plenty," *The Economist*, June 2, 1990, pp. 71–72. Note: For an excellent overview of global trade environment see "World Trade: Jousting for Advantage," *The Economist*, September 22, 1990, pp. 5–40, and Linda Hunter, "Europe 1992: An Overview," *Economic Review* (FRBD), January 1991, pp. 17–27.

17. Abraham F. Lowenthal, "Latin America: Ready for Partnership?" *Foreign Affairs*, Vol. 72, No. 1, 1992–93, pp. 75; Peter F. Drucker, "Trade Lessons from the World Economy," Ibid., Vol. 73, No. 1, 1994, pp. 99–108.

18. Adams, "Without GATT, There'd Be No NAFTA," *Laredo Morning Times*, December 17, 1993; George W. Grayson, "Mexico May Lead the Way in Breaking Down Trade Barriers," *Wall Street Journal*, September 20, 1985; "GATT Brief: The American Connection," *The Economist*, April 21, 1990, pp. 85–86. See also GAO, *The General Agreement on Tariffs and Trade: Uruguay Round Final Act Should Produce Overall U.S. Economic Gains*, vol. 2 (Washington, D.C.: July 1994), pp. 6–24.

19. Sidney Weintraub, *A Marriage of Convenience: Relations between Mexico and the United States* (New York: 1990), pp. 85–93.

20. Note: Mexican membership in regional and trade organizations includes GATT, ALADI, OAS, LAFTA, SELA, the UN, IMF, OPEC, APEC and the World Bank.

21. Salomon Brothers, *Emerging Market Research: Latin America*, March 30, 1994, p. 5; Bear Stearns, *Global Development*, March 25, 1994, p. 3, and *Latin America Watch*, April 20, 1994, pp. 6–7; "Debt and Equity Boom Brews as Mexico Awaits an Upgrade," *Euromoney Supplement*, January 1994, pp. 1–6; Banamex-Accival, "Mexico in the

OECD," *Review of the Economic Situation of Mexico*, September 1992, pp. 458–64; BMI, *Mexico 1994*, p. 95. Also see Albert Fishlow, Sherman Robinson, and Raul Hinajosa-Ojeda, "Proposal for a North American Regional Development Bank and Adjustment Fund," Conference Proceedings North American Free Trade, Dallas, June 14, 1991, pp. 15–23.

22. Cuauhtemoc Cardenas, "Misunderstanding Mexico," *Foreign Policy*, No. 78, Spring 1990, p. 123.

23. Robert H. Hayes and Gary P. Pisano, "Beyond World-Class: The New Manufacturing Strategy," *Harvard Business Review*, January-February 1994, pp. 77–86; "Europe in the Next Century," *Washington Post*, March 13, 1994; Diebold (ed.), *Bilateralism, Multilateralism and Canada in the U.S. Trade Policy*, pp. 1–36, 105–27. Also see David M. Gould, "Free Trade Agreements and Credibility of Trade Reforms," *Economic Review* (FRBD), 1992, pp. 17–21.

24. The White House Office of the Press Secretary, *Statement by the President [NAFTA]*, Washington, D.C.: August 12, 1992. Also see U.S. State Department, "U.S.-Mexico Relations," *GIST*, Bureau of Public Affairs, Washington, D.C.: July 31, 1992, and Richard Belous and Jonathan Lemco (eds.), *NAFTA as a Model of Development* (New York: 1995).

25. U.S. Department of Commerce, ITA, *Summary of the U.S.-Canada Free Trade Agreement*, January 2, 1988, pp. 2–42. Note: The earliest mention of a broad trade and investment agreement or "U.S.-Mexico Co-Production Zone" was presented by Ambassador Abelardo L. Valdez at a commencement address at Texas A&M University in College Station, December 12, 1980; see also Abelardo L. Valdez, "A Proposal for Establishing a United States-Mexico Co-Production Zone," *Law and Policy in International Business*, Vol. 20, No. 4, 1989, pp. 619–54. Representative William Richardson introduced the "co-production" concept or free trade bill to revitalize U.S.-Mexican trade in 1985, 1986, 1987; all failed to reach approval. See H. R. 1360, a bill "To revitalize trade between the United States and Mexico and to stimulate the international competitiveness of both countries," 101st Cong., 1st sess., March 9, 1989; Abelardo L. Valdez, "A Free Trade Zone Plan For U.S.-Mexico Border," *The Washington Star*, June 5, 1981.

26. *North American Free Trade Agreement between the Government of the United States of America, the Government of Canada and the Government of the United Mexican States 1993*, Vol. I and II (Washington, D.C.: 1994) (hereafter: *NAFTA: 1993*). For a review of objectives against both NAFTA and GATT, see *The Case against Free Trade: GATT, NAFTA, and the Globalization of Corporate Power* (San Francisco: 1993).

27. Mark Memmott, "Mexico Rivals Japan in U.S. Buys," *San Antonio Express-News*, May 27, 1994; "Exports to Mexico Soar After NAFTA," *USA Today*, May 25, 1994.

28. *NAFTA: 1993*, Chapter 14, pp. 1–16, and Annex VII—Resolutions, Specific Commitments and Other Items, pp. VII-1 to VII-U-14.

29. *NAFTA: 1993*, Article 1405: National Treatment, pp. 3–4, and Article 1406: Most Favored-Nation Treatment, p. 5; Ibid., Annex VII (B), p. VII-M-13–17; "Hacienda Approves Three New Banks," *El Financiero International*, April 11, 1994, p. 4; Hoyt, "Consider How NAFTA Helps Open Doors to New Markets," *Texas Banking*, April 1994, pp. 3, 12; Baker and McKenzie, *NAFTA Report*, Dallas, Texas, March 1994.

30. Knight-Ridder, "Mexican Government Sets Rules, Capital Requirements for Foreign Banks," press release, April 21, 1994; Deloitte Touche Tohmatsu International, *World Banking & Securities*, March 1994, pp. 13–14.

31. *NAFTA: 1993*, Articles 1411, transparency, p. 8.

32. Federal Reserve Board, *Regulation K: International Banking Operations*, 12 CFR 211 (Washington, D.C.: October 6, 1993). Note: Other applicable legislation includes the Federal Reserve Act (1913), the Bank Holding Company Act of 1956, the International Banking Act of 1978, and the International Lending Supervision Act of 1983. For details see U.S. Congress, House, Committee on Banking and Finance, *Compilation of Basic Banking Laws*, CP: 102–14, 102nd Cong., 2nd sess., 1992. Note: In December 1992 a U.S. Treasury-FRB study indicated that foreign-owned banks held 23 percent of all U.S. banking assets.

33. *NAFTA: 1993*, Annex VII (B), pp. VII-M-14–5.

34. *NAFTA: 1993*, Article 1410, p. 7 and, Article 1413, Consultations, pp. 9–10.

35. "Mexico: Turbulent Politics Raises Fresh Concerns about Peso Stability," *Lagniappe Letter*, April 1, 1994, p. 6; David LaGesse, "HBG [Henry B. Gonzalez—Chairman of the House Banking Committee] Questions Line of Credit to Mexico," *San Antonio Express-News*, April 22, 1994.

36. *NAFTA: 1993*, Annex VII, p. 7–M-1; U.S. Embassy Mexico, "Mexican Regulations for Banking and Other Financial Institutional under the NAFTA," February 1994.

37. U.S. Congress, House, Committee on Ways and Means, *Message from the President of the United States Transmitting the Uruguay Round Agreements*, 103d Cong., 2d sess., H. Doc. 103–316, vol. 1, September 27, 1994; Baker and McKenzie, *NAFTA REPORT*, Dallas, Texas, March 1994; Hoyt, "Consider How NAFTA Helps Open Doors to New Markets," *Texas Banking*, April 1994, pp. 3, 12; John A. Adams, Jr., "Without GATT, There'd Be No NAFTA," *Laredo Morning Times*, December 17, 1993.

38. The White House—Memo from USTR, Letter from the President to the Speaker, "Trade Agreement Resulting from the Uruguay Round of Multilateral Trade Negotiations" (Washington, D.C.: December 15, 1993), pp. 19–21. See also Final Act Embodying the Results of the Uruguay Round of Multilateral Trade Negotiations, Annex 1B, December 15, 1993, pp. 1–38.

39. Sallie Hughes, "Hacienda Sets Foreign Bank Rules," *El Financiero*, March 14, 1994.

40. *Diario Oficial*, December 27, 1993; Knight-Ridder, "Mexican Government Sets Rules, Capital Requirements for Foreign Banks," press release, April 21, 1994; Robert M. Barnett, "Mexico's New Foreign Investment Law," *San Antonio Lawyer*, Winter 1993–94, pp. 11–12. Also see U.S. Congress, Office of Technology Assessment, *U.S.-Mexico Trade: Pulling Together or Pulling Apart?*, ITE-545 (Washington, D.C.: October 1992).

41. *Diario Oficial*, April 28, 1995; Banco de Mexico, *The Mexican Economy 1995* (Mexico, D.F.: 1995), pp. 138–39.

Chapter 5

Investment in Mexico

Economic stability is only half the challenge. The other is growth. A nation must develop continually and Mexico, like all nations, requires a constant and productive flow of new technology and fresh investment capital in order to grow. The competition for capital investment around the world is intensive and Mexico needs to facilitate the investment process so that it can take its proper place among the world's advanced nations, and thus strengthen its sovereignty. . . . There is no way around these economic realities.

—Jaime Serra Puche (Secretary of Trade and Industry), May 18, 1989

The growth of the Mexican banking sector during the 1990's has been significantly impacted by an open economy approach to foreign investment as well as the creation and growth of an active securities market housed in the Mexican Stock Exchange—Bolsa Mexicana de Valores. As a small open economy, Mexican market capitalization is a tiny fraction of the global investment market. The reprivatization of the Mexican banks, with the ability to offer broader services, was seen in the early 1990's as the cornerstone to stability in the economy as well as vital to domestic industrial growth. Although in competition for the same sources of investment funds, a cooperative approach to investment growth has enhanced both bank and nonbank financial sectors. The Mexico 2000 Council noted, "For practical purposes, the potential supply of capital to Mexico is infinite, provided that the expected return in peso-denominated assets exceeds those of alternative assets in capital-rich industrial nations."[1] To facilitate such investment growth potential required a progressive evolution of Mexican investment laws to attract new foreign direct investment as well as lure home the return of millions of dollars in flight capital. An understanding of the evolution of the Mexican foreign investment regime and the rise of the Bolsa is paramount to an appreciation of the future growth of the U.S.-Mexican banking and financial markets.[2]

The investment climate in Mexico has changed dramatically over the past two decades. As Mexico looked to broaden its role in global markets, a shift in federal policy was slowly developed to transition the financial and industrial sectors away from a closed domestic economy. The results of this transformation demonstrated a number of common traits: productivity levels of domestically owned firms converging with foreign-owned companies doing business in Mexico, the degree of foreign ownership in Mexican industry is directly related to productivity, the productivity gap between Mexican and U.S. manufacturing sectors has slowly diminished, and finally, the rate of growth and productivity of Mexican industries is directly related to the amount of foreign investment.[3] Thus, foreign investment has been critical in both the direct and indirect portfolio areas. The capitalization of the Mexican Bolsa grew from approximately 7 percent of Mexico's gross domestic product in 1985 to over 45 percent in 1994. Efforts to expand portfolio investment proved very successful and resulted in the attraction of over $50 billion in cumulative foreign investment during the Salinas administration. However, the short-term liquid nature of new investment in Mexico coupled with the need to pay for a surge of new imports proved to be an unstabilizing influence. The shift in investment policy was accompanied by substantial changes in the Mexican foreign investment laws. These modifications evolved partly as a result of efforts to bring investment laws in line with NAFTA, yet moved broadly to facilitate wider foreign investment and ownership in Mexico. Notwithstanding the year-end 1994 devaluation, these changes have resulted in the dramatic expansion of the Mexican industrial and financial sectors.[4]

HISTORICAL PERSPECTIVE

Foreign investment in Mexico has had a rollercoaster evolution. Faced with the dilemma of acquiring much-needed foreign direct investment, successive administrations attempted to attract capital while not appearing to surrender Mexican sovereignty or undercut domestic Mexican ownership. As early as the Benito Juarez administration (1858–72), efforts were extended to allow foreign investment in hopes of expanding the Mexican economy. However, these earliest attempts to attract foreign investment were strongly influenced by a nationalistic sentiment and a desire to limit potential foreign economic influence and control. A fear of foreign intrigue has underpinned Mexican history for nearly 500 years.[5]

Substantial amounts of foreign investment from the United States, Spain, France, and Great Britain, primarily directed toward oil exploration, railroads, seaports, and mining, began to flow into Mexico during the Porfirio Diaz reign (1876–1910).[6] Nevertheless, Mexico experienced a severe financial debt crisis (not unlike the 1980's) in the early 1880's, presided over by London financiers. As the British bankers and the government worked persistently to restructure over 16 years of Mexican default debt, U.S. investors such as railroad tycoon Jay Gould, in partnership with former General U.S. Grant, bought and profitably consolidated a large number of the Mexican railroad lines.[7] The Diaz administration opened Mexico to foreign investment and linked the country to the world economy. The National Bank of Mexico was established, public utilities were expanded, and new factories were constructed. In an additional effort to restructure the external debt and stabilize the economy, and although Mexico was the largest silver producing country in the world, the Mexican government adopted the gold standard in May 1905.[8] Eventually, foreign interest achieved monopolistic control over the Mexican railroad system and basic natural resources. American investment alone exceeded $1 billion by 1910, more than the total capital owned by all Mexican investors. However, foreign investment was interrupted in 1910 by the revolutionary period that lasted for over a decade. As rival armies crisscrossed Mexico in search of a dominant leader, new external capital investment dwindled to a halt. The postrevolution Constitution of 1917 limited foreign ownership of land and direct majority ownership of virtually all sections of the economy. Although foreigners were granted the limited rights to own property in Mexico, the so-called "Calvo Clause" required outsiders and expatriates to renounce the right to invoke the protection of their sovereign governments in the event of conflict over property title or expropriation. The federal government of Mexico assumed virtually unlimited power over corporate charters, property rights, and ownership.[9]

In response to xenophobic concerns, many large, foreign-owned agricultural operations were expropriated between 1926 and 1940. Post-revolutionary foreign investment in Mexico was led by the United States, followed by England, France, Spain, and Italy. Land reform considerations of the constitutionally protected "ejido" programs for small farmers held priority over most foreign investment.[10] The first "petroleum"-related laws under Part 4, Article 27 of the Constitution of 1917 were passed in 1925 and augmented by a controversial Expropriation Law in 1936. In 1937–39, foreign-owned railroads and the oil industry were abruptly confiscated by the government. The nationalization of Mexico's oil industry was regarded domestically as a bold move and dramatic symbol of Mexican economic independence. However, this pattern of government expropriation sent shock waves through the foreign investment community, dropping Mexico from favor with most key foreign banks and multinationals.[11]

Investment in Mexico virtually dried up during the early 1940's. In 1944 the Mexican legal system began to allow controlled or "limited" foreign investment and granted the Secretariat of Foreign Relations unusually wide discretionary controls over the interjection of foreign capital. Intended to both selectively attract new foreign investment and halt wartime capital flight, the result was the establishment of the 49 percent foreign ownership rule as the maximum allowed investment in most Mexican industries. Although controls were strict, the postwar period from 1946 through the mid-1950's saw a more favorable approach toward foreign investment. Inflow of investments was primarily for capital equipment, infrastructure, and construction in the manufacturing sector.[12]

In the 1960's, the government began a program (or policy) of "reserved exclusivity," which limited or excluded foreign ownership from government-mandated sectors deemed strategic to the economy. Timber and mining were reserved in exclusively Mexican ownership in 1961, followed by legislation in 1965 that limited foreign ownership in banking and financial services, such as brokerage and insurance. By the early 1970's, tighter foreign exclusion regulations were imposed on steel, paper products, glass, cement, aluminum, and fertilizers. In 1973 limited foreign ownership to minority status was allowed. On March 9, 1973, the Mexican government approved the Law to Promote Mexican Investment and Regulate Foreign Investment or Foreign Investment Law (FIL). The FIL outlined guidelines for the 49–51 percent rule for foreign ownership of Mexican enterprises which were the bases for all foreign investment for over two decades. This law virtually excluded any form of extensive foreign investment in banking and financial services. Capital expansion stagnated and manufacturing alone could not thrive—in a closed economy—and lift Mexican production. Two additional laws further regulated foreign investment in Mexico—the 1973 Technology Transfer Law and the Law of Invention and Trademarks of 1976. Nevertheless, the decade of the 1970's languished in government mismanagement and waste, overregulation, and a further deterioration of the domestic manufacturing base, thus hampering exports that would generate hard currency. The nationalization of commercial banks in 1982 sent yet another discouraging signal to potential foreign investors. Mexico, from 1982 to 1984, was not competitive for worldwide investment funds.[13]

After a period of fiscal paralysis, during the mid-1980's, the de la Madrid administration undertook a plan to dismantle the old-style protectionism policies and to develop a more progressive investment plan, as well as to improve the image of the Mexican economy. Mexico, along with most nations in Latin America, in the late 1980's endorsed a neoliberal economic policy that stressed the removal of all barriers that formerly insulated the domestic economy from foreign participation or competition. Attracting new direct foreign investment was crucial to the justification of the shift in policy. Although they combatted high inflation rates, the initial efforts allowed for only modest investment growth from 1984 to 1987. In addition to an aggressive debt-for-equity swap program, substantial changes in the foreign investment law were made in 1989, on the eve of initial negotiations toward NAFTA.[14] One unique aspect of the 1989 law was the establishment of a rule to allow a maximum foreign investment of $100 million in fixed assets. In announcing the new 1989 investment law guidelines, Secretary of Trade and Industry Jiame Serra Puche stressed, "Mexico needs to facilitate the investment process . . . and growth . . . there is no way around these economic realities."[15] Mexico once again felt confident and was open for business (see Figure 5-1).

Figure 5-1
Cumulative Flow of Direct Foreign Investment as Measured by the National Foreign Investment Commission (Millions of U.S. Dollars)

Year	New Direct Investment	Percent Change	Cumulative Direct Foreign Investment	Percent Change
1973	287.3	51.3	4,359.5	7.1
1974	362.2	26.1	4,721.7	8.3
1975	295.0	-18.6	5,016.7	6.2
1976	299.1	0.1	5,315.8	6.0
1977	327.1	9.4	5,642.9	6.2
1978	383.3	17.2	6,026.2	6.8
1979	810.0	111.3	6,836.2	13.4
1980	1,622.6	100.3	8,458.8	23.7
1981	1,701.1	4.8	10,159.9	20.1
1982	626.5	-63.2	10,786.4	6.2
1983	683.7	9.1	11,470.1	6.3
1984	1,442.2	110.9	12,899.9	12.5
1985	1,871.0	29.7	14,628.9	13.4
1986	2,424.2	29.6	17,053.1	16.6
1987	3,877.2	60.0	20,930.3	22.7
1988	3,157.1	-18.6	24,087.4	15.1
1989	2,499.7	-20.8	26,587.1	10.4
1990	3,722.4	48.9	30,309.5	14.0
1991	3,565.0	-4.2	33,874.5	11.8
1992	3,599.6	0.1	37,474.1	10.6
1993	4,100.0	14.3	43,200.0	21.6
1994	10,973.0	167.6	54,173.0	25.4
1995	6,964.0	-36.5	61,137.0	12.9

Source: Banco de Mexico; SECOFI.

The outward orientation of the new Mexican economic strategy assumed both steady growth and stable exchange markets as well as increased binational trade and investment. Mexico's rise of confidence sparked a keen interest in both the private sector and government to position the country in the mainstream of world affairs. The Mexico-U.S. Business Committee, a binational private sector initiative, captured the essence of the challenge facing Mexico and their trading partners in their 1987 annual report:

Mexico alone will be hard pressed to meet all of its needs for new industrial plant, modernization of existing operations, infrastructure, and advanced technology. Foreign lending and equity investment by both overseas and Mexican investors can play extremely important roles in the country's development in the years ahead. Mexican policy reforms that promote the international competitiveness of the economy will encourage foreign and domestic businesses to invest in production for the world market. The results of these investments will include an accelerated economic recovery and an increase in Mexico's standard of living.[16]

FREE TRADE AND THE NAFTA MANDATE

The conclusion of NAFTA in 1993 foretold the advent of a more open investment atmosphere in Mexico. The new Foreign Investment Law, incorporat-

Figure 5-2
Foreign Investment in Mexico: 1988–95 (Billions of U.S. Dollars)

	Net Increase Direct Investment	Cumulative Total Investment
1988	$ 3.2	24.1
1989	2.5	26.6
1990	3.7	30.3
1991	4.8	33.9
1992	5.4	37.5
1993	5.5	43.2
1994	5.1	54.2
1995	5.9	61.1

Note: Over 40% of all direct foreign investment in Mexico has flowed into the country during the Salinas administration.

Source: SECOFI.

ing the rules contained in NAFTA, was completed in late 1993 and implemented in early 1994. The law has opened over 80 percent of the Mexican economy to outside foreign investment.[17] Inflow of capital into Mexico has been split between the Bolsa and direct capital improvements in both industrial and infrastructure projects. Large new foreign investments have had a tremendous impact on both monetary policy and economic growth, and raised concerns over the possibility of capital flight from the Bolsa in times of crisis. Foreign direct and portfolio investment inflow to Mexico has risen from $14.5 billion in 1991, to $17.3 billion in 1992, to $22.5 billion in 1993—during this three-year period 32.2 percent entered Mexico as direct investment and 67.8 percent as portfolio investment.[18]

Over the past five years over two-thirds of the direct foreign investment has originated from the United States.[19] Annual U.S. investment in Mexico has far exceeded inflows from Europe (12–14%), Asia (2–4%), and Canada (1.0–2%). The Japanese share of total investment in Mexico, under 2 percent in 1993, has increased in recent years to about 8 percent and is slightly ahead of investments made in the early 1980's. Since 1988, investment in the Bolsa estimated at $14 billion dollars soared to a capitalized level of over $200 billion at year-end 1993. Direct foreign investment has primarily been placed in (1) manufacturing and construction—IBM, Kimberly Clark, Celanese, XEROX; (2) chemical—DuPont; (3) transportation and communications—AT&T, Siemens, Hewlett Packard; (4) financial services—American Express, GE Capital, Arrendadora International; (5) automotive—General Motors, Chrysler, Ford; and (6) food processing—Nestlé, Anderson Clayton, Coca-Cola (Femsa).[20] Although direct foreign investment has continued annually, election year jitters slowed 1994 inflows below the 1992–93 pace. Total foreign investment in Mexico capital markets averaged $55 billion during early 1994, up $11 billion from year-end 1993. Inflow levels of new capital investment were projected to resume after the August 21 presidential election (see Figure 5-2).[21]

The Mexican financial sector is comprised of a diverse group of institutions which includes the commercial banks, securities firms, investment societies, financial leasing companies, insurance companies, credit unions, factoring companies, and money exchange houses. During the early 1990s regulation of these institutions was conducted by the Ministry of Finance and Public Credit (SHCP), the National Banking Commission (CNB), the Bank of Mexico, the National Securities Commission (CNV), and the National Insurance Bonding Commission.

FOREIGN CAPITAL INFLOWS AND THE GROWTH OF THE BOLSA

Since the reprivatization of the commercial banks, the Mexican government has made a strong commitment to foster domestic economic stability, while at the same time encouraging long-term direct investments. Foreign investment in Mexican securities, the most liquid emerging market in Latin America, can be by (1) direct stock purchase—usually B shares; (2) investment in the "neutral fund" or N shares—a trust arrangement by which a foreigner can obtain shares (series A shares) previously reserved to only Mexican nationals; (3) by acquiring American Depository Receipts (ADRs)—currently the most popular means to own Mexican securities and popular because problems with share ownership as well as currency exchange concerns can be minimized; or (4) by purchase of treasury bills (CETES) or dollar-denominated treasury bonds (tesobonos). Foreign investors have been given wide access to the Mexican securities market or Bolsa (see Figure 5-3).[22]

The Bolsa Mexicana de Valores, established in 1907 and located in the heart of Mexico City, became an active securities market in the mid-1970's. However, its meteoric growth can be traced from 1990 when high-profile, investor-quality stocks such as Telefonos de Mexico (Telmex), Gemex (soft drink bottles), Cementos de Mexico (Cemex), Tribasa and Bufete Industrial (construction), Vitro (glass products), Dina (trucking), Televisa (television and communications), and Cifra (retailing) attracted the attention of portfolio managers worldwide. In 1991–92, 20 of the top 200 traded stocks on the Mexican exchange comprised over 70 percent of the value of the Bolsa. A wider number of new issues have since broadened the market, yet a small concentration persists. Outside investors viewed the Mexican market in the early 1990's as a "growth" stock investment, motivated by rapidly appreciating peso-denominated assets in contrast to less risky investments in hard currency markets, that had a stagnant return in the 3–5 percent return range. Annual returns on the Bolsa between 1991 and 1994 of 18 to 26 percent were not unusual. Foreigners held over 55 percent of government-issued instruments and capital investment in the Mexican securities market in 1992–93, which exceeded $30 billion.[23]

In an additional effort to extend avenues for investment in Mexican companies, a series of dollar- and peso-denominated mutual funds were offered to attract institutional investors as well as new money from European and Asian

Figure 5-3
Foreign Investment in Mexican Stocks: 1993 (Amounts by Company—Millions of U.S. Dollars)

	ADRs	Free Sub-scription Shares	Nafinsa Nat'l Trust Fund	The Mexican Fund	Total	Pct.
Telmex A	414.2	132.5	0	29.3	576.1	2.08
Telmex L	13,542.2	433.2	0	44.3	14,019.8	50.73
Televisa	937.8	298.3	0	0	1,236.0	4.47
Cemex A	0	0	175.4	51.2	226.6	0.82
Cemex B	391.3	389.1	0	0	780.5	2.82
Cemex CPO	155.9	80.8	0	0	236.7	0.86
Banacci B	0	0	77.4	0	77.4	0.28
Banacci C	0	326.5	0	30.9	357.4	1.29
Cifra A	0	0	84.9	0	85.0	0.31
Cifra B	1,310.4	134.8	0	85.0	1,530.2	5.54
Cifra C	0	574.7	0	27.6	602.3	2.18
Carso	481.4	0	292.7	36.2	810.3	2.93
ICA	394.1	0	42.3	14.2	450.7	1.63
Vitro	244.9	0	160.8	19.3	425.0	1.54
Ttolmex	17.0	294.6	0	17.9	329.6	1.19
Kimber	0	13.0	533.6	41.1	587.7	2.13
Tamsa	141.1	0	33.0	0	174.1	0.63
Dina	215.5	1.7	0	0	217.2	0.79
Others	1,626.7	2,241.3	905.9	236.5	5,010.4	
Total	**19,872.5**	**4,920.5**	**2,306.0**	**633.5**	**27,732.5**	**100.0**
Pct.	**71.7**	**17.7**	**8.3**	**2.3**		**100.0**

Source: Banco de Mexico.

investors seeking a more diversified portfolio. Furthermore, Mexican stocks such as Telmex, Cemex, along with mutual funds such as the Mexico Fund, the Mexico Equity and Income Fund, and Emerging Mexico Fund were listed on the New York Stock Exchange in 1992. Vitro is listed on the Nasdaq. A fixed income fund, the First Mexico Income Fund, is listed in London and the Mexican Investment Company is traded in Luxembourg. With inflation dropping to the low double-digit range, NAFTA in process, the stability of the Salinas government and a large dose of hype—the Bolsa became the hottest global investors' market of the early 1990's (see Figure 5-4).[24]

FOREIGN INVESTMENT LAW OF 1993

In late December 1993, the Congress of Mexico authorized the Secretariat of Commerce and Industrial Development (SECOFI) to begin sweeping changes in Mexican foreign investment rules. Since 1926, the foreign investment law has been gradually modified to meet the changing political and economic policies of Mexico.[25] Trends of nationalization, a closed domestic economy approach, expulsion of foreign corporate ownership (primarily U.S. in the 1920's and 1930's) and expropriations, and efforts to generate a more open economy after the economic downturn of the 1980's have each in their time impacted foreign investment in Mexico.

Figure 5-4
Securities and Investments Offered for Sale in Mexico

Capital Markets

Variable Income	Stocks	Insurance and Bonding Companies Brokerage Firms, and Industrial Commercial and Services Activities
Fixed Income	Debentures	Industrial, Commercial and Services Subordinated and with Capitalized Yield at Maturity
	CPI	Real Estate Equity Certificates
	BBD	Bank Development Bonds
	BORES	Urban Renewal Bonds
	BBI	Infrastructure Bank Bonds
Mutual Funds	SIC	Regular Mutual Funds
	SID	Fixed Income Mutual Funds
	SINCAS	Venture Capital Mutual Funds
Derivative Products	Warrants	

Money Market Funds

Government Securities	CETES	Treasury Bills
	Bondes	Federal Development Bonds
	TESOBONOS	Dollar-Denominated Treasury Bonds
	AJUSTABONOS	Inflation-Adjustable Bonds
Bank Instruments	PAGARE	Bank Promissory Notes
	ABs	Bankers Acceptances
	CDBs	Bank Certificates of Deposit
Private Companies	PRENDARIOS	Collateral Bonds
	PC	Commercial Paper
Warehouse Companies	BPs	Warehouse Bonds
Metals	CEPLATA	Silver Certificates
	CENTENARIOS	Gold Coins

Source: Banco de Mexico

A chief factor in this evolution, on how to handle direct and indirect foreign investment, was the scope or level of foreign ownership, generally conveyed by limiting non-Mexican ownership to no more than 49 percent. The benchmark for foreign investors in recent years was the 1973 Foreign Investment Law, that proved to be both restrictive and regressive to the Mexican financial community. However, the first substantive change in the law grew out of the government's effort to attract foreign investors to buy government-owned businesses, thus generating revenue for the treasury. To facilitate this new approach, one of the most sweeping revisions occurred in May 1989, shortly after Salinas took office. These investment regulation changes were a signal to both Mexican private industry and outside investors that the country clearly wanted to abandon the closed-door policies of the 1970's and early 1980's, and move toward an internationalization of the Mexican economy.[26]

The new investment regulations established the means to attract greater foreign investments by allowing up to 100 percent ownership in many industries dealing with export activities, in an effort to generate much-needed inflows of trade dollars. To accomplish this new thrust, rules on joint ventures were liberalized, a pledge was made to reduce bureaucratic red tape and more investment routes were opened to participation in the lucrative tourism sector (primarily new guidelines on property ownership via trust), thus creating a means to bolster foreign exchange. To stress the significance of the change from the 1973 foreign investment policy, SECOFI offered its most extensive economic policy statement to date, thus setting the tone for what was hoped would be the emerging "new" Mexican economy:

Economic development is not an event. It is an evolutionary process. The world economy has changed significantly in the 16 years since the former [1973 investment law] investment regulations were passed. The developed nations have become increasingly interdependent, particularly in terms of the international movement of capital, the development of commercial markets, and the utilization of the technology essential to an advanced society. Mexico will now launch a program to attract investments from around the world, Mexico welcomes and encourages foreign investment. The day of passive expectation is over.[27]

The 1993 Foreign Investment Law largely completed the two-decade-long process to open the Mexican economy to foreign direct investment. The new 1993 investment law stressed national treatment in most foreign investment and has three primary parts: (1) a restatement of those activities considered "strategic areas" that are exclusively reserved for the state; (2) a review of investment and corporate activity largely reserved for Mexican individuals and corporations (to include the allowable percentage of foreign investment); and (3) the role, composition, and powers of the National Commission on Foreign Investment (CNIE).[28]

Foreign investment is defined as the *participation* of foreign investors in any proportion in the capital stock of Mexican corporations and the *formation* of Mexican corporations comprised of a majority of foreign capital. Existing laws embodied in the Mexican Constitution concerning oil exploration (Article 27) and the "restricted zone" (Article 21, Section I) still apply.[29] The restricted or prohibited zone, first entered into Mexican law in 1925, is defined for national security purposes and sovereignty considerations as the strip of Mexican national territory that is 100 kilometers (62.14 miles) wide along the border and 50 kilometers (31.07 miles) inland from the beaches. Further special incentives were created to allow companies to locate manufacturing plants or maquilas (in-bond production sharing) in a 13–mile, duty-free zone along the northern frontier. Investment in industry and tourism in the restricted zone is second only to the combined capital investment and output of Mexico City and Monterrey. Nevertheless, Mexico had thus taken care to expand and facilitate all possible foreign investment opportunities to northern U.S.-Mexican border industrial growth as well as to the direct investment in resort-tourism locations along the coast. An example of the impact of the loosening of Mexican investment laws and improved relations between investors and government officials is the boom of resort and condominium development in Baja California.[30]

STRATEGIC AREAS

The government of Mexico has historically maintained exclusive control over key territorial, transportation/communication, mineral extraction, and power generation sectors. While most of the following strategic areas are protected by both tradition and the Constitution, foreign investment in support services and sales of equipment (often guaranteed and paid for by the government) to those sectors has grown tremendously. In 1993–94 there was little likelihood that the following sectors reserved by the state in the new investment law, and which also appeared in the 1973 law, would be further diminished. However, after the devaluation and economic crisis of 1994–95 oil exploration, the railway system, electricity, and seaports were reevaluated for privatization. The most controversial sector is the status of the national oil company PEMEX. Initial strategic sectors exclusively reserved to the state include:[31]

- Petroleum and other hydrocarbons
- Issuance and minting of coins/currency
- Basic petrochemicals
- Radioactive minerals
- Telegraph
- Postal Services
- Control of ports
- Nuclear energy generation
- Satellite communications
- Radiotelegraphy
- Railways
- Electricity

In each of the above sectors, though deemed strategic areas, there has been substantial inflow of foreign capital investment, loans, and transfer of technology to improve efficiency and profitability. PEMEX is a prime leader in the use of new technology and loans. The Mexican electrical industry, facing expectations of increased urban and industrial demand, is experiencing major growth as are the telephone, railway, and petrochemical sectors. The future challenge for the Mexican government will be the opening of new investment areas, normally reserved for Mexican investment only. Privatization of the airports, seaports, and railroads will be gradually removed from the reserved list. This assessment has been under closer review as the nation looks to attract more foreign investment. Laws and policy interpretations are expected to be very fluid in light of the late-1994 devaluation.[32]

Modifications in the investment laws have allowed for innovative approaches to large projects that have a potential binational impact. Prior 1993 projects in the border region were nearly fully funded and controlled by the two national governments. An excellent example of such governmental funding is the completion in early 1996 of the $44 million Nuevo Laredo waste treatment facility. A second, more innovative project that fits with the public-private approach is the 700–megawatt Samalayuca II power plant south of Ciudad Juárez. This project is the first of ten cooperative ventures scheduled for construction between 1996 and 2002. A consortium led by General Electric Corporation worked closely with El Paso Energy, Intergen, and a Mexican partner, Groupo ICA. The $650 million power facility will lease the facility for 20 years after completion, under the guidelines of an 80 percent financing package developed by the Ex-im Bank and the Inter-American Development Bank. In the wake of the 1994 devaluation such foreign third-party financing assumed most of the Mexican risk. At the end of the primary lease the project will pass ownership to the Federal Power Commission of Mexico. This build-lease-transfer arrangement is the first of its type in Mexico.[33]

INVESTMENT OWNERSHIP RESERVED FOR MEXICANS

To the extent possible under the guidelines of NAFTA, Mexican investors and corporations have been given priority "with a clause of exclusion of foreigners" in the industrial and commercial areas of ground transportation, tourism, messengers and parcel services, ownership of retail gasoline stations, radio and television broadcasting (except cable television), credit unions, and development banks. However, foreign investment will be permitted up to a given percentage of ownership in a broad category of domestic activities. Foreign investment of up to 10 percent is allowed in production cooperatives and up to 25 percent investment in commercial air and freight services. Pursuant to the phase-in period established by NAFTA, up to 30 percent foreign investment will be allowed in financial holding companies, bank credit institutions, as well as brokerage operations. Minimum capital penetration rules will apply until at least 2001.[34]

Also impacted by NAFTA will be a further three-tiered, ten-year phase-in of international ground transportation of passengers, tourism, and freight services between points within Mexico as well as the location and administration of passengers and auxiliary services related to bus and truck terminals. Given the size and potential for growth, these are significant service sectors. Foreign investment will be able to actively participate via the following investment time schedule:

- As of December 18, 1995, up to 49 percent of capital stock ownership allowed in a Mexican Corporation.

- As of January 1, 2001, up to 51 percent of the capital stock of a domestic company.

- As of January 1, 2004, up to 100 percent of the capital stock, *without* the need to obtain a favorable decision from the Commission.

The most sweeping foreign investment changes regarding ownership and acquisition are now allowed in a broad number of previously protected industries with up to 49 percent penetration. In the nonbanking areas, extended access was permitted in insurance, bonding, foreign exchange houses, bonded warehouses, as well as leasing and factoring companies. Insurance industry analysts estimate a potential market of $50 billion in premiums over the next decade. The 49 percent rule is further extended to the printing and publication of newspapers within Mexico, cable television, manufacture of firearms and munitions, and most aspects of basic telephone service. Furthermore, foreign investors will have broadened access to commercial fishing within the 200–mile coastal exclusive zone off both coasts, access to participation in harbor services such as piloting and integral port management, railway maintenance and management, and fuel and lubricant supply to ships, aircraft, and rail equipment.[35]

More importantly, the new law permits the Commission authorization to review and waive the 49 percent rule when increased ownership is in the best interest of all involved parties. Areas in which a larger percentage will be applicable include oil and gas well-drilling services, pipeline construction, franchise of cellular phone services, legal services, management of air terminals and increased investment in "private" educational services at all levels (see Figure 5-5).

THE NATIONAL COMMISSION ON FOREIGN INVESTMENT

The National Commission on Foreign Investment (CNIE), first created in 1925 and reaffirmed in 1973 and 1989, is governed by a board of nine cabinet ministers—Interior, Foreign Relations, Finance, Energy and Mines, Commerce and Industrial Development, Communications and Transportation, Labor, and Tourism—and is charged with the development of policy guidelines as well as the review of all new foreign investment applications. The Secretary of Commerce and Industrial Development chairs the Commission with the assistance of an Executive Secretary and staff. There is no private sector representative on the CNIE. However, in 1991, a nonprofit organization, the Mexican Investment Board (MIB), was created to promote and facilitate foreign investment in Mexico. With the increased emphasis on privatization of a broad number of government-owned enterprises, the attraction of new direct foreign investment became a priority of the Commission. Such investment was seen as crucial to a smooth

Figure 5-5
Foreign Investment by Major Economic Blocs (Millions of U.S. Dollars)

	Cumulative 1989-1993		1994*		Cumulative 1989-1994	
	Value	% Part.	Value	% Part.	Value	% Part.
Total	18,287.6	100.0	3,319.1	100.0	21,606.7	100.0
North America	11,994.1	65.6	2,015.5	60.7	14,009.6	64.8
Canada	330.4	1.8	16.3	0.5	346.7	1.6
United States	11,663.7	63.8	1,999.2	60.2	13,662.9	63.2
Other American Countries	1,374.3	7.5	138.3	4.2	1,512.6	7.0
Western Europe	3,399.1	18.6	961.4	29.0	4,360.5	20.2
Germany	654.0	3.6	93.3	2.8	747.3	3.5
Belgium	194.1	1.1	0.2	0.0	194.3	0.9
Denmark	54.6	0.3	2.4	0.1	57.0	0.3
Spain	199.4	1.1	60.4	1.8	259.8	1.2
France	843.9	4.6	9.1	0.3	853.0	3.9
Ireland	46.8	0.3	0.0	0.0	46.8	0.2
Italy	25.3	0.1	8.8	0.3	34.1	0.2
Netherlands	464.8	2.5	258.3	7.8	723.1	3.3
Portugal	1.1	0.0	0.0	0.0	1.1	0.0
United Kingdom	849.3	4.6	528.1	15.9	1,377.4	6.4
Luxembourg	65.8	0.4	0.8	0.0	66.6	0.3
Sweden	38.5	0.2	9.2	0.3	47.7	0.2
Switzerland	826.8	4.5	18.1	0.5	844.9	3.9
Other	6.7	0.0	0.2	0.0	6.9	0.0
Eastern Europe	6.2	0.0	0.2	0.0	6.4	0.0
Asia	420.7	2.3	174.7	5.3	595.4	2.8
Japan	370.5	2.0	155.9	4.7	526.4	2.4
Other	50.2	0.3	18.8	0.6	69.0	0.3
Other Countries	221.2	1.2	1.5	0.0	222.7	1.0

*To June 1994

Source: General Directorate of Foreign Investment, SECOFI.

transition to broaden private sector development. In addition to reprivatizing hundreds of government-owned enterprises, the commission has been active in attracting capital to expand private construction in the tourism sector, long a prime generator of hard currency. Furthermore, domestic private investment during 1994 was responsible for assisting in the completion of nearly 6,000 miles of new toll roads in all areas of the country. Lastly, Mexico attracted a tremendous amount of investment in industrial equipment and systems as well as infrastructure improvements. These investments proved critical to allowing Mexico to both retool its industrial base and make a significant contribution to economic recovery after the devaluation of December 1994. Although crippled after the devaluation, industrial capacity in Mexico during 1995–96 ranked among the best in the world.[36]

To attract new capital and accomplish an improved investment environment required a more open approach to investment in Mexico. Applications for new investment as well as variances with percentage market penetration have a 45 "working days" (9–10 weeks in Mexico) processing time frame. In the event the Commission does not act within the time allotted, the application will be considered approved as presented. The Commission is charged with evaluating each application based on the nature and impact on employment and training of workers, the level of technological contribution and transfer, environmental impact and compliance with SEDESOL codes, and finally, the overall contribution of the applicant's potential to increase the competitiveness of the Mexican production base. Once approved, all foreign investment in corporate activities and joint venture participation are to be filed with the National Foreign Investment Registry within 40 working days following incorporation and/or inception of the investment in Mexico. Records of the Registry are not available to the public. Finally, the December 1993 Foreign Investment Law abrogates the March 1973 rules, which were titled the Law to Promote Mexican Investment and Regulate Foreign Investment.[37]

AN ECONOMY IN TRANSITION

As an emerging industrial and financial market, Mexico is greatly influenced by investment trends worldwide.[38] NAFTA further intertwines the North American region and U.S. monetary policy will have a significant influence on Mexico. Economists at Banamex optimistically concluded, in early 1994, that if interest rate increases are permanent and Mexico's inflation continues downward, a reduction in the rate differential between both nations will translate into less outside investment in the money markets. While the growth and economic stability of the five years ending in mid-1994 cannot be overlooked, it was clear that government planners and economists underestimated the impact of the increased amount of foreign investment as well as the increase in interest rates in the United States. There emerged an implied mandate on the next president and administration of Mexico, to be selected in August 1994, to continue to attract billions in direct and indirect investment dollars to expand the infrastructure, modernize factories, and create jobs to reduce the possibility of social instability (see Figure 5-6).[39]

The outlook for continued economic growth in the 1994–95 period seemed very promising. As Mexico struggled to recover from a mild recession in 1993, as well as the attention placed on the significance of the NAFTA passage, investors gradually expanded investments. In addition to expanded highways, the government anticipated the privatization of the national railroad systems, seaports, and a number of airports. In 1994, Mexico received $12.15 billion in foreign investment, two-thirds consisting of direct foreign investment (nearly twice the 1993 level of $4.9 billion) and the balance in portfolio investments. Foreign investment in the Bolsa in 1994 was up 61.5 percent over 1993. Nearly half (45.4 percent) was in ADRs, 41.5 percent in general stock issues, and 13.1 percent in the NAFIN Trust Fund. The 1994 investment activity brought the

Figure 5-6
Direct Foreign Investment by Sector (Millions of U.S. Dollars)

Sector	Cumulative Value 1989-1993 (Millions of Dollars)	Percent Partici- pation	Value in 1994 Millions of Dollars	Percent Partici- pation
Total	24,437.5	100.0	8,026.2	100.0
Agricultural	199.2	0.8	8.0	0.1
Industrial	8,403.3	34.4	3,505.9	43.7
Manufacturing	7,611.5	31.1	3,204.0	39.9
Mining	200.6	0.8	12.0	0.1
Electricity and Water	0.9	0.0	8.6	0.1
Construction	590.3	2.4	281.3	3.5
Commerce	2,718.4	11.1	635.7	7.9
Transport and Communications	5,306.2	21.7	678.6	8.5
Financial Services	3,765.5	15.4	103.0	1.3
Community Services	4,044.9	16.6	2,505.4	38.6

Source: SHCP.

historical total of all foreign investment in Mexico to over $70 billion (see Figures 5-7 and 5-8).[40]

As Mexico continues to compete for new foreign investment it will be more attractive "because of its favorable situation vis-à-vis other Latin American and Eastern European nations."[41] The new investment regime in Mexico has taken years to gestate. Foreign investors are attracted by both the potential for growth and progressive expansion of both the banking and industrial sectors. As William Orme noted in his timely pre-NAFTA publication *Continental Shift*, "For Mexico, NAFTA isn't just a trade pact. It's a seal of good economic housekeeping for investors." The privatization and stability of the banking and financial services sectors are the focal point and catalyst for future direct investment and growth.[42]

Figure 5-7
Cumulative Direct Foreign Investment in Mexico

Country of Origin	Cumulative Total through 1994 (Millions of Dollars)	Percent Partici- pation	Jan-Jun 1995 (Millions of Dollars)	Percent Partici- pation
Total	50,401.0	100.0	5,663.4	100.0
United States	30,625.6	60.8	2,720.3	48.0
United Kingdom	3,703.4	7.3	68.8	1.2
Germany	2,611.7	5.2	158.1	2.8
Switzerland	1,884.7	3.7	13.8	0.2
Japan	2,389.5	4.7	110.2	
France	1,655.5	3.3	72.6	1.3
Spain	988.0	2.0	32.6	0.6
Netherlands	1,070.3	2.1	397.7	7.0
Canada	817.3	1.6	530.5	9.4
Sweden	385.2	7.6	0.9	N/A
Italy	80.8	0.2	1.2	N/A
Others	4,189.0	8.3	1,556.7	27.5

Source: Annex to the Primer Informe de Gobierno del Presidente Ernesto Zedillo, p. 76.

Figure 5-8
Authorized Foreign Investment (Millions of Dollars)

Period	Year Total	Direct Investment	Portfolio Investment	Cumulative Total
1984	1,442.2	1,442.2	-	12,899.9
1985	1,871.0	1,871.0	-	14,628.9
1986	2,424.2	2,424.2	-	17,053.1
1987	3,877.2	3,877.2	-	20,930.3
1988	3,157.1	3,157.1	-	24,087.4
1989	2,913.7	2,499.7	414.0	27,001.1
1990	4,978.4	3,722.4	1,256.0	31,979.5
1991	9,897.0	7,015.2	2,881.8	41,876.5
1992	8,334.8	5,705.1	2,629.7	50,211.3
1993	15,617.0	4,900.7	10,716.3	65,828.3
1994	12,113.0	8,026.2	4,083.9	77,942.2

Sources: SECOFI; Annex to the Primer Informs de Gobierno del Presidents Ernesto Zedillo.

All seemed on track until the late fall of 1994. The Mexico miracle of the Salinas administration developed during early 1990's was the envy of emerging countries worldwide and viewed as an investor's dream. Inflation was at its lowest level in over two decades, the economy had diversified away from a dependence on oil exports, and unemployment was in the 3 percent range. Both new foreign investment and large volumes of consumer goods flooded Mexico in 1994. However, the economic stability and respectability so long in the making was dashed during Christmas 1994. The dynamics of a growing economy, domestic politics, and financial trends in world markets were to attract worldwide attention and concern to Mexico. The events of late 1994 and 1995 in Mexico would have global impact on the emerging economies as well as currency values both in the United States and abroad.

NOTES

1. David Goldman and Evan Kalimtgis, "Risk Analysis of the Cost of Capital in Mexico," Mexico 2000 Council, June 10, 1993. Note: See also Santos Flores, "Making Money on the Bolsa," *Mexican Business Review* (Fort Worth: May 1994), pp. 29–40.

2. For an excellent overview of the Mexican securities market, see Santos Flores, *An Industry Analysis of the Mexican Securities Market* (Fort Worth: June 1994).

3. Pedro Aspe, *Economic Transformation: The Mexican Way*, pp. 164–66.

4. James Blears, "Global Goals of the Bolsa," *Business Mexico*, 1994, pp. 31–34; Geri Smith, "Salinas Will Pay for Peace," *Business Week*, January 24, 1994; Anthony DePalma, "Fortunes and Fear in Mexican Stocks," *New York Times*, April 12, 1993; Business Monitor International (BMI), *Mexico 1994* (London: June 1994), p. 84; U.S. Embassy, *Mexico: Foreign Investment Report* (Mexico, D.F.: Winter 1994/1995), pp. 3–13.

5. Francois Chevalier, *Land and Society in Colonial Mexico: The Great Hacienda* (Berkeley: 1963), pp. 1–334; Charles C. Cumberland, *Mexico: The Struggle for Modernity* (New York: 1968), pp. 1–374; Charles Allen Smart, *Viva Juarez! The Founder of Modern Mexico* (New York: 1963), pp. 1–436.

6. Jose Ayala and Jose Blanco, "El Nuevo Estado y la Expansion de las Manufac-turas Mexico, 1877–1930," as seen in Rolando Cordera (ed.), *Desarrollo y Crisis de la Economia Mexicana* (Mexico, D.F.: 1995), pp. 13–44.

7. "Mexico and Her Obligations," *The Commercial and Financial Chronicle*, Vol. XXXVI, June 2, 1893, pp. 603–4; "General Investment News: Jay Gould-General Grant-Mexico," Ibid., p. 623.

8. "Mexico's Adoption of the Gold Standard," *The Chronicle*, Vol. LXXX, April 22, 1905, pp. 1146–47.

9. Camin and Meyer, *In the Shadow*, pp. 1–80, 104; Jaime Suchlicki, *Mexico*, pp. 98–131; "The Mexican Crisis," *The Chronicle*, Vol. XL, June 1885, pp. 752–53; "Mexican Central Railway Company, Limited: Twelfth Annual Report," Ibid., Vol. LIV, May 7, 1892, pp. 763–65; John Rogers and Adrian Zubikarai Arriola, "Mexico," *Latin Law* [supplement of *Latin Finance*], January-February 1996, p. 20. Note: Mexico in 1911 was the number three oil-producing country in the world. See also Henry B. Parkes, *A History of Mexico* (Boston: 1960), pp. 285–334.

10. Eyler N. Simpson, *The Ejido: Mexico's Way Out* (Chapel Hill: 1941).

11. Camin and Meyer, *In the Shadow*, pp. 99–120, 132, 136, 141, 150–56; Castenada, "Revolution and Foreign Policy: Mexico's Experience," pp. 391–417; Government of Mexico, *The True Facts about the Expropriation of the Oil Companies' Properties in Mexico* (Mexico City: 1940), pp. 1–270; Banamex, "The Past," *Review of the Economic Situation of Mexico* (Mexico D.F. : March 1995), pp. 57–69. See also Donald F. Harrison, *United States-Mexico Military Collaboration During World War II*, unpublished disser-tation, Georgetown University (Washington, D.C.: 1976), pp. 19–32.

12. U.S. Embassy, Mexico, *Mexico: Foreign Investment Report* (Mexico City: Fall/Winter 1993), pp. 1–75; Camin and Meyer, *In the Shadow*, pp. 161, 165, 194; Aspe, *Economic Transformation*, p. 164.

13. Matt Moffett, "Ahead of Itself," *Wall Street Journal*, September 24, 1993; Camin and Meyer, *In the Shadow*, pp. 212–20. Also see Wouter van Ginneken, *Socio-economic Groups and Income Distribution in Mexico* (New York: 1980), pp. 1–230; and Baker and McKenzie, *Investment and Manufacturing in Mexico: Legal Aspects*, pp. 1–30.

14. Banamex, "Mexico: Change and the Present," *Review of the Economic Situation of Mexico* (Mexico, D.F.: August 1992), pp. 384–87.

15. Blears, "Global Goals of the Bolsa," *Business Mexico*, 1994, pp. 31–34; SECOFI press release, "Mexico Liberalizes Foreign Investment Regulations to Stimulate Domes-tic Growth" (Mexico, D.F., May 15, 1989); John Purcell and Dirk Damrau, *Mexico: A World Class Economy in the 1990s* (New York: August 1990), pp. 1–15. Note: For the most concise review on the evolution of NAFTA see William A. Orme, Jr., *Continental Shift: Free Trade and the New North America* (Washington, D.C., 1993), pp. 1–235.

16. Mexico-U.S. Business Committee, *Report of the Advisory Group on Capital De-velopment for Mexico*, XLII Plenary (New Orleans: November 1987), p. 20.

17. *Diario Oficial*, December 27, 1993. See also NAFTA, Chapter 11, "Investment, Services and Related Matters," and Chapter 12, "Cross-Border Trade in Services," Washington, D.C., 1994; Banamex, "NAFTA: More Competition, More Assurances," *Review of the Economic Situation of Mexico* (Mexico, D.F.: January 1994), pp. 10–14.

18. Banamex, "Outlook for 1993," *Review of the Economic Situation of Mexico*, pp. 109–26; Serfin, "Foreign Investment in Government Securities," *El Indicador* (New York: May 1993), p. 1

19. Banamex, "Foreign Investment," *Review of the Economic Situation of Mexico*, p. 547.

20. Robin Bulman, "Political Woes May Hinder Mexico Investment Growth," *Journal of Commerce*, June 27, 1994; Eric D. Randell, "Mexican Stocks Poised for Gains," *USA Today*, March 1, 1994; Sergio Sarmiento, "Stock Market Takes a Breather," *El Financiero* (Mexico: March 13, 1994); BMI, *Mexico 1994*, pp. 8, 85–87.

21. Grupo Financiero Fina-Value, *Economic Perspectives*, January-March 1994, pp. 8–11; BMI, *Mexico 1994*, p. 87; "Foreign Investment Shows Positive Trend," *Mexico Service*, March 5, 1993, pp. 1–3.

22. Damian Fraser, "Edging Closer to U.S. Standards," *Financial Times* (London), February 7, 1994; Robert Herman, "Mexico's Tesobonos Market Appeals to Risk-Wary Investors," *Journal of Commerce*, July 27, 1994. Note: Tesobonos are short-term obligations of the Mexican government, denominated in U.S. dollars yet required to be purchased and redeemed in Mexican pesos. By early 1994, 17 Mexican companies offered ADRs on New York exchanges.

23. Laura Carlson, "Making Money in Difficult Times," *Business Mexico*, November 1993, pp. 4–7; Claire Poole, "Too Late?" *Forbes*, January 22, 1992, pp. 196–200; Craig Torres, "Investors Focus on Long Term in Mexico City," *Wall Street Journal*, January 25, 1994 ; BMI, *Mexico 1994*, pp. 80–81, 113–17. Note: In May 1993, Telmex accounted for half of the value of the Bolsa; by September 1994 the amount dropped to 37 percent.

24. Randall, "Mexican Stocks Poised for Gains," *USA Today*, March 1, 1994; Michael R. Sesit, "U.S. Investors Keep Buying Foreign Issues," *Wall Street Journal*, July 25, 1994. Note: The five largest recipients of U.S. stock portfolio investments from December 31, 1989 to March 31, 1994 were, in order, Britain ($38.6 billion), Japan ($34.8 billion), Mexico ($11.6 billion), Hong Kong ($9.7 billion), and Germany ($6.8 billion); source: Scudder; Probursa; The Mexico Fund; and Latin American Fund; Emerging Mexico.

25. *Diario Oficial*, January 21, 1926; July 7, 1994; March 9, 1973; May 15, 1989; December 27, 1993.

26. U.S. Embassy, *Mexico: Foreign Investment Report*, Winter 1994–95, pp. 3–7.

27. SECOFI press release, "Mexico Liberalizes Foreign Investment Regulations to Stimulate Domestic Economic Growth" (Mexico, D.F.: May 15, 1989).

28. Telegram, U.S. Embassy in Mexico to U.S. Department of Commerce, re: Foreign Investment Law, January 27, 1994; Laffan y Mues, "Mexico's New Law of Foreign Investment" (Mexico, D.F., December 1993); BMI, *Mexico 1994*, pp. 101–4.

29. Serfin, "Report of Banco de Mexico," *El Indicador*, p. 1; BMI, *Mexico, 1995–97* (London: July 1995), pp. 129–30.

30. Camin and Meyer, *In the Shadow*, pp. 89–90; "Mexico on the International Financial Markets," *Review of the Economic Situation of Mexico*, March 1994, pp. 127–31; Ernest Sander, "A Boom in Baja," *Austin American-Statesman*, July 31, 1994. See also 1992 Mining Law.

31. BMI, *Mexico 1995–97*, pp. 87–91; U.S. Embassy, Mexico, *Mexico: Economic and Financial Report* (Mexico, D.F.: Fall 1995), pp. 85–92; Banamex, "Liberalization of Investment Flows between Signatory Countries," *Review of the Economic Situation of Mexico*, January 1994, pp. 13–14.

32. *Diario Oficial*, December 27, 1993; Kevin G. Hall, "Foreign Firms Help Mexico Power Up," *Journal of Commerce*, July 5, 1994; Justin Bicknell, "Offer Fails to Electrify Investors," *El Financiero*, July 18, 1994; U.S. Embassy, Mexico, *Mexico: Foreign In-*

vestment Supplement, January 1994, pp. 1–11. Note: Control and management of sea and airports was not in the 1973 law.

33. Andrew Downie, "Power Plant Near Juarez Gets Go-ahead," *Houston Chronicle*, May 4, 1996; Carlos Angulo P., "The 'Mexican Risk' Factor in Credit Transactions," presentation at the Border Trade Alliance conference February 19, 1996, Mexico, D.F., pp. 1–7.

34. BMI, *Mexico 1995–97*, pp. 87–88.

35. U.S. Embassy, *Foreign Investment Supplement*, January 1994, pp. 1–11; David Bennett, "Insurance in Mexico Seen as Golden Opportunity," *San Antonio Express*, July 27, 1994.

36. BMI, *Mexico 1995–97*, p. 88; U.S. Embassy, *Mexico: Foreign Investment Report*, Winter 1994–95, pp. 22–24.

37. *Diario Oficial*, March 9, 1973; May 15, 1989; December 27, 1993.

38. Banamex, "Financiamiento Externo: Tasas en Estados Unidos, sus efectos sobre Mexico," *Estudios Economicos*, June 13, 1994, pp. 1–5.

39. George W. Grayson, "Jefe Diego Challenges the PRI," *The San Diego Union-Tribune*, July 24, 1994.

40. "Foreign Investment in Mexico during 1994," *El Mercado de Valores* (Mexico, D.F.: March-April 1995), pp. 29–36; U.S. Embassy, *Mexico: Foreign Investment Report*, Winter 1994–95, pp. 64–65.

41. "Mexico on the International Financial Markets," *Review*, March 1994, p. 131. See also Mark A. Ludwig (ed.), "The Mexican Stock Market: What Next?" *U.S. /Latin Trade*, June 1994, pp. 38–39, 42, 46, 48; Banamex, "Mercados Emergentes: Mercados de Capitales," *Estudios Economicos*, June 20, 1994, pp. 1–7; Bill Cormier, "U.S., Canadian Investors Like the Mexican Economy, but . . . ," *San Diego Union-Tribune*, July 24, 1994.

42. Orme, *Continental Shift*, pp. 37–40; Robert S. Gay, "Mexico's Surprising Growth," *Bankers Trust Research*, August 19, 1994, pp. 1–4; Oliver Grewe, "Emerging Capital Markets in Latin America," *Economic and Financial Prospects*, Swiss Bank Corporation, August 1994, pp. 1–3.

Chapter 6

The Christmas Surprise: Devaluation 1994

Currency overvaluation is the villain.
—The IMF, April 1994

Mexico's currency is overvalued by 20% and by now needs an urgent solution. The atmosphere of speculative attacks dramatizes that a solution has been postponed all too long.
—Rudi Dornbusch, May 1994

The year 1994, and the economic crisis that followed in 1995, will in time become a benchmark in modern Mexican history. Never in recent history have so many significant events impacted not only Mexico, but also the interface of Mexico with the world at large. As has been well chronicled in numerous publications, Mexico, for nearly a decade prior to the devaluation of December 1994, had worked to avoid the economic instability so common in the recent past and position itself as a stable, world-class economy—poised to be a significant regional leader and respected in the world at large. Economic reforms and an expanded industrial base became the focus of national policy. Mexico's merchandise exports nearly doubled from $31 billion in 1988 to $61 billion in 1994. During the same period, Mexico attracted foreign investment amounting to $103 billion, of which over $31 billion was foreign direct investment. Foreign reserves increased from $6.4 billion to $24.5 billion. Although overall domestic growth was sluggish during 1993, by early 1994 inflation—an indicator that dominated the policies of the Salinas administration—dropped to a 22–year low of 7.1 percent.[1]

For many in Mexico, the Christmas surprise of 1994 was not a surprise at all—there are those who predicted long before the devaluation that "something always happens in an [Mexican] election year." The memory of the two previous administrations concluding their terms in office with a ''snap'' devaluation of the peso has never been forgotten. Accompanying each adjustment in the value of the peso was a vicious cycle of devaluation-inflation-recession-devaluation, a trend Mexico wanted to avoid.[2] While investors in the early 1990's yearly became more bullish about prospects for growth and profits in Mexico (some even calling for Mexico to be upgraded to investment grade), representatives in both the government of the United States and the Salinas administration were coy in their assessments regarding the stability of the Mexican economic situation, beginning in early 1994. For international investors and the financial markets, all indicators pointed to a stable presidential transition in the fall of 1994 and a profitable year. Many miscalculated the economic dynamics and change underway in Mexico. A look at the events that unfolded in Mexico in 1994, as well as a look at the analysis and the response from Washington, D.C., Mexico City, and other world capitals, provides an excellent insight into the pressures on an emerging nation striving to be a respected world-class economic player.[3]

It is important to note that the seeds of the economic instability were sown long before the devaluation of late 1994. The government of Mexico, staffed by an energetic group of technocrats, had pursued a bold restructuring of the economy and the monetary policy. Economic activity in 1993 had been sluggish, due in part to the uncertainties surrounding the ratification of NAFTA. The gradual decline of the budget surplus and an expansion of loans by government-run development banks maintained a balanced economy, marked primarily by an overwhelming preoccupation with single-digit inflation.[4] In the private sector, despite high interest rates, commercial banks loosened credit standards allowing loans to grow rapidly. Between 1988 and 1994, loans to the public sector quadrupled as a percentage of GDP. The heaviest concentration of outstanding credits was in mortgages, credit cards, real estate, and construction. Although not instantly apparent or reported, the rapid expansion of credit led to serious deterioration in the quality of loan portfolios at most Mexican banks. Increased consumer consumption was supported and underpinned by the investment in highly liquid capital instruments. The current account deficit, backed predominantly by tremendous inflows of foreign capital—direct foreign investment expanded 63.8 percent during 1994 from $4.9 billion in 1993 to over $8.2 billion by late December—was financed through the issuance of short-term dollar-denominated Mexican government tesobonos.[5]

However, the status of the 1994 current account deficit, which received the lion's share of the news after the devaluation in December 1994, was the outward measure of events that—in their sum total—during the year signaled the signs of major economic instability. Mexico's current account deficit grew from 1.4 percent of GDP in 1988 to 7.7 percent of GDP in 1994. According to IMF data, Mexico's current account deficit averaged 5 percent of GDP from 1990 to 1993, as compared to Argentina with a current account deficit average of 1.9 percent of GDP and Brazil with an average current account *surplus* of 0.1 percent. Nevertheless, the "Mexican Miracle," as fashioned by the Salinas administration and embraced by governments, financial analysts, and investors throughout the world, was touted as the most significant economic reversal and return to a solid fiscal footing in recent memory. The contentious debate over, and conclusion of, the North American Free Trade Agreement in late 1993 was intended, according to some projections, to flush out the weakness in the Mexican economy and government. The reliance on Salinas and his support base in the United States sustained the heady process without exposing the weak underside of the Mexican economy. The fact that many major New York, European, and Asian investors remained fully invested in Mexico right up to the year-end devaluation of the peso is a sign of either confidence or major misjudgment of not only the Mexican economy, but also a misjudging of the larger cultural and political events that undercut the thinking of most corporate bank executives, market analysts, and investment portfolio managers.[6]

NAFTA AND THE ZAPATISTAS

In time, full volumes will be written about the events of 1994–95. The implications of this phenomenal period and the ramification to the image, investor confidence, domestic recovery, political stability, and growth of Mexico will be years in reassessment. The dynamics of 1994 involved political intrigue, social adjustments, and economic dimensions seldom found in one nation. The review of the following chronicle of events and actions prior to the December devaluation is crucial to an understanding of the magnitude of the resulting 1995 economic crisis that would culminate in a massive foreign financial intervention in January-February 1995, to prevent a total collapse of the Mexican economy and a domino effect on banks, investors, and government guarantees worldwide. The euphoria over the prospects and economic recovery of Mexico in the early 1990's gave way to instability in emerging markets worldwide—known as the "tequila effect"—in early 1995 and beyond.[7]

The North American Free Trade Agreement was signed in late 1993 and went into effect on January 1, 1994. The ability and finesse of the Salinas administration to enter into this trade agreement, given the historical reluctance of even appearing to have substantive ties with the United States, was formidable. To seal the deal the Mexican government had done the utmost to picture Mexico in the best light—a declining inflation rate, an active stock market, a reiteration of the ease of investing in Mexico, new intellectual property laws, more transparent borders open to new business, the promise of a vast consumer market, and the appearance of political stability. Mexico, a GATT participant since 1986, gained global attention with membership in the Asia Pacific Economic Cooperation (APEC) in November of 1993, and selection for the Organization for Economic Cooperation and Development (OECD) in April 1994. Financial analysts both in the U.S and abroad, as late as mid-December 1994, voiced positive, yet guarded, recommendations on the course of the Mexican economy and investment opportunities. One leading New York financial analyst presented an article that listed the "20 Reasons Mexico Won't Devalue." Few, if any, public or private investor reports disputed these conclusions.[8]

While it was common knowledge in some financial circles that the peso was overvalued an estimated 10–12 percent during late 1993 and early 1994, most, such as a December 1993 IMF report (comparing Mexico to Thailand), assessed the situation with generalized statements, such as a surge in capital inflows in Mexico could "challenge macroeconomic stability." Such broad assessments could be applied to most newly industrialized nations, if not all of Latin America. Financial authorities in Mexico were not convinced that the peso was overvalued based on such evidence as the strong performance of exports and nationwide productivity gains.[9] Nonetheless, foreign investment in the Mexican market doubled from $28.7 billion in 1992 to over $57 billion by year-end 1993. In January 1994 the Bolsa was valued at over $200 billion, with foreigners holding one-third of all publicly traded Mexican stocks. The future looked very bright.[10]

On New Year's Day, 1994, in one of the most remote areas of Mexico, in the southern state of Chiapas close to the Guatemalan border, a group of disgruntled Mayan peasants, in what they termed a "Zapatista" uprising by the Zapata National Liberation Army or EZLN, launched an attack against the Mexican government. The mere presence of opposition, in an election year and in the wake of the Salinas administration's efforts to secure NAFTA that focused a tremendous amount of attention on Mexico, was seen as unthinkable. The articulated complaints against the Salinas government by the Zapatista group played easily into the anti-NAFTA groups that had worked for over three years to derail a regional trade agreement. Although vocal, the Zapatista uprising was contained in the Chiapas area and the Salinas government moved swiftly to defuse the embarrassment. Investors watched closely but saw no major signs that the government would not handle the situation. The peso closed the month of January trading at 3.1063/$.[11]

In February 1994, the Federal Reserve Board noted that Rudi Dornbusch, an economist at MIT, had publicly suggested the peso is overvalued. In a seemingly unrelated event at the time, the Federal Reserve increased the federal funds interest rate from 3 percent to 3.25 percent on February 4, the first of six increases of the benchmark rate to occur in 1994, since mid-1992.[12] Mexico's net currency reserves increased by 10.4 percent from $26.4 billion at the beginning of February to $29.1 by month-end.[13] During the month the International Monetary Fund (IMF), the Federal Reserve, and the Treasury all privately expressed concern about the steadily increasing current account deficit. All three agencies agreed, any sudden reversal of capital flows could trigger economic instability in Mexico, resulting in a major disruption in world financial markets. IMF directors urged Mexico to lower its current account deficit as well as to create programs to strengthen domestic savings and maintain high levels of public savings. Pent-up demand after years of austerity during the 1980s and the lure

Figure 6-1
International Average Savings Rates (Percent of GDP)

	1988-84	1988-91	1991-94
Japan	33.88	33.43	33.51
Developing countries	25.10	25.55	25.47
Industrial countries	21.00	19.73	20.36
European Union	21.15	19.30	20.26
Mexico	18.25	15.35	16.69
United States	15.90	14.93	15.41

Source: Baring Securities.

of cheaper imported foreign products shifted disposable income from savings to consumption. Between 1988 and 1994 the IMF reported that Mexico had one of the lowest domestic saving rates in the world, averaging only the equivalent of 16.69 percent of GDP, as compared with an average of 25.47 percent and 20.36 percent for developing and industrialized countries, respectively. One leading Mexican bank concluded, in defense of the low savings rate, that foreign investment more than made up for the savings shortfall.[14] Oddly enough, the United States was one of the few nations with a savings ratio lower than Mexico, at 15.41 percent (see Figure 6-1). The Federal Reserve Bank of New York, in a broad overview of Latin America, noticed the same pattern in Mexico as the IMF, and concluded, "insufficient domestic savings resembles that of the late 1970's, an episode that culminated in the debt crisis of 1982."[15] This was the strongest warning statement to date on the status of the Mexican economy, yet no alarms were set off to address the situation.

In mid-February, Secretary of the Treasury Lloyd Bentsen met with President Salinas and Finance Minister Pedro Aspe. Bentsen's staff had forewarned the Secretary about the economic concerns in Mexico, stating that tight monetary and fiscal policy during 1993 and continuing into 1994 (the primary target being the goal of single-digit inflation and the passage of NAFTA) had "dampened economic activity." Furthermore, "the stance of fiscal and monetary policy is easing in the run-up to the election year and as a response to the recent events in Chiapas. Interest rates have already declined and there is evidence that the economy is recovering to a more satisfactory growth rate." Regarding Mexico's response to rising U.S. interest rates and the peso exchange rate policy, the briefing paper noted, "The economy only remains slightly vulnerable to a significant increase in the dollar [Fed funds] interest rates," and concerning the exchange rate, "the Mexicans understand the dangers of pegging the rate and intend to pursue a pragmatic, flexible exchange rate policy." In fact, rising U.S. interest rates, which doubled during 1994, had a tremendous impact on the Mexican economy. By reducing the relative attractiveness of high-yielding short-term tesobonos, investors had an alternative to invest in U.S. Treasury Bills. The peso closed the month of February at 3.20/$. While apprehensive, there was as yet no consternation at the U.S. Treasury. Private investment in all sectors

Figure 6-2
Cost of Funds, Banco de Mexico: 1994–95 (Monthly Percentage)

	1994	1995
January	13.22	29.81
February	11.96	35.98
March	11.53	56.82
April	14.16	70.26
May	17.03	57.86
June	17.18	46.39
July	17.82	41.42
August	17.16	37.10
September	16.73	34.61
October	15.96	37.08
November	16.34	47.54
December	16.96	46.54

Source: Banco de Mexico.

of the economy and Bolsa remained brisk. However, privately held concerns over the course of the Mexican economy and the stability of the financial system were confirmed and reached a significant transition point in March.[16]

THE ASSASSINATION OF COLOSIO

In retrospect, March was possibly the pivotal period prior to the 1994 devaluation, and provides the best potential glance at the onset of the resulting economic crisis in Mexico. Early in the month it became apparent that the peso could not sustain increased pressure, falling 6 percent against the dollar in the free market. The U.S. Treasury expressed concern about the decline of the peso in an internal memo that concluded, ''The Bank of Mexico faces a dilemma with the recent decline of the peso . . . the Bank may also view a slight depreciation of the peso as desirable to help stimulate export growth.''[17] While Mexico remained committed to maintaining price and exchange rate stability, the central bank indicated to representatives at the Treasury and the Federal Reserve that it would not hesitate to further raise interest rates to assure the financing of the current account deficit. The Banco de Mexico sets the average cost of funds, known as the CPP, yet there is little indication that the overall marginal rates were drastically raised during 1994 (see Figure 6-2).[18]

By mid-March, a day after Alfredo Harp Helu, President of Mexico's biggest bank, Grupo Financiero Banamex-Accival (Banacci), was kidnapped, an internal Treasury report on the Mexican economy determined that, ''The Mexican government does not seem to be overly concerned and considers it [the value of the peso] a natural adjustment in the wake of the huge capital inflows after NAFTA was approved by the U.S. Congress . . . the situation [in Mexico] merits our continued close attention.''[19] While most were focused on the economic situation and the value of the peso, the Mexican presidential race (held every six years) moved into the spotlight. The smooth transition to a new president was deemed critical to domestic stability and investor confidence in Mexico. These hopes were soon dashed.[20]

On March 23, 1994, PRI presidential candidate Luis Donaldo Colosio was assassinated while campaigning in the northern border town of Tijuana. The first high-level political assassination since Alvaro Obregon was murdered ten days after he was elected president in 1928, Colosio's death sent shock waves throughout Mexico and panicked foreign markets.[21] Colosio had been the front-runner in the campaign and was almost certain to become the next president of Mexico. Both the IMF and Treasury at once realized that the death of Colosio intensified uncertainty in the financial markets, which within hours triggered massive capital outflows.[22] The day following the assassination, Salinas suspended all financial operations in Mexico and closed the stock market, the currency exchange houses, and the banks. In an effort to insure stability and head off any unwarranted speculation and disruption, Secretary of the Treasury Bentsen and Federal Reserve Chairman Alan Greenspan issued a joint statement providing an immediate $6 billion swap facility to Mexico. Their concerns were well-founded. U.S. investors owned over $56 billion in Mexican stocks, or 27 percent of the total capitalization of the Mexican Bolsa. The peso strengthened slightly on the news of the swap facility; however, from March 23 to April 15, foreign reserves declined by $10.8 billion. The Banco de Mexico intervened six times and sold over $6 billion in foreign currency reserves to defend the peso. At month-end PRI campaign chairman for Colosio, Ernesto Zedillo Ponce de Leon, was selected the new PRI presidential candidate.[23]

The widening current account deficit, concern over capital flight, political unrest, and monetary tightening in the United States reflected by rising interest rates, caused what the OECD determined, ''growing expectations that there would have to be either a realignment or a significant adjustment of policies to defend the existing exchange-rate system.'' From mid-March onward the peso came under increased attack, remaining close to the top of the fluctuation band established by the government. At the end of the first quarter, the trade deficit reached $4.3 billion, 19 percent higher than the same period in 1993 (see Figure 6-3).[24]

Faced with continuing pressure on the currency, the OECD determined that the Mexican government had the following exchange rate options and monetary considerations:

- maintain the exchange-rate commitment, by tightening domestic monetary conditions or using the stock of international reserves, to the extent necessary to defend the exchange rate;

- increase the rate of depreciation of the exchange-rate band to try to ''engineer'' a gradual real depreciation;

- make a substantial once-off devaluation and re-peg the value of the currency against the dollar;

Figure 6-3
U.S. Fed-Funds Interest Rates: 1991–96

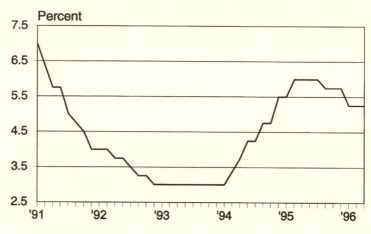

Source: Federal Reserve.

- float the exchange rate and establish an alternative nominal anchor (for example, an inflation target).[25]

The Mexican response to the pending peso valuation problem was that the economy was on course, NAFTA is working, and "Mexico is less affected because we are less vulnerable."[26] Furthermore, it was noted by analysts in Mexico that the currencies of some European countries had lost similar or greater value in their efforts to defend their currency. Additionally, many countries with dynamic expanding economies have sustained large current account deficits for many years. In an economic report by Banamex it was noted that, "Mexico's economic health is better than other nations . . . ," moreover, a number of factors make it difficult for "speculative attacks to harm the Mexican peso."[27]

a. In contrast to the European monetary system, in Mexico there is no futures market with which to speculate with resources greater than one's own;

b. Strictly speaking, there is no free convertibility of the peso, that is, pesos are not traded outside Mexico; there is therefore, better control over peso transactions;

c. Only Mexican banks can make loans in pesos and they are not easily accessible to foreign investors that might use such resources to speculate, buying dollars;

d. When borrowing in pesos to deposit in dollars, a high cost is incurred, hard to compensate for by a devaluation;

e. A devaluation from speculative pressures does not loom on the horizon and a competitive one would not only be unnecessary but counterproductive; and

f. To sustain the value of the currency, one should combine *credible measures* in the area of interest rates, exchange rates and the handling of reserves.[28]

The political unrest in Mexico, along with rising U.S. interest rates, increasing from 3.5 in March 1994 to 3.75 in April 1994, began to impact a growing number of foreign investors who, encouraged by the Ministry of Finance and the Banco de Mexico, began to shift out of long-term securities into short-term bonds. The action was intended to allow investors an option and comfort to cover any perceived exchange risk exposure.[29] Rising U.S. interest rates also began to cut corporate earnings in Mexico, as well as hamper cash flow and new capital investment. In response to the demand for dollars, the Banco de Mexico poured an additional $3 billion of its international reserves into the exchange markets during the weeks following the death of Colosio. From the end of March, Mexico's net international currency reserves fell 32 percent from $25.7 billion to $17.5 billion at the end of April. Rumors of a devaluation began to persist, causing increased speculative swings in the value of the peso. The U.S. Treasury and IMF dedicated greater attention to the Mexican situation, noting the Dornbusch analysis that the peso was significantly overvalued not 10 percent, but closer to the 20 percent range, thus influencing the conclusion of an IMF memorandum to the Treasury on April 22, 1994 concerning the situation in Mexico that stated, "Currency overvaluation is the villain. *Bottom line*: Some real appreciation might have been expected, but what has happened is excessive ... the peso is overvalued 20 percent." (see Figure 6-4).[30]

As the Banco de Mexico continued to issue large amounts of tesobonos to raise funds to attack the "villain" and defend the peso, the United States, Mexico, and Canada hastily announced the formation of the North American Financial Group (NAFG) on April 26. This trilateral consultative group or so-called "forum" was created to provide an intergovernmental, structured method for the review of economic and fiscal policy issues concerning Mexico as well as a clearinghouse for actions involving exchange swap facilities. Additionally, this standing credit facility would expand the pool of resources available in each country to maintain orderly exchange markets. Each country had reciprocal privileges to draw on the others' currency in amounts equivalent to the limits of the swap facility. The amounts set in the swap facility had three components: (1) The U.S. contribution of $6 billion on March 24, with the Treasury and the Federal Reserve each providing up to $3 billion; (2) an agreement between the Bank of Canada and the Bank of Mexico for a swap agreement for CAN $1 billion; and (3) the Federal Reserve and the Bank of Canada reaffirmed an existing swap agreement in the amount of $2 billion.[31] In internal memos at the Federal Reserve, it was becoming more and more evident that the economic peso situation in Mexico was deteriorating. The Federal Open Market Committee (FOMA) felt this announcement would help confirm U.S. support of Mexico's economic policies and settle the financial markets. However, the question remained, could the situation be salvaged? On the same day that the NAFG was

Figure 6-4
Key Monetary and Economic Indicators: 1993–95 (Billions of U.S. Dollars)

	Net. International Currency Reserves	Current Account Deficit Quarterly	Peso/U.S. $ Monthly Average	Federal Rate %
1993				
Dec	$24.886bn	5.347bn	3.1050	3.00
1994				
Jan	26,405		3.1075	3.00
Feb	29,152		3.1115	3.25
Mar	25,720	6.859	3.2841	3.50
Apr	17,504		3.3536	3.75
May	17,323		3.3120	4.25
June	16,396	7.352	3.3607	4.25
July	16,596		3.4007	4.25
Aug	17,024		3.3821	4.75
Sep	16,239	7.651	3.3998	4.75
Oct	17,478		3.4158	4.75
Nov	12,763		3.4426	5.50
Dec	6,101	7.318	5.3250	5.50
1995				
Jan	4,261		5.5133	5.50
Feb	9,493		5.6854	6.00
Mar	6,609	1.075	6.7019	6.00
Apr	8,548		6.2996	6.00

Source: IMF.

announced, Under Secretary of the Treasury Lawrence Summers noted in a briefing paper to Secretary Bentsen, in advance preparation for a meeting with Aspe, ''The Bank of Mexico has reportedly been intervening to support the peso with an estimated $6–8 billion of its foreign currency reserves . . . Mexico's dependency on financing of its large account deficit from largely volatile foreign portfolio investments remains a serious problem.''[32]

Nevertheless, investors demonstrated a high level of concern but no panic about the direction of the Mexican economy. The greatest concern of the officials at the Treasury was the prevention of any unnecessary reaction in the financial markets. The public spin on the situation in Mexico, by both U.S. and Mexican officials, was optimistic and a bit overstated given the urgency of the predicament. On the evening of the same day (April 26) that Summers briefed Bentsen, he told broadcast news service CNBC, ''Mexico is fundamentally sound and has a fundamentally sound currency. . . . We are very encouraged about the situation in Mexico.'' Bentsen also publicly restated his confidence that Mexico was ''on the right economic path''; while Aspe was a bit more careful in responding to a question on a further depreciation of the peso's exchange rate, replying, ''That's a market-oriented thing.''[33]

By May, the Salinas government increasingly realized that it was under a tremendous amount of pressure. Of prime concern was the fall presidential election. Investor confidence continued to erode as the situation with the "market" compounded, due to the potential uncertainty of the election. Although the PRI had been in power for over six decades, the 1993–94 mini-recession and depreciation of the peso brought into question the success of the Salinas administration's (and thus the PRI's) economic policies. In less than a month the level of reserves dropped by over $10 billion. The U.S. Treasury intensified its monitoring of the Mexico situation throughout the month, in addition to visits by Bentsen, with U.S. Ambassador to Mexico James Jones and Summers, meeting with Under Secretary of Finance Guillermo Ortiz. U.S. interest rates were raised again in May. Close observers again discounted the rising rates and hoped that the Mexican government's repeated policy of an "aversion" to devaluation would hold true.[34]

By the summer of 1994 the focus of the Salinas administration was to closely monitor the economy, in order to avoid any more economic or political surprises. The vocal opposition, dominated by the rise of popular National Action Party (PAN) candidate Diego Fernandez de Cevallos, began to stress the problems with the economy and social concerns that are always a part of the feud between the opposition parties and the PRI.[35] In June, the U.S. Embassy advised the Treasury that economist Rudi Dornbusch had, in a pointed and direct speech, told a private business group in Guadalajara that the peso was overvalued in the 20–25 percent range. These so-called private comments by Dornbusch became public, irritating many at the Banco de Mexico and in the Mexican government. While fundamentally correct, an "outsider's" comments can have a negative impact on the fragile Mexican economic system. At issue is the perception of confidence in the direction of the country and the creditworthiness of investments and loans. Nonetheless, the Dornbusch solution was to "turn the peso loose to float or preferably declare [sic] an abrupt 20 percent devaluation of the peso and a fixed rate thereafter." The Embassy cable further noted, "Given the prestige of Dornbusch in such matters, his remarks on devaluation of the peso cannot but have an effect on the exchange markets as well as on the thinking of his ex-students Salinas and Aspe."[36] Aspe's private response to the Dornbusch warnings was that he was "a dangerous man."[37]

At stake was the presidential election, but more important for the long term was the competitiveness and investment quality of the Mexican economy. Politically, the power of the PRI had begun to erode for the first time in decades. Key governorships and municipality elections had gone to the opposition PAN party in Baja California, Jalisco, Chihuahua, and Guanajuato. Mexican corporate and banking leaders began to have increased apprehension on the course of the economy, especially given the fact that there was a tradition of devaluation at the end of a Mexican president's constitutionally mandated, single six-year term. To position themselves, a number of Mexican multinationals such as Cemex, Vitro, Femsa, Bufete Industrial, and Tribasa had already expanded their operations outside of Mexico, both broadening their market and having access to a steady flow of hard currency.[38] Nonetheless, all these companies—while yearly more globally diversified—were closely tied to the fortunes of the domestic Mexican economy.

Unemployment began to trend upward and substantive efforts at a peace plan in Chiapas were rejected by the Zapatista rebels. Disgruntled farmers and ranchers, known as the El Barzon movement, had shut down banks in northern Mexico demanding an end to foreclosures and interest payments on overdue loans. In mid-June, the government announced a plan in conjunction with the banks to restructure an estimated $3.35 billion in bad loans, held by over 25,000 small- and medium-sized businesses. Loan loss reserves covered only about 40 percent of the volume of nonperforming loans. The Mexican banking system during the first half of 1994 had not recovered from the downturn in 1993, as indicated by the past due loan ratio that climbed to 7.67 percent, a relatively high level considering the conservative standards used to classify overdue loans.[39] By mid-year bank profits were severely impacted by further deterioration of asset quality. Although extensive attempts were made to raise new capital and generate more income from securities trading and foreign exchange reserves, Banamex, Bancomer, Banca Serfin, Banco Mexicano, Banco Internacional, and Multibanco Comermer had a considerable drop in profitability by the end of the second quarter. The mounting losses in the banking sector wiped out the gains, made possible by the reprivatization of the banks only two years earlier and eventually diminished their independence as they became daily more dependent on the government for support.[40]

In the weeks prior to the fall presidential election, there was a heightened reliance on tesobonos to support the peso. The issuance of the tesobonos was the prime avenue for the central bank to defend the peso. Mexican financial officials still advocated that the peso was not overvalued. Foreign investors found the tesobonos attractive as a hedge against exchange risk as well as political or financial turmoil. However, by July it was not "if" but "when" would the peso be devalued. Analysts at the Fed noted in an internal report that "The question boils down to how much Mexico will have to spend to maintain the band, and how long it can sustain the cost in reserves."[41]

More and more investors were substituting peso-denominated CETES with dollar-backed tesobonos. During 1993, the nominal value of new placements of tesobonos was the equivalent of 51.1 billion pesos ($17 bn) while new CETES issues totaled 209.4 billion pesos ($70 bn). In 1994, new tesobonos totaled 424.6 billion pesos ($129 bn)—an increase of 676 percent, while CETES totaled 147.5 billion pesos ($44.6 bn) for a decline of 34.2 percent. In July 1994 alone the central bank sold over $900 million in tesobonos in the secondary market. The high one-year rates were very attractive to investors with a spread over one-year U.S. Treasuries of about 362 basis points, "a nice pick-up in return on a security that has the highest short-term credit rating given by S&P, and that is now entitled to redemption in dollars!"[42] The peso closed the month of July down 1.2 percent in value at an average of 3.40/$.

At the beginning of August, the Mexican currency reserves were at $17 billion down over $7 billion from January. By now enough data were available to signal financial markets worldwide that a peso adjustment or devaluation in the short to medium term was likely. However, based on reports of increased levels of foreign direct investment (up over $9 billion or 30 percent over the previous year), persistent assessments from market analysts predicted a slight strengthening in the Mexican and a possible quicker lifting of the recession that had persisted since 1993.[43] Thus the surprise expressed by the market leaders and analysts in New York and abroad during the postdevaluation period after December 20; that they were caught by surprise is clearly overstated. They had invested in Mexico for high yields, fully aware of the volatile nature of the overvalued peso—especially in an election year. Furthermore, reports such as the press coverage given to the comments by Dornbusch were widely known. Billions in American pension funds (over 12 million individuals had retirement pensions and mutual funds associated with investments in the Mexican market) were one area that was highly exposed from August until the eventual December devaluation and crisis. In the days surrounding the presidential election, concerns surfaced about the eventual outcome and its impact on the economy and value of the peso.[44] Thus, it was hoped that the transition to the next administration in Mexico would settle such fears. Although Zedillo was a part of the administration in a number of capacities, it is now apparent that he did not know the full extent of the pending currency crisis. Salinas, aware of the actions of the previous two administrations to devalue, concerned about the outcome of the election, and preoccupied with his place in history, was not going to devalue the peso.[45] By the time of the election, events and actions all but telegraphed the need for direct action to adjust the currency policy to reflect the changes in the value of the peso. On August 16 the Federal Reserve raised interest rates from 4.25 to 4.75 percent. In Mexico, on the day before the election, the Bank of Mexico raised the floor of its exchange rate band from 3.104 to 3.25, to discourage a rapid appreciation of the peso after the election. The move was short-lived. In the week after the August 23 election of Zedillo, the peso lost 1 percent in value against the dollar.[46] The expected postelection surge in foreign investment failed to materialize. In Washington the Federal Reserve, having already gone through currency and loan problems with Mexico in the 1970's and 1980's, prepared for the worst. In a mid-August staff report to Chairman Greenspan and Vice Chair Blinder entitled "The Implied Probability of a Peso Devaluation," the possibilities of more serious problems beyond a devaluation were stressed:

The increased difference between tesobono and U.S. interest rates . . . suggests that not only has the perceived risk of devaluation increased, but that the perceived risk of the Mexican government defaulting or otherwise abrogating the terms of its liabilities, or suspending the convertibility of its currency, may also have risen.[47]

As the transition of the reins of power from Salinas to Zedillo were being arranged during early September in Mexico City, a heated internal debate among the Salinas insider group ensued concerning the handling of the peso and the economy. In an effort to encourage the appreciation of the peso, the Banco de Mexico adjusted the floor of the exchange rate band from 3.250 back to 3.104; however, the peso continued to trade between 0.8 and 1.3 percent from the ceiling of the band. Salinas and his economic advisors were fully aware of the deteriorating condition of the peso.[48] There was no good time to devalue, and Salinas—in pursuit of the directorship of the newly formed World Trade Organization—was not going to allow any such a devaluation shock to occur while he was still president. One last hope was to insure that the pending negotiations on the "Pacto," scheduled for mid-September, would address the fragile state of the peso. Many of the goals outlined in the eventual outcome of the Pacto, drafted primarily by the Salinas administration, were agreed to by Zedillo and his transition team. To have his mark on the final agreement, Zedillo changed the name of the Pacto from the "Pact for Stability, Competitiveness, and Employment" to the "Pact for Well-Being, Stability, and Growth," echoing his campaign slogan of "Well-being for your Family."[49] Even though the current account deficit was in a rapid decline, the government concluded that as long as foreign capital inflow continued, inflation was low, and productivity was up—no new pressure should be placed on the value of the peso. In hindsight, the very outline of the Pacto spelled doom.[50]

The Pacto represented a pivotal agreement impacting all sectors of the Mexican economy by setting the targets for wage and pricing policies, the federal budget, foreign exchange, and macroeconomic goals. The Pacto, concluded on September 24, 1994, left no room for error or economic instability. In hopes of further reducing inflation in 1995, the exchange rate band (already at the upper limit) in the agreement set a goal to depreciate the peso at NP .0004 per day or about 4–4.25 percent per year. The government planned to balance the budget while increasing public sector spending on infrastructure by 25 percent via joint ventures with the private sector. Price hikes on gasoline, electricity, as well as wage increases were set at 4 percent. Projected GDP for 1995 was to expand to 3.8 percent. The plan was bold, and well received in the investment community (see Figure 6-5).[51]

During the week after the announcement of the Pacto, a period that should have shown a marked recovery in the strength of the peso, it instead took another dip with the murder of the secretary general of the PRI, Jose Francisco Ruiz Massieu, a close advisor to Zedillo.[52] In Washington, both the Federal Reserve and Treasury privately questioned both the political unrest and the short- and long-term projections of the new Pacto. The decision to maintain a fixed exchange rate policy, in view of the fact that the peso was significantly overvalued, caused concern that the Pacto was more cosmetic than substantive. Given the slim margin of error due to the peso trading near the upper limit of the band, both the inflation target and the exchange rate forecast were clearly much too ambitious. Furthermore, the current account deficit was a very high 7 percent of GNP. The Zedillo plan for "gradual, long-term adjustment rather

Figure 6-5
U.S. Interest Rates: Effect on Mexico

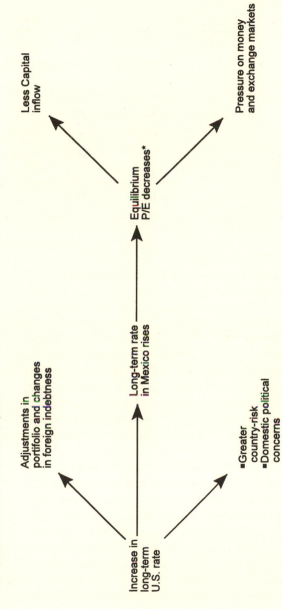

Sources: Department of Economic Research; Banamex.

Figure 6-6
Foreign Investment in Mexican Equity: August 1994 and 1995 and December 1994
(Millions of U.S. Dollars)

	August 1994	December 1994	August 1995	Percent Annual Change	Percent Year to Date Change
ADR's	33,356.9	21,162.9	16,621.0	-50.2	-21.5
Free Subscription Shares	13,526.4	8,079.0	6,784.2	-49.8	-16.0
Neutral Fund	7,191.3	4,348.4	3,042.5	-57.7	-30.0
Mexico Fund	1,311.0	765.6	679.8	-48.1	-11.2
Intermediate Market	3.3	15.6	42.7	1,203.0	174.0
Warrants	5.3	23.7	9.3	74.8	-60.8
Total	**55,394.2**	**34,395.2**	**27,179.5**	**-50.9**	**-21.0**

Source: Mexican Stock Exchange, "Indicadores Bursatiles," December 1994 and August 1995.

than immediate adjustment" fell short of expectations.[53] The peso closed the month of September trading at 3.3998/$.

In essence the Pacto, the key agreement that had guided inflation lower since 1987, did not have the desired effect of strengthening the peso, and its fate was held suspect due to the political unrest and continued high volatility in the financial markets.[54] A second internal confrontation occurred in early October between Salinas and Zedillo over the issue of the value of the peso. Salinas again refused to budge. Officials at the highest levels in the U.S. Treasury, the U.S. Embassy in Mexico City, the State Department, and the Federal Reserve held nearly a dozen meetings with Mexican government and central bank officials during October. At the core of these discussions was the Mexican government's staunch defense of the fixed exchange rate (against the U.S. dollar) and the possibility the United States was willing to offer financial support via the swap agreements. This assumption on the part of Mexican officials concerning the arrangement of a swap facility was based on their experience over the preceding year. On three distinct occasions, in November and December 1993 and again in March 1994, after the assassination of Colosio, a mix of permanent and temporary currency swap facilities was arranged by the U.S. and/or Canadian government and the Bank of International Settlements.[55] However, the swap facility was created to be used in time of crisis, not as a routine vehicle to prop up the currency or, as officials at the Federal Reserve noted, "the swap lines are intended to deal with what are viewed as transitory market disturbances, not to buttress an unsustainable exchange rate regime."[56] By month-end, Secretary Bentsen was advised by an internal memo prior to a meeting with Finance

Minister Pedro Aspe that the "hopes for a stable postelection period and resumption of capital inflows have not materialized" and the peso is very "vulnerable."[57]

Mexico's net international currency reserves dropped 27 percent from $17.5 billion in late October to $12.7 billion by the end of November. During the final weeks prior to the devaluation there was a marked increase in violence in Chiapas. The news of renewed fighting in Chiapas and the fact that the Fed raised the rates from 4.75 to 5.5 percent in mid-November caused investors to sell pesos, and rumors in Mexico spread that the banks were running short of dollars. Goldman Sachs, based mainly on the news of the joint venture announcement between AT&T and Groupo Alfa to enter the communications market in Mexico, dropped its "buy" recommendation for the cornerstone Mexican stock—Telmex. The peso fell to its weakest position of the year at 3.4501/$, only 0.21 percent from the ceiling of the band. To combat the weakening peso the Banco de Mexico was forced to intervene with an injection of $2.25 billion (see Figure 6-6).[58]

It is quite possible that November 20, 1994 was the pivotal day for the Salinas administration with regard to how to address the peso situation. At a meeting on this date attended by President Salinas, Pedro Aspe, President-elect Ernesto Zedillo, Jaime Serra Puche, Arsenio Farell, Miguel Mancera, and Luis Tellez the position of the government regarding the peso was debated around three possible actions, according to Aspe:

We proceeded to ponder the advantages and disadvantages of performing a "small devaluation of 10% to 15%." The group made a review of the pros and cons of this alternative, ending up with a division of opinions between those who wanted its immediate implementation, those in favor of letting the exchange rate float freely and those supporting a drastic tightening of monetary policy to increase rates significantly. The last group rejected devaluation, arguing that it would break up the Pacto and bring back high inflation and a turn to wage-price spiral.[59]

The only course of action agreed to was for the incoming Zedillo government to support the Pacto and to prepare for the transition of the new administration.

A NOT-SO-FELIZ NAVIDAD

In spite of government efforts to negotiate with the Zapatistas and the positive words for a peaceful settlement offered by Zedillo at his inauguration on December 1, hostilities in Chiapas continued in early December. With the current account deficit at $7.31 billion and the currency reserves dropping daily from the end of November total of $12.7 billion, the situation was now critical. To attract needed funds for the Mexican government would require that (1) interest rates be significantly increased on Mexican bonds (which could further dampen growth projections), (2) the United States and/or an international group would

step forward to assist, or (3) the peso must be "allowed greater depreciation."
On December 5–6 both the Federal Reserve in Washington and the Banco de
Mexico knew that an adjustment in the exchange rate band would occur and
steps were taken to shore up the financial position of the Mexican government.[60]
Though implied, the term "devaluation" was not used by either government
with relation to change in the exchange rate. In a memo from Summers and
Jeffery Shafer on December 5 titled "Mexico: Planning For The Next Stage,"
the Federal Reserve concluded that "the new Mexican Administration will not
be able to sustain its existing exchange rate regime, we need to take a look at
options . . . reserves are now only slightly above the critical $10 billion thresh-
old. Another bad week would get them there quickly. They seem to have used
up all the easy ways to boost reserves."[61] Preliminary questions were posed in
the Summers-Shafer memo that would set the stage for U.S. response to the
pending crisis:

1. Should we look for an early opportunity to meet (Summers with Ortiz's successor)
   to explain what we would be prepared to do and not prepared to do in the event of
   further pressure and any change on the exchange rate regime?
2. What complementary policy changes might be necessary to restore domestic and external balance as part of an adjustment in the exchange rate regime? Would we want
   to engage the IMF in a more serious effort than we have done to date?[62]

At what exact moment, and by whom, the final decision to address the
exchange rate issue was made is still not clear, and will probably not be for
years to come. Both the Clinton and Zedillo administrations realized the magnitude of the situation, but no one foresaw the swiftness of reaction in the
markets and the resulting impact on emerging markets worldwide.[63] All proceeded in hopes of a solution, short of a radical devaluation. On December 9,
as the Mexican government released its 1995 budget emphasizing a 4 percent
growth and inflation targets, President Clinton delivered extensive remarks at
the Summit of the Americas in Miami on the rise of free trade, lower inflation,
economic growth, reduced tariffs, and "stabilized currencies" in the hemisphere—noting it was just one year to the day since the signing of the North
American Free Trade Agreement.[64]

During the week prior to the December 19–20 devaluation, Mexico endeavored to attract more capital. The mounting short-term nature of the tesobono
investments, along with the more attractive three-month U.S. Treasury Bills that
were yielding nearly 6 percent, prevented any substantive effort. Although a
number of analysts still heralded Mexico's recovery and investment quality, the
path to an adjustment in the exchange rate band was imminent.[65] As late as
mid-December the Swiss Bank Corporation, calling Mexico "a changed country
. . . it has already passed the threshold of economic stabilisation," promoted the
country as a prime candidate for an investment grade rating.[66] Their review of
the accomplishments of the Mexican government to stabilize the economy since

1990 reflected the numerous changes underway in the country, yet like most investors worldwide, they underestimated the magnitude of the imbalance being created by a combination of increased trade levels, a rigid exchange rate policy, and the tremendous level of short-term investments. To combat the rumors, representatives of the Mexican government began to express some reluctance about the Pacto's goal of 4 percent economic growth in 1995, yet held steadfast to the position that Mexico would, according to Zedillo's new Finance Minister Jaime Serra Puche, "stick with its current peso policy and not devalue."[67] The same day Serra made his bold endorsement of the currency policy, the peso traded at its lowest point in over three years, 3.470/$. Frantic meetings were called in Mexico City, Washington, D.C., and New York City capital markets to reassure investors.[68]

Mexico's outstanding tesobono obligation, all due in 1995, had reached a staggering $30 billion and the foreign exchange reserves fell below $10 billion, an amount determined necessary to sustain credible finances.[69] The government was on the verge of default by December 18. Meetings between government officials, parties to the Pacto, and the business community on December 19 resulted in a refusal to accept a move to directly float the peso. In retrospect, allowing the peso to float and informing the investment community of the reasons for the action might have lessened the ensuing economic crisis. Thus, on December 20, the government announced an easing of the pressure on the exchange rate by widening the peso/dollar exchange rate band. The widening of the band was interpreted by the surprised and uninformed financial markets worldwide as a radical devaluation which, within hours, devalued the peso by 15 percent.[70]

The announcement by the Mexican government was made in a complete vacuum—as little or no advance contact was made with Washington or the IMF. Zedillo had carried over very few of the key economic officials who had dealt with Washington during the Salinas administration. Furthermore, there were no contingency plans to introduce stabilizing measures to reassure the financial markets, such as an announcement to raise domestic interest rates, tighten fiscal controls, contact the IMF for a line of credit, or reassessment of the targets set in the Pacto. The government tried and failed to portray the situation as a minor exchange rate adjustment, not a devaluation. On December 21, the actions by the government resulted in the outflow of over $4 billion in foreign reserves and on December 22, Mexico announced it would freely float the peso. The lack of economic countermeasures, planning, or even adequate public relations to inform and calm the major capital markets created a "crisis of confidence." Concerns about the ability of the new Zedillo administration to handle the situation heightened fears of complete default—based on the fact that by early January 1995, Mexico would quickly diminish its remaining reserves (about $6 billion) to redeem short-term, dollar-indexed and denominated tesobono obligations.[71]

The full impact of the devaluation would not be felt until after the new year.

On Christmas Day, Mexico City and the nation was calm and quiet. There was a somber reaction to the devaluation. During the ensuing weeks initial steps were begun to ensure a stable transition. Although default on a broad array of loan covenants and agreements was always possible, much too much was at stake to allow the Mexican economy to fully disintegrate. In a press release from the U.S. Treasury on December 27, Summers urged calm. "Recent movements in the value of the Mexican peso have gone beyond what can be justified by Mexican economic fundamentals. We are confident in the underlying soundness of Mexican economic policies . . . and recognize that extensive depreciation is in no one's interest."[72]

NOTES

1. Banamex, "Mexico's Achievements," *Review of the Economic Situation of Mexico* (Mexico D.F.: August 1994), pp. 362–80; Pedro Aspe Armella, *El Camino Mexicano de la Transformacion Economica* (Mexico, D.F.: 1993), pp. 1–210; Catherine Mansell Carstens, *Las Finanzas Populares en Mexico* (Mexico, D.F.: 1995), pp. 71–157; Jaime Suchlicki, *Mexico: From Montezuma to NAFTA, Chiapas, and Beyond* (Washington: 1996), pp. 132–56; Banamex, "NAFTA: More Competition, More Assurances," *Review of the Economic Situation of Mexico* (Mexico, D.F.: January 1994), pp. 10–14; Sergio Sarmieto, "Central Bank Autonomy May Get Mexico Back on the Growth Track," *Wall Street Journal*, June 4, 1993, p. A15; Banco de Mexico, *The Mexican Economy 1995* (Mexico, D.F.: June 1995), pp. 30–33, 43. Note: One investment firm in Mexico, InverMexico, categorized the economic crisis of 1995 as "without a doubt, one of the worst in modern history." See InverMexico Grupo Financiero, *62nd Meeting of Economic and Securities Research* (Mexico, D.F.: 1996), p. 8.

2. Note: The principal peso devaluations greater than 20 percent accrued in February 1982 (37.7%), August 1982 (44.03%), December 1982 (113.29%), July 1985 (41.89%), November 1987 (45.04%), and December-February 1995 (74.07%).

3. U.S. Congress, Senate, Committee on Banking, Housing, and Urban Affairs, *The Peso Crisis and the Administration's Proposed Loan Guarantee Package for Mexico*, S. Hrg. 104–164, 104th Cong., 1st sess. (Washington, D.C.: 1995); Sergio Sarmiento, "Of Devaluation and Purges," *El Financiero International* (hereafter *EFI*), August 30, 1993, p. 3; Robert Gay, "Mexico Soon Will Be Investment Grade," *Bankers Trust Research*, December 14, 1993, pp. 1–4; Tom Petruno, "Global Money—Free Flows, Free Falls," *Los Angeles Times*, March 21, 1995.

4. Jose Angel Gurria Trevino, "Modernization of the Mexican Economy," *El Mercado de Valores* (Mexico City: May-June 1994), pp. 18–30; Banco de Mexico, *The Mexican Economy 1995*, pp. 1–58.

5. OECD, *Mexico 1994–95: OECD Economic Surveys* (Paris: September 1995), pp. 3–6, 17–19, 27–28; Banamex, "Emerging Economies: Foreign Investment," *Review of the Economic Situation of Mexico* (Mexico, D.F.: August 1994), pp. 389–92; "1993 Inflation Hits 21 Year Low," *Mexletter*, Vol. XXXVI, No. 2, February 1994, pp. 1–4; "Foreign Investment in Mexico During 1994," *El Mercado de Valores*, March-April 1995, pp. 29–36.

6. OECD, *Mexico 1994–95*, pp. 6–16; Shahid Javed Burki and Sebastin Edwards,

"Causes and Lessons of the Mexican Crisis," *El Mercado de Valores*, September-October 1995, pp. 24–25; Rudi Dornbusch, "Now, for Mexico's Next Miracle: Democracy," *Business Week*, April 4, 1994, p. 19. Note: See also IMF, *Balance of Payments Statistics Yearbook*, Part 1 (Washington, D.C.: 1995), pp. 510–15

7. InverMexico, *62nd Meeting*, pp. 31–33; E. Henry Urquidi, "Latin American Equity Derivatives," *Latin Finance* (supplement), February 1996, pp. 10–14.

8. Banamex, "Mexico As Seen through the OECD," *Review of the Economic Situation of Mexico* (Mexico, D.F.: August 1994), pp. 381–82; John A. Adams, Jr., "Without GATT, There'd Be No NAFTA," *Laredo Morning Times*, December 17, 1993; David Malpass, "20 Reasons Mexico Won't Devalue," *Latin America Watch*, Bear, Stearns & Co., April 21, 1994, pp. 7–8; William Kail, "Analyst: Bank Won't Allow Inflation," *The News* [Mexico, D.F.], December 9, 1994.

9. Banco de Mexico, *Report on Monetary Policy: January 1, 1995–December 31, 1995* (Mexico D.F.: January 1995), pp. 11–14.

10. Susan Schadler, Maria Carkovic, Adam Bennett, and Robert Kahn, "Recent Experiences with Surges in Capital Inflows," *Monetary Fund Occasional Paper*, No. 108 (Washington, D.C.: December 1993), pp. 5, 11, 29; Gary Newman, "Volatility Remains," *Business Latin America*, January 24, 1994, p. 3; Yves Maroni, "Mexican Exchange Rate Policy," Federal Reserve Board (FRB), January 28, 1994, Doc. No. 94–4.

11. Tom Barry, *Zapata's Revenge: Free Trade and the Farm Crisis in Mexico* (Boston: 1995), pp. 155–71; Robert Reno, "Anti-NAFTA Screeching in Fear, Not Reason," *Houston Chronicle*, September 12, 1993, p. 1F; Frank Swoboda, "President Woos Labor on NAFTA," *Washington Post*, October 5, 1993, p. C1; Ross Perot and Pat Choate, *Save Your Job, Save Our Country: Why NAFTA Must Be Stopped Now* (New York: 1993), pp. 1–110; Gary Newman, "Turmoil in Mexico," *Business Latin America*, January 17, 1994, p. 1. See also Andres Oppenheimer, *Bordering on Chaos*, pp. 16–36; USTR, "Correcting the Record: Response of the Office of the U.S. Trade Representative to the Perot/Choate NAFTA Book" (Washington, D.C.: September 2, 1993), pp. 1–74, and Autonomedia, *Zapatista!—Documents of the New Mexico Revolution*, December 31, 1993–June 12, 1994 (New York: 1994), pp. 1–340. Note: The EZLN took the name of Emiliano Zapata, a peasant leader and champion of land reform during the 1910 Mexican Revolution.

12. "More Moves Ahead," *Investors Business Daily*, February 21, 1996, p. B1.

13. Banco de Mexico, *The Mexican Economy 1995*, p. 37. Note: The highest level of reserves occurred on February 15, 1994 at $29.225 billion.

14. Banamex, "Savings from Abroad," *Review of the Economic Situation of Mexico* (Mexico, D.F.: March 1994), pp. 120–25. See also Banco de Mexico, *The Mexican Economy 1994* (Mexico, D.F.: 1994), pp. 163–68.

15. IMF, *Annual Report of the Executive Board for the Financial Year Ended April 30, 1994*, pp. 81–82; Memorandum from Michael Hood to McCauley, "Investment and Savings in Latin America," Federal Reserve Board of New York (FRBNY), February 3, 1994, Doc. No. 94–10; OECD, *Mexico 1994–95*, pp. 7–8. See also U.S. Embassy, Mexico, *Mexico: Economic and Financial Report—Fall 1995* (Mexico City: 1995), pp. 24–25; Banco de Mexico, *The Mexican Economy 1995*, pp. 11–12; Ariel Buira, *The Main Determinants of Savings in Mexico*, prepared for the Conference on the Role of Savings in Economic Growth, Federal Reserve Bank of Dallas, Houston, Texas, March 18–19, 1994; and Richard Alm and David M. Could, "The Saving Grace," *The Economic Review* (FRBD), Third Quarter 1994, pp. 45–48.

16. U.S. Treasury Department, memo from Assistant Secretary of the Treasury for International Affairs Jeffery R. Shafer to Secretary of the Treasury Lloyd Bentsen, "Briefing for Your Meeting in Mexico City, Thursday, February 17, 1994," February 10, 1994, Treasury Doc. Nos. 3284–307; Ibid., "Bi-Weekly Report on Mexico," February 15, 1994, Doc. Nos. 709378–80; Banco de Mexico, *The Mexican Economy 1995*, pp. 39–40.

17. U.S. Treasury Department, memo to Under Secretary Lawrence H. Summers and Shafer, "Peso Volatility Moderates" March 8, 1994, Treasury Doc. No. 3280. See also Banamex, "Banco de Mexico: Independence and Monetary Policy," *Review of the Economic Situation of Mexico* (Mexico, D.F.: July 1994), pp. 312–13.

18. Note: The Banco de Mexico is primarily concerned with the overall monetary policy and is charged in the Constitution, Article 20, paragraph 6 to "pursue the stability of the purchasing power of the domestic currency." See Banco de Mexico, *The Mexican Economy 1995*, pp. 35–53.

19. U.S. Treasury, "Bi-Weekly Report on Mexico," March 15, 1994, Treasury Doc. Nos. 716935–37; Banco de Mexico, *The Mexican Economy 1995*, p. 40.

20. Geoffrey Dennis, "The Mexican Rally: A One-Two from Camacho and Greenspan," *Latin America Watch*, March 22, 1994, pp. 5–6. Note: Harp was released on June 28, 1994 after a high ransom was paid and additional high profile kidnappings occurred throughout the year.

21. Gary Newman, "Asessing the Damage in Mexico," *Business Latin America*, April 4, 1994, p. 1; Newman, "A Mexican Tragedy," Ibid., March 28, 1994, p. 1.

22. GAO, *Mexico's Financial Crisis: Origins, Awareness, Assistance and Initial Efforts to Recover* (Washington, D.C: February 1996), pp. 52–59; Newman, "A Mexican Tragedy," p. 1; Newman, "Assessing the Damage in Mexico," p. 1.

23. Suzanne Bilello, "Mexico: The Rise of Civil Society," *Current History*, Vol. 95, pp. 85–86; Memo from Summers to Bentsen, April 26, 1994, Treasury Doc. 3247–3253; Liz Capo and Ted Merz, "Experts Believe Mexican Finances Will Pass Test: Others Fear Assassination Will Reinforce Perception of Instability," *Austin American-Statesman*, March 25, 1994, p. A10.

24. Banamex, "The State of the Economy: A Graphic Synthesis," *Review of the Economic Situation of Mexico* (Mexico, D.F.: June 1994), pp. 267–68; Banco de Mexico, *The Mexican Economy 1995*, pp. 36–41.

25. OECD, *Mexico 1994–95*, p. 32.

26. Banamex, "Emerging Economies: Capital Markets," *Review of the Economic Situation of Mexico* (Mexico, D.F.: June 1994), p. 275.

27. Banamex, "Monetary Policy," Ibid., p. 269.

28. Ibid., pp. 269–72

29. Banco de Mexico, *The Mexican Economy 1995*, pp. 41–44.

30. Cable from U.S. Embassy in Mexico to U.S. Department of State, "Paper Views Effect of Colosio Death on Currency Exchange" (translation of article from *La Jornada*), April 6, 1994, State Dept. Doc. No. A-45; Rudi Dornbusch, "Stabilization, Reform, and No-Growth" (FRBNY), May 1994, Doc. Nos. 10000308–338; Letter, author and recipient unidentified, April 22, 1994, U.S. Treasury Doc. Nos. 187–88.

31. U.S. Treasury, "Joint Statement by the Finance Ministers and Central Bank Governors of Canada, Mexico and the United States" (Washington, D.C.), April 26, 1994.

32. Ibid.; Memo from Shafer to Summers, "Briefing for This Year's Meeting of the U.S. Mexico Binational Commission," May 6, 1994, Treasury Doc. Nos. 3159–196;

Memo from Summers to Bentsen, April 26, 1994, Treasury Doc. Nos. 3247–53.

33. Federal News Service, Washington, D.C., April 26, 1994. Note: In an unrelated event the police chief of Tijuana investigating the Colosio assassination was murdered on April 28, 1994.

34. Cable from U.S. Embassy in Mexico to U.S. Treasury Department, "Mexico Economic Recovery: Not Quite Yet," May 1994, State Department Doc. No. A-141; Memo from Shafer to Summers, "Briefing for Dinner Hosted by [name deleted]," May 6, 1994, Treasury Doc. Nos. 3197–211. See also OECD, *Mexico 1994–95*, p. 116; Banamex, "Effects of Higher U.S. Interest Rates," *Review of the Economic Situation of Mexico* (Mexico, D.F.: March 1994), pp. 121, 125.

35. Leon Lazaroff, "A Rising Star," *Business Latin America*, June 13, 1994, p. 3.

36. Cable from U.S. Embassy in Mexico to U.S. Treasury Department, "Peso Devaluation Urged by MIT's Rudi Dornbusch," June 1994, State Department Doc. No. A-166. See also Rudiger Dornbusch, Alejandro Werner, Guillermo Calvo, and Stanley Fisher, "Mexico: Stabilization, Reform, and No Growth," *Brookings Papers on Economic Activity*, Vol. 1, 1995, pp. 253–315.

37. David Wessel, Paul Carroll, and Thomas Vogel, "How Mexico's Crisis Ambushed Top Minds in Officialdom, Finance," *Wall Street Journal*, June 6, 1995, p. A3.

38. Joel Millman, "Cementing Latin America," *Forbes*, February 26, 1996, pp. 45–46.

39. Thomson Bank Watch, "Declining Fortunes," *Latin Finance*, November 1994, pp. 30–42.

40. Talli Nauman, "Movement Strikes Financial Heart of Mexico," *El Financiero Internacional*, February 28, 1994, p. 13; Thomson Bank Watch, "Declining Fortunes," pp. 40–42; OECD, *Mexico 1994–95*, pp. 34–38.

41. E-Mail from Weir to Bentley, July 6, 1994 (FRBNY), Doc. No. 10001567, as seen in Senator Alfonse D'Amato, "Report on the Mexican Economic Crisis" (Washington, D.C.: June 29, 1995), pp. 17–19 (hereafter MEC D'Amato). See also GAO, *Mexico's Financial Crisis* (Washington, D.C.: February 1996), pp. 60–66.

42. U.S. Embassy, Mexico, *Mexico: Economic and Financial Report Fall 1995*, p. 45; E-Mail from Weir to Bentley, July 19, 1994, FRBNY, Doc. Nos. 10001571, 10001577, as seen in MEC D'Amato; Chris Aspin, "Hot Money Levels Raise Fiscal Concern," *EFI*, March 24, 1994, p. 1.

43. "Stock Market Moves Higher," *Mexletter*, August 1994, pp. 1–2; Robert S. Gay, "Mexico's Surprising Growth," *Bankers Trust Research*, August 19, 1994, pp. 1–4.

44. Steve Kamin and John Morton, "The Implied Probability of a Peso Devaluation," August 19, 1994 (FRB), Doc. No. 94–119, pp. 1–2.

45. Alejandro Ramos, "WTO: Sorry, Charlie [Carlos]," *EFI*, November 28, 1994, p. 6; Wessel, Carroll, and Vogel, "How Mexico's Crisis Ambushed Top Minds In Officialdom, Finance," *Wall Street Journal*, June 6, 1995, p. 1; Steve Kamin and David Howard, "Options for Mexican Exchange Rate Policy," August 17, 1994 (FRB), Doc. No. 94–115.

46. Memo from Timothy Geithner to Bentsen, October 27, 1994, U.S. Treasury Doc. No. 702667; Cable from U.S. Embassy in Mexico to Treasury Department, "Mexican Financial Weekly," August 29, 1994, p. 2, State Department Doc. No. 244.

47. Memo from Siegman to Greenspan and Blinder, August 19, 1994; and Kamin and Morton, "The Implied Probability of a Peso Devaluation," August 19, 1994, pp. 1–2 (FRB), Doc. No. 94–119. Note: The Central Intelligence Agency (CIA), since the early

summer of 1994, had repeatedly warned U.S. government officials of the real possibility of a devaluation and their concern for the impact of the presidential election and the Mexican economy. See MEC D'Amato, p. 18.

48. Pedro Aspe, "Mexico's Ex-Finance Minister Sets the Record Straight," *Wall Street Journal*, July 15, 1995, p. A15.

49. Steve Kamin, "Mexico's New Pacto" (FRB), Doc. No. 94–144, September 29, 1994; Robert Gay, "Mexico: The Pacto and the Peso," *Banker Trust Research*, October 6, 1994, pp. 1–4.

50. Geithner to Bentsen, October 17, 1994, Treasury Doc. No. 702667; Anthony De Palma, "Waiting for the Other Peso to Drop," *New York Times*, September 18, 1994; Adam Cordery, "Staying the Course," *Business Latin America*, October 3, 1994.

51. E-Mail from Laura Weir (FRB), Doc. No. 10004106, September 26, 1994; Robert S. Gay, "Mexico: Moving toward Transparency," Bankers Trust Research, November 7, 1994, p. 4. See also "Orthodoxy, Continuity, Prudence and Predictability, Economic Pillars of Zedillo's Program," *El Economista*, September 9, 1994. Note: The Pacto was ratified on November 21, 1994.

52. "The Specter of Instability," *Mexletter*, October 1994, pp. 1–3.

53. Summers to Bentsen, "Mexico Maintains Current Exchange Rate Policy in Renewal of 'Pacto'," Treasury Doc. No. 001760, September 27, 1994; Susan Charrette to Bennett, "Renewal of Mexico's Annual Economic Pact" (FRBNY), Doc. No. 10003844–48, September 28, 1994.

54. "Fiscal Policy: To Spend or Not to Spend Is Zedillo's Question," *Mexico Service*, December 2, 1994, pp. 3–5.

55. GAO, "Mexico's Financial Crisis," February 1996, pp. 80–81.

56. Siegman to Greenspan, Background Material for October 20 Visit by President-elect Zedillo's Advisor Luis Tellez" (FRB), Doc. No. 94–149, October 19, 1994.

57. Memo from Geithner to Bentsen, Treasury Doc. No. 702660–2, 64, 67, October 27, 1994. See also Clay Chandler, "Treasury Had 3 Early Peso Alerts," *San Antonio Express-News*, March 3, 1995, p. 1E.

58. E-mail from Laura Weir (FRBNY), Doc. No. 1732A, November 14, 1994; Memo [OASIA] to Summers, Treasury Doc. No. 001390, November 14, 1994; Memo from Shafer to Bentsen, "Bank of Mexico Intervenes to Support a Weakening Peso," Treasury Doc. No. 001207, November 18, 1994; Summers to Bentsen, "Update on Peso," Treasury Doc. No. 000764, November 22, 1994. See also "Panacea or Placebo: 3 Reasons Why Devaluation Won't Help," *Mexico Service*, November 18, 1994, pp. 4–5.

59. Aspe, "Mexico's Ex-Finance Minister Sets the Record Straight," p. A15

60. Memo to Summers and Shafer, "Mexico: Planning for the Next Stage," Treasury Doc. No. 001209–10, December 5, 1994; Comments by Banco de Mexico officials, Mexico City, February 19, 1996.

61. Memo to Summers and Shafer, "Mexico: Planning," December 5, 1994; Laura Weir, "FRBNY Market Insight Mexico: Period 11/15/94–12/15/94" (FRBNY), Doc. No. 94–170, December 1994.

62. Memo to Summers and Shafer, "Mexico: Planning," December 5, 1994. Note: This memo contained four questions, two of which (numbers 2 and 4) were still classified as "secret" as of mid-1996. Questions 1 and 3 appear in the text.

63. Georg Junge, "Emerging Market Countries in Global Financial Markets," *Economic and Financial Prospects*, Swiss Bank (Basel: February 1996), pp. 10–13. Note:

The country economies most directly impacted included Brazil, Argentina, the Philippines, Turkey, Venezuela, Hungary, and Thailand.

64. White House, "Remarks on Goals of the Summit of the Americas in Miami, Florida," *Weekly Compilation of Presidential Documents*, Vol. 30, December 9, 1994, pp. 2485–89.

65. Carl Ross, "The Mexican Current Account: Balancing the Books," *Bankers Trust Research*, December 19, 1994, pp. 1–8; "Peso Weakens to Record Low," *San Antonio Express-News*, December 16, 1994.

66. "Mexico—Candidate for Investment Grade," *Economic and Financial Prospects*, Swiss Bank Corporation, No. 6, December-January 1994, pp. 1–4.

67. Craig Torres, "Mexico's Goal for '95 Growth May Be Tough," *Wall Street Journal*, December 16, 1994, p. A6.

68. "The Morning After," *Business Latin America*, January 9, 1995; "Ex-Finance Chief Defends Actions in Peso Crisis," *Journal of Commerce*, July 20, 1995; "Treasury and Federal Reserve Foreign Exchange Operations," *Federal Reserve Bulletin*, Vol. 81, No. 3, March 1995, p. 247.

69. Memo to Geithner, "Contact with Mexicans Before They Do Something," Treasury Doc. No. 702690, December 19, 1994.

70. Knight-Ridder, "Emerging Market Debt: Mexico Bradies Active on Peso Devaluation," 1:37 P.M., December 20, 1994, pp. 1–4; "Mexico Drops Efforts to Prop Up Peso, Spurring 15% Fall and Eroding Credibility," *Wall Street Journal*, December 23, 1994, p. A3; Leslie Eaton, "Peso's Woes: A Very Familiar Diminuendo," *New York Times*, December 25, 1994; "On the Brink," *LatinFinance*, March 1996, pp. 14–17. Note: In the *LatinFinance* article, Lawrence Summers was named by the publication "1996 Man of the Year."

71. Guillermo Guémez García, "Comments to the 'Board Trade Alliance' on the Strategy and Evolution on the Economic Adjustment in Mexico," Banco de Mexico (Mexico D.F., February 19, 1996); Craig Torres and Paul Carroll, "Mexico Puts Economic Steps on Hold until Fallout from Peso's Plunge Settles," *Wall Street Journal*, December 27, 1994; David Gould and William Gruben, "The Roots of Mexico's Peso Crisis," *The Southwest Economy* (FRBD), vol. 1, 1995, p. 11.

72. U.S. Treasury, Press Release, December 27, 1994, Treasury Doc. No. 707160.

Chapter 7

Crisis of Confidence: 1995

> The current situation in Mexico arises from a loss of confidence—and its fallout. There is a prospect of a vicious circle, as this loss of confidence chokes off Mexico's access to funds and creates financial and economic distress, perpetuating investor unwillingness to invest in Mexico.
> —Secretary Robert E. Rubin, January 25, 1995

> In all frankness, I reiterate that the devaluation will have painful effects. But with equal frankness I emphasize that united, we can ensure that those effects are transitory and that they turn into a decisive step towards a stage of growth with stability.
> —Ernesto Zedillo, January 3, 1995

The ramifications of the 1994 devaluation of the Mexican peso were staggering. For a nation on the path of both economic recovery and a return of investor credibility, the shock of devaluation—the third such major currency crisis during the last three presidential administrations—was devastating. In a few short hours Mexico lost what had taken years of economic restructuring to achieve. Although Ernesto Zedillo had been president less than three weeks, the blame for the debacle rested solely on the shoulders of the outgoing Salinas administration. The fact that Wall Street and other investment markets worldwide claim to have been taken by surprise and "missed" the signals that resulted in the Mexican crash is a bit overstated. Although the overvaluation of the peso had been analyzed and discussed in financial markets worldwide, no single warning was heeded regarding the pending peso collapse. The *Economist* noted that "financial markets did a rotten job as economic watchdog in Mexico. First they were too eager to throw money at it . . . and then they abruptly decided to get out.''[1] The fact that the Salinas administration, with the full knowledge of the Banco de Mexico and despite numerous U.S. warnings, avoided the need to alter the currency policy to reflect the true value of the peso and thus maintained the value of the peso at an unrealistic, artificially high level only made the crash more devastating in the end. Foreign as well as Mexican investors were confident that the Mexican economy was one of the safest investments of all the emerging markets worldwide. In an ex post facto assessment of the devaluation, the *Institutional Investor* noted that "the greatest mistake Mexico watchers made, stems from the way human psyche is hard-wired: observers displayed a basic inability to envision *complete calamity*."[2]

During the first few weeks following the devaluation there was general dismay and mild panic as foreign investors reacted to cut their losses and move their portfolio investments out of Mexico. The mood in Mexico was somber. The foreign exchange markets were hyperactive as the trading value of the peso was fueled largely by speculation. The peso lost 40 percent of its value and briefly soared to 10 peso/$ in a number of U.S.-Mexico border towns and in the key port city of Veracruz, where the supply of dollars dried up overnight. As the Bolsa tumbled, investors, bankers, world monetary organizations, exporters to Mexico, and most importantly, the U.S. government began to assess the damage and options for an after-the-fact solution to a crisis that could have extreme consequences on both the U.S. and Mexican banking sector as well as the economy of each country. As an immediate short-term measure, Secretary Bentsen, on December 21, 1994, authorized the activation of the swap line for $6 billion that had been set up following the Colosio assassination.[3] At jeopardy was not only the status of the banking industry but also the retirement savings of millions of American investors that had pension investments directly in or tied to the Mexican capital markets. Furthermore, the devaluation of late 1994 was so sudden, many felt its impact and aftermath far exceeded the most recent Mexican currency crashes in 1982 and 1986, due in large part to the broader exposure of the Mexican economy and currency policies to the whims of foreign investors and the overwhelming secondary impact—the tequila effect—on the emerging market economies worldwide, most particularly Latin America.[4] Mexico had become the bellwether model and barometer of progressive growth, privatization, and regained economic stability. The nations of Latin America were collectively recovering from overregulation by authoritarian domestic government as well as a need and desire for foreign investment capital to assist in a globalization of the regions economies. Mexico's bullish approach at restructuring its economy, embracing free trade, amending restrictive investment laws, and privatizing unprofitable government-owned businesses was considered the prototype to emulate. While the importance and influence of Mexico was not universally agreed to by all observers, the fact remains that then and now, events in the Mexican economy are now and forever very pivotal to financial market stability both regionally and worldwide.[5]

Comparison of the 1994–95 devaluation and crisis with the currency crashes in the 1980's demonstrate that in 1994, while the overall Mexican economy and

Figure 7-1
Mexico: Then and Now

	1987	1993/94
Budget Balance (% of GDP)	-14	0
Public Sector Debt (% of GDP)	77	25
Interest Payments (% of GDP)	20	3
Inflation (%)	159	7
Short-term Interest Rates (%)	96	15
Private Investment (% of GDP)	11	18
Direct Foreign Investment ($Bn)	3	7
Manufacturing Prod. Index	100	148
Oil exports (% of total)	31	14
Total trade flow ($Bn)	46	141
# of Public Enterprises	617	210
Foreign Portfolio Investment ($Bn)	-1	28
Real exchange rate index	64	102
Private Consumption (% of GDP)	66	72
Trade balance ($Bn)	9	-18
Foreign reserves ($Bn)	6	6

Source: Bankers Trust Research.

government deficits were vastly improved, the current account balance hampered an orderly transition of capital flows in a rising interest rate environment. The structural changes in the Mexican economy tended to overlook and/or neglect such imbalances. A comparison of the 1986–87 period with the most recent crisis demonstrate that Mexican public finances in 1993–94 were in better shape and inflation was at its lowest level in over two decades, dropping from almost 160 percent in 1987 to under 10 percent in 1994. Privatization reduced government-owned businesses from over 1,000 in 1982 to 210 in 1994. Private investment was up a full 7 percentage points of GDP, resulting in a 48 percent rise in manufacturing productivity. Two of the most sticking indicators is that foreign portfolio investment rose to $28 billion in 1994 from a net outflow of $1 billion in 1987; while at the same time foreign reserves, so critical to the eventual devaluation in late 1994, were at substantially the same level as 1987— $6 billion. One factor impacting each of the devaluations over the past two decades, that has always been hard to quantify, is the intangible yet real psychological repercussions on the people of Mexico. Attention to financial fundamentals undercut domestic confidence and a perceived era of growth and economic recovery. Mexico's primary problem in 1994–95 was a liquidity crisis (see Figure 7-1).[6]

However, unlike 1987, the nature and magnitude of the crisis that ensured during late 1994 and 1995 is further accented by the fact that, while massive investment debt was involved in addition to a radical currency devaluation, this was not the sole problem of the banking and financial sector in the United States; there was also a crisis that held broader implication to three mutually distinct, yet inexplicably connected entities: (1) an enormous broad base of over 12 million "individual" American investors (U.S. residents held about 90 percent of foreign-owned tesobonos, worth over $16 billion), (2) the full involvement and response of the U.S government to address the crisis, and (3) the heightened role of worldwide monetary agencies such as the International Monetary Fund, Bank of International Settlements, Japanese External Bank, and the World Bank. Unlike the previous monetary crisis of the 1980's, this was not a case of poorly timed bad loans or banker haste to capitalize on flush reserves of petrodollars. Nor was the devaluation and resulting crisis purely a function of the year-old North American Free Trade Agreement. The imminent complication to regional currency stabilization as well as the viability and consequences on the banking sector was of prime concern to policy and monetary experts not only in Washington, but also in leading financial markets worldwide. A total economic collapse in Mexico followed by a run (or even uncertainty) on the U.S. dollar could dramatically impact the British, Germans, and Japanese.[7]

CONGRESSIONAL GRIDLOCK

The Clinton administration, a clear champion of improved relations with Mexico as well as the catalyst for the passage of NAFTA in the fall of 1993, was faced with few options with regard to the support of Mexico. A furious round of meetings and negotiations in both Mexico City and Washington, D.C., began—first, to explore whether the worldwide banking community would respond with assistance (which they declined), and second, to allow deliberations by the U.S. Congress to address a rescue package or "bailout" of the Mexican currency crisis.[8] While Congress debated, Mexico daily throughout January was on the verge of total default. To relieve the short-term financial pressures, the Treasury advanced $250 million to Mexico on January 11 and requested the IMF to make a bridge loan available. On January 12, 1995, the president proposed a $40 billion loan and guarantee package for Mexico and sought approval by Congress to move forward with a plan to provide short-term funds and long-term guarantees to restructure both the internal and external debt. With a newly seated Republican majority in the House of Representatives, a result of the November 1994 mid-term elections, the debate turned away from a program to assist Mexico but instead focused on an inquiry as to what happened within the U.S. government concerning knowledge of the Mexican economic situation and a classic Washington ritual of—who knew what, and when. Officials of the Clinton administration on numerous occasions during January stressed that Mexico made critical errors in its macroeconomic policy. Secretary of the Treasury Robert Rubin noted in testimony before the House Banking Committee, "In retrospect, Mexico could and should have managed this situation better. By the time authorities let the peso go, they lacked the resources to counter market disorder."[9] In the meantime, not less than ten different legislative drafts were considered by Congress during the early weeks of 1995 to provide financial aid to Mexico. Opponents of a package to assist Mexico argued that any action would be nothing more than a bailout of Wall Street investors.[10] The Clinton administration, as is evident in congressional testimony by Federal Reserve Chairman

Alan Greenspan, stressed the timely role of a U.S. guarantee proposal as well as the magnitude of the Mexican crisis:

The objective of the proposed guarantee program is to halt the erosion in Mexico's financing capabilities before it has dramatic impacts far beyond those already evident around the world. This program in my judgement is the least worst of the various initiatives which present themselves as possible solutions to a very unsettling international financial problem. Our concerns are not so much with potential losses to the American taxpayer, which we believe will be minimized, but with what economists call moral hazard where the active involvement of an external guarantor distorts the incentives perceived by investors. Thus, appropriate conditionality must be associated with the guarantee to underline the fact that it is being provided at high cost and on rigorous terms in exceptional circumstances. Moreover, Mexico's economic policies are the key to ensuring that the guarantee facility actually does help to stabilize the Mexican economic and financial situation; ultimately only sound policies that are sustained over time will restore investors' confidence in Mexico.[11]

Although President Clinton appealed directly to the Congress during his State of the Union address on January 25 to approve a loan guarantee package for Mexico, the prospects of an agreement to provide congressional assistance seemed unlikely. On January 26, the IMF agreed to lend Mexico $7.58 billion, the largest loan in the fund's 50–year history. However, two other factors had a tremendous impact on any congressional response: first, a bailout package to address the crisis in Mexico did not fit into the legislative plans of the newly elected Republican majority in the House of Representatives, and second, the White House could not obtain sufficient support from the Democratic members of Congress. This standstill resulted in the Mexican financial situation further deteriorating, looming threats to diminish the value of the U.S. dollar in foreign exchange markets, and ultimately an erosion of any consensus in Congress to develop a plan to assist the Mexican financial crisis.[12]

As the Clinton administration and Congress searched for a solution, Mexico reviewed its options. During the early weeks that followed the devaluation, the newly elected Mexican government was faced with a challenge that far exceeded any previous monetary crisis experienced by Mexico. Zedillo and the Minister of Finance, Guillermo Ortiz, expected the peso to settle at 4 peso/$ by mid-January. To achieve renewed stability would require a massive plan to restore domestic confidence and reassure foreign investors that Mexico was a safe investment. This would be difficult, as the Bolsa dropped to its lowest level since April 1994 and foreign investment came to a halt. In the wake of the crisis the central bank was concerned about capital flight as banks reported difficulty rolling over dollar-denominated consumer deposits, as well as other short-term sources of dollar financing. Furthermore, in a 1994 agreement between the Banco de Mexico and the International Monetary Fund, it was expected that the Mexican bank would require only an estimated 10 billion pesos during all of

1995 to stabilize the banking sector. However, by late January 1995, the central bank had already used 40 per cent of the annual allotment.[13]

Investor confidence was paramount to obtaining both much-needed capital and to insure the country would not default on its already large loans and accounts due to international lending agencies, commercial banks, and individual investors. President Zedillo and Finance Minister Ortiz began to shape both a public opinion and an economic recovery plan that would require both swift action and much-needed credibility.[14] The government at once began to review options with leading investment banks to address first the short-term tesobono problem and assistance in providing capital to reduce speculation in the foreign exchange markets. Foreign commercial banks both in the United States and abroad were supportive of a plan to stabilize the currency crisis but none were willing to take the lead. Fresh memories of the Brady bond negotiations of the late-1980s caused a great deal of apprehension among foreign lenders. The second step was to work with the United States, Canada, and the Bank of International Settlements (BIS) to pool $18 billion into a currency stabilization fund.[15] The third initiative was to establish and put in operation a futures or forward peso-dollar market to provide investors with a means to hedge their investments. Within the floating exchange rate regime the central bank "allowed" the Chicago Mercantile Exchange to explore reopening its peso-dollar futures market.[16] Lastly, the Mexican government announced the need to reduce the federal budget, increase exports to generate hard currency, and a bold plan to limit credit in 1995 "to a level consistent with an average inflation of about 15 percent."[17] These optimistic plans failed to sway the U.S. Congress or foreign commercial banks. By late January, Mexico began to approach an increasingly greater risk of defaulting on its extensive foreign debt. No country had defaulted on government bond debt since World War II.[18]

THE LEAST WORST SOLUTION

Additional attempts were made by the White House to compromise and overcome both the gridlock and reluctance of Congress, to no avail. By Monday, January 30 rumors surfaced in the financial markets worldwide that Mexico faced imminent default. Faced with the prospects of a massive default and disruption of financial markets worldwide, at 10:30 P.M. CST the White House abandoned all efforts to obtain congressional approval, and decided the best course was unilateral action to provide loans to Mexico.[19] The new White House plan and solution, relying heavily in the IMF and the World Bank, included a $50 billion multilateral assistance package, announced formally on Tuesday the 31st, anchored by the availability of $20 billion from the Exchange Stabilization Fund (ESF). The Clinton administration's announcement came on the same day that the Senate Banking Committee began hearings on the peso crisis.[20] The ESF was established during the early New Deal era, pursuant to section 10 of the Gold Reserve Act of 1934 and placed under the control of the president and

Figure 7-2
The Old and the New: A Comparison of the Mexico Plans

Funding Source	Old Plan	New Plan
U.S. Treasury	Guarantees of up to **$40 billion** of long-term Mexican bonds	Commitment of **$20 billion** from Exchange Stabilization Fund for:
	Commitment of **$9 billion** from Exchange Stabilization Fund for short-term swaps of dollars for pesos	▪ Short-term swaps ▪ Mid-term swaps ▪ Guarantees of long-term Mexican bonds
International Monetary Fund	**$7.8 billion** in direct loans	**$17.8 billion** in direct loans
Bank of International Settlements	**$5 billion** in direct loans	**$10 billion** in direct loans
Latin American countries	None	**$1 billion** in short-term swaps
Canada	None	**$1 billion** in short-term swaps
Commercial Banks	**$3 billion** in new loans	**$3 billion** in new loans
Total	**$64.8 billion**	**$52.8 billion**

Source: Washington Post.

the secretary of the treasury, to be used to intervene in foreign currency markets to support the value of the dollar. Three types of support provided by the ESF would serve as a basis for the Mexican financial package: short-term swaps, swaps with maturities of 3 to 5 years, and securities guarantees with maturities of 5 to 10 years. Additionally, the use of the ESF with Mexico did not represent a president. The United States has had a swap line with Mexico since 1941 and the Treasury has provided dollars to Mexico through short-term swap arrangements five times since 1982. The new "swaps" or loan package proposal to assist Mexico would include elements of all three provisions of the ESF and offered more flexibility to advance funds to Mexico than did the early January congressional proposals. Furthermore, additional funding by other international agencies would be made available, primarily $18 billion from the Washington-based International Monetary Fund, $10 billion from the Swiss-based Bank of International Settlements, and private commercial banks pledged new loans in excess of $3 billion (see Figure 7-2).[21]

Some in the U.S. Congress and in Mexico, such as Jorge Castañeda, who rejected the bailout and cynically called the loan package "at least the greatest event in Mexico since the arrival of Cortés," complained that the president used "executive privilege" and circumvented normal monetary procedure, and Zedillo followed suit by agreeing to the financial package without consulting the

Mexican Parliament. Nonetheless, the impact of settling the currency market jitters was very beneficial.[22] The condition of the loans via the ESF involved the negotiation of a detailed agreement to obtain broad support from international lending agencies, hemispheric cooperation, and most importantly, collateral from Mexico to guarantee payments. As one report noted, the initial stage of the Mexican bailout was "no panacea"; the key to a structured recovery rested in the return of foreign investor confidence and domestic political stability.[23]

Once the commitment was made by the Clinton administration, it took three weeks for the treasury and central bank officials of both countries to draft a multipurpose commercial agreement and guidelines on the access of short- and medium-term funds, reporting procedures, a clear definition of repayment mechanisms, and government management of the economic structure, money supply, and targets of the budget. Rubin and Ortiz signed an extensive rescue package on February 21, 1995.[24] Four basic documents defined the use and management of the $20 billion provided by the United States in the economic stabilization package:

Framework Agreement—defining term and conditions, this served as the umbrella document of the borrowing of U.S. "resources" to support the Mexican economy and currency base. Conditions included the economic policies Mexico will follow, eligibility for financing, how U.S resources may be used, how the United States will be repaid, and how satisfaction of these conditions will be determined.[25]

Medium-term Agreement—specifies the term and conditions for medium-term (up to 5 years) swaps between countries. Under this agreement, for every purchase of dollars for pesos, Mexico will deposit a corresponding amount of pesos in a U.S. Treasury account at the Banco de Mexico. To cover the U.S. risk, this agreement specifies the interest rate the United States will charge.[26]

Guarantee Agreement—specifies the terms and conditions for the issue of securities issues by Mexico. No guarantees can be issued for payment of principal and interest due more than 10 years after issuance of the guaranteed debt securities. The fee structure for the guarantees will increase with greater outstanding use to encourage Mexico to seek regular private market sources of financing.[27]

Oil Proceeds Facility Agreement—establishes a mechanism to provide an assured source of repayment of U.S. resources. Under the agreement Petroleos Mexicanos (PE-MEX) will instruct its foreign customers to make payments for exports of oil, oil products, and derivatives into an account at a U.S. bank. The bank, in turn, will be under "irrevocable instructions" to transfer funds to a Banco de Mexico account at the Federal Reserve Bank of New York. If Mexico fails to repay the United States under any of the financing agreements, the U.S. Treasury is entitled to set off its claims against these funds.[28]

The primary objective of the financial assistance package was to allow Mexico to overcome its liquidity crisis by meeting the short-term obligations and restructuring its long-term debt. The plan to accomplish stabilization of the Mexican economy anticipated a broader number of participants in the support of the crisis and enhanced safeguards. For the first time in Mexico's history, crude oil and oil products were tied to the repayment schedule. The Mexican central bank and government were also required to report to the U.S. Treasury, on a weekly and monthly schedule, such items as all account balances, investment trends, inflation projections, money supply patterns, and how money raised with U.S guarantees would be repaid. In all, over 100 economic and monetary indicators are filed on an ongoing basis by the Mexican government to allow the U.S. Treasury and IMF to track the progress of the economic recovery. The emphasis on timely and accurate reporting of economic statistics is based on the fact that the IMF recounted that, prior to December 1994, outdated reports masked the true volatility of hard-currency reserves. Moreover, the United States reserved the right to deny any request for funds if the Treasury determined the use to be inappropriate, and the United States reserved the right to accelerate Mexico's outstanding obligation if Mexico failed to comply with certain key provisions of the agreement. Although the plan and its reporting requirements were viewed as harsh and draconian by many in Mexico and the United States, it proved to be a pivotal step in preventing additional economic unrest.[29]

NO MAGIC CURE

The opposition to the plan came from diverse groups both in the United States and Mexico. In the United States, opponents stressed the fact that investors should have known the level of risk in Mexico and thus should bear the brunt of any loss, just as they would reap any investment gains. Some critics of U.S. assistance to Mexico asserted that the situation was a short-term problem that would pose no obstacle to the U.S. economy. Furthermore, some opponents pointed out that the overheated and fragile Mexican economy could not absorb investment losses due to the fact that the middle and lower class would be taxed the most—both in real terms and as a result of diminished purchasing power due to higher prices and inflation. Some felt that the problems prior to the crisis of 1994 were equally related to the debt burden of the reconstructed loans from the 1970's and 1980's.[30] But the most sensitive issue in the minds of many Mexicans was the surrendering of further control over the national petroleum reserves. While the Mexican Constitution of 1917 prohibited foreign exploration and control of petroleum leases in Mexico, there was no restriction on the use of proceeds from revenues derived from the export of crude oil and petroleum products. The implied control by Mexico of domestic oil and gas reserves has been the catalyst of much antiforeign sentiment and mistrust. By 1994, the annual generation of hard currency of over $7 billion in income due to oil exports proved critical to justifying the bailout plan in both the United States and with worldwide monetary agencies. The Zedillo administration was truly faced with an economic and historical dilemma with regard to the handling of the oil issue (see Figure 7-3).[31]

Figure 7-3
Petroleum Production: 1980–94

	Crude Oil (thousand b/d)	Natural Gas (mmcfd)
1980	1,936.0	3,548
1981	2,313.0	4,061
1982	2,746.4	4,246
1983	2,665.5	4,054
1984	2,684.5	3,753
1985	2,630.5	3,604
1986	2,427.7	3,431
1987	2,540.6	3,498
1988	2,506.6	3,478
1989	2,513.3	3,572
1990	2,548.0	3,652
1991	2,675.8	3,634
1992	2,667.7	3,584
1993	2,673.5	3,576
1994	2,685.0	3,625

Sources: Pemex, *Statistical Yearbook*, 1994; press reports.

With the Clinton Plan inked in late February 1995, the U.S. Congress turned its attention to conducting hearings to assess the rationale, impact, and cost of the Mexico rescue agreement. During the process of lengthy congressional hearings that stretched from early March to July, the Congress attempted to understand the true impact of the crisis. Three very critical issues tested the validity of the actions taken to stabilize Mexico, while at the same time raising further monetary concerns both at home and abroad in emerging markets: (1) the status of the declining value of the dollar in the wake of the peso crisis, (2) the impact on the Mexican economy and social structure to absorb drastic tightening of the economy, and (3) the impact on the already fragile banking sector in Mexico.[32]

The first problem that began to command worldwide attention in late February and early March 1995 was the decline of the dollar against major currencies, primarily the Deutsche mark, the Swiss franc, and the yen. Due to a broad sell-off of dollars in tandem with the peso, a widespread perception surfaced in foreign exchange markets that the United States would suffer because of its close ties with Mexico and thus not move rapidly enough to defend its currency. Some analysis expressed concern that defending the peso would prove difficult given the magnitude of the Mexican crisis, and thus the U.S. dollar experienced its own currency "crisis of confidence" on world exchange markets.[33] The decline of the dollar, falling 15 percent against most major currencies, had been evident since early 1994 primarily because of the tremendous trade deficit, running over $160 billion yearly. Additional pressure surfaced due to disparity between U.S. interest rates and those of various G-7 countries, primarily Germany, and the shift by some foreign central banks of their foreign exchange reserves out of dollars and into other hard currencies. Some felt that the Mexican crisis so consumed the time and resources of the U.S. Treasury that the newly confirmed secretary, Robert Rubin, initially underestimated the magnitude of the problem and the impact on the dollar as well as poorly handled Treasury's effort to convey the extent of the Mexican situation to Congress.[34] Rubin, a seasoned Wall Street trader, brought a real world market perspective to his new job—a somewhat shocking occurrence for those accustomed to bureaucratic Washington. Others within the administration identified the broader reasons for the dollar weakness. In response to questioning on the dollar's decline, Federal Reserve Chairman Greenspan noted, "it is doubtless symptomatic of some of the underlying problems confronting the longer-term health of the economy: inadequate national savings, continuing large budget deficits and a persistent current account imbalance."[35]

The second, broader issue was the reaction in Mexico to yet another austerity plan. While the February U.S.–Mexico financial agreement provided both short-term and long-term support to the Mexican economy, it also contained a harsh formula to restore a balanced economy and investor confidence. During the early weeks of March, Mexico drew its first medium-term swap in the amount of $3 billion. The Banco de Mexico announced it would redeem all tesobonos in dollars to ease any foreign investor anxiety. These actions and monies went to satisfy tesobono obligations and did little to address both the rise in interest rates and the ballooning inflation. Domestically, these measures were swift. In anticipation of a wave of inflation the money supply was drastically curtailed. The fiscal austerity program restricted economic activity and growth by limiting credit, raised the value-added tax (VAT) from 10 percent to 15 percent, mandated spending cuts of 10 percent by the government (mirroring a 2 percent contraction of the economy), and resulted in an increase in consumer prices. Gasoline prices were immediately increased by 35 percent, to be followed by an 0.8 percent increase per month for the balance of 1995. In like fashion electricity prices were increased by 20 percent and food prices shot up. During the first quarter of 1995 the retail sector sales dropped over 10 percent and the construction industry came to a virtual standstill, creating increased urban unemployment that rose to 5.7 percent in March as compared to 3.2 percent at the end of 1994.[36]

The economic decline in the Mexican domestic sector during 1995 demanded that those with exportable products and services find new customers or drastically cut output. As the recession slowly gripped Mexico during all of 1995, a number of distinct areas demonstrated better-than-average growth for much of the year. Tourism and energy exports remained strong. The industrial sectors of chemicals and plastics, wood products, metals, and paper products contributed to a merchandise export jump of 40 percent in the first quarter to $19.4 billion from $13.8 billion a year earlier.[37] Due to the large capital investment in new manufacturing systems, transportation services, and equipment during much of the early 1990's, Mexico was in an ideal situation to open new foreign markets (primarily in Central and South America and the Caribbean) that had previously been ignored. The diversification of the Mexican export sector has assisted the economy to recover in a shorter time frame. However, the increased export industries were not able to create enough jobs to absorb losses in the construction, agricultural, and retail sectors. Notwithstanding the recession of 1995, Mexico continued to attract substantial sums of investment capital in the maquila, energy, auto, tourism, and telecommunication sectors, as well as funding for the privatization of rail and port facilities. Most notable, the maquiladora industry had the largest annual growth in its three-decade history. New plant locations and expansion of existing facilities increased maquiladora employment by over 12 percent during 1995.[38]

The Mexican domestic economy weathered the worst of the postdevaluation recession during 1995, though overall GDP growth for the year was a dismal −7 percent, inflation soared to 50 percent, and the recovery has been measured and difficult. Capitalization in the Mexican Bolsa dropped from $195 billion in November 1994 to $91 billion in December 1995. The rigid fiscal policies of the Zedillo administration, while not popular at home, have sent a clear signal to the investment markets that Mexico is again open for business. Thus, to shorten the financial cycle was paramount. During the first half of 1995 the Mexican budget had a surplus. After the 1982 currency crisis, it took eight years before the Mexican public sector was able to issue bonds in the international market. In contrast, by June 1995, less than six months after the crash of the peso, Bancomext issued a $300 million bond offering. New issues followed with a billion dollar United States of Mexico floating rate issue, a Deutsche mark issue by NAFIN, and a securitized paper offering by Banamex. As exports increased, Mexico's leading privately owned corporations have also been successful in placing short-term, dollar-denominated notes in the international market: Cemex–cement, Gemex–bottling, Groupo Posadas–resorts and hotels, Hylsamex–steel, Bufete Industrial–construction, and Corporacion Industrial San Luis–mining and auto parts. During 1995, ten Mexican companies sold debt issues for a total of $3.3 billion versus $5 billion in 1994, which represented 20.4 percent (32.5% in 1994) of total corporate debt in Latin America. The Mexican public sector issued more debt in the foreign market during the first three quarters of 1995 than it did in any year between 1990 and 1992.[39]

BANKING ON THE BRINK

After nearly a decade of government ownership following the nationalization of all financial institutions in 1982, Mexican banks were reprivatized in 1992. After the government had completed the conversion, it allowed newly organized banks to file for charters in 1994. By year-end 1994, Mexico had 32 private sector banks with an aggregate asset base of over $160 billion. By early 1995, six of the largest banks reported assets of $111 billion, representing 70 percent of the industry—Banamex, Bancomer, Serfin, Mexicano, Comermex, and Banco Internacional (BITAL). These key banks along with a cross-section of foreign-owned subsidiaries in Mexico offered a full line of banking services. However,

Figure 7-4
Mexico: Ratio of Past-Due Loans to Total Loans: 1979–96

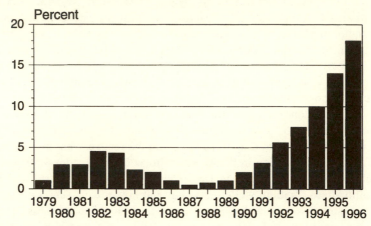

Source: Banco de Mexico.

the transition from government-owned to private sector had been costly for both the investors groups that purchased the banks and, more importantly, to the customer base that was for the most part underserviced. The entire Mexican banking industry was under tremendous pressure during 1993–94 to profitably expand operations. Domestic reluctance over the passage of NAFTA and a mild recession in 1993 began to progressively undermine the banking system. The currency devaluation of December 1994 threatened to collapse an already fragile situation affected by three critical indicators: asset quality, capitalization, and liquidity (see Figure 7-4).[40]

Immediately following the reprivatization of the banks there was an aggressive trend to lend. Consumer credit increased 43 percent in 1992–93, according to the Comision Nacional Bancaria de Valores (CNBV) or National Banking Commission, thus the potential rise of nonperforming loans.[41] The eventual high levels of past-due loans by late 1993 were caused by a number of factors: the depreciation of the peso, high interest rates, and the sluggish economy. Furthermore, the banking system was not prepared for the new demand. Reflecting on what some have termed the "lost generation of bankers," referring to the nationalized period during the 1980's, Eduardo Fernandez, director of CNBV, noted that "when the credit boom hit there were not enough bank officers adequately trained in granting credit."[42] By year-end 1994, and prior to the devaluation, Mexican banks reported past-due loans ranging from 9 to 14 percent of their portfolios. As borrowers failed to service the debt obligations, the banking system was required to increase provisions for loan losses. At the same time, the Federal Reserve noted that the Mexican banks were adversely impacted, "in light of the need for a higher capital cushion to counter the effects of changing asset values caused by fluctuations in the peso-dollar exchange rate and interest rates.''[43] What followed was liquidity difficulties due in large measure to the volume of dollar-dominated funding given the volatility of the peso-dollar exchange rate. Throughout 1993–94, Mexican banks maintained a high reliance for peso funding, based on interest rate–sensitive instruments. Further compounding the financial ramifications were the political uncertainties, such as the Colosio assassination that required the Banco de Mexico to intervene on a regular basis thereafter to shore up the currency and the domestic banking system.[44] In response to high interest rates and skyrocketing debt, a coalition of farmers and ranchers from northern Mexico and middle-class urban home owners formed "El Barzon" in 1993. El Barzon has grown into a national debtors' movement pressing banks and the government for debt-relief programs in order to reduce a flood of loan defaults that have led to foreclosures across the country. Members are reported to have bad loans amounting to over $12 billion. This broad-based organization, in order to gain attention, has withheld loan payments, staged massive rallies, forced some banks to temporarily close, and has had modest success in having the government both recognize and respond to this critical situation. Opponents of El Barzon stress that the movement has merits but does not warrant borrowers receiving total debt forgiveness.[45] In reviewing the stability of the banks and the bad loan situation, the IMF in early 1995 concluded:

Mexican banks do not have a foreign currency exposure problem. The Government moved two years ago to limit foreign borrowing by commercial banks and to restrict open market exchange positions. The system as a whole is in balance as between foreign-currency-denominated assets and liabilities. Rather, the weakness is one of old-fashioned bad loans. With bank capital of about 8–10 percent of assets . . . the banks appear to be in a precarious position.[46]

The devaluation followed by a sudden interest rate hike and an economic downturn only aggravated loan payments. In response to the crisis, Moody's lowered the credit rating for long-term foreign currency deposits at the two largest banks, Banamex and Bancomer, from Ba1 to B1. Banks essentially stopped lending in the wake of the crisis. As the government looked for ways to address the peso crisis, investors also voiced concern about the need to reschedule the troubled debt. In rapid order the government augmented the financial sector investment laws, developed new programs to restructure consumer and commercial debt payments, and examined means to provide needed capital to the banks. Coverage under FOBAPROA—Fondo Bancario de Proteccion al Ahorro (Banking Fund to Protect Savings), the Mexican equivalent of the Federal Depository Insurance Fund (FDIC), was expanded by the Banco de Mexico to provide dollar-denominated liquidity for banks that experience short-term U.S. dollar funding pressure. Initially, the fund had experienced difficulty maintaining adequate reserves due in large part to the bailout of the Groupo Financiero Cremi-Union in mid-1994.[47] In mid-1995, FOBAPROA received

Figure 7-5
Average Nominal Annual Interest Rates

	Bank's Average Cost of Funds (CPP)	28-Day Treasury Bills	90-Day Treasury Bills	TIIP Interbank Rate
1987	94.64	94.85	103.70	N/A
1988	67.64	69.12	63.77	N/A
1989	44.61	45.01	44.71	N/A
1990	37.07	34.77	35.04	N/A
1991	22.56	19.28	19.87	N/A
1992	18.78	15.62	15.88	N/A
1993	18.56	14.85	15.39	18.00
Jan 1994	13.22	10.52	10.75	11.75
Feb 1994	11.96	9.45	9.80	10.52
Mar 1994	11.53	9.73	10.31	11.04
Apr 1994	14.16	15.79	15.92	19.17
May 1994	17.03	16.36	17.44	20.24
Jun 1994	17.18	16.18	16.74	18.89
Jul 1994	17.82	17.06	17.38	21.17
Aug 1994	17.16	14.27	14.76	18.37
Sep 1994	16.73	13.75	14.15	17.76
Oct 1994	15.96	13.80	13.98	17.62
Nov 1994	16.34	13.94	15.54	19.54
Dec 1994	16.96	18.51	20.37	28.01
Jan 1995	29.87	37.25	39.23	46.11
Feb 1995	35.98	41.69	41.65	54.02
Mar 1995	56.82	69.54	71.20	86.03
Apr 1995	70.26	74.75	71.50	85.33
May 1995	57.86	59.17	54.71	60.53
Jun 1995	46.39	47.25	47.31	49.49
Jul 1995	41.42	40.94	39.72	42.92
Aug 1995	37.10	35.14	35.88	37.57

Source: Banco de Mexico.

supplemental capitalization in the amount of $2 billion from a joint loan from the World Bank and a group of international private banks. In response to the economic shocks and deteriorating loan situation the Mexican government implemented and expanded several existing programs to assist the banks.[48]

In an effort to augment capital at selected banks, the Banco de Mexico developed a program whereby FOBAPROA would purchase subordinated debt with a maturity of five years. This subordinated debt would then allow the troubled banks to maintain minimum capital ratios. In essence, the FOBAPROA facility is intended to serve as a last resort source of short-term, dollar-denominated funding. The first three banks to receive assistance were Serfin, Comermex, and Internacional. Initial interest charged for funds from the facility was 20 percent, yet by late 1995 this was raised to 25 percent. Although borrowings under this facility peaked in April 1995 at $3.5 billion; by year-end Probursa, Promex, Atlantico, Bancrecer, Banoro, and Banorte had been recapitalized. Furthermore, in 1995, nonperforming loans nationwide never improved below 14 percent (see Figure 7-5).[49]

In August 1995 the Mexican government announced the Apoyo Inmediato a los Deudores de la Banca (ADE) or Immediate Support Agreement to Bank Debtors. The ADE debt relief program offered immediate interest rate relief for up to 18 months and allows for long-term debt restructuring. The borrowers' interest rates are adjusted down, in most cases below the bank's cost of funds. Each participating bank is provided an interest subsidy by the government to repay the difference in the reduced rates. Through the first quarter of 1996, this program has cost the government nearly $2 billion. A secondary program to assist in the restructuring of loans, known as Unidades de Inversiones (UDIs) or Units of Investment, was initiated in 1995. The UDI program was designed to assist mortgage holders and small businesses by establishing a repayment schedule based on inflation-indexing terms, thus reducing the cash flow burden on borrowers. The borrowers pay a real rate of interest on the appreciated balance. Furthermore, in many cases the UDIs allowed nonperforming loans to become performing. Initial participation in the UDI program was limited, yet increased when interest rates began to rise in September-October 1995. The program assisted banks by allowing them to place as much as 20–30 percent of their loan portfolios, including nonperforming loans, into UDIs and then move them off their books. Additionally, the banks retain full recourse on the loan and in effect receive an income subsidy from the government by exchanging their nonperforming loans for government notes paying nominal yields. The total estimated cost of this program to the Mexican government has been $3 billion as of March 1996.[50]

Two primary steps were taken in 1995 to supplement bank capital. The first was the Programa Emergente de Capitalizacion Temporanea or PROCAPTE (Emergency Program for Temporary Capitalization), to cope with capital shortfalls caused by the need to have adequate loan loss reserves and cover balance-sheet growth induced by the peso devaluation. Participating banks are required to maintain a total risk-based capital ratio in excess of 8.5 percent and an equity ratio in excess of 2 percent. Six banks, Serfin, Inverlat, Internacional, Confia, Centro, and Obrero borrowed $6.5 billion in March 1995. By mid-1996 only Confia remained in the program. However, the complexity of the facility and reluctance of financial markets to endorse the program diminished its full potential.

The final and most significant long-term action to attract additional capital to the Mexican banking system was the further liberalization of laws to allow for greater participation by both existing shareholder and foreign investors. Individual investors would be permitted to own up to 20 percent of a financial holding company, up from 15 percent. Two key provisions of the investment section of NAFTA were modified in February 1995. First, foreign companies that have established or are able to establish, subject to approval by the Finance Ministry, a bank in Mexico under NAFTA will be permitted to acquire between 51 and 100 percent controlling interest in an individual Mexican bank. Designed to facilitate further equity injections into Mexico's troubled banks, the new rules excluded the three largest banks, Banamex, Bancomer, and Banca Serfin; these three control about 50 percent of the total commercial banking assets. The new law made it possible for the next three largest banks, Banco Mexicano, Multibanco Comermex, and Banco Internacional, to be eligible for foreign acquisition. The second significant change was in the aggregate market share limitations on foreign ownership. The aggregate market share, previously limited to 9 percent during 1995 under NAFTA and stipulated to increase to 15 percent by January 1, 1999, was increased to 25 percent. Plans to phase out the aggregate market share limitations remained targeted for the year 2000.[51]

While the various loan relief programs have tended to overlap, the net effect on the banking sector and economy has been mixed but promising. In response to the grass-roots clamoring of El Barzon, a large number of loans have been restructured. The ADE program, for example, put an interest rate cap on 1.67 million loans, representing 79 percent of the loans the government planned to refinance under this debt-relief program—with the goal of helping nonperforming loans to become current as well as making it easier for the borrowers to make payments.[52] New foreign capital was injected into the banking system with the February 1995 changes in the bank investment law. During 1995, Spain's Banco Bilbao Vizcaya bought controlling ownership of Banco Probursa and in mid-1996 Bilbao also acquired Banca Cremi and Banco de Oriente. Negotiations by the Bank of Nova Scotia to joint venture with Inverlat (with a nonperforming loan ratio of 16.40 percent in June 1995) was concluded in early 1996. Other foreign investment includes GE Capital's 13 percent stake in Grupo Financiero Serfin and the establishment by Bank of Boston of a subsidiary operation in Mexico City.[53]

The impact of the 1994 devaluation and the decline of the banking system has most impacted the Mexican consumer. The cost in both the short run and over the next three to four decades will be in the tens of billions of dollars. To prevent total default, consumer interest payments have been gradually shifted into the future. By year-end 1995, Mexico had received a total of $17 billion in funding under the support agreements. Two formal IMF visits had been conducted during the year, along with numerous official consultations between Mexican and U.S. agencies. About $7 billion had flowed through Mexico's special funds account at the Federal Reserve Bank of New York, averaging $25 million in oil revenue deposits per day. There have been no set-offs. Nonperforming loans continued to be absorbed by the government to insure the banking system would not collapse. In March 1996, the Mexican government estimated that the cost associated with the restructuring of the banking sector, via some seven programs developed in 1995, had a net present value of $12 billion or 5.5 percent of the 1995 GDP. However, these new and complex programs and their impact on internal accounting procedures and external reporting have created problems for both regulators and investors in tracking the true condition of the banking sector on a regular basis. At year-end 1996, the Mexican banking sector remained in poor but guarded condition. Although exports surged to a ten-year high and the country posted a 26 percent inflation rate, foreign investment was slowly returning.

NOTES

1. "Judge and Jury," *Economist*, October 7, 1995, p. 18. See Also David Wessel, Paul B. Carroll, and Thomas T. Vogel, "Peso Surprise: How Mexico's Crisis Ambushed Top Minds in Officialdom, Finance," *Wall Street Journal*, June 6, 1995, p. 1; Pedro Aspe, "Mexico's Ex-Finance Minister Sets the Record Straight," Ibid., July 14, 1995, p. A15.

2. U.S. Congress, Senate, Committee on Banking, Housing, and Urban Affairs, *The Mexico Peso Crisis and the Administration's Proposed Loan Guarantee Package to Mexico*, S. Hrg. 104–164 (Washington, D.C.: March 10, 1995), pp. 1–36, 61–70, 362–63, 365–67; Craig Torres, "Mexico's Devaluation Stuns Latin America—and U.S. Investors," *Wall Street Journal*, December 22, 1994, p. 1; Debbie Galant, "Why Wall Street Missed Mexico," *Institutional Investor*, May 1995, p. 75; Bernard D. Kaplan, "Most Economists Got It Wrong on Mexico," *Laredo Morning Times*, January 28, 1995; Rudi Dornbusch, "We Have Salinas to Thank for the Peso Debacle," *Business Week*, January 16, 1995, p. 20. See also Jorge G. Castaneda, "Ferocious Differences," *Atlantic Monthly*, July 1995, pp. 68–76, and Moises Naim, "Mexico's Larger Story," *Foreign Policy*, Summer 1995, pp. 119–21.

3. Memo from Lawrence Summers to Bob Rubin, "Mexican Devaluation," December 21, 1994, Treasury Doc. No. 002025–6. Note: Summers also commented on future trade patterns, "Mexico's devaluation will make American exports more expensive in Mexico and Mexican exports cheaper in the United States. This is likely to swing $5 billion in trade between the United States and Mexico over the next two years."

4. Thomas Vogel, "Mexico Worries Spread to Emerging Markets," *Wall Street Journal*, January 31, 1995, p. C1; White House, *Weekly Compilation of Presidential Documents*, Vol. 31, pp. 45–46; Lester C. Thurow, *The Future of Capitalism: How Today's Economic Forces Shape Tomorrow's World* (New York: 1996), p. 225. Note: Other countires prone to currency/liquidity problems include: Chile, Argentina, Thailand, Malaysia, Brazil, Indonesia, and the Philippines.

5. Georg Junge, "Emerging Market Countries in Global Financial Markets," *Prospects*, February 1996, pp. 10–13: "Mexico Heralds, Not Another 1982 Debt Crisis, Just a Different One," *Latin American Weekly Report*, January 12, 1995, p. 1; "South Americans Still See Mexico's Ills Hurting Them," *Wall Street Journal*, February 2, 1995, p. A10; Associated Press, "Latin Markets Hit by Peso Hangover," *San Antonio Express-News*, January 16, 1995, p. E1; Gary Springer and Jorge L. Molina, "The Mexican Financial Crisis: Genesis, Impact, and Implications," *Journal of Interamerican Studies and World Affairs*, Summer 1995, Vol. 37, pp. 74–78; "For Mexico, a Hard Year Ahead," *Washington Post*, March 12, 1995.

6. Carl W. Ross, "Mexico: Fundamentals Are Much Better This Time Around," *Perspectives on Emerging Markets*, February 21, 1995, p. 26; Robert Gay, "Postmortem on Mexico's Financial Crisis," *Bankers Trust Research*, February 9, 1995, pp. 1–3; Statement by Alan Greenspan, Chairman, Federal Reserve before the Committee on Foreign Relations, U.S. Senate, January 26, 1995, as seen in *Federal Reserve Bulletin*, Vol. 81, March 1995, pp. 261–64; David Hale, "The Price Was Right," *Washington Post National Weekly*, June 10, 1996, p. 25.

7. Juan J. Walte and Mark Potok, "Failing Economy at the Root of a Deepening Restlessness," *USA Today*, March 23, 1995; U.S. Treasury, "Beneficiaries of U.S. Guar-

antees," Washington, D.C.: January 25, 1995; "Misunderstood NAFTA," *Investor's Business Daily*, February 13, 1996; Thurow, *The Future of Capitalism*, p. 228.

8. U.S. Treasury, Memo, "Treasury's Efforts to Inform Congress about the Administration's Response to the Mexican Economic Situation" (Washington, D.C.: April 6, 1995); Ibid., press release, "Statement by Robert Rubin before the House Committee on Banking and Financial Services, U.S. House of Representatives" (Washington, D.C.: January 25, 1995); Knight-Ridder, "Mexico Loan Plan Gains D.C. Support: Perot Blasts $40 Billion Bailout Effort," *San Antonio Express-News*, January 14, 1995.

9. U.S. Treasury, "Statement of Robert E. Rubin before the House Committee on Banking and Financial Services, U.S. House of Representatives," Treasury Doc. 710344–48, January 25, 1995. See also White House, "Remarks on Loan Guarantees for Mexico," *Weekly Compilation of Presidential Documents*, Vol. 31, January 18, 1995, pp. 75–77.

10. Public Citizen, "One Year Later: NAFTA Disaster!" (Washington, D.C.: circa 1995), p. 1; Jorge Castaneda, "Did Someone Say 'I Told You So'?" *Los Angeles Times*, March 8, 1995. See also Howard J. Wiarda, "After Miami: The Summit, the Peso Crisis, and the Future of U.S.–Latin American Relations," *Journal of Interamerican Studies and World Affairs*, Vol. 37, No. 2, Spring 1995, pp. 43–68.

11. Knight-Ridder, press release, "Text of Greenspan's Prepared Testimony to House on Mexico" (Washington, D.C.: January 25, 1995).

12. Knight-Ridder, press release, "Clinton Pleads for U.S. Congress to Approve Mexico Aid Package" (Washington, D.C.: January 25, 1995); Ibid., "Text of Greenspan's Prepared Testimony to House on Mexico," January 25, 1995; Kevin Merida and Ann Devroy, "Mistrust Led to Death of Initial Loan Plan," *Washington Post*, February 1, 1995; Craig Torres and Tim Carrington, "IMF Agrees to Lend $7.58 Billion to Mexico, Endorsing Rescue Plan," *Wall Street Journal*, January 27, 1995.

13. Banco de Mexico, *Report on Monetary Policy for 1996* (Mexico D.F.: January 1996), pp. 10–22; U.S. Department of Treasury, "Monthly Report by the Secretary of the Treasury Pursuant to the Mexican Debt Disclosure Act of 1995" (Washington, D.C.: May 31, 1995), pp. 1–8; Craig Torres and Paul Carroll, "Mexico Puts Economic Steps on Hold until Fallout from Peso's Plunge Settles," *Wall Street Journal*, December 27, 1994; Torres, "Mexico's Central Bank Struggles As Reserves Reach Severe Lows," Ibid., February 3, 1995; Al Taranto, "The Year of Trading Dangerously," *El Financiero International*, December 26, 1994, p. 6.

14. Knight-Ridder, "Full Text of Zedillo Speech on Economic Plan" (Mexico, D.F.: January 3, 1995); "Credibility Lost" [editorial], *El Financiero International*, January 2, 1995, p. 6.

15. Guillermo Ortiz, "How We're Handling the Peso Crisis," *Wall Street Journal*, January 5, 1995. Note: The plans outlined by Minister Ortiz in early January 1995 and his mention of a "stabilization fund" predated the final U.S.-Mexico agreement and foretold one of the key elements in the White House package to assist Mexico, the ESF at the U.S. Treasury; also the final U.S. package had $20 billion earmarked, again very similar to the Ortiz estimates.

16. Guillermo Guemez, "Comments to the Border Trade Alliance on the Strategy and the Evolution of the Economic Adjustment in Mexico," Board of Governors, Banco de Mexico (Mexico D.F., February 19, 1996); "Peso Futures: The Next Hedging Instrument," *Mexico Service*, February 10, 1995, pp. 4–6; Chicago Mercantile Exchange, *Mexican Peso: Futures and Options* (Chicago: 1995), pp. 1–8. Note: Four variables influence

the futures, or forward price of the peso—(1) the cash market, or spot price, (2) U.S. interest rates, (3) Mexican interest rates, and (4) time to expiration (number of days until the forward date).

17. Ortiz, "How We're Handling the Peso Crisis," *Wall Street Journal*, January 5, 1995. See also Daniel Dombey, "Sacrifice for All: Zedillo's Economic Package Predicts Austerity Measures," *El Financiero International*, January 9, 1995, p. 14.

18. Lawrence H. Summers, "After the Storm—Latin American Finance: A Progress Report," presentation at the Conference of the Americas, New York City, September 29, 1995.

19. Ann Devroy and Clay Chandler, "Clinton Bypasses Congress, Provides Loans to Mexico," *Washington Post*, February 1, 1995; "U.S. Lends Mexico $20 Billion: Clinton Abandons Proposal Needing Congressional OK," *San Antonio Express-News*, February 1, 1995, p. 1; Martin Crutinger, "Fed Feared Default: Clinton Had No Choice on Mexico Aid," *Laredo Morning Times*, February 2, 1995.

20. White House, "Message to the Congress on the Financial Crisis in Mexico," *Weekly Compilation of Presidential Documents*, Vol. 31, March 9, 1995, pp. 390–91. Note: For a detailed assessment on the authority to use the ESF, see memo from Edward S. Knight to Robert E. Rubin, Treasury Doc., February 21, 1995, and Testimony of Knight, General Counsel of the U.S. Treasury Department before the Subcommittee on General Oversight and Investigations, House Committee on Banking and Financial Services, April 6, 1995.

21. U.S. Congress, Senate, *The Mexico Peso Crisis*, March 10, 1995, pp. 407–12; U.S. Treasury, press release, "Testimony of Treasury Secretary Robert E. Rubin: House Committee on Banking and Financial Services," RR-71 (Washington, D.C.: February 9, 1995); Ibid., "The Multilateral Program to Restore Financial Stability in Mexico" (Washington, D.C.: January 31, 1995); Steven Pearlstein and John Berry, "Mexico Aid Plan Contains Major Changes," *Washington Post*, February 1, 1995.

22. Tod Robberson, "Mexican Financial Markets, Politicians Cheered by Clinton Initiative," *Washington Post*, February 1, 1995. See also Jorge G. Castaneda, *The Mexican Shock: Its Meaning for the U.S.*, pp. 177–254.

23. Knight-Ridder, "Market Analysis: Market Reaction Shows U.S. Aid Plan Is No Panacea," February 21, 1995; Geri Smith, "Can Zedillo Push Democracy—and Keep the Lid On?" *Business Week*, February 20, 1995, p. 61.

24. "Impone EU Severas Medidas a Mexico," *El Manana*, February 22, 1995; Knight-Ridder, press release, "Market Reaction Shows U.S. Aid Plan No Panacea," February 21, 1995.

25. United States and Mexico, "U.S.–Mexico Framework Agreement for Mexican Economic Stabilization" (Washington, D.C.: February 21, 1995), pp. 1–13.

26. Ibid., "Medium-Term Exchange Stabilization Agreement," February 21, 1995, pp. 1–15.

27. Ibid., "Guarantee Agreement," February 21, 1995, pp. 1–20.

28. Ibid., "Oil Proceeds Facility Agreement," Annex A, February 21, 1995, pp. 1–34. Also see U.S. Treasury, "Summary of Agreements: Fact Sheet on United States Support for Mexico," Washington, D.C.: February 21, 1995; "U.S. Aid Brings Tough Rules," *Houston Chronicle*, February 26, 1995; and Testimony by Jeffrey Shafer, Asst. Sec. of the Treasury for International Affairs, before the House Subcommittee on Western Hemisphere and the House Subcommittee on International Economic Policy and Trade of the Committee on International Relations, Treasury News Release, February 22, 1995.

29. GAO, *Mexico's Financial Crisis: Origins, Awareness, Assistance, and Initial Efforts to Recover* (Washington, D.C.: February 1996), pp. 109–23; Dean Foust, "What the IMF Needs Is a Good Alarm System," *Business Week*, February 20, 1995, p. 55.

30. John Weeks, "The Contemporary Latin American Economies: Neoliberal Reconstruction," as seen in Sandor Halebsky and Richard L. Harris (eds.), *Capital, Power, and Inequality in Latin America* (Boulder: 1995), pp. 109–32: Antony De Palma, "Mexicans Ask How Far Social Fabric Can Stretch," *New York Times*, March 12, 1995, p. 1, 20; Thurow, *The Future of Capitalism*, pp. 224–29; Duncan Green, *Silent Revolution: The Rise of Market Economies in Latin America* (London: 1995), pp. 84–87, 200–210.

31. GAO, *Mexico's Financial Crisis*, pp. 117–22; Dean Faust, "Tough Love in Mexico: Realities of the U.S. Bailout," *Business Week*, March 6, 1995, pp. 30–32; Lorenzo Meyer, *Mexico and the United States in the Oil Controversy, 1917–1942* (Austin: 1972), pp. 14–19, 54–59, 172–79. See also Government of Mexico, *The True Facts about the Expropriation of the Oil Companies' Properties in Mexico* (Mexico, D.F.: 1940), pp. 1–270; White House, "Message to the Congress on the Financial Crisis in Mexico," *Presidential Documents*, Vol. 31, March 9, 1995, pp. 390–91.

32. U.S. Congress, Senate, *The Mexico Peso Crisis*, March 9–10, 1995, pp. 185–449.

33. David E. Sanger, "Dollar Dips As the Peso Falls Again," *New York Times*, March 10, 1995, pp. D1–2; Daniel Dunaief, "Rumors Roil Bank Stocks, Debt As the Peso Dives to a New Low," *American Banker*, March 10, 1995; Elgar von Schmidt, "Mexico's Austerity Plan Deserves Its Mixed Reviews: Linkage of U.S. and Mexican Economies Is Sure to Trigger Further Downside Probing in the Currency Market," Knight-Ridder (New York: March 15, 1995).

34. Hobart Rowen, "Lack of Confidence in Rubin Is Contributing to Dollar's Decline," *Washington Post*, March 12, 1995; Kevin Muehring, "The Trader at Treasury," *Institutional Investor*, January 1996, p. 46. For a contrary view see Albert Hunt, "A Wall Streeter Makes Good in Washington," *Wall Street Journal*, April 11, 1996, p. A21.

35. John Berry, "Dollar Stabilizes, Ending a Four-Day Tumble," *Washington Post*, March 9, 1995. See also Berry, "Dollar Keeps Falling Against Yen and Mark," Ibid., March 7, 1995.

36. Anthony De Palma, "Mexico Outlines an Economic Plan of Extended Pain," *New York Times*, March 10, 1995, p. A1; Paul B. Carroll and Craig Torres, "Mexico Unveils Programs of Harsh Fiscal Medicine," *Wall Street Journal*, March 19, 1995; "Mexico on the Mend," *Business Latin America*, April 3, 1995, pp. 1–3; U.S. Treasury, "Monthly Report by the Secretary of the Treasury [on Mexico]" (Washington, D.C.: May 31, 1995), pp. 1–6; OECD, *Main Economic Indicators* (Paris: September 1995), pp. 67–71. Note: Certain foods and beverages have a 6 percent VAT.

37. Robert S. Gay, "Mexico: Exports Keep Economy Afloat," *Bankers Trust Research*, May 18, 1995, p. 1.

38. John A. Adams, Jr., "Window on the Future: Mexico 1996," *Twin Plant News*, January 1996; "Has Mexico Finally Turned the Corner?" *Mexico Service*, May 5, 1995, pp. 1–8; Paul Carroll, "Peso Shockwaves Ripple through Mexico," *Wall Street Journal*, January 9, 1995, p. A6; Sidney Weintraub, "The Mexican Economy: Life after Devaluation," *Current History*, March 1995, pp. 108–13; John M. Nagel, "More for the Money," *El Financiero International*, January 16, 1995, p. 10. See also U.S Treasury, *Monthly Report by the Secretary of the Treasury*, June 30, 1995, and July 31, 1995.

39. U.S. Treasury, "Monthly Report by the Secretary of the Treasury" (Washington, D.C.: October 1995), pp. 18–22; OECD, *Main Economic Indicator*, p. 67; Carl W. Ross,

"Mexico: Balance of Payments Update," *Bankers Trust Research*, August 3, 1995, pp. 1–3; Geri Smith, Stanley Reed, and Elisabeth Malkin, "Mexico: A Rough Road Back," *Business Week*, November 13, 1995, pp. 104–7; Ruben Marquez Gallegos, "Mexico: A Corporate Finance Update," *Corporate Finance in Latin America 1996*, March 1996, pp. 102–12.

40. Federal Reserve Board, "Condition of the Mexican Banking System" (Washington, D.C.: May, 16, 1995); "Can the Banks Be Saved," *Mexico Service*, January 13, 1995, pp. 11–12.

41. Robert S. Gray, "Mexican Banks: Coping with Credit Risk," *Perspectives on the Americas*, November 22, 1993, pp. 16–17; David R. Luhnow, "Mexico's Banks Booming, but Borrowers Wary of Rates,"*San Antonio Express-News*, March 21, 1993.

42. Michael Tangeman, "The Once, and Future, Banking Crisis," *Institutional Investor*, November 1995, pp. 119–21.

43. Federal Reserve Board, "Condition of the Mexican Banking System," p. 2.

44. U.S. Treasury, press release, remarks by Lawrence H. Summers to the Brookings Institution (Washington, D.C.: March 3, 1995), pp. 1–8; Craig Torres, "Mexico Banks Hang in 'Delicate Balance'," *Wall Street Journal*, January 31, 1995, p. A16.

45. Dianne Solis, "In Mexico, a New Kind of Rebel Emerges," *Wall Street Journal*, September 2, 1995; Carmina Danini, "El Barzon Debtors Group Takes on Mexican Banks," *San Antonio Express-News*, July 16, 1995, p. 5A; Knight-Ridder, "Mexico: Rural Group Says Banks at Risk of Bankruptcy for Bad Loans" (Mexico City: March 8, 1995); Philip True, "5 Year Drought Shoves Northern Mexico Toward Disaster," *San Antonio Express-News*, May 19, 1996, p. 6A.

46. IMF, Memorandum, Karin Lissakers to Jeff Shafer, re: "More on Mexican Commercial Banks" (Washington, D.C.: January 6, 1995), IMF document 704706.

47. Daniel Dombey, "Banks Take Devaluation Beating," *El Financiero International*, January 9, 1995, p. 3; Craig Torres, "Mexican Banks Post Big Loss on Peso's Fall," *Wall Street Journal*, January 17, 1995.

48. Banco de Mexico, *The Mexican Economy 1995*, pp. 113–24; Craig Torres, "Mexico Overhauls Banks Amid Turmoil," *Wall Street Journal*, March 6, 1995, p. A10.

49. Federal Reserve Board, "Condition of the Mexican Banking System," pp. 9–11; Enrique de la Madrid and Javier Cavito (CNBV), conference presentation, "The Mexican Banking System," New York City, January 1996; U.S. Treasury, *Semi-Annual Report to Congress by the Secretary of the Treasury on Behalf of the President* (Washington, D.C.: December 1995), pp. 16–18.

50. Al Taranto, "How Much Is Enough?" *El Financiero International*, August 28, 1995, p. 1; Federal Reserve Board, "Mexican Banking System," p. 8; Jim Freer, "Coping with the Crisis," *LatinFinance*, October 1995, pp. 30–32.

51. *Diario Oficial*, February 15, 1995. See also *Diario Oficial*, November 17, 27, 1995; "Mergers and Acquisition Laws 1996," *LatinFinance*, January 1996, pp. 20–23; "Foreign Financial Institutions Face Revised Limits," *Inter-American Trade and Investment Law*, Vol. 3, December 8, 1995, p. 1; Skip Edmonds, "Mexican Banks Open to Foreign Investors," *Financial Industry Issues* (FRBD), First Quarter 1995, pp. 1, 4.

52. Freer, "Coping with the Crisis," *LatinFinance*, p. 30; Bloomberg, press release, "Mexico's Debt-Relief Plan Restructures 79% of Targeted Loans" (Mexico, D.F: February 6, 1996).

53. Lloyd Harris, "The Spanish Conquest," *Mexico Business*, December 1995, pp. 8,

10; Craig Torres, "GE Capital Corp. to Acquire 13% of Mexico's Serfin," March 21, 1995; Karen Gullo, "Mexican Bankers Say They'll Pull through Financial Crisis," *Laredo Morning Times*, March 13, 1995; Knight Ridder, press release, "Mexico Opts for Solid Foreign Bidder in Cremi Sale" (Mexico, D.F.: June 10, 1996).

Chapter 8

Tequila Hangover: Impact of the Peso Crisis on Argentina

Because the Mexican model has been so widely watched, and so widely emulated, and is so salient in the minds of investors, what happens in Mexico has implications that go far beyond Mexico, or even Latin America. Indeed all you have to do is sit at a Reuters screen, and see that the Thai baht has done such and such because of changing views about investor confidence in Mexico, or that South African interest rates have moved thus and so, or that Argentine bank stocks have performed a certain way—to see that the stakes involved in what happens in Mexico go far beyond Mexico, and go far beyond Latin America.
—Lawrence H. Summers (Under Secretary of the Treasury),
January 20, 1995

During the past decade Mexico has been a key barometer of the economic activity and growth in Latin America. As an emerging world economy, Mexico has encountered a wide range of economic situations that have spilled over to its neighbors to the south—radical currency devaluations, an international debt crisis, political intrigue, as well as a formidable competitor for foreign direct investment and new markets. In contrast to economic distress, Mexico has been viewed by some as the model of wide-scale privatization of a vast number of previously government-owned banking, business, and industry. The experiences of Mexico, as well as the reaction of outside investors to Mexico's relative position of stability, have had a distinctive influence (referred to as the "Tequila Effect" or "Hangover" in the popular press)[1] on the larger economies of the region—most significantly Brazil, Venezuela, Chile, Colombia, and Argentina.[2] Of these nations, Argentina has been uniquely impacted by (and oftentimes compared to) the economic fortunes of Mexico. Thus, this section will review and examine the influence of Mexico on the financial and commercial markets of Argentina.

BACKGROUND

At the beginning of the decade of the 1990's a significant economic shift began throughout Latin America. The idea, promoted by many but articulated by the Bush administration, that a free-trade zone would span the entire Western Hemisphere, open once closed markets, and instill encouragement to a region emerging from decades of stagnation was fostered primarily by a bankrupt policy known as import-substitution industrialization (ISI). Latin American leaders were under the false impression that the best way to enhance their economies was to artificially protect the domestic industrial and distribution base by excluding or limiting foreign competition.

Some economic sectors in the region did show brief periods of economic independence, most notably Mexico and Venezuela, during the oil boom of the early 1970's. However, in the process, the norm was that domestic industries throughout the hemisphere deteriorated, new direct foreign investment dramatically declined, most were excluded from international capital markets, technology transfer was impeded, and a major regional hemispheric market was— by its closed door policies and actions—cut off from the rest of the world.[3] One observer noted:

The industrialists got lazy because they didn't have to compete with anyone—including their fellow countrymen—and the products they manufactured became inferior and overpriced. Uncompetitive islands of economic and political instability resulted.[4]

Mexico and Argentina emerged as two of the "uncompetitive islands" and economic casualties of the late 1970's and early 1980's—stagnation, debt, and inflation caused both nations to discard ideas of a closed economy and embrace a broader scope of free trade on both a regional and, eventually, a global scale. In 1990, the spirit of the "Enterprise of the Americas" proposed by President George Bush and followed by years of adjustment resulting in the Summit of the Americas in late 1994, envisioned a free-trade zone from Alaska to the Tierra del Fuego by the turn of the century.[5] Within the conceptual framework of the General Agreement on Tariffs and Trade (GATT), and following the lead of the Canada-U.S. Free Trade Agreement (CUSFTA) concluded in 1988, trade liberalization and the free-trade dialogue began to flourish in the region.[6] For example, Brazil, Uruguay, Paraguay, and Argentina formed a common market called Mercosur; the Andean nations of Bolivia, Colombia, Peru, Ecuador, and Venezuela reduced cross-border trade barriers; Chile and Mexico signed a free-trade pact in 1991; and Mexico and Venezuela opened trade talks with the Central American nations. Mexico opened a dialogue with the United States in 1991 to draft the North American Free Trade Agreement (NAFTA) that, in its

Figure 8-1
Latin America Inflation Profile (Percentage Yearly Inflation)

	1990	1991	1992	1993	1994	1995	1996*
Mexico	29.9	18.8	11.9	8.0	7.0	51.9	26.3
Peru	7,650	139.2	57.7	39.5	15.4	10.2	9.8
Colombia	32.0	26.8	25.1	22.6	22.6	22.8	18.5
Chile	27.3	18.7	12.7	12.2	8.9	7.8	5.3
Argentina	1,344	84.0	17.2	7.4	3.9	1.6	1.0

*forecast.

Source: IMF.

final form in 1993 included Canada. Andres Velasio, a top Chilean trade ne-gotiator noted in 1992, "In today's Latin America, free trade is almost a fad" (see Figure 8-1).[7]

The fad was bolstered by significant political and economic changes through-out the region. "Freer" trade—trade is never truly without some form of barriers both real and imagined—was augmented by the emergence of free mar-ket, democratically led nations hemisphere-wide. The reduction of authoritarian state oversight was embodied in a wave of privatization of enterprises once inefficiently controlled by government auspices. Although Mexico was hailed worldwide as the model for privatization, the country grappled to insure a solid economic footing. The reprivatization of the Mexican banking system was the most extensive sector cut from full government control. However, the euphoria of the fresh new investment in the financial services sector and the advent of NAFTA resulted in excesses in granting domestic credit by undercapitalized banks. Government industries, such as hitherto protected "strategic industries" like Petroleos Mexicanos (PEMEX) and Ferrocarriles Nacionales de Mexico (FNM), as well as seaports and harbors, airports and airlines continue to be evaluated for privatization. The recent crisis has resulted in the accelerated ef-forts both to deregulate and attract private investors.[8]

Thus, the nations of Latin America began the decade of the 1990's pursuing remarkably similar open-door-free-market policies and objectives. In addition to trade liberalization and privatization, fiscal discipline emerged and was imper-ative to address the debt crisis that crippled Latin finance markets and invest-ment. The larger national economies of Latin America critically needed access to international credit markets crucial to growth and development.[9] By the early 1990's, Mexico and Argentina embarked on bold programs to be both regional and world players in economic and trade matters. In these efforts, Mexico, in early 1994, emerged as the regional benchmark and primary influence for the rebirth of investment, commerce, and free trade.[10]

The first element toward a more open economy involved the political con-science and will to realign with the broader financial and trade trends brought about by an emerging, interrelated global economy. In 1988–89, Mexico under Carlos Salinas de Gortari and Argentina under the administration of Carlos Saul

Figure 8-2
Net Capital Flows to Latin America (Billions of U.S. Dollars)

	1990	1991	1992	1993	1994	5 yr total
Argentina	-1.9	3.6	11.2	10.5	10.5	33.9
Brazil	5.3	0.8	8.8	9.0	13.0	36.9
Chile	3.0	0.8	3.5	2.8	3.1	13.2
Colombia	0	-0.8	0.2	2.2	3.1	4.7
Mexico	8.2	24.9	29.5	30.9	11.5	105.0
Peru	0.9	0.5	2.7	2.7	6.0	12.8
Venezuela	-6.0	1.2	2.5	1.7	-5.2	-5.8

Sources: World Bank; IMF; CEPAL.

Menem launched domestic reforms and progressive, external trade-oriented programs. Both Mexico and Argentina introduced economic reform initiatives targeted to reduce inflation, enhance domestic production and exports, and encourage increased inflows of foreign capital. To accomplish this required changes in tariff schedules, investment laws, foreign access to capital markets, and a stronger regime of protection for intellectual property rights. With these and other modifications the reluctance of foreign investors, in the wake of the 1980's debt crisis, began to diminish. Foreign direct investment and portfolio investment as well as the repatriation of large sums of flight capital began to flow back not only to Mexico and Argentina, but all of Latin America in increasing amounts, starting in 1990 and peaking in mid-1994. Less than a year prior to the onset of the Mexican crisis, the vice chairman of Citicorp—a key corporate player in financial services and debt restructuring throughout the hemisphere—proclaimed, "The Latin Tigers Are Ready to Roar."[11] Mexico, with its bullish worldwide effort to be a larger global player, was the regional leader in the inflow of investment capital. The net capital inflow to Mexico between 1990 and 1994 exceeded $100 billion, surpassing the combined total for the same period in Argentina, Brazil, Chile, Colombia, Peru, and Venezuela (see Figure 8-2).[12]

EXCHANGE RATE CONTROLS

Mexico and Argentina embarked on a parallel course with regard to hard-currency policies and more open markets. By 1990–91 both governments made exchange rate policy a critical element of their pro-foreign investment and anti-inflationary strategies. Argentina, the smaller of the two economies, was unable to control the hyperinflation in the late 1980's and thus abolished most foreign exchange controls in early 1990.[13] Investment in Argentina and repatriation of profits, dividends, and capital in hard currency was freely permitted. In early 1991 a hard-currency monetary policy, the Convertibility Plan, was adopted that pegged the Argentine peso at parity, to the U.S. dollar at an exchange rate of 1:1.[14] The central bank, Banco Central de la Republica Argentina, was charged with the responsibility to monitor circulation, thereby tying money supply growth to the level of exchange reserves. To insure parity to the dollar a currency board system was implemented. Beginning in 1992, the economy became more dollarized and, until early 1994, inflows of capital more than compensated for the steadily widening external gap. As liquidity expanded, the economy experienced an average 7.4 percent GDP growth. By 1994, aggravated by large capital outflows and looming recession, it was estimated that efforts to maintain the peso/dollar peg along with the narrowing of the intervention range resulted in the peso being in excess of 40 percent overvalued.[15]

In late 1987, Mexico replaced the old two-tier system and took a more flexible approach. To insure a measure of control the peso was allowed to float within a tightly monitored exchange rate band fixed initially at 3.0562/U.S.$1. The upper limit of the band increased daily at the rate of .0004 pesos. During the period from 1990 to mid-1994, inflation improved and foreign investment freely moved to Mexican markets. Mexico's emergence from recession, the conclusion of NAFTA, and the attractive nature of Mexican investments overlooked structural problems with the Mexican peso and the banking system.[16] In an overview of the currency situation in Latin America, *Euromoney*, in March 1994, was one of the few publications to, early on, signal pending problems with the Mexican economic structure:

There has been some concern that the peso could weaken towards the top of the current band or even that there could be a discrete devaluation because of the increase in the size of the current account deficit and because the currency is overvalued against the dollar. . . . Balance of payments developments in the next year will be the crucial macroeconomic influence on the sustainability of the current arrangement.[17]

THE CHRISTMAS SURPRISE

Efforts by the Salinas administration to lower inflation, restore confidence in the capital markets, and rid Mexico of decades of economic and political intrigue were dashed on December 20, 1994. Although the peso had been devalued daily within the guidelines established by an agreement between the government, business, and labor to keep wages and prices under control (known as the ''Pact for Stability, Competitiveness and Employment'' or PACTO), governmental reserves dipped to dangerously low levels by mid-December. During much of 1994, the Salinas government had avoided any devaluation due to the fall 1994 presidential election. Even though the peso was between 18 and 20 percent overvalued, most experts predicted there would be no devaluation.[18] In December the situation boiled over. In response to the pending crisis, newly elected president Ernesto Zedillo was forced to widen the exchange rate band in which the peso was traded, thus setting off a wave of drastic devaluation of the currency. Steve Hanke, a close observer of economic events in both Mexico and Argentina noted:

The peso was allowed to trade within a tolerance band of some plus or minus 3%. The band "crawled" downward daily, allowing an annual peso depreciation of about 4% against the dollar. To keep the peso within this band, the Mexican central bank had to manage simultaneously both the peso-dollar exchange and the peso money supply. This is an almost impossible balancing act.[19]

The initial 15 percent devaluation mushroomed to 30 percent in March and by year-end 1995 exceeded 50 percent. Mexico had lost confidence in its ability to control the peso and international markets were further flustered by the seemingly unexpected series of events started in late December. The devaluation can clearly be laid at the feet of the Salinas administration.[20] The impact of these actions echoed throughout Latin America, as investors moved swiftly to reduce their exposure and investments in the region. The Mexican "Tequila Effect" on its neighbors was swift and unsettling—for example, the Argentine central bank reported that in early 1995 over U.S.$ 8.2 billion in bank deposits fled the country and the Argentine stocks dropped roughly 38 percent; investors backed away from Brazil, and the Peruvian stock market in Lima suffered its sharpest decline in six years on January 10, 1995.[21]

Initial efforts to shore up the Mexican peso failed, with the result that the peso was allowed to freely float on December 22, 1994. Institutional and portfolio investors lost confidence in Mexico, resulting in a disintermediation in excess of $25 billion from Mexico in less than a four-week period. In the wake of the Mexican turmoil, Zedillo announced an austerity plan known as the Programa de Emergencia Economica, and accepted the "sacrificial" resignation of Finance Secretary Jaime Serra Puche. The initial reaction by international markets and investors was to withdraw a substantial portion of their investments from Mexico. The rate of capital flight, coupled with a lack of confidence in the Banco de Mexico and the crisis, nearly collapsed the Mexican economy and the government.[22]

In late February 1995, after any hopes of action by the international banking community or the U.S. Congress, the Clinton administration (in cooperation with the IMF) announced a bold $51 billion financial package and loan guarantees to shore up the Mexican government and banks.[23] The funds in this package were composed of a mix of direct aid and guarantees jointly underwritten by the U.S. government via the Treasury and the Federal Reserve, the International Monetary Fund (IMF), the Bank for International Settlements (BIS), and the World Bank. In congressional testimony on March 9, 1995, Alan Greenspan stated that the administration's action to put together a bailout package was valid and represented the "least worst solution" to the Mexican crisis. Millions of U.S. investors held direct and indirect investments, primarily in pension funds, tied to the Mexican economy.[24]

The reaction both in Latin America and capital markets worldwide was swift. As noted, investors—primarily in liquid portfolio accounts—were swift to withdraw investments from all the countries in the region. The quick response by countries throughout the region was that "we are not Mexico." Argentina, for example, did not have the short-term tesobono buildup that Mexico had. Yet unfortunately, due to the high profile of Mexico—as evidenced by its ability to attract large sums of investment, the admission to the OECD in early 1994, the optimism associated with the conclusion of NAFTA, and the high profile possibility that President Salinas would be selected as the first General Secretary of the World Trade Organization (WTO)—many equated these events with stability, success, and a return to economic growth; with what some called the "Mexican Miracle." These events as well as the reaction to the reverberations of the crisis on the Argentine economy are instructive.[25]

ARGENTINA: THE TEQUILA EFFECT

The economic hangover induced by the Mexican crisis is measured largely in the way in which Latin American nations responded to the broader economic repercussions. Central to the Argentine response was the viability of the policies of the Menem administration and the actions of Finance Minister Domingo Cavallo. Since the early 1990's, Cavallo has been the primary architect of the restructuring of the Argentine economy. The fallout of the Mexican crisis had a tremendous bearing on efforts to restore confidence in the Argentine economy and stimulate growth. Cavallo had been a principal planner in the "convertibility" scheme—pegging the exchange rate of the peso to the dollar. In the wake of Mexico's attempt to convince Wall Street financiers that the adjustment of late December was not a severe problem, Cavallo conducted an in-person public relations blitz with investors in New York in January, and later in March 1995 in Europe, centered around the theme that "Argentina isn't Mexico." In retrospect, March and April were the pivotal months for Argentina.[26] Although Cavallo projected a GDP growth for 1995 in the 4.5–6 percent range and the acceleration of privatization efforts, Wall Street fund managers were fearful of the overdependence on short-term foreign capital that had historically proved disruptive in both Mexico and Argentina. By his strategy and actions, Cavallo confirmed that the Mexican crisis was in fact a potentially destabilizing influence on the fragile Argentine economy.[27]

Credible action was needed in a number of areas. Within the guidelines of the Convertibility Plan, Cavallo and the central bank president, Roque Fernandez, increased dollar reserves, minimum cash requirements for banks were lowered, and banks were allowed to freely hold and handle U.S. dollars. As with Mexico, financing the current account deficit and establishing confidence proved paramount. The initial response from the foreign capital markets was positive but guarded. Into early 1995, unemployment paralleled the rising trend in Mexico; unemployment in Argentina was at 18.4 percent in May and dropped to 16.4 percent in October. Capital flight strained the liquidity of the banks and Menem was facing reelection in May 1995. Thus the pressure to avert high interest rates, runaway inflation or an abandonment of the economic policy could trigger a devaluation and a Mexican-style crisis.[28]

Well aware of the influence created by the deterioration of the Mexican economy, the Menem government worked to restore confidence both at home and abroad. The interrelationship of three elements would prove pivotal—the banking sector, the role of the IMF, and the viability of the Convertibility Plan and the Currency Board. The interworkings of these three factors would determine the outcome of the Menem-Cavallo plan to thwart a financial crisis. By April, shortly before the election, the main impediment to recovery and stability was the weakness of the banking system.

BANKING: ON BORROWED TIME

In the months prior to the reverberations from the December 1994 devaluation in Mexico, Argentine banking was "booming"—bank loans had grown from less than $1 billion in 1989 to $45.7 billion in mid-1994, and bad loans were reported to be low. The Argentine banking system is very concentrated. While the five largest banks accounted for 20 percent of total deposits in the banking system, the largest 20 banks control 80 percent of the financial markets. However, in early 1995 concern rose over the growing instability of the banking sector, caused by a fourfold increase in interest rates and the explosive growth of bad loans and the capital flight. Nonetheless, these events did not substantially impact the May presidential election, as Menem won carrying over 50 percent of the popular vote and 10 of the 14 provinces. His major opposition, Jose Octavio Bordon of the Center-Left Party—FREPASO, invoked a contrary view on the Mexican crisis saying, in the closing days of the campaign, "that Argentina was not suffering from the tequila effect so much as the champagne effect: a heady sense of unreality." Notwithstanding the Menem reelection, there was a looming banking crisis.[29]

By the start of the second quarter of 1995 Argentine banks suffered both a wave of insolvency and disintermediation of core deposits. The Argentine Banking Association (Asociacion de Bancos Argentinos—ADEBA) reported that between December 20, 1994 and March 2, 1995 the banks had lost $4.2 billion in deposits. The funds were removed to new investments in Europe and America, yet strangely an estimated 10 percent of the flight capital went to dollar-denominated accounts in neighboring Uruguay. While Uruguay is not routinely considered a "safe" haven for investment, one can only speculate that this was intended to diversify risk.[30]

According to Argentine central bank data, capital flight can be partly attributed to the reduction of the number of banks from 205 to 150.[31] Deteriorating loan quality, inefficient banking systems, and the fact that, according to the central bank, "the Argentine financial system faced a crisis of systemic liquidity" are additional reasons for the wave of insolvency. While there was a modest increase in return deposits, the net outflow from late December 1994 to

October 1995 exceeded $5 billion. Year-end bank deposits struggled to regain the "pre-tequila" level. To further complicate matters, tax revenues were over 10 percent below the previous year's collection, this despite an increase in the VAT rate from 18 percent to 21 percent (VAT provides 38 percent of total revenues for Argentina versus 17 percent for Brazil and 18 percent for Mexico). One bright spot was that inflation remained below 2 percent. Nevertheless, one primary measure of the Argentine strategy to recovery is the ability to attract financial backing in the international market.[32]

IMF: THE RETURN OF FOREIGN CAPITAL

As the banks grappled with survival, the government worked to shore up the country's overall international financial position. To prevent a Mexican-like collapse, foreign creditors and the IMF strongly encouraged a tight fiscal control, a reduction in imports, and a restructuring of the banking system. Of considerable concern was the shortfall of tax revenues and the high unemployment.[33] In the aftermath of the bailout of Mexico, Argentine officials, primarily with the coordination of the IMF, were able to secure a number of loans, and structure a bond offering as well as lines of credit. The package included a mix of private and public sector funding, an international debt restructuring to include a $1.6 billion loan from the IMF to underpin the government, $8.7 billion from commercial banks' guarantees and placement of "solidarity bonds," and a $1 billion line of credit from the BIS (secured by shares of stock in the state-owned oil and gas company—Yacimientos Petroliferos Fiscales, YPF—the largest company based in Argentina). Two final components included a $300 million loan from the World Bank to facilitate and speed up the Argentine banking system mergers and privatization, and the "Bono Argentino" offering, a public sector loan structured by the leading investors and companies for a $1 billion loan (line of credit), repayable in three years.[34]

In this last case, the bonds will be applied to private sector tax payments to the government—a form of advance payment redeemable at a future date. In addition to the above financial package, Argentina continues an obligation on its Brady debt. Furthermore, in August, to dispel any doubts about its ability to access international markets, Argentina issued a one billion Deutsch mark ($717 million), five-year bond offering. This was the first public bond issue by the Menem government since the Mexican devaluation and it established a much-needed benchmark for future private sector borrowing. At year-end 1995, J. P. Morgan Bank agreed to a $350 million loan, based on the confidence that Argentina would not devalue the peso. Learning from the pitfalls of the Mexican experience, one analysis noted, "Argentina will continue to be rewarded for being one of the only countries in recent history to fend off a speculative attack by using orthodox, pro-market economic policies—namely, severe tightening of fiscal policy and monetary conditions."[35]

CURRENCY BOARD

The true test of the impact of the Mexican crisis on the Argentine economy was the viability and survivability of the currency board established in April 1991. Currency boards are not a new concept. First established by the British in the second half of the nineteenth century to assist in the management of their vast colonial network, a currency board offers to exchange domestic currency for foreign exchange at a fixed rate, on demand, and under all circumstances. It insures this currency framework by fully backing the domestic monetary base with a foreign-reserve currency and by setting the exchange rate as a matter of public policy.[36] The effort in Argentina to halt the hyperinflation of the late 1980's was very effective. With the Argentine peso fully convertible into U.S. dollars at a rate of 1 to 1, the monetary system was literally backed by U.S. dollar reserves. The currency board system functions much like the turn of the century U.S. gold standard, except paper pesos are fully convertible to dollars instead of gold. A currency board is intended to be an institutional agreement to separate monetary and fiscal policy. As one observer noted, it prevents monetary policy from becoming the handmaiden of fiscal policy. Furthermore, the currency board prevents the major engine of inflation—the central bank—from printing pesos without the adequate backing of American dollars reserves.[37]

In a dissenting evaluation of the Argentine convertibility program and the reaction to the Mexican crisis, Harvard economist Jeffrey Sachs indicated that the four-year-old currency board system "aggravated Argentina's recession [in 1995] because it made it difficult for the central bank to act as lender of the last resort." Sachs based his comments on the side effects of a Phillips Curve movement that increased unemployment from 5.8 percent in 1991 to a high of 18 percent in mid-1995. However, the impact of the Mexican currency crisis on capital flight from Argentina and the weak Argentine banking sector proved pivotal to the downturn of the economy. Nevertheless, the Menem-Cavallo approach to support and maintain the Convertibility Plan has proved, at least during 1995, the prudent course of action. Furthermore, the IMF and World Bank have replaced the central bank system as the lender of last resort.[38]

As the "tequila effect" influenced a decrease in capital from a growing number of weak Argentine banks, the Menem administration was hard-pressed to show substantial short-term benefits of the currency board during the early months of 1995. The Mexican crisis provoked a collective investor retreat, further causing domestic credit to collapse. The only bright spot for both Argentina and Mexico was the rise in exports. Export earnings in Argentina surged 36 percent to a record $21 billion. What is significant is that the currency board prevented the government or central bank from creating worthless money to bail out the troubled bankers—a short-term fix, yet as history has demonstrated the root of a long-term problem usually resulting in economic stagnation and hyperinflation; thus, the loss of investor/depositor confidence.[39]

Relieved at the announcement by the Clinton-IMF stability package for Mexico, Menem and Cavallo—though challenged by the pressures of the pending election and the ongoing banking slump—worked consistently to restore foreign investor confidence. According to President Menem, to have abandoned the currency board would have caused the return of runaway inflation, devaluation, and most likely the defeat at the election polls, "for 50 years, we devalued in Argentina, and every time, it was worse."[40] However, with the banking system reeling from the capital flight, it was hard to convince both domestic opponents of speculation and foreign investors that currency stability was paramount. Argentina more so than any other nation, has had an instructive currency board legacy. From 1890 to 1935 a board functioned well, yet gave in to prevailing fashions, in the mid-1930's, to establish a central bank. There are only two primary advantages to a central bank and national currency: the seignorage gained through the "inflation tax" and the national symbolism attached to a nation having its own money in circulation. Furthermore, Argentina and all of the Latin American markets have always been vulnerable to a rise in global interest rates. When Menem was elected president in 1989, annual inflation was 4,924 percent, dropped to 3.9 percent in 1994, and averaged 1.7 percent (CPI) in 1995.[41]

PERSPECTIVE

In the aftermath of the Mexican peso devaluation, analysts focused on the secondary impact to economies throughout the Latin American region. Faced with tough decisions and a need to restore depositor and investor confidence both at home and abroad, the Menem-Cavallo response was to distance Argentina from any direct or indirect association with the Mexican crisis. During 1994 financial analysts had expressed pre–Mexican crisis concern about the Argentine economy due to—increased public spending, low tax collection, a weak, "over-banked" banking system, interest rate concern, bad loans, and a potential for a fiscal deficit in 1995. Thus it was imperative that the Menem government move swiftly beginning in January 1995 to identify new sources of investment, restore and improve the banking system, and maintain the convertibility policy anchored by the currency board. Nonetheless, foreign investor and domestic confidence waned in early 1995 sparking capital flight and an increase in the domestic interest rate. A solid election victory in May, followed by the return of some capital flight funds and support of the currency board augmented with a broad package of IMF loans and guarantees sustained the Argentine economy. As one analysis noted, "Mexico devalued while Argentina defended its currency."[42]

Although problems remain with the restructuring of the Argentine banks, by year-end 1995 inflation remained at an all-time low, unemployment was trending lower, and an estimated $7 billion of $8 billion capital that left in early 1995 had returned. Investors and analysts that watched Mexico now closely watch Argentina as a possible model for developing country economic and monetary stability. Local interest rates in Argentina dropped below 6 percent in 1996, inflation is nonexistent, and international reserves far exceeded the pre–Mexican crisis levels. Mexico in contrast ended the year with inflation of 51.97 percent, a strained banking sector, and a plunging GDP. The Zedillo administration gradually moved closer to a dollar-based economy—validating a de facto situation that has strongly considered an Argentine-style currency board—a system that has matured and gained credibility as a result of the Mexican crisis. David Hale, Chief Economist at Kemper Financial Services noted, ''The introduction of a currency board would not be able to eliminate financial risk premiums overnight, but, if supported by an adequate international financial aid package, it would be a bold policy gesture for signalling Mexico's commitment to correcting the breach of promise which . . . took place on December 20th.''[43] Nonetheless, the prime concern for the establishment of a currency board in Mexico is the need to require massive amounts of foreign reserves to guarantee a fixed rate for the peso. Some estimate Mexico will need as much as $50 billion in foreign reserves—coincidentally the same amount as the February 1995 bailout package.[44]

Thus, in the year following the Mexican peso devaluation Argentina and the Menem-Cavallo policy persevered. Avoiding the temptation to make short-term decisions that would lead to short-term gains, Argentine economic policy in 1995 focused on a strategy to avoid the bankrupt policies of the past in favor of solid planning and stabilization that will have long-term gains for the nation. At the height of the Mexican crisis and its repercussion on Argentina and the region, the *Economist* captured the essence of the ongoing challenge faced by nations endeavoring to be monetarily stable and globally competitive:

In the wake of the Mexican economic crisis, it is early to jump to the conclusion that exchange-rate pegs are foolhardy, and that keeping controls on capital inflows is a necessary precaution. This would be a mistake. Exchange rate pegs play a useful role in fighting inflation; the trick is to ensure that the currency in question does not become grossly overvalued. Nor is short-term foreign capital necessarily dangerous; what is dangerous is depending too much on it. The real secret of economic success is tight fiscal and monetary policies and a programme of deep structural reforms which, among other things, increase domestic saving.[45]

The 1995 Argentine economic adjustment to the impact of the Mexican crises as well as a realization of the structural financial problems within Argentina was formidable. Having reduced inflation from nearly 5,000 percent to zero in half a decade did not insure adequate economic growth. During the early months of 1996 Cavallo and Menem could not agree on the best means to speed Argentina's recovery, lower unemployment, and stabilize tax revenues. The rumors of discord between the two regarding the course of the Argentine economic policy concluded in the departure of Cavallo in late July 1996. The challenge to improve the sluggish economy passed to the president of the Central Bank, Roque Fernandez. There were no plans to drastically alter economic policy away from the congressionally approved market-oriented convertibility program championed by Cavallo.[46]

NOTES

1. Ali Qassim, "Peso Panic: Buenos Aires Is Trying to Calm Post-Mexico Alarm," *The Banker*, Vol. 145, May 1995, pp. 43–44. Note: The effect of the Mexican economic crisis on Latin America has been routinely referred to in the media as the "tequila effect." This reference to Mexico's woes has gained global recognition. For a contrary opinion on the influence of the 1994–95 Mexican crisis, see Harvey D. Shapiro, "Tequila Effect? What Tequila Effect?" *Institutional Investors*, October 1995, pp. 263–64.

2. Carl Ross, "Latin America: Current Issues in Sovereign Risk," *Perspectives on the Americas*, Bankers Trust Research, July 21, 1994, pp. 8–15; "The Brazilian Model," *Latin American Economy and Business* (hereafter *LAEB*) (London: May 1995), p. 1; "Deficit Sounds Early Warning on Peru," *LAEB*, November 1995, p. 1; "Mexico Heralds Not Just Another 1982 Debt Crisis, Just a Different One," *Latin American Weekly Report* (hereafter *LAWR*) (London: January 12, 1995), p. 1; "Brazil: 'It Is Not Enough to Be Different'," *LAWR*, March 9, 1995, p. 104; Jonathan Kandell, "The Chilean Model II?" *Institutional Investor*, October 1995, pp. 267–69.

3. "Carnival Time Again for Latin Borrowers," *Euromoney*, September 1990, pp. 155–61; G. Bruce Knecht, "U.S. Banks Are Boosting Foreign Loans Despite Billions in Losses During 1980's," *Wall Street Journal*, October 5, 1995.

4. "Five Latin Ministers Embrace Free Trade," *Wall Street Journal*, September 13, 1990, p. A 18. Also see Riordan Roett, "Trends of the Trade," *Latin America Trade Finance 1995–1996*, September 1995, pp. 32–38.

5. The White House, *Enterprise for the Americas Initiative: A Vision for Economic Growth in the Western Hemisphere* (Washington, D.C.), February 1992, pp. 1–11; Robert A. Pastor, "The North American Free Trade Agreement: Hemispheric and Geopolitical Implications," *The International Executive*, Vol. 36, January-February 1994, pp. 3–31; Peter Morici, "An Architecture for Free Trade in the Americas," *Current History*, Vol. 95, February 1996, pp. 61–65.

6. Manuel R. Agosin and Ricardo Ffrench-Davis, "Trade Liberalization and Growth: Recent Experiences in Latin America," *Journal of Interamerican Studies and World Affairs*, Vol. 37, No. 3, Fall 1995, pp. 9–58; Howard J. Wiarda, "After Miami: The Summit, the Peso Crisis, and the Future of U.S.-Latin American Relations," Ibid., Vol. 37, No. 2, pp. 43–68; "Back to Beggar My Neighbour," *LAEB*, April 1995, p. 1. Also see Peter Morici, "Export Our Way to Prosperity," *Foreign Policy*, Winter 1995–96, pp. 3–17.

7. David K. Diebold and Natalie Bej, "Latin America: Trade Objectives Beyond U.S.-Mexico Negotiations," *The International Executive*, Vol. 33, July-August 1991, pp. 25–29; Thomas Kamm, "Latin Links: South American Nations Tear Down Trade Barriers, Creating a Jigsaw Puzzle of Regional Groups," *Wall Street Journal*, September 24, 1992, p. R6; Robert S. Gay, "The Americas: Forging a Free-Trade Zone," *Perspectives on the Americas*, Bankers Trust Research, July 21, 1994, p. 19; "Free Trade from Alaska to Argentina by 2005 (Maybe Sooner)," *Latin American Index*, Vol. XXIII, No. 22, December 31, 1994, pp. 1–12. Note: Chile joined Mercosur in June 1996.

8. "Oil-Mexico: A Trade-Off," *LAEB*, February 1995, p. 24; "Privatization-Mexico:

Chickens Come Home,'' Ibid., April 1995, p. 16; ''Mexico Vows to Step Up Pace and Extent of Deregulation and Privatization as Part of Program to Restore Stability,'' *Latin American Index*, Vol. XXIV, No. 2, February 5, 1995, pp. 1–8; Moises Naim, ''Mexico's Larger Story,'' *Foreign Policy*, No. 99, Summer 1995, pp. 112–30; John A. Adams, Jr., ''Window on the Future: Mexico 1996,'' *Twin Plant News*, January 1996, pp. 9–13.

9. ''Brady Strategy: Rest in Peace,'' *Wall Street Journal*, January 22, 1990, p. A1.

10. Maurice Obstfeld, ''International Currency Experience: New Lessons and Lessons Relearned,'' *Brookings Papers on Economic Activity* (Washington, D.C.: 1995), pp. 170–1. Note: In 1994 Mexico ranked fifth behind the United Kingdom, China, France, and Germany on the top ten list of ''Recipients of U.S. Manufacturing Investment,'' *Investors Business Daily*, December 21, 1995, p. A4.

11. William R. Rhodes, ''The Latin Tigers Are Ready to Roar,'' *Wall Street Journal*, December 31, 1993. Also see Pedro Aspe Armella, *El Camino Mexicano de la Transformacion Economica* (Mexico: 1993), pp. 1–214.

12. Chris Iggo, ''Latin Exotics,'' *Euromoney: The 1994 Guide to Currencies*, March 1994, pp. 2, 14; Paul Beckerman, ''Central-Bank 'Distress' and Hyperinflation in Argentina, 1889–90,'' *Journal of Latin American Studies*, Vol. 27, Part 3, October 1995, pp. 663–82; Banamex, ''Brazil, ¿Competencia para America Latina?'' *Estudios Economicos: Mercados Emergentes* (Mexico, D.F.: December 5, 1994), pp. 1–3.

13. Miguel A. Kiguel and Pablo A. Neumeyer, ''Seigniorage and Inflation: The Case of Argentina,'' *Journal of Money, Credit, and Banking*, Vol. 27, No. 3, August 1995, pp. 672–82. Note: According to 1993 GNP data, Argentina with a GNP of $244 billion, is the third largest economy in Latin America behind Brazil, $472 billion, and Mexico, $325 billion. Source: World Bank Atlas, 1995, as seen in *Investors Business Daily*, November 30, 1995, p. B1. Also see The World Bank, *Argentina: Reforms for Price Stability and Growth* (Washington, D.C.: 1990).

14. Beckerman, ''Central-Bank 'Distress','' *Journal of Latin American Studies*, p. 680. Note: Some view the Argentine ''quasi-currency board'' scheme as short-lived (notwithstanding averting a devaluation in 1995) and limited in scope because they do not have the ability to act as a lender of last resort; see Carlos Zarazaga, ''Argentina, Mexico, and Currency Boards: Another Case of Rules Versus Discretion,'' *Economic Review* (FRBD), Fourth Quarter 1995, pp. 14–24.

15. Iggo, ''Latin Exotics,'' *Euromoney*, p. 14; Oliver Grewe, ''Argentina's Foreign Trade Pattern: Mexico Redux?'' *Economic and Financial Prospects*, Swiss Bank Corporation, October-November, 1995, pp. 10–11; Scott Weeks, ''Breach of Faith: Critics of Devaluation Point to Lessons from Mexico, but Laud Argentina,'' *LatinFinance*, September 1995, pp. 47–48. See also Securities and Exchange Commission, *Annual Report of The Republic of Argentina*, Form 18–K (Washington, D.C.: November 30, 1995). Note: The Brookings Institute, in its annual 1995 report, stated that the Argentine peso has undergone a real appreciation of more than 60 percent.

16. Anthony De Palma, ''Waiting for the Other Peso to Drop,'' *New York Times*, September 18, 1994.

17. Iggo, ''Latin Exotics,'' *Euromoney*, pp. 16–17; David Malpass, ''20 Reasons Mexico Won't Devalue,'' *Latin America Watch*, Bear, Stearns & Co., April 21, 1994, pp. 7–8; Robert S. Gay, ''Too Much Pessimism on Mexico?'' *Perspectives on the Americas*, Bankers Trust Research, July 21, 1994, pp. 16–17.

18. Malpass, ''20 Reasons Mexico Won't Devalue,'' *Latin America Watch*, April 21, 1994, pp. 7–8; Debbie Galant, ''Why Wall Street Missed Mexico,'' *Institutional Investor*,

May 1995, pp. 73–76; Robert Gay, "Mexico: The Pacto and the Peso," *Bankers Trust Research*, October 6, 1994, pp. 1–4; "Panacea or Placebo: 3 Reasons Why Devaluation Won't Help," *Mexico Service*, November 18, 1994, pp. 4–5.

19. Steve H. Hanke, "Pegged Out," *Forbes*, January 16, 1995, p. 119.

20. "Mexico: Salinas's Grim Legacy," *LAEB*, February 1995, pp. 4–5; Mark Fineman, "Mexican Currency Plunges in Value," *Austin American Statesman*, December 23, 1994, p. 1; David Asman, "Mexico's Modernization: Phase II," *Wall Street Journal*, October 5, 1994, p. A16.

21. U.S. Embassy, *Mexico: Economic and Financial Report* (Mexico, D.F.: Spring 1995), pp. 1–95; "Argentina: Market Nerves Threaten Plan Cavallo," *LAEB*, October 1995, p. 6; "We Are Different from Mexico," *LA Weekly Report*, January 1995, p. 27; Gary L. Springer and Jorge L. Molina, "The Mexican Financial Crisis: Genesis, Impact, and Implications," *Journal of Interamerican Studies and World Affairs*, Vol. 37, No. 2, Summer 1995, pp. 57–81; "Latin America Learns Lessons: Sober Reactions Prevent Hangover from 'Tequila Effect'," *Washington Post*, June 4, 1995, p. A8. Note: Argentina and Brazil were the two primary countries singled out by the Federal Reserve as being adversely impacted by the Mexican crisis; see *Federal Reserve Bulletin*, Vol. 81, No. 3, March 1995, p. 242, and Vol. 81, No. 8, August 1995, p. 764.

22. "Zedillo's Second Economic Package," *LAEB*, April 1995, pp. 4–5; Knight-Ridder, "Mexico Peso Focus: Catharsis in 1995, Stability in 1996?" Wire Service Report, December 19, 1995, pp. 1–9. Note: Serra was replaced by former Secretary of Communications and Transportation Guillermo Ortiz. For details of the U.S. response, see U.S. Congress, Senate, Committee on Banking, Housing, and Urban Affairs, *The Peso Crisis and the Administration's Proposed Loan Guarantee Package for Mexico*, S. Hrg. 104–164, 104th Cong., 1st sess., 1995.

23. U.S. Department of the Treasury, "Statement of Treasury Secretary Robert E. Rubin: Mexico Agreement Signing Ceremony," Washington, D.C., February 21, 1995; Ibid., "Guarantee Agreement among the United States Department of the Treasury and the Government of the United Mexican States," February 21, 1995. Note: Under the guidelines of the Mexican Disclosure Act of 1995, the Secretary of the Treasury, "on behalf of the president," is required to provide the Congress a monthly report on the status of the Mexican crisis.

24. Knight-Ridder: "Clinton Pleads for U.S. Congress to Approve Mexico Aid Package," January 25, 1995; "Greenspan's Prepared Testimony to the House on Mexico," January 25, 1995; "Congress May Convene to Discuss aid [to Mexico]" (New York and Mexico City), February 6, 1995; Statement by Alan Greenspan, Chairman, Board of Governors of the Federal Reserve System, before the Committee on Foreign Relations, U.S. Senate, January 26, 1995, as seen in the *Federal Reserve Bulletin*, Vol. 81, No. 3, March 1995, pp. 261–64. Note: At year-end 1995, $13.5 billion had been advanced by the U.S. Treasury from the ESF and $13.5 billion had been provided by the IMF: the combined total was $27 billion.

25. OECD, *Mexico 1994–95: OECD Economic Surveys* (Paris: September 1995), pp. 1–154. Note: The OECD, established in 1961, is primarily charged with trade expansion and economic growth. In an effort to expand regional trade initiatives Argentina is a member of an OECD subgroup known as DNMEs—Dynamic Non-Member Economies. Other members include Brazil, Chile, Chinese Taipei, Hong Kong, Malaysia, Singapore, and Thailand. See *OECD Letter*, October 1995, Vol. 4/8.

26. Gordon Matthews, "Jitters over Argentina Hit Shares of Boston Bank," *American*

Banker, Vol. CLX, No. 44, p. 1; Calvin Sims, "Argentina, a Victim of Mexico's Fall, Tries to Recover," *New York Times*, March 12, 1995, p. F14; Jorge A. Vilches, "Argentina Holds Out Against Short-Sighted Shorts," *Wall Street Journal*, March 17, 1995, p. A11; Matt Moffett and Jonathan Friedland, "The Big Game: Taking a Huge Risk, Argentina Intentionally Deflates Its Economy," Ibid., March 21, 1995; Robert S. Gay and Patricia Artigas, "Argentina's Great Gambit," *Bankers Trust Research*, March 29, 1995, pp. 1–11.

27. "A Conversation with Domingo Cavallo," *Financial World*, February 1, 1994; " 'Not Mexico' This Time Figures: Bid to Make Convertibility More Credible," *LAWR*, January 26, 1995, p. 35; "Play on the Fear of Devaluation," *LAWR*, p. 39; Knight-Ridder, "Argentina Reportedly Secures 1 bln dlrs from Privatization," November 9, 1995, p. 1; Matt Moffett and Jonathan Friedland, "Argentina Is Seeking More IMF Funding As Fallout from Mexico Crisis Continues," *Wall Street Journal*, March 10, 1995, p. A10.

28. Carl W. Ross, "Argentina: Politics and Unemployment Are Lingering Problems," *Bankers Trust Research*, October 20, 1995, pp. 1–3; "Argentina: Worries Mount—Fiscal Deficit and Unemployment," *LAEB*, January 1995, p. 6; "Argentina: On a Wing and a Prayer," Ibid., February 1995, p. 6; Jonathan Friedland, "Foreign Investors Bet on a Bright Future for Argentina Despite Recent Woes," *Wall Street Journal*, May 21, 1995. Note: Argentines are likely to accept high unemployment in exchange for price and exchange rate stability, due to generous unemployment compensation programs that offer 18 months' pay, thus acting as a disincentive to active job search and reemployment.

29. Norman Peagan, "Argentine Banks Face a New World," *Euromoney*, March 1994, pp. 98–99; "Argentina: The Banking Crisis," *LAEB*, April 1995, p. 6; "Memen Triumphs," Ibid., p. 6; "Expensive Crutches," *The Economist*, April 8, 1995, p. 66. Note: Citibank and Bank of Boston have a large retail banking operation in Argentina; subsidiary arrangements are conducted by American Express Bank, Bank of America, Chase, Chemical, Morgan, Bankers Trust, Republic National, Bank of New York, Norwest, and Firstar Bank of Milwaukee.

30. "Savers Redefine 'Safe'," *LAWR*, May 4, 1995, p. 182. Note: Uruguay has a very small undeveloped capital market and meager investment indicators to include: 45 percent inflation, a trade deficit that has more than doubled in the past two years to nearly $900 million, a fiscal deficit which doubled to 10 percent of GDP, and a rapidly growing external debt, accumulating since 1991, of $9 billion.

31. Knight-Ridder, "Argentine Banks Reduced," January 5, 1996; Ibid., "Argentine Central Bank Head Says Banking System Inefficient," January 2, 1996.

32. Miguel Angel Ortiz, "Argentina: Banking Profile," *LatinFinance*, November 1995, Supplement, pp. 6–7; "The Banking Crisis," *LAEB*, p. 6; "Jittery: Bank Deposits Say It All," Ibid., July 1995, p. 6; Lisa Sedelnik, "Ahead of the Curve," *Latin Finance*, October 1995, p. 65; Carl W. Ross, "Argentina's Provinces: The Last Bastions of Statism and Big Government," *Bankers Trust Research*, June 28, 1995, pp. 1–3. Note: Argentine provinces receive roughly 50 percent of VAT revenues collected by the federal government.

33. "Tough Time: Cavallo Haggles with the IMF," *LAEB*, September 1995, p. 6; "Tax Fall Gives Cavallo IMF Headache," Ibid., November 1995, p. 6; Knight-Ridder, "Argentina Will 'More Than Comply' with IMF Targets," December 1, 1995, p. 1. Note: At year-end 1995, past-due tax obligations exceeded $2 billion.

34. "Back from the Brink," *LAEB*, April 1995, p. 6; "The Banking Crisis," Ibid.,

May 1995, p. 6; "Cavallo's SOS," *The Banker*, April 1995, p. 96; "Argentina Calls on Banks for $1bn 'Support' Bond to Emphasize Confidence," *Euroweek*, March 24, 1995, p. 33.

35. "The Return of the Rescheduler," *LAEB*, October 1995, p. 1; Paul Kilby, "Argentina Makes Its Mark," *Latin Finance*, October 1995, p. 57; Ariel Berschadsky and Carl W. Ross, "A New Trading Range for the Argentine/Mexican Par Bond Spread," *Perspectives on Emerging Markets*, Bankers Trust Research, June 2, 1995, pp. 14–15; Knight Ridder, "Argentina Confirms $350 Million Loan Deal with J. P. Morgan," January 2, 1996. Also see Robert Gay and Patricia Artiga, "Argentina's Great Gambit," Ibid., March 29, 1995, and Andrew Brady, "Trading Points," *Barron's*, February 28, 1994, p. 54. Note: The principal payments on Brady bonds are secured by the U.S. Treasury but interest payments are the obligation of Argentina.

36. Owen F. Humpage and Jean M. McIntire, "An Introduction to Currency Boards," *Economic Review*, Federal Reserve Bank of Cleveland, Vol. 31, No. 2, 1995, pp. 2–11. For a detailed overview on the evolution of the currency board, see Anne J. Schwartz, "Currency Boards: Their Past, Present, and Possible Future Role," *Carnegie-Rochester Conference Series on Public Policy*, Vol. 39, December 1993, pp. 429–59.

37. Steve H. Hanke, "Why Argentina Is Solid," *Forbes*, May 8, 1995, p. 42; "Argentina Tests the Currency Board," *LAEB*, March 1995, p. 1; Robert L. Hetzel, "Currency Boards: A Comment," *Carnegie-Rochester Conference Series on Public Policy*, Vol. 39, December 1993, pp. 189–93. Note: Countries with or considering a currency board include Hong Kong, El Salvador, Singapore, Estonia, Malaysia, the Philippines, and Panama (dollarized economy). For a contrary view of the historical impact of the gold standard, see Christopher J. Neeley and Goeffrey E. Wood, "Deflation and Real Economic Activity Under the Gold Standard," Federal Reserve Bank of St. Louis, *Review*, Vol. 77, No. 5, September-October, pp. 27–37.

38. Knight-Ridder, "Sachs Says Convertibility Deepened Argentine Recession," December 13, 1995; Guillermo Calvo, *Money, Exchange Rates, and Output* (Cambridge: 1996), pp. 127–175. Note: The Phillips Curve is a graph that *attempts* to show the menu of choices an economy has in seeking an acceptable balance between unemployment and inflation.

39. Ali Qassim, "Peso Panic," *The Banker*, March 1995, pp. 43–44; "Expensive Crutches," *The Economist*, April 8, 1995, p. 66; Ross, "A New Trading Range for the Argentine/Mexican Par Bond Spread," *Perspectives*, June 2, 1995, pp. 14–15; "Backlash Ripples Across Region," *Financial Times* (London), October 6, 1995.

40. "The World Bank and Argentina," *LAEB*, July 1995, p. 28; Steve H. Hanke, "The Great Modernizer," *Forbes*, September 11, 1995, pp. 126–30; Knight-Ridder, "Forecasters Bullish," January 3, 1996; Ibid., "Argentine December CPI up 0.1% vs. November," January 4, 1996; "Menem: The Devil's Real Name is Devaluation," *Business Week*, August 28, 1995, p. 45.

41. Steve H. Hanke, "The Curse of Central Banking," *Forbes*, September 25, 1995, p. 72; Grewe, "Argentina's Foreign Trade Pattern: Mexico Redux?" Ibid., pp. 10–11.

42. Scott Weeks, "Breach of Faith," *Latin Finance*, September 1995, p. 47; "The Mexico Syndrome, and How to Steer Clear of It," *The Economist*, March 18, 1995; Roberto Salinas-Leon, "The Importance of Money," *Journal of Commerce*, October 16, 1996, p. 6A.

43. U.S. Congress, Committee on Banking, Housing, and Urban Affairs, David Hale, "Emerging Markets After the Mexican Crisis," *The Peso Crisis and the Administration's*

Loan Guarantee Package for Mexico, S. Hrg. 104–164, 104th Cong., 1st sess., 1995, p. 92.

44. Knight-Ridder. "Cavallo Admits Argentina's Banks Still Hurt from Mexico," December 1, 1995, pp. 1–3; Ibid., "Argentina Today," November 14, 1995, p. 1; Pablo Mass, "Argentina: Business Outlook," *Business Latin America* (London), December 11, 1995, pp. 4–5; Michael Tangeman, "The Once, and Future, Banking Crisis?" *Institutional Investor*, November 1995, pp. 119–25; Sara Calian, "Emerging-Market Funds Are Reviving," *Wall Street Journal*, January 19, 1996, p. C23; Palacio National: Estados Unidos Mexicanos, "Oficina del Vocero Economico Alejandro Valenzuela" (Mexico, D.F., January 10, 1996); Steve Hanke, "Mexico Still Needs a Currency Board," *Wall Street Journal*, February 22, 1995; and for a contrary view, see William R. Cline, "Mexico Too Leveraged to Set Up Monetary Board," *Financial Times* (London), February 28, 1995; "Mexico and Argentina," *Review of the Economic Situation of Mexico*, No. 850, September 1996, pp. 301–8.

45. *The Economist*, April 8, 1995, p. 66.

46. Gabriel Escobar, "Argentine Economic Czar Ousted," *Washington Post*, July 27, 1996, p. A20; Calvin Sims, "President Ousts Finance Chief in Argentina," *New York Times*, July 27, 1996, p. 21; Jonathan Friedland, "Argentine Finance Chief Faces Dilemma," *Wall Street Journal*, July 29, 1996, p. A8; Jeb Blount, "Cavallonomics without Cavallo?" *Latin Trade*, October 1996, pp. 30–32.

Chapter 9

Back from the Abyss

By virtue of history, character and ambition, Mexican people do not easily give in nor do they allow their fundamental unity to become weak. From the moment the crisis broke out, we Mexicans took action with clear vision and determination, with fortitude and with discipline. We were aware then, as we are now, that we would only overcome the adversity with effort and perseverance.

—Ernesto Zedillo, April 16, 1996

The recovery of the Mexican economy and banking system is pivotal to the stability of both Mexico and financial markets worldwide. The events of the past decade are instructive given the impact and influence of the emerging Mexican economy on world markets. Because the Mexican model has been so extensively watched, so widely emulated, and is so salient in the minds of investors, what happens in Mexico has implications that go far beyond Mexico, or even Latin America.[1] The response to the 1994–96 Mexican recovery is as important as the events that caused the currency crisis. Given the fact that the economic fundamentals were relatively sound during much of the early 1990's, Mexico has been able to gradually recoup at a surprising pace from the worst recession since 1932. In the wake of efforts to tighten domestic credit, increase the rate of savings, maintain wage restraint, shore up the banking sector, and reduce the federal budget, Mexico did not interfere with a critical emphasis to allow the free flow of imports and exports. Unlike previous economic disruptions, barriers (both tariff and nontariff) were not placed on imports. It had become a standard solution in Mexico to address domestic economic problems with exorbitant import duties and exchange controls—both slowing recovery and undermining the banking sector.[2]

Figure 9-1
Mexico Stabilization Funds: 1995 (Millions of U.S. Dollars)

	USA	Canada	Spain	IMF	Total
January 11	500	59	-	-	599
13	500	59	-	-	599
31	-	-	1,000	-	1,000
February 2	2,000	237	(1,000)	-	1,237
6	-	-	-	7,725	7,725
March 14	(1,000)	(118)	-	-	(1,118)
14	3,000	-	-	-	3,000
April 19	3,000	-	-	-	3,000
May 19	2,000	-	-	-	2,000
July 5	2,500	-	-	-	2,500
6	-	-	-	2,023	2,023
24	-	-	-	-	-
August 1	(2,000)	-	-	-	(2,000)
1	2,000	-	-	-	2,000
28	-	-	-	1,643	1,643
October 13	(700)	(83)	-	-	(783)
December 20	-	-	-	1,633	1,633
Total	**11,800**	**154**	**0**	**12,024**	**24,978**

Sources: Banco de Mexico; U.S. Department of the Treasury.

While exports from the United States to Mexico sharply declined in 1995 (contracting 10 percent, following a 21 percent increase in 1994), southbound American goods demonstrated modest increases in 1996. Correspondingly, there was a significant drop in 1995–96 of foreign imports from Europe and Asia. Maintaining an open-market approach in the wake of the peso crisis was the direct result of the market access parameters embodied in the North American Free Trade Agreement as well as the Zedillo administration's ongoing strategy to open, stabilize, and further globalize the Mexican economy. The export-import policies were directly tied to improvements in the economy. Evidence of an economic turnaround is oftentimes transparent in the evolving stages, yet in the case of Mexico clear signs of recovery were evident by early 1996.[3] Compared with the sharp economic decline during the first half of 1995, the recovery appeared in its earliest stages to be very gradual. Nonetheless, such seemingly rapid recovery somewhat surprised and pleased the capital markets and international monetary agencies that prepared the U.S.-IMF financial recovery package in early 1995. These agencies were some of the same groups that missed and/or failed to recognize and plan for the advent of the 1994 devaluation. Of the total $50 billion U.S.–IMF aid package, only a little over half— $27.8 billion—was used by Mexico, and this high outstanding balance was reduced to $20 billion by mid-1996. Although some members of the G-7 disagree with the expanded role of the IMF, by default, the Mexican crisis solidified the role of the IMF as the lender of last resort to the third world during liquidity crises (see Figure 9-1).[4]

The Mexican economic recovery, while not accomplished in a vacuum, is not complete without a perspective on the disruption created in the surrounding domestic economic and social structure. For the past ten years Mexico has been a country in transition. Economic reform, political intrigue, the advent of open markets and "free trade" as well as global significance of Mexican industrial production and investor opportunities have forever altered Mexico's position among emerging industrial nations. In this segment the focus will be on an assessment of those trends, lessons, and opportunities that will have an influence on Mexico for the balance of the decade and beyond. Emphasis will center on the banking, investment, and commercial aspects of Mexico's future—fully mindful of concerns such as the political, environmental, and social changes constantly in process. There will be no shortage of books and inquiry dealing with these equally important aspects as the full measure of the transition of Mexico over the past decade is researched and analyzed in the years to come.[5]

As has been discussed, a number of variables have impacted the varying course of Mexico's recent roller-coaster path of economic stability and instability over the past two decades. Such variables or trends have tremendous significance on the future course of the Mexican economy and provide a benchmark for future responses to currency crisis in other emerging countries. The lessons of the Mexican economic experience and crisis as well as the stability of the currency markets and banking system depend substantially on the following: (1) the openness of the investment regime, (2) the soundness of the banking sector, (3) the return of predevaluation levels of foreign direct investment, (4) the prospect for and safeguards against future devaluations, and (5) the influence of external interest rates on the ability of the Mexican economy (and government) to cope with the pressures and risks of global factors that could impact the course of the nation's economic policy and security. In so doing, Mexico has emerged as a barometer for investment and growth potential for all of Latin America, as well as a gage for economic development for emerging nations worldwide.[6]

INVESTMENT

The crisis of 1994–95 has resulted in Mexico emerging as one of the most open investment areas of Latin America. Thus, the path to full, if there is such a level, economic recovery in Mexico will be measured largely in the degree of both domestic and foreign investor confidence. The importance of both direct and portfolio investment to the growth of the Mexican economy is paramount to the recovery and stability of the banking sector. In late February 1996, a Mexican government spokesman boldly declared the economic recession to be over. The significance of such a declaration, on the first annual anniversary of the U.S.–IMF-orchestrated loan package was an implied attempt—holding much symbolism for Mexico—to put the past in perspective and concentrate on the future. Although the economic indicators and statistics may not have fully supported such a claim, foreign investment in the Mexican Bolsa increased 15 percent in the first quarter of 1996. In spite of the fact that direct foreign investment fell over 50 percent in 1995 to $4.5 billion, Mexico posted an overall $7.3 billion trade surplus (representing only about two-tenths of 1 percent of the U.S. GDP), the first since 1990. And in spite of the 1995 economic crisis, Mexico remained the third largest U.S. export market, behind Canada and Japan. Many forget that Mexico, while in the crisis recovery mode during 1995, continued to outperform all but a few nations. Furthermore, Mexico, according to Finance Secretary Guillermo Ortiz, met the two major challenges in the post-devaluation crisis period: adjustment of the current account imbalance and the repayment of a high percentage of the short-term, dollar-denominated debt—thus, the troublesome 1994–95 $30 billion in tesobono debt was retired by the end of the first quarter of 1996.[7]

By 1996, Mexico maintained a more stable monetary policy and budgetary controls than in 1994–95. Austerity measures resulted in high interest rates, a weak currency, high tax rates, limited government spending, and wage controls, all intended to hold down domestic consumption and imports. Rising consumer interest rates that exceeded 100 percent in 1995 dropped to 30 percent by mid-1996. The bellwether 28–day CETES were at 25 percent by July. Additionally, Mexico looked to the indirect external markets to initially stimulate the economy. During the last half of 1995, Mexico sold seven large bond capitalization packages in the international market. The first foray in the U.S. bond market since 1994 occurred in January 1996 with an offering of $1 billion of five-year dollar-denominated bonds. The bonds were priced at par to yield 9.75 percent (U.S. Treasury bills at the time were yielding 5.30 percent). During 1996 Mexico raised over $15 billion in long-term debt to retire more expensive short-term debt and to reduce interest costs. As Mexico strives to restructure its debt, 1997–1999 will involve significant capital investments. In addition to the reentry into world capital markets, the recovery was fueled by the inflow of hard currency from two distinct industrial sectors: the domestic Mexican manufacturing export sector and the growing maquiladora industries.[8]

Further evidence of the strong recovery potential of the economy is the globalization of a number of Mexico's key industries since the late 1980's and early 1990's. The growth of a solid, diversified industrial base proved vital to weathering the 1994–95 recession and diminished liquidity constraints that cause business disruption. Select Mexican industrial and commodity products were especially in demand worldwide. At a time when the domestic economy was contracting, Mexican producers of products ranging from cement and steel to bulk tortilla and tequila exports were able to diversify into new or expanded global markets.[9] The composition of Mexican exports in the 1990's is a far cry from the days when petroleum sales dominated over two-thirds of the economy. By 1996 the export composition was very broad—manufactured goods accounted for 82 percent, oil and oil products 11 percent, and agricultural goods 7 percent. However, the export-led surge by the large multinational Mexican firms did not lessen the strain on a number of other key sectors. Hardest hit were the small and medium-sized businesses as well as the domestic construction industry that could not obtain either loans at reasonable rates nor had the ability to break into international markets to earn hard-currency income.[10]

While some languished in the shadow of the 1994–95 recession, the maquiladora sector had the largest growth year in the history of the three-decade-old, Mexican-originated production-sharing program. Rivaling only the income generated by the export of oil products and the fortunes of the Mexican tourism industry, the maquila sector took full advantage of the peso devaluation and opened over 400 new locations and expanded operations at 625 facilities in 1995. The attractiveness of Mexican production sites, improved infrastructure enhancements during the early 1990s, moderate utility cost, and low relative unit labor cost as well as the use of Mexico as an export base of operations attracted billions of dollars in foreign investment away from competitive locations in El Salvador, Chile, Venezuela, Costa Rica, and emerging locations on the Pacific Rim. The unexpected windfall of direct foreign investment in new and expanded maquiladoras is expected to continue for the balance of the decade. Moreover, direct investment in new facilities and expansion of existing operations is expected to exceed $10 billion during 1996–97 and $45 billion by the year 2000. U.S. firms and investors will inject over half of the new investment resources and the balance will be equally divided between European and Asia investors. Maquila employment by the year 2000 will jump from 700,000 to over 1 million due to the increase in manufacturing facilities from 2,200 in 1996 to over 3,000 by the end of the decade. The ability to sell maquila products in the domestic Mexican market as well as the continuing worldwide demand will further encourage enhanced production methods, speed new technology transfer, and insure a steady flow of much-needed foreign direct investment.[11]

Two trends to watch will be whether other emerging markets are able to attract both portfolio and direct investment away from Mexico, and the impact of transfer pricing taxation rules on the competitiveness and profitability of offshore manufacturing in Mexico. While Mexico is well positioned during the balance of the decade compared to other countries in Latin America, the primary competition for investor funds will be with emerging markets in Eastern Europe and Asia. U.S. export performance in Latin America during the 1980's was significantly impeded by the geographic concentration of investment in East and Southeast Asia, where Japanese firms enjoyed a competitive advantage via keiretsu (industrial group) investments. As the economies of Latin America improved by the early 1990's, there was an imperceptible but substantial shift in U.S. investment. Thus, closer to home, Mexico will be for some years to come the bellwether for the nations of Latin America. The downside phenomenon of the "Tequila Effect" of 1994–95 will have a corresponding positive upside during the good economic times of the late 1990's—a prosperous Mexico will allow other economies in the region to follow suit. Furthermore, as Mexico becomes more creditworthy, U.S. investors, many of which perceive there is a special, protected relationship between the two countries, will return in force. Signs of this were evident as early as the second quarter of 1996.[12]

The second item that could impact investment in the maquila manufacturing sector will be the reaction to and the implementation of a taxation framework for transfer pricing—the costing of intrafirm transfers on goods, services, and production-related intangibles. As joint U.S.–Mexico tax talks evolved during the early 1990's, transfer pricing was one concept that Mexican officials quickly embraced. The Mexican taxing authority, the Secretaria de Hacienda y Credito Publico (''the Hacienda'')—well aware of the importance of hard foreign currency generated by the maquiladora industry—looked to expand further sources of tax revenues. The Mexican intent has been to gradually replicate U.S. tax standards. The United States has had one of the most complex corporate tax regimes in the world for multinationals engaged in the manufacturing processes which have a high concentration of transfer pricing. Since 1991, Mexico has worked to incorporate transfer pricing standards in its tax code that correspond with world standards of other OECD members, most specifically the United States.[13] Mexico's interest in addressing transfer pricing is threefold: (1) replication of world tax standards in the expanding multinational production sector, (2) develop limits on the multinational's ability to engage in valuation manipulation due to transfer pricing accounting, and (3) as federal budgets are tightened, transfer pricing taxation is a lucrative source of much-needed revenue. Mexico's efforts closely parallel U.S. intracorporate transfer tax regulations found in Section 482 of the U.S. Income Tax Code. The initial Mexican regulations were in place by 1992, and by 1994 agents of the Hacienda began the first multinational transfer pricing audits. As of January 1995, the Hacienda determined that maquiladora operations should charge an ''arm's length'' price for the services they provide to their U.S. affiliates. The maquiladora sector has been the prime target of such audits as the gradual concept of ''production cost'' incurred at maquila facilities shifts under the accounting treatment from cost to profit centers. Historically, cost center accounting has been exempt from most annual Mexican corporate income, inventory, and asset taxation. In 1995 the maquila tax exemptions began to be phased out. As Mexico enhances its implementation of audits on transfer pricing, tax revenues from maquilas will be shifted from the United States (or foreign parent) to Mexico, effectively redirecting or reducing U.S. tax revenues.[14]

Problems arise with the transfer pricing tax efforts due mainly to concerns on how to compare the typical financial components and profitability of a maquila with the balance sheets of nonmaquila manufacturers. The OECD guidelines advocate a cost-plus approach, since most maquiladoras are paid on a ''time and material'' basis, recognizing the fact that their upstream operations manufacture or partially assemble component parts for the final downstream assembly location elsewhere. Moreover, since the U.S. parent company generally receives a full foreign tax credit for the taxes paid offshore in Mexico, the means by which transfer pricing is calculated could make it a noncreditable expense against the parent company's U.S. tax obligation. Thus, the implementation and impact assessments on transfer pricing taxation have become a major foreign corporate concern in Mexico since late 1994. As Mexican transfer pricing regulations increasingly resemble the U.S. tax code, the likelihood for at least partial implementation is expected by 1997–98. From 1998 until 2001, rules will be solidified in advance of the 2001 market access modifications under NAFTA. While concern has been expressed by many multinationals, compliance with the transfer pricing requirements should not diminish the viability of both competitive and profitable maquiladora manufacturing and assembly operations in Mexico. Furthermore, direct foreign investment in a broad cross-section of the Mexican economy will include expanded market entry under NAFTA, which will eliminate nearly all investment and cross-border service restrictions in value-added services such as telecommunications, food processing, railroads, natural gas transportation, electrical generation, and limited sections of the oil industry. Thus, one key to investment in Mexico is to become familiar with the continuing changes in the market access and taxation rules.[15]

One additional item is a yet to be fully interpreted official statement by the Mexican government in the October 23, 1996 issue of the *Diario Official* that outlines what may become crucial guidelines for all future treatment of maquila operations. This decree effectively amends the Maquiladora Law of December 22, 1989 and modifications made on December 24, 1993 prior to the implementation of NAFTA. Key elements of the new decree bring into question (1) the amount of production a maquila facility can sell directly into the domestic market—when such activities "affect the national non-maquiladora industry," (2) provisions to suspend a manufactures maquila permit, (3) import and export quotas, as well as (4) clear implications on the tax treatment of all portions of maquila operations. Given the provisions in NAFTA to allow the phased increase with which maquilas can sell in the Mexican domestic market from 1994–2000, there could be a clear conflict in both the spirit and letter of the new decree with trade accords currently in place.

The repercussions of October 1996 maquila amendments are hard to measure, as is the full rational behind its seemingly punitive treatment of maquiladoras. The introduction of the decree could be the reaction to concern over a number of seemingly unconnected items. While Mexico is concerned about the domestic economic recovery, they are also concerned with "sovereignty" issues and the impact of foreign investment and market share on the political, social, and economic framework. Additionally, the new regulation adds more teeth to generate an untouched source of additional tax revenue that is sorely in demand by the central government. Lastly, indirect irritation in Mexico over the Helms-Burton Act restricting trade with Cuba, as well as the ongoing fight over exportation of tomatoes and avocados (not allowed in the United States for over 81 years) could have contributed to the hard line by the Mexican government.

The new maquiladora decree could be an indication that hardliners in the PRI would like to reject the aggressive market-oriented reform during the 1990s. The July 1997 national elections in Mexico will have significant impact on the economic policy. If the PRI is soundly returned to offices nationwide, it could bring about a resurgence in nationalism that further rejects the policies of the neo-liberal technocrats to further privatize and open the economy. Given the impact of the maquila sector on the Mexican economy it is difficult to envision any moves that would cause investors to look elsewhere.

DEVALUATION AND DEBT

Devaluation and debt have been the twin hallmarks of economic instability not only in Mexico but in most of Latin America for decades. International efforts—first by the money center banks after World War II and in the past two decades by international monetary agencies, managed jointly by the International Monetary Fund, World Bank, Bank of International Settlements—have worked to foretell as well as forestall economic precariousness and currency developments that have radical consequences. Mexico has averaged a radical currency devaluation or debt crisis every six years over the past three decades, and in December 1994 essentially lost control over its short-term economic destiny. This cycle has been driven by numerous factors: a common thread of uncontrolled debt (internal and external), periods of rising external interest rates, ineffective government leadership, overvaluation of the peso, uncontrolled inflation, and a poor understanding of the ramifications of short-term portfolio investments. These same factors at varying times have also combined to stagnate much of the Latin American region.[16]

Exchange rate policies, particularly in Mexico, have had a distinct political overtone, as each successive government since the early 1960's has attempted to balance nationalism, limited foreign ownership, development of natural resources, and growth with boom and bust economic cycles (see Figure 9-2). Oftentimes these actions were based on poor assumptions and triggered by external events over which Mexico had little or no control—such as the oil embargo of 1973–74, the demise of oil markets in the mid-1980's, and rising interest rates in the United States during 1994. With these historical events in mind, the government and central bank are acutely aware of the economic challenges. Finance Minister Ortiz noted that in addition to the stability of the banking sector, care will always be needed in the management of the currency markets: "the expected flow of foreign investment in the country, a very probable positive trade balance, a favorable public debt-payment schedule are elements to reduce the risk of pressure on the peso exchange rate."[17]

Thus, it should be anticipated that there would be a great deal of analytical assistance to prevent or reduce a future volatile currency crisis. In the case of Mexico, numerous efforts have been made to monitor debt levels, inflation, investment, and budgets in hopes of avoiding the debacle of radical devaluation. The pegged or managed exchange rate system, notwithstanding the high growth rate and tremendous influx of direct foreign investment, was expected to be a means to stabilize the economy. It was hoped or assumed that the "technocrats" of the late 1980's and early 1990's had in some way studied and learned from

Figure 9-2
Mexico: Peso Value, 1900–97

Years	Pesos per dollar	Years	Pesos per dollar	Years	Pesos per dollar
1900	2.06	1933	3.50 [3]	1965	12.50
1901	2.11	1934	3.60	1966	12.50
1902	2.39	1935	3.60	1967	12.50
1903	2.38	1936	3.60	1968	12.50
1904	1.99	1937	3.60	1969	12.50
1905	2.02	1938	4.52 [4]	1970	12.50
1906	1.99	1939	5.19	1971	12.50
1907	2.01	1940	5.40 [5]	1972	12.50
1908	2.01	1941	4.85	1973	12.50
1909	2.01	1942	4.85	1974	12.50
1910	2.01	1943	4.85	1975	12.50
1911	2.01	1944	4.85	1976	19.95
1912	2.01	1945	4.85	1977	22.73
1913	2.08	1946	4.85	1978	22.72
1914	3.30 [1]	1947	4.85	1979	22.80
1915	11.15 [2]	1948	5.74 [6]	1980	23.25
1916	23.83	1949	8.01 [7]	1981	26.22
1917	1.91	1950	8.65	1982	96.48 [9]
1918	1.81	1951	8.65	1983	143.93
1919	1.99	1952	8.65	1984	192.60
1920	2.01	1953	8.65	1985	371.70
1921	2.04	1954	11.34 [8]	1986	923.50
1922	2.05	1955	12.50	1987	2,209.70
1923	2.06	1956	12.50	1988	2,281.00
1924	2.07	1957	12.50	1989	2,641.00
1925	2.03	1958	12.50	1990	2,945.40
1926	2.07	1959	12.50	1991	3,071.00
1927	2.12	1960	12.50	1992	3,110.00
1928	2.08	1961	12.50	1993	3.10 [10]
1929	2.15	1962	12.50	1994	3.25
1930	2.26	1963	12.50	1995	6.42
1931	2.65	1964	12.50	1996	7.75 [11]
1932	3.16	1965	12.50	1997	8.25 [11]

1. First semester, 2.24 national gold; second semester, 4.36 paper money.
2. Paper money (1915 & 1916).
3. 3.60 until November 8, 1933.
4. 3.60 until March 18, 1938.
5. 4.85 from October 1, 1940.
6. 4.85 until June 21, 1948.
7. 8.65 from June 18, 1949.
8. Arithmetical average of exchange rates: 8.65 until April 18, 1954 and 12.50 from April 19, 1954.
9. Four major devaluations: February, August, September and November.
10. On 1 January 1993 the "nuevo peso" was implemented to a one digit value.
11. Forecast: Values for 1996–1997 are annual average exchange rates (peso/$).

Sources: 1900 to 1928: *Anuario Estadistico de los Estados Mexicanos*, 1941, p. 934.
1929 to 1964: Banco de Mexico, S.A.
1965 to 1993: *Statistical Abstract of Latin America*, Vol. 30, part 2, p. 1140.

past devaluations and debt crises. Economic growth, respect among their peers, and investor confidence were critical to Mexico in the decade of the 1990's. There was no better spokesman than the dynamic presentations by a host of young, U.S.-trained Mexican politicians and business entrepreneurs. An entire generation of leadership—Salinas, Zedillo, Serra Puche, Aspe, Zabludovsky, among others—had been prepared, both educationally and by service in the corporate sector and the Mexican government, to open the Mexican economy, gain global investor recognition, and smooth out the peaks and valleys of the Mexican economic roller coaster.[18]

The "Mexican Miracle" was to be the legacy of the technocrats, buoyed by a neoclassical economic policy. A series of PACTOs to maintain harmony between labor, management, and the government set a "crawling peg" against the dollar to stabilize the peso and reduce inflation. It was not that the policy was flawed, rather the pegged exchange rate was not adhered to. Wages, interest rates, prices, and the currency were increasingly indexed to inflation. A sweeping privatization-diversification-investment strategy was developed to lift the Mexican industrial base to recognized world-class standards. An emphasis on intense foreign investment and low inflation was seen as the twin pivotal solution to avoid the debt crisis of the 1970's and 1980's. Additionally, diversification of the Mexican export mix away from a concentration on oil exports and privatization was seen as a key to attracting more multinational investment in Mexico. In late 1994, against the backdrop of one of the most rapidly expanding economies, a liquidity crisis, due in large measure to the overvalued peso and short-term nature of foreign portfolio investment, shattered the dreams and plans of the neoliberal technocrats. The very success of the economy, the investment atmosphere, and the implied "image" of a stable risk environment in Mexico lay foundered in an old-school approach via rigid domestic politics and egos that failed to respond to repeated indicators of the pending demise of the peso. The fragile economic dynamics associated with capital flows, interest rates, and debt payments were overlooked in the rush to promote investment in Mexico. One clear example of a little-noticed financial market fluctuation that has had and will continue to have dramatic impact is the fact that a one percentage-point increase in the cost of capital equals an increase of $1.6 billion in annual Mexican debt service, assuming all debt were at a floating rate. A reduction in the level of the internal and external debt will be paramount to a determination of the chances for potential future debt default. The cost to the economy, in terms of development and growth, given the impact of such interest rate rises as well as to investor confidence, is enormous and erratic. Interest rate swings coupled with the capacity of investors to instantaneously move funds to markets with either/or less risk or higher yields proved volatile not only to Mexico, but also to a host of emerging markets worldwide.[19]

All indications are that the Mexican government and central bank have been placed under close monitoring by the International Monetary Fund and World Bank as well as observers from the U.S. Treasury. Beyond the stabilization of economy and currency in the most recent post-1994 devaluation, these external monetary agencies have begun an extensive new era of international currency management, monetary policies oversight, and debt-service review in Mexico that far exceeds any previous efforts.[20] Critical elements recommended for economic recovery and to prevent future devaluations include expanding the tax base, a flexible value-added tax (VAT), external debt reduction, further streamlining of governmental budgets at all levels, and enhanced programs to encourage (or mandate) increased domestic savings. The role of the "PACTO" concept in Mexico, the intention to indirectly develop a consensus over a semi-managed economy will receive extensive review during the balance of the decade. One option is to restructure the national economic development plan around the Industrial Policy and International Foreign Trade Program drafted in May 1996 by the Zedillo administration.[21] This new industrial program, yet to be proven, resembles the framework developed by the Ministry of International Trade and Industry or MITI during the 1970's in Japan.

Closely associated with the stability of the peso is the relevancy of a currency board scheme, most often touted by the 1995–96 Argentine experience. To fix the value of the peso directly to the dollar is viewed as politically shortsighted in such a potentially volatile economy and has yet to be substantiated. The importance and relevance of once seemingly benign indicators, such as large current account shortfalls, especially if they are justified by large foreign investment and presumable positive domestic growth, were forever changed by the Mexican crisis of 1994–95. And economic enhancement to lessen dependence on foreign capital flows would be the gain from a second wave of privatization of the final portion of government-owned businesses and facilities. New private investment in the air and seaports, railroads, chemical firms, and closely held petroleum sector has the potential to net the government $100 billion by the year 2000. Furthermore, the de facto forward trading of peso futures on the Chicago Mercantile has made tremendous strides to dollarize the Mexican economy. While there is perceived to be a great deal of political uncertainty with the floating currency concept, as the peso rebounds and inflation drops great care will be needed to insure the peso does not become artificially overvalued. Noted Mexican economist Roberto Salinas-Leon observed: "While the peso is a medium of exchange—it will not return to prominence—until it is once again a stable store of value."[22]

BANKING: MEASURED RECOVERY AND CONSOLIDATION

Implications for further financial unrest in Mexico during the balance of the decade are hinged on the recovery and viability of the banking sector. Simply attracting new investment and temporarily stabilizing the economy will not allow Mexico to escape further insecurity. Since late 1993, the financial institutions have been plagued with a series of problems: bad loan portfolios, capitalization problems, loss of market share to nonbank entities, and the absence of profits.

Thus, the weak banking system has been a significant contributor to the constriction of the economy, both as a drain on capital resources to sustain the shaky financial system and a negative impact on the inability of domestic banks to increase lending. In spite of the fact that Mexico returned to the international private capital markets in less than a year after the devaluation of late 1994, on a level considered unimaginable, overdue domestic loans tripled during the same time period. Standard & Poor's calculated that the direct investment to support the beleaguered banking sector could eventually cost the government ''up to'' 12 percent of GDP, more than double the initial bailout estimates of 70 billion pesos, or 5 percent of GDP.[23] Economists at *El Financiero* reckon that for the period from January 1995 to March 1996 the Mexican government spent $16 billion (115–120 billion pesos) in a variety of programs to prop up the banking system. At year-end 1996, the federal government adjusted the bank bailout cost to 212.3 billion pesos, or 8.51 percent of GDP. Speaking to the national meeting of the Mexican Bankers Association, Lawrence Summers, Deputy Secretary of the Treasury, capsulized the state of Mexican banking, ''The banking system was not without problems before the onset of the [1994–95] crisis. There was too much emphasis on the *quantity* of lending and too little emphasis on the *quality* of lending.''[24]

Efforts to speed the recovery of the banking system have involved an ongoing struggle by the Zedillo administration to reform and privately recapitalize the weak institutions, backed by Mexican governmental programs to assist the restructuring of overdue loans and the absorption of bad loans. At the same time it is important to provide depositors protection and investors incentives to deposit in the banks. Beyond the domestic efforts to strengthen the banking system, Mexico has further liberalized the investment laws to attract foreign direct investment. The prospects for the future stability of Mexican banking depend on a number of interrelated factors that are crucial to the return of domestic depositor confidence as well as long-term capital investment. Important revisions in the banking law became effective February 16, 1995. The entire Mexican banking sector, with the exception of the three largest financial groups—Banamex, Bancomer, and Serfin—are eligible for foreign acquisition. These three banks, with combined total assets of $70 billion, are among the top eight largest financial institutions in Latin America.[25] Modifications to the law significantly reduced the market share restrictions under NAFTA (previously requiring 100 percent investment in any bank acquired in Mexico) and enhanced the ability for foreign banks to gain a major presence in the Mexican financial market. Furthermore, a single investor could directly or indirectly own up to 20 percent of the total voting stock. The widening of the foreign investment law to attract investors into the banking sector placed the need for investment capital above nationalistic pride. Mexican banks will spend the balance of the decade clearing bad loans and strengthening their balance sheets. The long-range outcome will potentially have four results:

1. adequate foreign investment will assist in the stabilization of the banking sector, lower interest rates, and make more credit available;

2. if foreign direct investment becomes too overweighed in the banking-financial sector, there is the potential this could cause a backlash in Mexico that would call for pre-1992 limited foreign control and investment;

3. if the new 1995 investment laws do not attract ample new investment capital, there is a strong implication that investment rules could be further relaxed;

4. competition from foreign banks will be an important factor in the composition of the Mexican financial sector by the turn of the century. Those institutions providing niche financial services and new technology will have significant market share.[26]

The irony of the post-devaluation bank crisis and credit crunch is that the Mexican government by mid-1996 owned controlling interest in a substantial portion of the same banking system it privatized in 1991–92. Government intervention to purchase large portions of troubled loan portfolios is evidence that the industry's predicament runs deeper than first suspected. The gain realized by the Mexican treasury in the reprivatization of the 18 leading banks was effectively wiped out in the aftermath of the 1994 peso devaluation. Some argue that the way in which the bank privatization was accomplished contributed to the eventual economic crisis of 1995–96. Mexican banks in 1991 had been sold or "reprivatized," on the average, at a pricey 3.1 times book value and 15 times earnings. Eager new owners, many with no previous banking experience, attempted to rapidly recoup their investments and expanded credit at an unprecedented rate. The overall loan quality of portfolios quickly deteriorated due to insufficient credit and risk analysis, and fraud was prevalent. The role of the banks to assist in the economic development of the nation was quickly diminished and limited to collection on bad loans. Furthermore, at the time of the 1990–91 privatization and deregulation, adequate regulations were not established to prevent excesses in the banking system.[27]

By 1995–96 it was evident that in addition to opening the banking sector to more direct investment, additional reforms were needed to increase the solvency of the system. In addition to raising reserve requirements, the National Banking Commission and the government began a series of reforms that will require three to five years to fully implement. The prime agent to insure that the banks are liquid and solvent is the government. Finance Secretary Ortiz, from the earliest stages of the crisis, stressed that "no savers or creditors in Mexican banks will sustain any loss whatsoever."[28] To accomplish this, steps were taken to bolster the deposit insurance system, interest rate subsidies were developed for borrowers, and banks received short-term credits against long-term repayments as well as the pooling of bad loans outside the banks' portfolio. To assist with the recovery extensive plans were drafted to facilitate securitization of financial assets, modify outdated bankruptcy laws, encourage nonbank growth to provide consumer loans, and enhance the extensive bank deposit insurance system. In the wake of shrinking credit and falling savings, the Hacienda began an effort to encourage banks to establish new branch banks nationwide. These efforts, along with new pension reform legislation, are expected to stimulate internal savings, which in the long run will contribute to the stabilization of the economy. Extensive branch expansion is expected by Multibanco Mercantil Probrusa (70 percent owned by Spain's Banco Bilbao Vizcaya), which plans to quadruple locations from 150 to over 600 by the end of the decade. Branching is also expected by Banco Bital and Banco Santander. One of the leading results of new foreign investment in Mexican banking during the 1990's is that it will speed the implementation of "change" via new products, expertise, and the introduction of new technology throughout the financial system.[29]

Another outcome of the Mexican crisis will be an effort to prevent future occurrences. To do this will require transparency and disclosure. Mexico, as well as all of Latin America, has for decades had policies and accounting methods that did not conform with global financial standards. For the most part accounting systems were based on inflation models and tended to both undervalue and delay accurate information on the true nature of financial data. The transparency of economic data and accounting procedures via internationally accepted standards are critical for both the market and private sector monitoring to keep the economy under close scrutiny. Such uniform policies will help recognize early danger signs and signal recommendations for the appropriate action before any situation erupts into a crisis. Timely data along with accurate analysis and risk management will need to prevail to insure the integrity of the reporting system.[30]

One of the most substantive changes will be the implementation of U.S.-styled Generally Accepted Accounting Principles, or GAAP, by year-end 1996. This change, one of the most profound financial events in this century, will significantly alter all future Mexican accounting and banking practices. Initial changes under GAAP will cause the financial picture of banks to be even worse. In the case of nonperforming loans, Mexican banks only consider the total interest owed as past due. Under GAAP, when a borrower misses a payment past 90 days the entire amount of the loan, principal and interest, is considered nonperforming. Historically, Mexican banks have been reluctant to recognize bad loans and losses. The amount of past-due loans system-wide in 1996 was estimated to be 18–20 percent; thus under new GAAP standards nonperforming portfolios could more than double (30–40 percent). While the target is in the 3–4 percent range, a 10 percent nonperforming loan rate was sufficient to trigger the U.S. savings and loan crisis in the 1980's. These changes under GAAP, coupled with increased loan-loss reserve requirements, will put additional strain on the capital base as well as cut earnings of most Mexican banks. Nevertheless, Bancomer was the first bank to provide against bad loans, creating a loan loss reserve of 4.2 billion pesos during the first half of 1996.[31]

Additional Mexican bank reform will include the use of mark-to-market accounting for securities to report the market value and new rules on capital adequacy. Tighter controls will be placed on credit cards, due to the massive losses in 1994–95. When interest rates more than doubled in 1995, credit card debt jumped 26 percent. In an effort to assist the financial industry, credit bureaus launched their initial entry in 1995 to collect and disseminate credit information. A full service credit tracking system will not be available until 1998–99. The banking industry trimmed over 20,000 jobs in 1995–96 in efforts to downsize operations. The growth in new bank branches is not expected to have a major job creation impact, due to smaller staffing requirements owing in large part to the use of newer technology and systems. Furthermore, nonbank financial organizations such as the partnerships of U.S. insurer Aetna with Bancomer and GMAC with Grupo Financiero Abaco will expand over the balance of the decade.[32]

FOREIGN BANKS TO THE RESCUE

By 1996 all of Mexico's leading 18 banks had received funding from the government, as bad debt portfolios soared. New capitalization requirements and higher loss reserves placed a strain on even the largest banks. To inject additional capital into the system the banks turned to foreign investors. While interest in bank investment was high during the first year of NAFTA, the mood changed as most U.S. bankers took a wait-and-see attitude.[33] Potential U.S. investors have expressed concern about the extent to which the three largest Mexican banks are protected. Some have also indicated they see no benefit in acquiring even 100 percent of small troubled banks, given the complexity of government regulation and the condition of the overall banking sector. Nevertheless, the Bank of Boston and First National Bank of Chicago opened offices in Mexico City, primarily to service large multinational companies.[34] In contrast to and following the lead of Spain's Banco Bilbao Vizcaya, the Bank of Montreal acquired 16 percent of Mexico's second largest financial group, Bancomer, for an estimated $460 million. In return, Bancomer will have the options, after seven years, to obtain ten million shares of the Bank of Montreal. In a more complicated transaction the Bank of Nova Scotia, no stranger to Mexico, purchased from FOBAPROA (the equivalent of the FDIC) the Inverlat Group for $50 million. With the initial shares purchased and an option on subordinated debt, the Bank of Nova Scotia will own between 39 and 55 percent of Inverlat by March 31, 2000. To begin lending again, an additional $125 million in capital had to be injected into Inverlat. Both acquisitions provide a broad foreign entree into a growing retail market for bank services at a time when Mexican bank assets are about as inexpensive as they have ever been. These acquisitions and future investment will only be successful with adequate capitalization, prudent credit-risk controls, and a long-term market share strategy.[35]

MEXICO: IMPACT ON LATIN AMERICA

Much of the external financing in Latin America is provided by the United States. The linkage to the region is both old and tested. American bankers have for the most part reduced their broad exposure in Latin America, especially after the debt crisis of the 1970's and 1980's when the volatility of the region threatened bank stability in the United States. As U.S. banks faced tougher reserve requirements they began to lose some market share to less regulated European financial institutions. Although the Mexican crisis of 1994–95 surfaced many of these old concerns, loans by commercial banks to the region totaled over $17.5 billion in 1995, with over 20 percent placed in December. San Francisco-based Bank of America was the primary agent bank lending $2.7 billion in 1995, followed by Chase Manhattan, Citicorp, and J. P. Morgan.[36] Even so, by 1996 foreign debt among all Latin American countries surged 8 percent to over $700 billion. The spillover effect of the peso crisis on the three biggest economies south of Mexico—Brazil, Argentina, and Venezuela—will take years to be fully corrected. The World Bank reported that overall Latin American growth shrank from 5 percent in 1994 to 0.6 percent in 1995.[37] The market economy and globalization of regional trade, distribution, and manufacturing will help to speed the recovery. Additionally, due to the ongoing process to privatize most banks in Latin America, there will be an enormous demand for new technology. Thus the region could require as much as $350 billion in infrastructure investment over the next 15 years. Projections for growth in Latin America, as noted by Lawrence Summers, are vastly different from the patterns of the "lost decade":

From 1982 to 1990, Latin America growth stagnated at an average 1.5 percent annual rate, with a sharp 4 percent fall over 1982 and 1983. Had today's crisis been even half that bad, Latin America would have lost a full $150 billion in output over the next three years—a loss that would have quickly translated into lost opportunities for U.S. businesses. Instead, most expectations are for Latin America to enjoy 2.5 percent growth this year [1995], with a recovery to 3.5 percent by next year [1996] and annual rates as high as 5 percent for years after.[38]

The speed at which Latin America will prosper is directly linked to the stability (both real and perceived) and recovery of the Mexican economy. Coupled with the regional recovery is the expansion of the North American Free Trade Agreement. After the Summit of the Americas, held in early December 1994, a number of Latin American nations, particularly Chile, were anxious to join NAFTA. When membership in NAFTA was delayed, Chile joined the southern cone countries of Argentina, Brazil, Paraguay, and Uruguay in the MERCOSUR trading bloc in mid-1996. While the regionalization of free trade is important, care must be taken not to allow the euphoria of NAFTA to create economic expectations that are difficult to implement and accomplish. Discussions on the incorporation of additional NAFTA partners will not take place until 1997, after the fall 1996 U.S. presidential elections, at which time the key focus will be on the labor and environmental concerns. Latin America as a region has many challenges in the years ahead, yet expects growth in 1996–97 to be in the 2.4–2.6 percent range. While no country in the region is among the top 25 richest economies in terms of GNP per capita, the potential for the collective financial, industrial, and commercial growth is tremendous. As the regional economic crunch subsides, Latin America will see a trend toward more domestic acceptance of privatization and free market economic policies, thus enhancing the attraction of foreign investment.[39]

IMPLICATIONS FOR INTERNATIONAL FINANCE

Mexico during the past decade has had one of the most colorful and dramatic economic transformations in comparison to any emerging country worldwide. Efforts to position the nation as a world-class economy required tremendous change and acceptance of new economic and international requirements during the late 1980's and early 1990's. In addition to being a regional leader, Mexico was one of the pioneers of market-oriented economic reform and the first emerging nation to be granted OECD membership in over two decades. Diversification of the economy and expansion of trade worldwide far exceeded even the gains made with the completion of NAFTA in 1993. Such dynamic growth and global thinking attracted investors at an unprecedented rate, taxing the ability of the Mexican market to absorb and manage the new investment within parameters of the changing domestic economy.

In addition to economic opportunities and challenges, political turmoil both overshadowed and undercut a feeling of confidence. A loss of confidence disrupted cash flows and brought into question exchange rate controls. Monetary and fiscal policies showed laxness as the current account reached 8 percent of GDP backed by short-term debt instruments. The peso, throughout 1994, weakened to the point that it was overvalued by at least 20 percent. This, together with the uprising in Chiapas, uncertainties associated with the presidential election, deterioration of the commercial banking sector, the blend of direct and portfolio foreign investment, the pressure of the first year of NAFTA, rising U.S. interest rates, and shortsighted planning as well as a lack of timely leadership proved a volatile mix. The economic challenges caused by the crisis were neither the result of NAFTA nor a referendum on its viability. There will remain no concrete consensus on what caused the Mexican crisis; however, it is clear that the deterioration of macroeconomic fundamentals and liquidity problems triggered the final stages of the devaluation.

The fact that worldwide money center managers and investment advisors either missed or discounted the information and trends during 1993–94 will require extensive future evaluation. Notwithstanding the fact that many felt they had a good understanding of the events and dynamics occurring in the Mexican economy, more investors from the United States, Europe, and Asia had more money invested in Mexico than in any emerging market investment ever on record. Second, there appeared to be an implied feeling that there would be some form of a "warning" if conditions in Mexico were to deteriorate. In spite of the fact that indicators pointed to an overheated economy, even prior to the Colosio assassination in March 1994—after which it was only a matter of time before the "band" in which the peso was traded would have to be widened or, in market terms, devalued. Thus, the Mexican crisis provides an excellent example and lesson on how macroeconomic fundamentals can help in forecasting which countries are most likely to face a balance-of-payments predicament.

In addition to not fully appreciating the dynamic factors over which they had no control, such as a doubling of Fed fund interest rates in the United States during 1994, Salinas and his advisors quite possibly took on an air that, given the emergence of the Mexican economy in the NAFTA era, they were somehow "too big to fail." This could partly account for the comparison by the technocrats with the economic swings in such countries as Italy, who had historically maintained larger current account deficits and survived. After the Mexico experience, large current account deficits will not soon be viewed as harmless. Nonetheless, the crash of December 1994 sent shock waves first through Latin America, and then worldwide to both the markets of the industrialized G-7 and the emerging nations looking to Mexico as a model of passage from third- to first-world status. The impact of the Mexican devaluation undoubtedly taught markets worldwide lessons in volatility and liquidity.

The trend toward large capital flows into emerging market countries should always be reason for concern. While confidence in the overall economic structure is paramount, there are no guarantees of an advance warning during a currency crisis. Once viewed as benign, country risk assessments and liquidity levels are foremost. Current account balances should generally not exceed 2.5–3.0 percent of GDP, anchored by a high public sector savings rate. As domestic demand increases imports during 1997–98, it will be important for Mexico to closely monitor the current account within the 2–3.0 percent range of GDP. In today's liberalized financial markets, emerging national domestic growth and stability—economic, social, as well as political—must be carefully gauged when attracting or investing large sums of short-term foreign investments. In addition to keeping speculative capital under control, incentives are needed to encourage long-term direct foreign investment. And emerging market opportunities will abound as more countries expand privatization programs, relax investment laws, and strive to globalize their economies. Such steps should be carefully monitored and transparent. In the event of a future liquidity crisis both the national treasury of the country involved and the portfolio claims by investors are more likely to suffer greater losses.

While relaxed investment laws have attracted new capital for the Mexican banking sector, the challenge remains to further strengthen the financial industry. The reluctance of U.S. commercial banks to expand in Mexico will gradually subside as the economy improves. Substantive entry into retail banking will most likely be accomplished by U.S.-Mexican border banks that have a tremendous knowledge of the market and culture. Expansion of banking services in Mexico will hinge on the regulatory environment, transparency of reporting, new technology, and availability of managerial talent.

The most frightening aspect of the Mexican peso crisis was how dangerously close Mexico came to defaulting on all its debt. The full magnitude of the decision by the Clinton administration to take action on the eve of Mexico falling into default, after U.S. congressional assistance was deemed scuttled, may never be known or fully appreciated. In addition to the $20 billion U.S. portion of the financial package (repaid in full by January 1997), one indication as to the magnitude of the crisis was that the World Bank and the IMF each made the largest loans ever allowed to a single country. Furthermore, the unprecedented U.S.-IMF financial support package was the largest international aid response since the Marshall Plan in 1948. Thus, the 1994–95 Mexican crisis was not a situation that could be ignored.

As a result of the Mexican economic crisis, the world was made acutely aware that economic and political events in Mexico have tremendous significance on both global financial markets and the stability of emerging markets. The line between stable emerging markets and catastrophe will always be fine. As with the case of Mexico and its rise to world prominence, it will be advisable to heed the capital flows caused by investment dynamics and the viability of the banking sector of such emerging markets in the years to come.

NOTES

1. U.S. Treasury, press release, Lawrence H. Summers, "Our Mexican Challenge," presentation at the Georgetown University Law Center, Washington, D.C., January 20, 1995.

2. David Gould, "Mexico's Crisis: Looking Back to Assess the Future," *Economic Review* (FRBD), vol. 2, 1995, pp. 2–5; Allan D. Brunner, "U.S. International Transactions in 1995," *Federal Reserve Bulletin*, Vol. 82, No. 5, May 1996, pp. 383–35; Bloomberg, press release, "Rubin Says Data Suggests Mexican Economic Recovery Underway" (Washington, D.C.: March 1, 1996). Note: The nominal GDP drop in 1932 was 15 percent while the real per capita GDP declined 8.1 percent in 1982 and 9.1 percent in 1983. The mass media generally refer to the 1932 figure when commenting on the Mexican crisis of 1994–95.

3. "Monetary Policy Report to the Congress," *Federal Reserve Bulletin*, Vol. 92, No. 4, April 1996, p. 301; "Is the End In Sight?" *Latin American Monitor: Mexico*, January 1996, pp. 4–7. Note: The Federal Reserve data tracked both in Washington and at the Dallas Fed indicated that "the decline [caused by the devaluation of 1994] in Mexican real economic activity may have ended" in November 1995.

4. Keith Phillips, "New Business Cycle Indexes for Mexico Point to Economic Expansion," *The Southwest Economy* (FRBD), Vol. 2, 1996, p. 10; InverMexico, "62nd Meeting of Economic and Securities Research" (Mexico, D.F.: January 1996), pp. 26–

29; Bloomberg, "Salomon's Purcell Raises Mexico Weighting, Cuts Brazil, Chile" (New York and Mexico, D.F: May 14, 1996), p. 1; Robert Gay, "A Robust Recovery: Will It Last?" *Perspectives on Emerging Markets*, February 1996, pp. 2–3; Enrique Rangel, "Economy Is Rebounding in Mexico as Market Soars," *Dallas Morning News*, April 2, 1996; Anna J. Bray, "IMF Hopes a New $48 Bil Fund Will End Mexico-Style Problems," *Investor's Business Daily*, April 23, 1996, p. B1. See also SECOFI, *Industrial Policy and International Foreign Trade Program* (Mexico, D.F.: May 1996), pp. 20–22; "G-7 Face Time," *Investor's Business Daily*, July 1, 1996, p. B1; Margorie Deans and Robert Pringle, *The Central Banks* (New York: 1994), pp. 104–9. Note: Great Britain and Germany abstained from the IMF executive board vote on the 1995 Mexican aid package.

5. For an example of post-1994 devaluation analysis, see Castaneda, *The Mexican Shock: Its Meaning for the U.S.* (New York: 1995); Marcario Schettino, *El Costo del Miedo: La Devaluacion de 1994–1995* (Mexico, D.F.: 1995); Domenec Biosca, *100 Soluciones Para Salir de la Crisis* (Madrid: 1995); Sidney Weintraub, "The Mexican Economy: Life After Devaluation," *Current History*, March 1995, pp. 108–13; Andres Oppenheimer, *Bordering on Chaos: Guerrillas, Stockbrokers, Politicians, and Mexico's Road to Prosperity* (New York: 1996); Stephen D. Morris, *Political Reformism in Mexico: An Overview of Contemporary Mexican Politics* (Boulder: 1995); and Wayne A. Cornelius, *Mexican Politics in Transition: The Breakdown of a One-Party-Dominant Regime* (San Diego: 1996).

6. For an excellent overview of the Mexico crisis, see Edwin M. Truman, "The Mexican Peso Crisis: Implications for International Finance," *Federal Reserve Bulletin*, Vol. 82, March 1996, pp. 199–209. See also Craig Torres, "Mexican Finance Aide's Glass Is Half Full," *Wall Street Journal*, October 18, 1996, p. A10.

7. Banco de Mexico, "Monetary Policy Program for 1996" (Mexico, D.F.: January 1996), p. 40; Deborah L. Riner, "For Mexico's Zedillo, Path to Reform Gets Steeper," Knight-Ridder Financial News Forum, New York, May 9, 1996, pp. 1–3; Sidney Weintraub, "NAFTA Benefits Flow Back and Forth Across the Rio Grande," *Wall Street Journal*, May 11, 1996, p. A11; Robert Gay, "Peso Volatility and the Mexican Cete Market," *Bankers Trust Research*, February 1, 1996, pp. 1–4; Sherry Kuczynski, "Who Should Get Credit for U.S. Export Boom," *Investor's Business Daily*, May 10, 1996, p. B1; Knight-Ridder, "Ortiz Says Mexico Has Met the Two Major Challenges" (Mexico, D.F., December 13, 1995). See also remarks by Ambassador Jesus Silva-Herzog to the Border Trade Alliance (BTA), El Paso, Texas, June 24, 1995.

8. David Malpass, "Mexico: Austerity Program Continues," *Global Notes*, Bear Stearns, April 16, 1996, p. 9; David Hale, "The Price Was Right," *The Washington Post National Weekly Edition*, June 16, 1996, p. 25; Dan Dorrow, "Mexico: Signs of an Incipient Recovery," *Latin American Economics*, Merrill Lynch, February 21, 1996, pp. 1–4.

9. "Top 100 Publicly Traded Companies," *Latin Trade*, August 1996, pp. 42–53. Note: Mexico's top ten industrial/service companies in 1996 include: Telmex, Vitro, Alfa, Cifra, Cemex, Carso, Visa, Femsa, Panamco, and Comercial Mexicana.

10. Victoria Griffith, "Forging Ahead," *LatinFinance*, March 1996, pp. 55–57; Joel Millman, "Mexican Tortilla Firms Stage U.S. Bake-Off," *Wall Street Journal*, May 10, 1996, p. A6; Rick Wills, "Construction Still Hurting," *El Financero International*, May 13, 1996, p. 9; "The Current Condition of Mexico's Economy," *El Mercado de Valores*, February 1996, pp. 21–28; Presentation by U.S. Ambassador James R. Jones, 39th An-

nual Session of the Southwestern Graduate School of Banking (SMU), Dallas, Texas, May 30, 1996. Note: Tequila exports grew over 40 percent in 1995 to $56 million.

11. Press release, National Palace, "Financial Markets Report" (Mexico D.F.: December 6, 1995), pp. 1–16; Fred Rosen, "Manufactured Exports Spur Modest Hope," *El Financiero International*, March 25, 1996, pp. 1, 9. Note: Of the maquila industry's total added value in mid-1996, 50 percent was paid in wages, 29 percent in overhead, 14.5 percent in profit, and 6.5 percent in raw materials, freight, and packing.

12. Deidre McFadyen, "Mexico on a Wall Street Comeback," *El Financiero International*, May 6, 1996, p. 8; Richard Lawrence, "Latin America Nips Asia's Heels as Growth Picks Up in S. Hemisphere," *Journal of Commerce*, September 20, 1996, p. 2A; Geri Smith, "Staying Afloat Quite Nicely, Thank You," *Business Week*, April 8, 1996, p. 56. See also John H. Dunning and Rajneesh Narula, "Transpacific Foreign Direct Investment and the Investment Development Path: The Record Assessed," *Essays in International Business*, No. 10 (Columbia: May 1994), pp. 1–55; and Kenichi Ohmae (ed.), *The Evolving Global Economy* (Boston: 1995), pp. 100–101, 142–44.

13. John McLees, "Doing Business in Mexico under the U.S.-Mexico Income Tax Treaty: Initial Thoughts," *Tax Notes International*, November 1992, pp. 995–1003.

14. Mark Nehoray, "Transfer Pricing in Mexico: A Window of Opportunity for Maquiladoras," *Twin Plant News*, November 1995, p. 31; Luis Manuel Perez de Acha, "Examining the Mexican Transfer Pricing Laws," *Tax Notes International*, June 1994, pp. 1487–89.

15. Nehoray, "Transfer Pricing in Mexico," pp. 31–32; John McLees, John Wilkins, and Ignacio Valdes, "Extension of Mexican Assets Tax Complicates Transfer Pricing for Maquiladoras," *Tax Notes International*, May 1995, pp. 1619–30; Lorraine Eden, "Searching for A CUP: The Harmonization of Transfer Pricing Rules in North America," *Proceedings of Competitiveness in International Business and Trade* (San Diego: May 22–25, 1996), Vol. I, pp. 235–49; USTR, "Mexico: 1996 National Trade Estimate" (Washington, D.C.: April 1, 1996), pp. 1–7; "Pemex a Case Study for Mexico's Future," editorial, *San Antonio Express-News*, March 21, 1996, p. 2L.

16. For an overview of the IMF, see Harold James, *International Monetary Cooperation Since Bretton Woods* (New York: 1996), and on the so-called "lost decade," see Nora Lustig (ed.), *Coping with Austerity: Poverty and Inequality in Latin America* (Washington, D.C.: 1995).

17. "Resurrecting the Banking System," *El Financiero International*, April 8, 1996, p. 8.

18. Herminio Blanco and Peter M. Garber, "Recurrent Devaluation and Speculative Attacks on the Peso," *Journal of Monetary Economics*, Vol. 94, 1986, pp. 148–66; Alan Alford and Gabor Finaczy, "Predicting Devaluation," *Proceedings of Competitiveness in International Business and Trade*, Vol. I, pp. 273–85; Thurow, *The Future of Capitalism*, p. 2.

19. Geri Smith, "Staying Afloat Quite Nicely, Thank You," *Business Week*, April 8, 1996, p. 56; Alice Salgado and Al Taranto, "Debt Jitters Resurface," *El Financiero International*, April 15, 1996, pp. 1,3. Note: For a brief contrary view of the neoliberal economic model, see Cuauhtemoc Cardenas, "If You Were President of Mexico, What Would You Do?" *The International Economy*, February 1996, pp. 28–29.

20. Banco de Mexico, *Report on Monetary Policy for 1996*, January 1996, pp. 29–39; Edwin M. Truman, "The Mexican Peso: Crisis: Implications for International Finance," *Federal Reserve Bulletin*, Vol. 82, No. 3, March 1996, pp. 207–9; Anna J. Bray, "IMF

Hopes a New $48 Bil Fund Will End Mexico-Style Problems,'' *Investors Business Daily*, April 23, 1996, p. B1; John Preece, ''IMF Praises Gov't Policy,'' *El Financiero International*, May 5, 1996, p. 1. Note: By the end of 1997, Mexico and Russia will account for 49 percent of the IMF's outstanding loans.

21. SECOFI, ''Industrial Policy and International Foreign Trade Program,'' pp. 1–27; Alva Senzek, ''Whither Industrial Policy?'' *El Financiero*, May 20, 1996, p. 14. See also Clyde V. Prestowitz, Jr., ''Mandarin Strategies: Japan's Industrial Policy,'' in *Trading Places: How We Allowed Japan to Take the Lead* (New York: 1988), pp. 122–50.

22. David Hale, ''How to End Mexico's Meltdown,'' *Wall Street Journal*, January 19, 1995; Craig Torres, ''Peso's Stability Unnerves Some Mexicans,'' Ibid., May 2, 1996; George Junge, ''Emerging Market Countries in Global Financial Markets,'' *Economic and Financial Prospects*, No. 1, 1996, pp. 10–13; Andrew A. Reding, ''It Isn't the Peso: It's the Presidency,'' *New York Times Magazine*, April 9, 1995, pp. 54–55; Jonathan Kandell, ''The 'Dollarizing' of Argentinean Politics,'' *Institutional Investor*, June 1996, pp. 43–49; Gay, ''Peso Volatility and the Mexican CETE Market,'' *Bankers Trust Research*, pp. 1–4. Note: Notwithstanding the fact that Mexico has chosen to model its industrial plan after the MITI, Japan's top 11 commercial banks for year-end March 1996 suffered their largest annual loss since World War II, due to massive write-offs of bad loans.

23. ''Mexico's Bank Bailout Could Cost 12% of GDP,''*Investor's Business Daily*, March 1, 1996, p. B1; Knight-Ridder, press release, ''Mexico Puts Cost of Aid to Banks at 6.57% of GDP'' (Mexico, D.F., July 3, 1996).

24. Bloomberg, press release, ''Summers Urges Austerity by Mexico, Slam Bank Bailout'' (Cancun: March 15, 1996). See also Craig Torres, ''Opening of Mexico's Financial System Won't Bring Any Immediate Rewards,'' *Wall Street Journal*, October 24, 1994, p. A6; Anna J. Bray, ''Mexican Government Fiddles As the Peso Burns,''*Investors Business Daily*, November 7, 1995, p. B1; and Robert Collier, ''Shaky Mexico Banks Pose Threat to Recovery,'' *San Francisco Chronicle*, February 9, 1995.

25. Jim Freer, ''The Top 50 Banks,'' *Latin Trade*, July 1996, pp. 50–51. Note: Banamex ranks number 4, Bancomer number 5, and Serfin number eight; the balance of the top eight ranking is occupied entirely by Brazilian banks.

26. Skip Edmonds, ''Mexican Banks Open to Foreign Investors,'' *Financial Industry Issues* (FRBD), Vol. 1, 1995, pp. 1, 4. Note: The three biggest banks controlled over 50 percent of the commercial banking assets in Mexico in 1995–96.

27. Craig Torres, ''The Banking Disaster in Mexico Whipsaws: An Ailing Economy,'' *Wall Street Journal*, January 25, 1996, p. 1; John Preece, ''Government Increases Control over Banking System,'' *El Financiero International*, May 27, 1996, p. 3 ; ''Sefin's Bad-Debt Problems Continue,'' Ibid., June 3, 1996, p. 12; ''Recession Makes Mexican Government a Banker Again,'' *Laredo Morning Times*, December 6, 1995.

28. As seen in Scott Pardee, ''After the Fall: Why Mexico's Banks Will Rebound,'' *Mexico Service*, December 15, 1995, p. 8. Also see Ernesto Zedillo, ''Statement by the President at the Inauguration Ceremony of the Seventh Securities Market Convention'' (Mexico, D.F.: April 16, 1996).

29. Ibid.; John Rogers, ''Mexico,'' *LatinFinance: LatinLaw*, March 1996, p. 5; ''Resurrecting the Banking System,'' *El Financiero International*, April 8, 1996, p. 8; ''The Problem is the Banking System,'' Ibid., April 29, 1996, p. 5; Bloomberg, press release, ''Spain's Banco Bilbao, Probursa Plan to Quadruple Mexico Network'' (Mexico, D.F: May 10, 1996). Note: Banco Bilbao Vizcaya has operations in 30 countries; the Probursa

banking group was renamed "Banco Bilbao Vizcaya-Mexico" in July 1996. Furthermore, as of year-end 1995, there were an estimated 5,000 bank branches in Mexico.

30. Carlos Angulo P., "The 'Mexican Risk' Factor in Credit Transactions" (El Paso: February 1996), pp. 1–7; Todd C. Nelson and Ronald Cuming, "Harmonization of the Secured Financing Laws of the NAFTA Partners: Focus on Mexico," *National Law Center for Inter-American Free Trade* (Tucson: 1995), pp. 1–141.

31. Jim Cole, "Mexico Banks Face Hard 96 Preparing for U.S. Accounting Rules," Knight-Ridder (Mexico, D.F.: January 30, 1996); "Bank Support Plan Widened," *Mexico: Latin America Monitor*, February 1996, p. 7.

32. Bloomberg, press release, "Mexican Overdue Credit Card Debt Rises on Recession, Weaker Peso" (Mexico, D.F.: April 8, 1996); Ibid., "Mexico's 13 Big Banks Fired 9,729 Workers in 1995" (Mexico, D.F.: March 7, 1996); Lisa Fickenscher, "Credit Bureaus Poised for Leap into Mexico," *American Banker*, March 10, 1995; Kevin Hall, "Mexican Officials Tighten Regulations of Banks and Brokerage Houses," *Journal of Commerce*, July 16, 1996, p. A6.

33. Jim Freer, "U.S. Banks Look North, South," *United States Banker*, June 1992, pp. 42–43; William S. Haraf, "NAFTA Opens Doors to Mexican Markets for U.S. Banks," *Bank Management*, February 1993, pp. 11–24; Harvey Rice, "U.S. Banks Look South of the Border," Ibid., November 1992, pp. 44–46.

34. As of early 1996, 38 different banks were operating in Mexico, while over 72 foreign banks were approved to open operations in Mexico. Those with established offices in Mexico include: Citibank, Chase Manhattan Bank, J. P. Morgan, Bank of Boston, Chemical Bank, Bank of America, Republic Bank of New York, American Express Bank, Dresdner Bank, Banco Santander, Banque Nationale de Paris, ABN AMRO, Bank of Toyko, Banco Bilbao Vizcaya, Bank of Montreal, Bank of Nova Scotia, and the Fiji Bank.

35. Alicia Salgado and Al Taranto, "Foreign Banks to the Rescue," *El Financiero International*, February 26, 1996, p. 1; Salgado, "First Chicago Opens Mexico Unit," Ibid., p. 3; Craig Torres, "Bank of Montreal Deal Raises Questions," *Austin American-Statesman*, March 10, 1996, p. D4; Claudia Fernandez, "Canada to the Rescue," *Mexico Business*, May 1996, pp. 19–20. Note: In mid-1996, Spain's Banco Bilbao Vizcaya outbid Banco Promex (Mexico's seventh largest bank) to acquire Banco Cremi and Banco de Oriente, with a combined total of 153 branches. Also, the *Diario Oficial*, June 19, 1996 lists the registration of 412 foreign banks.

36. Bloomberg, press release, "Loans to Latin America Grow as Borrowers Put Finances in Order" (New York: February 8, 1996).

37. Ibid., "Mexico 'Tequila Effect' May Claim More Victims" (Miami: January 26, 1996); "Washington: Latin America Recovers," *Investors Business Daily*, April 24, 1996, p. B1; Jim Freer, "Bankers: U.S. Trails Europe in Financing Latin Projects," *Journal of Commerce*, October 17, 1996, p. 4A.

38. U.S. Treasury, press release, Lawrence H. Summers, "After the Storm—Latin American Finance: A Progress Report," presentation at Conference on the Americas, New York City: September 29, 1995. See also Pearl Bosco, "Latin American Banks Embrace Big Change," *Bank Systems and Technology*, April 1995, pp. 56, 58; and Lustig (ed.), *Coping with Austerity* (New York: 1995).

39. Shirley Christian, "Don't Let Mexico's Woes Spoil Our Commitments to Chile," *Wall Street Journal*, February 3, 1995; Bloomberg, press release, "Treasury's Shafer Says Mexican Economy is 'Turning the Corner' " (Washington, D.C.: February 2, 1996);

''Vital Signs: The World's 25 Richest Economies, Based on GNP Per Capita,'' *Investors Business Daily*, April 18, 1996, p. B1; Richard Lawrence, ''Latin America Nips at Asia's Heels as Growth Picks Up in S. Hemisphere,'' *Journal of Commerce*, September 20, 1996, p. 2A; Kevin Hall and Tim Shorrock, ''Foreign Business Beat a Path to Latin America,'' Ibid., October 9, 1996, p. 4A; Robert Batterson, ''Double Dealing on Latin Trade,'' Ibid., July 18, 1996, p. 7A.

Appendixes

Appendix

Appendix A

Mexican Banking and Financial Milestones, 1935–97

August 31, 1935	*Law of Mutual and Insurance E. & Inst.* • foreign investment up to 49% only • no single shareholder (individual) over 15%
March 9, 1973	*Law to Promote Mexican Investment and to Regulate Foreign Investment*
1974	*Law of Credit Institutions*: Multiple Bank Act
January 2, 1975	Securities Market Law • created brokerage house • up to 30% foreign investment possible • individual ownership to 10% • revamped Comision Nacional de Valores or CNV
1977	*Petrobonds*: created shares in trust at Nacional Financiera based on government oil resources
1978	*CETES*: First introduction of government treasury notes
1980	*Commercial Paper* authorized
1981	Bankers Acceptances authorized
September 1, 1992	Nationalization of the banks: Lopez Portillo
January 14, 1985	*Law of Auxiliary Credit Institutions* • governs factoring, leasing, credit unions, S&Ls, foreign exchange houses • foreign ownership up to 49%—factoring and leasing only
January 14, 1985	*Law of Investment Corporations* • investment funds, management "Sociadades de Inversion"
1986	*Money market accounts* (cuentas maestras) appeared

1988	*Deregulation* of interest rates on loans and deposits • reduced reserve requirements • terminated policy of compulsory allocations of credit to preferred sectors
July 18, 1990	*Law to Regulate Financial Groups* • Holding Company Act or "financial groups" • Holding company must control 51% of at least *3* financial entities • foreign investment limited to 'B' shares
June 1990	Constitutional amendment: to allow majority private sector ownership of Mexican commercial banks
July 19, 1990	*Law of Credit Institutions* • restored multiple bank or developing banks • A-B-C-L shares authorized
December 29, 1990	*Law of Bonding Institutions* • bonding groups "instituciones de finanzas"
January 91–July 92	*Bank privatization*—18 banks sold
September 1991	Eliminated remaining liquidity coefficient of 30%
December 1991	*Exchange controls* abolished
June 1992	"L" class shares approved for up to 30% foreign investment
September 1992	*Warrants*—approved for trading Mexican equity
December 27, 1993	New Foreign Investment Law
January 1, 1994	NAFTA placed into force
April 21, 1994	SECOFI: foreign bank requirements released
December 20, 1994	Devaluation: expansion of the Peso trading band
February 24, 1995	PROCAPTE Program: temporary capitalization
April 1, 1995	UDIs Program: debt restructuring
April 28, 1995	National Banking and Securities Commission
August 1995	Program for Banking System Debtors (ADE)
January 1997	GAAP rules to be in place at Mexican banks

Principal Regulators of Financial Institutions in Mexico:

• Mexican Constitution
• Ministry of Finance and Public Credit
• Banco de Mexico
• National Banking and Securities Commission
• National Insurance and Bond Commission

Appendix B

Foreign Investment Law, December 27, 1993

SECRETARIAT OF COMMERCE AND INDUSTRIAL DEVELOPMENT

Foreign Investment Law

CARLOS SALINAS DE GORTARI, Constitutional President of the United Mexican States, notifies its inhabitants:

That the Honorable Congress of the Union, through me, has directed the following

DECREE

"THE CONGRESS OF THE UNITED MEXICAN STATES DECREES THE:

FOREIGN INVESTMENT LAW

FIRST TITLE
GENERAL PROVISIONS

Chapter I
On the purpose of the Law

ARTICLE 1. This Law is public in nature, and general in observance throughout the Republic. Its objective is to establish rules in order to channel foreign investment to the country, and to ensure that this contributes to national development.

ARTICLE 2. For this Law, (the following definitions) will apply:

I. Commission: the National Foreign Investment Commission;

II. Foreign investment:

a) The participation of foreign investors, in any proportion, in the capital stock of Mexican corporations;

b) The formation of Mexican corporations with a majority of foreign capital; and

c) The participation of foreign investors in the acts and activities envisioned by this Law.

III. Foreign investor: non-Mexican individuals or entities, and foreign entities without corporate legal status;

IV. Registry: the National Foreign Investment Registry;

V. Secretariat: the Secretariat of Commerce and Industrial Development;

VI. Restricted Zone: the strip of national territory that is 100 kilometers [62.14 miles] wide along the borders and 50 kilometers [31.07 miles] inland from the beaches, as described in Article 27, Section I, of the Mexican Constitution; and

VII. Clause of Exclusion of Foreigners: the precise agreement or pact, that is part of the articles of incorporation/by-laws, which mandates that the corporations in question will not directly or indirectly admit foreign investors, nor corporations with a clause of admission of foreigners, as partners or stockholders.

ARTICLE 3. As a result of this Law, [investment] made by foreigners in the country with immigrant (*inmigrado*) status will be the same as Mexican investment, excepting [investments] made in the activities considered in the First and Second Titles of this Law.

ARTICLE 4. Any percentage of foreign investment will be able to participate in the capital stock of Mexican corporations, acquire capital assets, enter new fields of economic activity or manufacture new product lines, open and operate establishments, and expand or relocate already existing [establishments], excepting where stipulated in this Law.

The rules on the participation of foreign investment in financial sector activities, as set forth in this Law, will be applied without prejudice to that which is established in the specific laws for these activities.

Chapter II
On Reserved Activities

ARTICLE 5. The activities defined by the [applicable] laws, in the following strategic areas, are exclusively reserved for the State:

I.   Petroleum and other hydrocarbons;

II.   Basic petrochemicals;

III.   Electricity;

IV.   Nuclear energy generation;

V.   Radioactive minerals;

VI.   Satellite communications;

VII.   Telegraph;

VIII.   Radiotelegraphy;

IX.   Postal service;

X.   Railways;

XI.   Issuance of currency;

XII.   Minting of coins;

XIII.   Control, supervision and vigilance of ports, airports and heliports; and

XIV.   Others expressly indicated in the applicable legal conditions.

ARTICLE 6.   The following economic activities and corporations are exclusively reserved for Mexicans, or Mexican corporations with a clause of exclusion of foreigners:

I.   National ground transportation of passengers, tourism and freight, excluding messenger and parcel services;

II.   Retail gasoline stations and distribution of liquid petroleum gas;

III.   Radio broadcasting, and other radio and television services, excepting cable television;

IV.   Credit unions;

V.   Development banks, in accordance with the applicable laws; and

VI.   The rendering of professional and technical services that are explicitly shown in the applicable legal conditions.

Foreign investment will not be able to participate directly in the activities and corporations mentioned in this Article, nor through trusts, agreements, business or incorporation contracts, pyramid schemes, or [any] other mechanism that grants whatsoever control or participation, excepting that which is indicated in Title Five of this Law.

Chapter III
On specifically regulated activities and acquisitions

ARTICLE 7.   Foreign investment, in the ensuing economic activities and corporations, will be able to participate according to the following percentages:

I.   Up to 10 percent:

    a)   Production cooperatives;

II.   Up to 25 percent:

    a)   National air transportation;

    b)   Air taxi transportation; and

    c)   Specialized air transportation;

III.   Up to 30 percent:

    a)   Financial group holding companies;

    b)   Multiple bank credit institutions;

    c)   Stock exchange houses; and

    d)   Stock exchange specialists;

IV.   Up to 49 percent:

    a)   Insurance institutions;

    b)   Bond institutions;

    c)   Foreign exchange houses;

    d)   Bonded warehouses;

e)   Financial leasing companies;

f)   Financial factorage companies;

g)   Financial corporations of limited purpose to those cited in Article 103, Section IV, of the Credit Institutions Law;

h)   Companies cited in Article 12 Bis of the Securities Market Law;

i)   Representative fixed capital stocks of investment corporations and operating companies of investment corporations;

j)   Manufacturing and marketing of explosives, firearms, cartridges, ammunition and fireworks, excluding the acquisition and utilization of explosives for industrial and (mining) activities, or the manufacture of mixed explosives for use in said activities;

k)   Printing and publication of newspapers circulated exclusively in national territory;

l)   Series ''T'' shares of companies that own agricultural, livestock and forest property;

m)   Cable television;

n)   Basic telephone services;

o)   Fishing in fresh waters, coastal waters and in the [200 mile] exclusive economic zone, excluding aquaculture;

p)   Integral port administration;

q)   Harbor pilot services so that vessels can navigate in inner (waterways), according to the applicable law;

r)   Shipping companies devoted to the commercial operation of inland and coastal trade vessels, with the exception of tourist cruise ships and the operation of dredges and naval devices for port construction, protection and operations;

s)   Services connected with the railway sector, that consist of passenger services, maintenance and roadbed rehabilitation, switching, locomotive and rail car repair shops, organization and marketing of self-contained rail cars, domestic freight terminal operations, and railway telecommunications; and

t)   Fuel and lubricant supply for ships, aircraft and rail equipment.

The foreign investment participation limits, as set forth in this Article, cannot be exceeded directly nor through trusts, agreements, business or incorporation contracts, pyramid schemes, or any other mechanism that grants control or a participation greater to that established in the provisions, excepting that which is indicated in Title Five of this Law.

ARTICLE 8.   A favorable decision by the Commission is required in order for foreign investment to participate, in a percentage greater than 49 percent, in the following economic and corporate activities:

I.   Port services for vessels, so that they can carry out inland navigation operations, including towage, warp anchorage and lighterage;

II.   Shipping companies devoted to working exclusively with oceangoing ships;

III.   Administration of air terminals;

IV.   Private preschool, elementary, high school, junior college, college, and combined educational services;

V.   Legal services;

VI.   Credit information companies;

VII.   Securities rating institutions;

VIII.   Insurance agents;

IX.   Cellular telephone;

X.   Pipeline construction for the transmission of petroleum and [oil] derivatives; and

XI.   Drilling of oil and gas wells.

ARTICLE 9.   In Mexican companies, where foreign investment seeks to directly or indirectly participate in more than 49 percent of their capital stock, a favorable decision by the Commission is required only when the total value of assets of the companies involved, at the time the acquisition application is submitted, exceeds the amount annually determined by the Commission.

SECOND TITLE
ON THE ACQUISITION OF REAL ESTATE AND ON TRUSTS

Chapter I
On the acquisition of real estate

ARTICLE 10.   In accordance with the provisions of Article 27, Section I, of the Mexican Constitution, Mexican corporations with a clause of exclusion of foreigners, or that have entered into the agreement referred to in said provisions, will be able to acquire ownership of domestic real estate.

In the case of corporations whose statutes include the agreement referred to in Article 27, Section I, of the Constitution, the following will apply:

I.   They will be able to acquire ownership of real estate located in the restricted zone, that is to be used for non-residential activities, having to register said acquisition with the Secretariat of Foreign Relations; and

II.   They will be able to acquire rights to real estate in the restricted zone, that they will use for residential purposes, according to the provisions of the following Chapter.

Chapter II
On trusts for real estate in the restricted zone

ARTICLE 11.   Permission from the Secretariat of Foreign Relations is required in order for credit institutions to acquire rights, as trustees, to real estate located within the restricted zone when the purpose of the trust is to allow the use and development of such properties without establishing property rights over them, and the trusts will be:

I.   Mexican corporations without a clause of exclusion of foreigners, as provided in Article 10, Section II, of this Law; and

II.   Foreign individuals and entities.

ARTICLE 12.   The rights to the use and enjoyment of real estate located in the restricted zone will be understood, through the utilization and development of the same, which accordingly includes proceeds, products and generally any yield that result from profitable operations and exploitation by third parties or through the trustee institution.

ARTICLE 13.   The duration of the trusts referred to in this Chapter will be for a maximum period of 50 years, which can be extended for the same [period] through application by the interested party.

The Secretariat of Foreign Relations reserves the right to verify, at any time, observance of the conditions through which the permits and registries referred to in this Title are granted.

ARTICLE 14.   The Secretariat of Foreign Relations will decide on the permits referred to in this Chapter, taking into consideration the economic and social benefits that fulfillment of these transactions will mean to the Nation.

Every permit request that meets the indicated requisites will have to be granted, by the Secretariat of Foreign Relations, within 30 working days following the date it is submitted. Registrations, with the registrar referred to in Article 10, Section I, will have to be processed within a maximum period of 15 working days following the presentation of the application. Otherwise, the corresponding permit or registration will be considered granted.

THIRD TITLE
ON CORPORATIONS

On the setting up and modification of corporations

ARTICLE 15.   Permission from the Secretariat of Foreign Relations is required in order to form corporations. The clause of exclusion of foreigners, or the agreement provided in Article 27, Section I, of the Constitution, will have to be inserted into the statutes of corporations that are formed.

ARTICLE 16.   Permission from the Secretariat of Foreign Relations is required in order for established corporations to change their title or trade name, or modify their clause of exclusion of foreigners for the admission of foreigners.

FOURTH TITLE
ON INVESTMENT BY FOREIGN ENTITIES

ARTICLE 17.   Without prejudicing that which is established in international treaties and agreements that Mexico is party to, in order for foreign entities to be able to routinely carry out commercial transactions in the Mexican Republic, authorization from the Secretariat will have to be obtained for their subsequent registration in the Public Registry of Commerce, in compliance with the General Law of Business (Mercantile) Corporations, Articles 250 and 251.

Every application, in order to obtain the authorization referred to in the previous paragraph [and] that meets the corresponding requisites, must be granted by the Secretariat within 15 working days following the date it is submitted.

FIFTH TITLE
ON NEUTRAL INVESTMENT

Chapter I
On the concept of neutral investment

ARTICLE 18.   Neutral investment is that made in Mexican corporations or authorized trusts in compliance with this Title and will not be calculated in order to determine the percentage of foreign investment in the capital stock of Mexican corporations.

Chapter II
On neutral investment represented by documents issued by trustee institutions

ARTICLE 19.   The Secretariat will be able to authorize trustee (fiduciary) institutions to issue neutral investment documents that singularly grant, with respect to corporations, pecuniary rights to their holders and, accordingly, limited corporate rights, without giving their holders the right to vote in their Regular Shareholder's Meetings.

Chapter III
On neutral investment represented by a special series of stocks

ARTICLE 20.   The investment in stocks without voting rights, or with limited corporate rights, is considered neutral as long as prior authorization has been obtained from the Secretariat and, when applicable, the National Securities Commission.

Chapter IV
On neutral investment in financial group's holding companies, multiple banking institutions and brokerage firms

ARTICLE 21.   With prior opinions from the Secretariat of Finance and Public Credit, and the National Securities Commission, the Secretariat will be able to decide on neutral foreign investment through the purchase of common participation certificates issued by fiduciary institutions authorized to do so, whose patrimony is made up of representative series "B" shares of the capital stock of financial group's holding companies [or] multiple banking institutions, or representative series "A" shares of the capital stock of brokerage firms.

Chapter V
On neutral investment made by International Development Finance Corporations

ARTICLE 22.   The Commission will be able to decide on neutral investment that international development finance corporations seek to make in the capital stock of corporations, in accordance with the terms and conditions established in order to do so in the Regulation [internal rules] of this Law.

SIXTH TITLE
ON THE NATIONAL FOREIGN INVESTMENT COMMISSION

Chapter I
On the structure of the Commission

ARTICLE 23.   The Commission will be composed of the Secretaries of Government (Interior); Foreign Relations; Finance and Public Credit; Social Development; Energy, Mines and State-owned (Parastatal) Industry; Commerce and Industrial Development; Communications and Transportation; Labor and Social Welfare; and Tourism, who will be able to assign an Undersecretary as an alternate. Furthermore, those officials who have responsibility regarding the subjects dealt with may be invited to participate in the sessions of the Commission.

ARTICLE 24.   The Commission will be chaired by the Secretary of Commerce and Industrial Development, and in order to function it will have an Executive Secretary and a Committee of Representatives.

ARTICLE 25.   The Committee of Representatives will be made up of a public servant named by each of the Cabinet Secretaries who form the Commission, and it will have those powers delegated by the same Commission.

Chapter II
On the duties of the Commission

ARTICLE 26. The Commission will have the following duties:

I. To issue policy guidelines regarding foreign investment, and to design mechanisms in order to promote investment in Mexico;

II. To decide, through the Secretariat, on the legal basis of the participation of foreign investment activities and acquisitions that are specifically regulated, and when applicable on the terms and conditions, in keeping with Articles 8 and 9 of this Law;

III. To be the obligatory consulting agency on foreign investment issues for agencies and entities of the federal government;

IV. To establish the criteria for the application of legal and regulatory provisions on foreign investment, through the issuance of general resolutions; and

V. Other corresponding [duties] in accordance with this regulation.

ARTICLE 27. Duties of the Executive Secretary of the Commission:

I. To represent the Commission;

II. To report the resolutions of the Commission through the Secretariat;

III. To complete the studies assigned by the Commission;

IV. To present an annual statistical report to Congress on the performance of foreign investment in the country, that includes the economic sectors and regions where it is located; and

V. Other corresponding [duties] in accordance with this Law.

Chapter III
On the operation of the Commission

ARTICLE 28. The Commission will have to decide on applications submitted for its consideration within a period of time not to exceed 45 working days from the date of presentation of the respective application, according to the terms established in the Regulation of this Law.

In the event that the Commission does not make its decision in the time allotted, the application will be considered approved as presented. At the express request of the interested party, the Secretariat will have to issue the corresponding authorization.

ARTICLE 29. In order to evaluate the applications submitted for its consideration, the Commission will heed the following criteria:

I. The impact on employment and the training of workers;

II. The technological contribution;

III. Observance of the regulations on environmental matters as contained in the ecological codes that govern the issues; and

IV. In general, the contribution in order to increase the competitiveness of the country's productive base.

The Commission, when deciding on the legal merits of an application, will only be able to impose requisites that do not distort international trade.

ARTICLE 30. The Commission will be able to prevent acquisitions, through foreign investment, for national security reasons.

SEVENTH TITLE
ON THE NATIONAL FOREIGN INVESTMENT REGISTRY

ARTICLE 31.   The Registry will not be public in nature, and it will be separated into sections as established in its Regulation, which will also determine its organization and the information that will have to be filed with the Registry.

ARTICLE 32.   [The following] will have to be recorded in the Registry:

I.   Mexican corporations with foreign investment participation;

II.   Foreign individuals or entities that routinely carry out commercial activities in the Mexican Republic, and subsidiaries of foreign investors established in the country; and

III.   Stock or partnership, real estate, and neutral investment trusts, by virtue of which rights are derived in favor of foreign investment.

The obligation to register will be the responsibility of the individuals or entities referred to in Sections I and II (above), and in the case of Section III, the obligation will apply to the fiduciary institutions. The registration will have to be done within 40 working days following the date the corporation was formed, or [following] the act of foreign investment; from the legalization or registration with an official notary of the relative documents of the foreign corporation; or from the establishment of the respective trust or granting of beneficiary rights of the trust in favor of foreign investment.

ARTICLE 33.   The Registry will issue proof of registration when the following data is included in the application:

I. With respect to Sections I and II [above]:

   a)   Name, firm name or trade name, address, applicable date of incorporation, and the principal economic activity to take place;

   b)   Name and address of the legal representative;

   c)   Name and address of the persons authorized to receive and hear notices;

   d)   Name, firm name or trade name, nationality and applicable immigration status, address of the foreign investors abroad or in the country, and their percentage of participation;

   e)   Amount of capital stock undersigned and paid, or undersigned and payable; and

   f)   Estimated date for the operations to begin, and the approximate amount of total investment with its calendar schedule.

II. With respect to of Section II [above]:

   a)   Name of the fiduciary institution;

   b)   Name, firm name or trade name, address, and nationality of the foreign investment or the settlor foreign investors;

   c)   Name, firm name or trade name, address, and nationality of the foreign investment or the foreign investor's designated trustees;

   d)   Date of establishment, purposes and duration of the trust; and

   e)   Description, value, destination and, if applicable, location of the patrimony held in trust.

Once the proof of registration and its renewals are issued, the Registry reserves the right to ask for clarifications with respect to the information submitted.

The Registry will have to be notified of any modification to the information presented according to the terms of this Article, in accordance with that established in its Regulation.

ARTICLE 34.   In the formation, modification, transformation, merger, split, dissolution and liquidation of business (mercantile) corporations, companies and individual associations, and in general in all legal acts and proceedings where an individual or representatives participate, notary publics will require the persons or their representatives who must be recorded with the Registry, according to Article 32 of this Law, to accredit their registration before said registry, or in the event that the registration is being processed [that they submit evidence of] the corresponding application. If not accredited, the notary will be able to authorize the related public document, and he/she will report said omission to the Registry within ten working days following the authorization date of the document.

ARTICLE 35. The individuals who must be recorded in the Register will have to renew their proof of registration annually, for which it will suffice to submit an economic-financial questionnaire in accordance with the terms set in the respective Regulation.

ARTICLE 36.   Federal, state and municipal authorities are required to provide the necessary reports and certifications to the Secretariat, in order for [it] to perform its duties in accordance with this Law and its regulatory provisions.

EIGHTH TITLE
ON PENALTIES

ARTICLE 37.   When actions are carried out in violation of the provisions of this Law, the Secretariat will be able to revoke the authorizations that have been granted.

The statutory acts, agreements or partnerships declared null and void by the Secretariat for violating this Law will not have legal effect between the parties, nor will they be recognized with respect to third parties.

ARTICLE 38.   Infractions to that established in this Law and its regulatory provisions will be penalized according to the following:

I.   In the event that the foreign investment carries out activities, acquisitions or any other act that requires a favorable decision from the Commission in order to be performed, without this having been obtained beforehand, a fine of 1,000 to 5,000 salaries will be imposed;

II.   In the event that foreign legal entities routinely carry out commercial activities in the Mexican Republic, without having obtained authorization from the Secretariat beforehand, a fine of 500 to 1,000 salaries will be imposed;

III.   In the event of acts in violation of this Law or its regulatory provisions with respect to neutral investment, fines of 100 to 300 salaries will be imposed;

IV.   With respect to the obligations of those required to register, report or notify the Registry, in the event of an omission, late filing, [or] incomplete or incorrect submission of information, a fine of 30 to 100 salaries will be imposed;

V.   In the event of bogus/("a simulation of") activities, in order to allow the possession of real estate in the restricted zone, or for it to be at the disposal of foreign individuals or entities, or Mexican corporations without a clause of exclusion of foreigners, in violation of the provision in the Second and Third Titles of this Law, the violator will be assessed a fine of up to the total amount of the transaction; and

VI. In the event of other violations of this Law or its regulatory provisions, a fine of 100 to 1,000 salaries will be imposed.

For the purposes of this Article, salary means the general daily minimum salary in effect in the Federal District at the time the violation is determined.

In order to determine and impose penalties, the affected party will have to be heard first, and in the event of pecuniary penalties the nature and seriousness of the violation, the economic means of the violator, the time that transpired from the date the obligation was to be met to its fulfillment or regularization, and the total value of the transaction [must be] taken into consideration.

The imposition of penalties will be the responsibility of the Secretariat, with the exception of the infraction referred to in Section V of this Article, and those others related to the Second and Third Titles of this Law, that will be applied by the Secretariat of Foreign Relations.

The imposition of the penalties referred to in this Title will be without prejudice to corresponding civil or penal liability [that may apply].

ARTICLE 39.   The notary publics will report, include or attach the official notices that list the authorizations that must be issued, according to this Law, in the official records or appendices of the documents they execute. When they ratify documents in which such authorizations are not reported, they will be subject to the penalties as established in the corresponding notary laws and the Federal Law of Notary Publics.

TRANSITORY

FIRST.   This Law will enter into effect the day following its publication in the *Official Daily*.

SECOND.   It abrogates [the following]:

I.   The Law to Promote Mexican Investment and Regulate Foreign Investment, published in the *Diario Oficial*, March 9, 1973;

II.   The Organic Law of Section I, Article 27 of the Constitution, published in the *Diario Oficial*, January 21, 1926; and

III. The Decree that established the transitory need to obtain permission for the acquisition of goods by foreigners, and for the establishment or modification of Mexican corporations that have or might have [sic: tuvieren] foreign partners, published in the *Diario Oficial*, July 7, 1944.

THIRD.   It repeals [the following]:

I.   Articles 46 and 47 of the Federal Firearms and Explosives Law, published in the *Diario Oficial*, January 11, 1972; and

II.   All legal, regulatory and administrative provisions, of a general nature, that are contrary to this Law.

FOURTH.   While the Regulations for this Law are being prepared, the Regulation of the Law to Promote Mexican Investment and Regulate Foreign Investment, published in the *Diario Oficial*, May 16, 1989, will remain in effect over all that which is not contrary to [this Law].

FIFTH.   Foreign investors, and corporations with foreign investment, that as of the publication date of this Law have agreed upon programs, [met] requisites and [made] commitments with the Commission, its Executive Secretary, or the General Directorate of Foreign Investment of the Secretariat, will be able to submit an exemption of their compliance for the consideration of said General Directorate, so that [said] administrative agency will have to respond regarding the movement [of the material] through channels in a period not to exceed 45 working days from the presentation of the corresponding request. Those foreign investors who do not make use of the possibility of the referred to exemption will have to comply with the obligations previously defined, with respect to the indicated Commission, public entities and persons.

SIXTH.   International ground transportation of passengers, tourism and freight activities, between points within Mexico, and the service of administering passenger and auxiliary service bus and truck terminals, are exclusively reserved for Mexicans, or Mexican corporations with a clause of exclusion of foreigners.

Nevertheless, foreign investment will be able to participate in the [above] mentioned activities according to the following provisions:

I.   As of December 18, 1995, up to 49 percent of the capital stock in Mexican corporations;

II.   As of January 1, 2001, up to 51 percent of the capital stock of Mexican corporations; and

III.   As of January 1, 2004, up to 100 percent of the capital stock of Mexican corporations, without the need to obtain the favorable decision from the Commission.

SEVENTH.   Foreign investment will be able to participate in up to 49 percent of the capital stock of Mexican companies involved in the manufacture and assembly of parts, equipment and accessories for the automobile industry, without prejudice to the provisions of the Decree for the Promotion and Modernization of the Automobile Industry. As of January 1, 1999, foreign investment will be able to participate in up to 100 percent in the capital stock of Mexican corporations, without the need to obtain the favorable decision from the Commission.

EIGHTH.   Foreign investment will be able to participate in up to 49 percent of the capital stock of Mexican corporations involved in the sales activities of video-text services and packaged telephone selectors. As of July 1, 1995, foreign investment will be able to participate in up to 100 percent in the corporations dedicated to the mentioned services, without the need to obtain the favorable decision from the Commission.

NINTH.   The favorable decision of the Commission is required for foreign investment to participate in a greater percentage than 49 percent of the capital stock of corporations that are involved in building, construction and installation works activities. As of January 1, 1999, foreign investment will be able to participate in up to 100 percent in the capital stock of Mexican corporations involved in the same, without the need to obtain the favorable decision from the Commission.

TENTH.   For the purposes of the provision in Article 9, and whereas the Commission sets the amount of the total value of the assets that are referred to in said Article, the amount of N$85 million new pesos is set.

ELEVENTH.   The provisions in the Second Title, Chapter II, of [this Law], with all of the resulting benefits, will apply to foreign investors and Mexican corporations with a clause of admission of foreigners who hold real estate trusts in the restricted zone when this Law goes into effect.

Mexico, D.F., December 15, 1993. Dip. Fernando Rodríguez Cerna, President; Sen. Eduardo Robledo Rincón, President; Dip. Juan Adrián Ramírez García, Secretary; Sen. Antonio Melgar Aranda, Secretary.

In observance of that ordered under Article 89, Section I, of the Political Constitution of the United Mexican States, and for its due publication and observance, this Decree is issued [by] the Federal Executive Authority, in Mexico City, Federal District, this December 23, 1993. Carlos Salinas de Gortari.

Appendix C

Foreign Ownership Allowed in 1993 Investment Law

Percent Foreign Ownership Allowed in Restricted Sectors of the Economy

Sector	1993 Foreign Investment Law	NAFTA	1973 Foreign Investment Law
Primary			
Agriculture and Livestock	49	49	100 (government approval required)
Cooperative Production Societies	10	10	0
Fishing	49	49	49
Forestry	49	49	0
Industry and Manufacturing			
Auto Parts	49 rising to 100 in January 1999	49 rising to 100 in January 1999	40
Basic Petrochemicals	0	0	0
Bus/Truck Construction	49 rising to 100 in January 1999	49 rising to 100 in January 1999	40
Cable Television	49	49	0
Coal Mining	Not specified	49 (up to 100 with government approval until January 1999; thereafter 100 with no approval required)	34

Sector	1993 Foreign Investment Law	NAFTA	1973 Foreign Investment Law
Construction	49 (up to 100 with government approval until January 1999; thereafter 100 with no approval required)	49 (up to 100 with government approval until January 1999; thereafter 100 with no approval required)	Up to 100 with government authorization
Electricity	0	0	0
Minerals Mining (Ordinary Concession)	Not specified	49 (up to 100 with government approval until January 1999; thereafter 100 with no approval required)	49
Minerals Mining— Sulphur, Phosphorus and Ferrous Minerals (Special Concession)	Not specified	49 (up to 100 with government approval until January 1999; thereafter 100 with no approval required)	34
Munitions Manufacturing	49	49	49
Nuclear Energy	0	0	0
Petroleum and Other Hydrocarbons	0	0	0
Radioactive Minerals	0	0	0
Retail Gasoline and LPG	0	0	0
Secondary Petrochemicals	100	100	100
Tertiary Petrochemicals	100	100	100
Financial Sector			
Banking	30	100 with size and market share restrictions described above	30

Sector	1993 Foreign Investment Law	NAFTA	1973 Foreign Investment Law
Brokerage Houses	30	100 with size and market share restrictions described above	30
Credit Unions	0	0	0
Financial Groups	30	100 with size and market share restrictions described above	30
Financial Leasing	49	100 with size and market share restrictions described above	30
Foreign Exchange Houses	49	100	30
Insurance	49	100 with size and market share restrictions described above	30
Mutual Fund Companies	49	100	0
Other Services			
Bus and Truck Land Transportation of Passengers and Freight	0 (up to 49 in December 1995, 51 in 2001, and 100 in 2004)	0 (up to 49 in 1997, 51 in 2001, and 100 in 2004)	0
Bus Terminal Administration	0 (up to 49 in December 1995, 51 in 2001, and 100 in 2004)	Up to 100 with government authorization	Up to 100 with government authorization
Business Real Estate			
Restricted Zone	100 with government approval	100 with government approval	30-year trust
Unrestricted Zone	100 with government approval	100 with government approval	100 with government approval
Cable Television	49	49	0

Sector	1993 Foreign Investment Law	NAFTA	1973 Foreign Investment Law
Drilling Services for Oil and Gas	49 (up to 100 with government authorization)	49 (up to 100 with government authorization)	Up to 100 with government authorization
Mail	0	0	0
Maritime Services	49	49 (up to 100 with government approval)	0
Periodicals	49	49 for Mexican editions and 100 for foreign editions	100 with government approval
Port Administration	0	0	0
Private Educational Institutions	49 (up to 100 with government authorization)	49 (up to 100 with government authorization)	Up to 100 with government authorization
Radio	0	0	0
Railroads	0	0	0
Residential Real Estate			
Restricted Zone (within 100 km. of border or 50 km. of seacoasts)	50-year renewable trust	30-year renewable trust	30-year trust
Unrestricted Zone	100 with government approval	100 with government approval	100 with government approval
Satellite Communications	0	0	0
Telegraphic and Radio Telegraphic Services	0	0	0
Telegraphic Services	0	0	0
Television	0	0	0

Bibliography

There is a wealth of primary and secondary information on the topic of Mexican financial services, banking, investment, and free trade. It was imperative to review a broad cross-section of government documents as well as financial publications. Key financial groups and banks also produce a large volume of data. In the case of banking, much of the primary information is held by governmental agencies that release only condensed statistical data. Since the devaluation of the Mexican peso in December 1994, both the Mexican and U.S. governments have attempted to provide both timely and detailed information. The U.S. congressional hearings during early 1995 and the mandated U.S. Treasury monthly reports on the status of the Mexican economy, begun in May 1995, provide a wealth of information on the evolution of the recovery of the Mexican economy, banking system, and impact of NAFTA. A broad cross-section of Mexican government documents, banking sources, and secondary material is referenced. Since newspapers and financial periodicals played such a pivotal role in the understanding of the Mexican crisis and its impact on markets worldwide, an extensive article review is provided. Investment company reports, newsletters, and economic journals (the publication of all three has more than doubled during the early 1990's) provide a wealth of month-to-month analysis and broad perspective on the changing Mexican economy. Knight-Ridder Financial News and Bloomberg online news services provided timely data and day-to-day information that were not always covered in the mass media.

The appendixes include a number of key timely primary reference documents not readily available on the financial services section of NAFTA and the new Mexican investment and banking laws. These documents are crucial to any review and assessment of U.S.-Mexico cross-border banking, investment, and finance.

The bibliographical material on this topic, while never complete, contains as much up-to-date source material as was available to the author. These sources were key to this study and should provide an excellent foundation for future research.

OFFICIAL RECORDS AND DOCUMENTS: UNITED STATES AND MEXICO

United States

Border Environment Cooperation Commission. "Introduction and BECC's Function." El Paso: 1995.

California Trade and Commerce Agency. Lloyd Day (ed.). *NAFTA: California and the North American Marketplace.* 1994.

Comptroller of the Currency. Daniel E. Nolle. "Are Foreign Banks Out-Competing U.S. Banks in the U.S. Market?" Paper 94–5. Washington, D.C.: May 1994.

Federal Reserve Bank. *Federal Reserve Bulletin.* Washington, D.C.: March 1994 to September 1996.

———. North American Free Trade Agreement between the Government of the United States of America, the Government of Canada and the Government of the United Mexican States 1993. Vols. I and II. Washington, D.C.: 1994.

———. *Regulation K: International Banking Operations 10/93.* 12 CFR 211. Washington, D.C.: October 6, 1993.

INPAC. *Report to the United States Congress Concerning the Investment Chapter of the North American Free Trade Agreement.* Washington, D.C.: September 14, 1992.

ISTEA. Assessment of Border Crossings and Transportation Corridors for North American Trade. Washington, D.C.: March 7, 1994.

U.S. Bureau of the Census (CIR). Frank B. Hobbs. *Mexico's Total Employed, and Excess Labor Force: Future Prospects, 1985 to 2000.* CIR Staff Report No. 47. Washington, D.C.: March 1989.

U.S. Congress. House. Committee on Banking and Finance. *Compilation of Basic Banking Laws.* CP: 102–14, 102nd Cong., 2nd sess. Washington, D.C.: 1992.

———. House. Committee on Banking and Finance. *Export-Import Bank.* Serial No. 102–16, 102nd Cong., 1st sess. Washington, D.C.: 1991.

———. House. Committee on Banking and Finance. *Impact of Accounting and Regulation Procedures on the Third World Debt.* Serial No. 101–29, 101st Cong., 1st sess. Washington, D.C.: 1989.

———. House. Committee on Banking and Finance. *International Monetary Fund.* Serial No. 102–48, 102nd Cong., 1st sess. Washington, D.C.: 1991.

———. House. Committee on Government Operations. *The Federal Response to the Impact of Peso Devaluation on U.S. Border Business.* Report No. 98–579, 98th Cong., 1st sess. Washington, D.C.: November 18, 1983.

———. House. Committee on Ways and Means. *Implementation of the North American Free Trade Agreement.* H.R. 3450, Report No. 103–361, 103rd Cong., 1st sess. Washington, D.C.: November 4–15, 1993.

———. House. Committee on Ways and Means. *North American Free Trade Agreement Implementation Act.* Report No. 103–361, Part 1–3, 103rd Cong., 1st sess. Washington, D.C.: November 15, 1993.

———. House. Committee on Ways and Means. *Overview and Compilation of U.S. Trade Statutes.* CP: 103–1, 103rd Cong., 1st sess. Washington, D.C.: 1993.

———. House. Committee on Ways and Means. *To Revitalize Trade between the United*

States and Mexico and to Stimulate the International Competitiveness of both Countries. H.R. 1360, 101st Cong., 1st sess. Washington, D.C.: March 9, 1989.

———. House. Hearing of the Subcommittee on Economic Goals and Intergovernmental Policy. *The United States-Mexico Border Economic Situation.* 98th Cong., 1st sess. Washington, D.C.: August 1983.

———. House. Message from the President of the United States Transmitting the Uruguay Round Trade Agreement. 103rd Cong., 2nd sess., House Document 103–316, Vol. 1. Washington, D.C.: September 27, 1994.

———. House. NAFTA Congressional Fact Finding Mission to Laredo, Texas; comments by Tommy Tomko, plant manager of Packard Electric, October 17, 1993.

———. House. Office of Technology Assessment. *U.S.-Mexico Trade: Pulling Together or Pulling Apart?* ITE-545. Washington, D.C.: October 1992.

———. House. Southwest Border Surface Transportation: Investment in the Future, testimony by John A. Adams, Jr., Chairman Infrastructure Committee: Border Trade Alliance to the Subcommittee on Surface Transportation, 103st Cong., 1st sess. Washington, D.C.: March 15, 1994.

———. House. Subcommittee on International Development, Finance, Trade and Monetary Policy. *The U.S.-Mexican Free Trade Agreement.* 102nd Cong., 1st sess. Washington, D.C.: April 16, 1991.

———. House. Subcommittee on Trade of the Committee on Ways and Means. *Background Information and Compilation of Materials on Items 807.00 and 806.3 of the Tariff Schedules of the U.S.* Washington, D.C.: July 12, 1976.

U.S. Congress. Senate. Committee on Banking, Housing, and Urban Affairs. *The Mexican Peso Crisis and th Administration's Proposed Loan Guarantee Package to Mexico.* S. Hrg. 104–164, 104th Cong., 1st sess. Washington, D.C.: 1995.

———. Senate Joint Economic Committee, Subcommittee on Economic Growth, Trade and Taxes. *Free Trade and the United States-Mexico Borderlands.* 102nd Cong., 1st sess. Washington, D.C.: July 1, 1991.

U.S. Department of Agriculture. *Agriculture in a North American Free Trade Agreement: Analysis of Liberalizing Trade Between the United Stated and Mexico.* No. 246. Washington, D.C.: September 1992.

U.S. Department of Commerce. (ITA) *Financing the Border of Tomorrow: Progress Report on the U.S.-Mexico Border Infrastructure Finance Conference.* San Antonio: July 1993.

———. (ITA) *North American Free Trade Agreement.* Washington, D.C.: May 1991.

———. Office of Mexico. "Mexico—Vital Statistics." Washington, D.C.: 1993.

———. (ITA) "Successful Uruguay Round Launches Revitalized World Trading System." *Uruguay Round Update.* January 1994.

———. (ITA) *Summary of the U.S.-Canada Free Trade Agreement.* Washington, D.C.: January 2, 1988.

———. (ITA *U.S. Exports to Latin America and the Caribbean: A State-by-State Overview 1987–1990.* Washington, D.C.: March 1992.

———. (ITA) *U.S. Exports to Mexico: A State-by-State Overview 1987–1990.* Washington, D.C.: August 1991.

———. (ITA) *U.S.-Mexico Border Economic Development Task Force: Directory of Border-Related Programs.* Washington, D.C.: October 1994.

————. NAFTA Office. "NAFTA: 1995 Update." Washington, D.C.: March 11, 1996.

————. *U.S. Global Trade Outlook 1995–2000: Toward the 21st Century*. Washington, D.C.: March 1995.

————. William R. Cavitt. "The North American Free Trade Agreement." Director, Office of Canada, Conference on the Future of Trans-Atlantic Trade, Le Havre, France, May 3, 1994.

————. David C. Lund. "Foreign Banking in the United States." *Foreign Direct Investment in the United States: An Update*. Washington, D.C.: June 1993.

U.S. Department of State. "U.S.-Mexico Relations." *Gist*. Bureau of Public Affairs. Washington, D.C.: July 31, 1992.

U.S. Department of the Treasury. Memo, "The Multilateral Program to Restore Financial Stability in Mexico." Washington, D.C.: January 31, 1995.

————. Memo, "The Multilateral Support Effort." RR-27, Washington, D.C.: January 25, 1995.

————. "Monthly Report by the Secretary of the Treasury." Mexican Debt Disclosure Act of 1995, Washington, D.C.: May 1995-March 1996.

————. *Report to Congress on Foreign Government Treatment of U.S. Commercial Banking Operations*. Washington, D.C.: 1974.

————. "Semi-Annual Report to Congress by the Secretary of the Treasury on Behalf of the President." Mexican Debt Disclosure Act of 1995, Washington, D.C: June and December, 1995.

————. "U.S.-Mexico Framework Agreement for Mexican Economic Stabilization [and accompanying documents on medium-term swaps, guarantees, and oil proceeds facility agreement]." Washington, D.C: February 21, 1995.

U.S. Embassy, Mexico. *Foreign Investment Climate Report*. Mexico, D.F.: June 1989.

————. *Foreign Investment Climate Report*. Mexico, D.F.: August 1991.

————. *Mexico: Economic Trends Report*. Mexico, D.F.: November 1989.

————. *Mexico: Foreign Investment Report*. Mexico, D.F.: Fall-Winter 1993.

————. *Mexico's Economic and Financial Report*. Mexico D.F.: April 1993.

U.S. Environmental Protection Agency. *Summary: Environmental Plan for the Mexican-U.S. Border Area*. Washington, D.C.: February 1992.

U.S. General Accounting Office. *Cargo Preference: Effects of U.S. Export-Import Cargo Preference Laws on Exporters*. Washington, D.C.: October 1994.

————. *The General Agreement on Tariffs and Trade: Uruguay Round Final Act Should Produce Overall U.S. Economic Gains*. Washington, D.C.: July 1994.

————. *International Trade: Assessment of the Generalized System of Preferences Program*. Washington, D.C.: November 1994.

————. *International Trade: Combating Unfair Foreign Trade Practices*. Washington, D.C.: March 1987.

————. *International Trade: Strengthening Worldwide Protection of Intellectual Property Rights*. Washington, D.C.: April 1987.

————. *North American Free Trade Agreement: Structure and Status of Implementing Organizations*. Washington, D.C.: October 1994.

U.S. International Trade Commission. *The Impact of Increased U.S.-Mexican Trade on Southwest-Border Development Investigation, No. 332–223*. McAllen: 1986.

———. *Potential Impact on the U.S. Economy and Selected Industries of the North American Free Trade Agreement.* Washington, D.C.: January 1993.

———. *Production Sharing: U.S. Imports Under Harmonized Tariff Schedule Provisions 9802.00.60 and 9802.00.80, 1989–1992.* Washington, D.C.: February 1993 and February 1994.

———. *Production Sharing: U.S. Subheadings 9802.00.60 and 9802.0080, 1985–1988: Formerly Imports Under Items 806.30 and 807.00 of the Tariff Schedules of the United States.* Washington, D.C.: December 1989.

———. *The Year In Trade: Operation in Trade Agreements Program During 1995.* 47th Report. Washington, D.C.: August 1996.

U.S. Securities and Exchange Commission. *Annual Report of the Republic of Argentina.* Washington, D.C.: November 30, 1995.

U.S. Small Business Administration. *Opportunity in Mexico: A Small Business Guide.* Washington, D.C.: 1992.

U.S. Trade Representative. Mexico: 1996 National Trade Estimate. Washington, D.C.: April 1996.

———. 1990 Trade Policy Agenda and 1989 Annual Report of the President of the United States on the Trade Agreement Program. Washington, D.C.: 1990.

———. 1993 Trade Policy Agenda and 1992 Annual Report of the President of the United States on the Trade Agreement Program. Washington, D.C.: 1993.

———. Statement of PPG Industries, Inc. Regarding the Accession of the General Agreement of Tariffs and Trade (GATT), by Eugene L. Stewart et al. Washington D.C.: February 18, 1986.

———. Testimony of Ambassador Mickey Kantor Before the Subcommittee on International Trade, Committee on Ways and Means, U.S. House. Washington, D.C.: March 11, 1993.

———. Testimony by John H. Keck, President and CEO, Union National Bank of Texas, on the impact of NAFTA on the U.S.-Mexican Border and Financial Services. Washington, D.C.: September 4, 1991.

———. Understanding Between the Government of the United States of America and the Government of the United Mexican States Concerning a Framework of Principles and Procedures for Consultations Regarding Trade and Investment Relations. Ambassador Clayton Yeutter and Secretary Hector Hernandez Cervantes. Mexico, D.F.: November 6, 1887.

White House. Memorandum for the United States Trade Representative: Trade Agreement Resulting from the Uruguay Round of Multilateral Trade Negotiations. Washington, D.C.: December 15, 1993.

———. Report of the Administration on the North American Free Trade Agreement and Actions Taken in Fulfillment of the May 1, 1991 Commitments. Washington, D.C.: September 18, 1992.

———. *Weekly Compilation of Presidential Documents.* Washington, D.C.: 1995–1996.

Mexico

Banco de Mexico. "Economic Policy: Results." *Review of the Economic Situation of Mexico.* June 1993.

———. *The Mexican Economy.* Mexico City: 1990–95.

————. "Mexico: A Global Investment Forum." Presentation to the Mexico Investment Board. September 1995.

————. "Mexico: A Political Overview." *Mexico-US Trade Advisory*, July 1991.

————. Monetary Policy Program for 1996. Mexico, D.F.: January 1996.

————. Report on Monetary Policy for 1996. Mexico, D.F.: 1996.

————. Ariel Buira. "The Mexican Stabilization Program." As seen in *El Mercado de Valores*. Mexico, D.F.: November 1995.

————. Ernesto Zedillo, Director, FICORCA. "FICORCA Facility Agreement." Mexico City: August 6, 1987.

Comision Nacional Bancaria de Valores. "The Mexican Banking System." New York: January 1996.

Commission of Foreign Investment. *Foreign Investment: Legal Framework and Its Application*. Mexico, D.F: 1986.

Comite para la Promocion de la Inversion en Mexico. *Economic and Business Overview*. Mexico, D.F.: June 1990.

Diario Oficial. January 21, 1926. [Investment law]

————. March 9, 1973. [Foreign investment law]

————. September 1, 1982. [Bank nationalization]

————. August 15, 1983. ["Old" maquiladora decree]

————. August 15, 1983. [Revised maquila law]

————. May 16, 1989. [Investment law]

————. December 11, 1989. [Automotive content decree]

————. December 22, 1989. [Revised maquiladora decree]

————. December 24, 1993. [Amended maquila law to comply with NAFTA]

————. December 27, 1993. [New Mexican investment law]

————. April 21, 1994. [Foreign bank investment in Mexico]

————. April 1, 1995. [Decree creating UDIs]

————. April 28, 1995. [Creation of the National Banking and Securities Commission]

————. June 19, 1996. [Registration of foreign banks in Mexico]

Embassy of Mexico. Ambassador Jorge Montano. "Border Trade Alliance Fall Conference." Washington D.C.: October 4, 1994.

INEGI. Annual Reports. Mexico, D.F.: 1985–95.

————. *El Sistema Bancario y Financiero en Mexico, 1970–1982*. Mexico, D.F.: 1984.

Instituto Mexicano de Comercio Exterior. *Mexico 1982 In-Bond Industry*. Publication No. 629. Mexico, D.F.: 1983.

Press Office of the President of Mexico. *Mexico: On the Record*. Mexico City: October/November 1992.

SECOFI. "Mexico Liberalizes Foreign Investment Regulations to Stimulate Domestic Economic Growth." Press release, Mexico, D.F.: May 15, 1989.

Secretaria de Programacion y Presupresto. *Mexico: Economic and Financial Report*. Secretaria de Relaciones Exteriores. Consulado Economic Reports. Mexico, D.F.: 1992–96.

————. *Segundo informe de gobierno, anexo I*. Mexico City: 1978.

United Mexican States. "Discount and Par Bond Exchange Agreement: Implementation Part I of the 1989–92 Financing Package for Mexico—Citibank, N.A. as Closing Agent." Mexico City: February 4, 1990.

————. Foreign Investment Supplement. January 1994.

———. Mexican Government Financial Plan. Mexico, D.F.: February 21, 1996.

———. *Mexico: Economic and Financial Report*. Mexico D.F.: Summer 1994.

———. *Mexico: Foreign Investment Report*. Mexico, D.F.: Fall/Winter 1993.

———. Offering Circular for U.S. $1,000,000,000 in Floating Rate Notes Due 1997. Mexico, D.F.: July 14, 1995.

———. Telegram. Embassy to U.S. Department of Commerce, re: Foreign Investment Law. January 27, 1994.

———. Telex. "Mexican Regulations for Banking and Other Financial Institutions under the NAFTA." February, 1994.

———. *The True Facts about the Expropriation of the Oil Companies' Properties in Mexico*. Mexico, D.F.: 1940.

———. Javier Flores. "The Banking Automation Equipment Market in Mexico." Mexico, D.F.: 1994.

Zedillo, Ernesto. FICORCA: Banco de Mexico to the International Community, "FICORCA Facility Agreement." Mexico City: August 6, 1987.

———. Secretary of Public Education. "Mexico's Economic and Investment Climate." *Investing in Mexico*. The Conference Board No. 999. New York: 1992.

———. Statement by the President at the Inauguration Ceremony of the Seventh Securities Market Convention. Mexico, D.F.: April 16, 1996.

———. Terms of Emergency Economic Plan as Agreed to by All Sectors of the Mexican Economy. Mexico, D.F.: January 3, 1995.

Other

Canadian Embassy. Mexico, D.F. "NAFTA Year One: The Canadian Perspective." Mexico, D.F.: April 1995.

General Agreement on Tariffs and Trade. *Trade Policy Report: Mexico 1993*. 2 vols. Geneva: July 1993.

International Monetary Fund. *Balance of Payments Statistics Yearbook*, Vol. 46, Part I. Washington, D.C.: 1995.

———. "Factors Behind the Financial Crisis in Mexico." *World Economic Outlook*. Washington, D.C.: May 1995.

Organization for Economic Co-Operation and Development (OECD). *Main Economic Indicators*. Paris: September 1995.

———. *OECD Economic Surveys: Mexico 1994–95*. Paris: 1995.

———. "The OECD in the 1990s." Paris: July 1994.

———. "Unfinished Business in Mexico's Reforms." *OECD Letter*, Vol. 4/9, November 1995.

———. Colin I. Bradford, Jr. (ed.). *Strategic Options for Latin America in the 1990s*. Paris: 1992.

———. Raymond W. Goldsmith. *The Financial Development of Mexico*. Paris: 1969.

———. Wilson Peres-Nunez. *Foreign Direct Investment and Industrial Development in Mexico*. Paris: 1990.

United Nations. *Global Outlook 2000: An Economic, Social and Environmental Perspective*. New York: 1990.

World Bank. Sam Laird and Alexander J. Yeats. *Trends in Non-tariff Barriers of Developed Countries, 1966–1986*. Washington, D.C.: 1988.

NEWSPAPERS AND NEWSLETTERS

Newspapers

Houston *Chronicle*
Juarez, Mexico *Diario de Juarez*
Laredo *Morning Times*
London *Financial Times*
Los Angeles Times
Mexico City *Daily Bulletin*
Mexico City *Excelsior*
Mexico City *El Financiero*
Mexico City *The News*
Mexico City *La Reforma*
Monterrey, Mexico *El Norte*
New York *Barron's*
New York *Investor's Business Daily*
New York Times
New York *USA Today*
New York *Wall Street Journal*
Nuevo Laredo, Mexico *El Diario*
Nuevo Laredo, Mexico *El Manana*
San Antonio *Express-News*
Washington Post
Washington *Times*

Newsletters: Public and Private

Arlington, Mass. *Environmental Watch: Latin America*
Arlington, Va. *Pratt's Letter*
Atlanta *Journal-Constitution*
Austin *Capitol Update*
Austin *EnviroMexico*
Austin *Fiscal Notes* (Office of the Texas Comptroller)
Basel, Switzerland *Economic and Financial Prospects* (Swiss Bank)
Bethesda, Md. *LDC Debt Report*
College Station, Tex. *Border Community Development News*
College Station, Tex. *Texas Economic Outlook*
Concord *Latin American Law and Business Report*
Dallas *Financial Industry Issues* (Federal Reserve Bank of Dallas)
Dallas *TransActions* (Bristol)
El Paso *Border Frontiers* (Federal Reserve Bank of Dallas)
El Paso *The Southwest Economy* (Federal Reserve Bank of Dallas)
Fort Worth *Mexican Business Review*
Hong Kong *The International Report*
Houston *Economic Digest*
Houston *Mexico Finance*
Houston *NAFTA Update* (Price Waterhouse)

La Jolla, Calif. *Hemisfile*
Laredo *Border Business Indicators*
Laredo *Laredo Manufacturing Association*
Laredo *Mexico-U.S. Trade Advisory*
Laredo *NAFTA Digest*
London *Emerging Debt Markets Report* (Goldman Sachs)
London *Latin American Economy and Business*
London *Latin American Monitor*
London *Latin American Weekly Report*
London *Mexico & NAFTA Report*
Maplewood, N.J. *Mexico Business Monthly*
Mexico, D.F. *Analisis: Direccion de Estudios Economicos* (Probursa)
Mexico, D.F. *Mexican Economic Report*
Mexico, D.F. *Mexletter*
Minot, N.D. *Central North American Trade Corridor*
New York *Americas Trade and Finance*
New York *Economic Week* (Citibank)
New York *Free Trade Advisory*
New York *Latin America Watch*
New York *Myers World Trade Report*
New York *U.S. Investment Perspectives* (Morgan Stanley)
New York *World Banking and Securities* (Deloitte Touche)
Rockville, Md. *Mexico Service*
San Antonio *Lawyer*
San Antonio *Mexico Trade Letter*
San Antonio *Trade Commission of Mexico Newsletter* (Bancomext)
St. Louis *International Economic Trends* (Federal Reserve Bank of St. Louis)
Stuart, Fla. *Technology Latin America*
Waco, Tex. *The Perryman Texas Letter*
Washington, D.C. *Bank Policy Report*
Washington, D.C. *Ex-Im Bank Bulletin*
Washington, D.C. *Inside NAFTA*
Washington, D.C. *Japan Economic Report [JEI]*
Washington, D.C. *The Kiplinger Washington Letter*
Washington, D.C. *LA/C Business Bulletin* (USDOC)
Washington, D.C. *Latin American Index*
Washington, D.C. *NAFTA Review* (EPA)
Washington, D.C. *News from Washington* (The State of Texas)

ARTICLES

Adams, John A., Jr. "For Mexico, 1996 Will Bring Modest Economic Recovery." Knight-Ridder Financial News (New York), December 14, 1995.
———. "Laredo Banking: On the Front Line of Financing U.S.-Mexico Trade." *International Trade World* (Dallas), Spring 1993.
———. "Laredo in Transition." *Explore* (Laredo), January 1996.
———. "Marketing in Mexico: Overview of Doing Business South of the Border." *International Trade in the 1990s* (Midland), May 1990.

————. "Mexican Debt Review: The Background and Possible Solution." *Infonational Review*, July 5, 1989.

————. "Mid-year Assessment: Updating the Mexican Economy." *Twin Plant News* (El Paso), September 1995.

————. "Window on the Future: Mexico in 1996." *Twin Plant News* (El Paso), December 1995.

————. "Without GATT, There'd Be No NAFTA." *Laredo Morning Times*, December 17, 1993.

Agosin, Manuel R. and Ricardo Ffrench-Davis. "Trade Liberalization and Growth: Recent Experiences in Latin America." *Journal of Interamerican Studies and World Affairs*, Fall 1995.

"Alamo City Snares NAFTA Bank." *San Antonio Express-News*, March 26, 1994.

Alm, Richard. "Monterrey Radiates Economic Confidence." *Dallas Morning News*, April 13, 1992.

Alm, Richard and David M. Gould. "The Saving Grace." *Economic Review* (Federal Reserve Bank of Dallas [FRBD]), Third Quarter 1994, pp. 43–52.

Andreas, Peter. "U.S.-Mexico: Open Markets, Closed Borders." *Foreign Policy*, No. 103, Summer 1996.

"Argentine-Mexican Par Bond Spread." *Perspectives on Emerging Markets*, June 2, 1995.

"Asia Fears a Latin 'Dragon'." *Far Eastern Economic Review*, as seen in *World Press Review*, October 1991, p. 44.

Aspe, Pedro. "Mexico's Ex-Finance Minister Sets the Record Straight." *Wall Street Journal*, July 14, 1995.

Associated Press. "Foreign Investments Fleeing Instability." *Laredo Morning Times*, April 19, 1994.

Baca, Reynaldo and Dexter Bryan. "The 'Mexican Dream': Al Norte, and Home Again." *Los Angles Times*, April 12, 1981.

Baerrensen, Donald W. "Devaluation and Merchandising in Texas Border Cities." *Texas Business Review*, September-October 1982.

————. "Mexico's Assembly Program: Implications for the United States." *Texas Business Review*, November-December 1981.

————. "Unemployment and Mexico's Border Industrialization Program." *Inter-American Economic Studies*, September 1975.

Baker and McKenzie. *North American Free Trade Handbook* (Draft) (Dallas), March 1994.

Bamrad, Joachim. "Mexico: The Year of the Bank." *U.S./Latin Trade*, April 1994.

Banamex-Accival. "Financiamiento Externo: Tasas en Estados Unidos, sus efectos sobre Mexico." *Estudios Economicos*, June 13, 1994.

————. *Informe Anval* (Mexico D. F.), 1994.

————. "Mercados Emergentes: Mercados de Capitales." *Estudios Economicos*, June 20, 1994.

————. "Mexico en los Mercados Financieros Internacionales." *Examen de la Situacion de Mexico*, Vol. LXX, Marza 1994.

————. "Mexico in the OECD." *Review of the Economic Situation of Mexico*, September 1992.

————. "NAFTA: More Competition, More Assurances." *Review of the Economic Situation of Mexico*, January 1994.

"Banca Texana a Monterrey." *El Diario*, March 16, 1994.

"Bank Brawl Begins over Border Trade." *Mexico Service*, May 6, 1994.

"Banking." [Mexico] *The Europa World Yearbook*, Vol. II, 1993.

"Banks Act to Boost Their Capital Bases." *Euromoney*, January 1994.

Bannon, Jeffrey, James H. Holcombs, and Richard L. Sprinkle. "An Evaluation of Mexican Policy Toward Foreign Direct Investment." *Southwest Journal of Business and Economics*, Spring 1990.

Barnett, Robert M. "Mexico's New Foreign Investment Law." *San Antonio Lawyer*, Winter 1993–94.

Barro, R. "Latin Lessons in Monetary Policy." *Wall Street Journal*, May 14, 1995.

Batterson, Robert. "Double Dealing on Latin Trade." *Journal of Commerce*, July 18, 1996.

Bear, Sterns & Co. "Action on Capital Gains Should Lift Markets." *Economic Outlook*, October 1993.

———. *Global Development*, March 25, 1994.

———. "Mexican Interest Rates, Economy and Politics." *Latin American Watch*, April 20, 1994.

Beckerman, Paul. "Central-Bank 'Distress' and Hyperinflation in Argentina, 1989–90." *Journal of Latin American Studies*, October 1995.

Bennett, David. "Insurance in Mexico Seen as Golden Opportunity." *San Antonio Express-News*, July 27, 1994.

———. "$60 Billion NAD Bank Investment Projected." *San Antonio Express-News*, April 27, 1994.

———. "Slaying Jolts Financial Markets." *San Antonio Express-News*, March 25, 1994.

———. "Two Large Bankers Battling for Border Bucks." *San Antonio Express-News*, March 1, 1994.

Bicknell, Justin. "Offer Fails to Electrify Investors." *El Financiero*, July 5, 1994.

Black, Ken U. and William A. Staples. "The Impact of Peso Devaluations on Retailers along the U.S.-Mexico Border." *Southwest Journal of Business and Economics*, 1985.

Blears, James. "Global Goals of the Bolsa." *Business Mexico*, 1994.

Blond, David. "The World According to GATT." *Global Production*, March-April 1994.

Bolin, William H. and Jorge Del Canto. "LDC Debt: Beyond Crisis Management." *Foreign Affairs*, Summer 1983.

Bosco, Pearl. "Latin American Banks Embrace Big Change." *Bank Systems and Technology*, April 1995.

Boyd, Roy G., Kerry Krutilla, and Joseph McKinney. "The Impact of Tariff Liberalization between the United States and Mexico: An Empirical Analysis." *Applied Economics*, No. 25, 1993.

Brady, Andrew. "Trading Points." *Barron's*, February 22, 1990.

Braubach, Robert P. "The New United States–Mexico Tax Treaty: A Former Incentive for Conducting International Business." *San Antonio Lawyer*, Winter 1993–94.

Bray, Anna J. "IMF Hopes a New $48 Bil Fund Will End Mexico-Style Problem." *Investor's Business Daily*, April 23, 1996.

———. "Mexican Government Fiddles As the Peso Burns." *Investor's Business Daily*, November 7, 1995.

Brenner, Reuven. "The Pursuit of Poverty." *Wall Street Journal*, November 14, 1995.

Brock, William E. "Trade and Debt: The Vital Linkage." *Foreign Affairs*, Summer 1984.

Bulman, Robin. "Political Woes May Hinder Mexico Investment Growth." *Journal of Commerce*, June 27, 1994.

"Bush Pleased with Plan to Reduce Mexican Debt." *The Eagle*, July 25, 1989.

"Business International: Financial Performance of U.S. Investors in Latin America." *Business Latin America*, November 9, 1992.

Butler, Charles E. "Mexico's Foreign Trade and Balance of Payments." *Texas Business Review*, Vol. 56, November-December 1982.

Capitol Update, Vol. 13, No. 7, April 1, 1994.

Carlson, Eugene. "Japanese Companies Increase Presence Near Mexican Border." *Wall Street Journal*, December 22, 1987.

Carlson, Laura. "Ejido Reforms Spark Debate." *Business Mexico*, December 1991.

———. "Making Money in Difficult Times." *Business Mexico*, November 1993.

Carroll, Paul B. "Peso Shockwaves Ripple through Mexico." *Wall Street Journal*, January 9, 1995.

Carroll, Paul B. and Craig Torres. "Mexico Unveils Program of Harsh Fiscal Medicine." *Wall Street Journal*, March 10, 1995.

Castaneda, Jorge G. "The Devaluation: A Political Reflection." *Current History*, March 1995.

———. "Ferocious Differences." *Atlantic Monthly*, July 1995.

———. "Mexico at the Brink." *Foreign Affairs*, Winter 1985–86.

———. "Revolution and Foreign Policy: Mexico's Experience." *Political Science Quarterly*, September 3, 1963.

Castro, Richard. "Oil: Mexico's Social Solution." *Rocky Mountain News*, May 1, 1981.

"Central Bank Details Deficits, Surpluses." *El Financiero International*, May 3, 1992.

"Central Bank Releases 1993 Report." *El Financiero International*, April 11, 1994.

Chandler, Clay. "Mexico Predicts Early Repayment of Loans." *Washington Post*, April 6, 1995.

Chant, John F. "The Financial Sector in NAFTA: Two Plus One Equals Restricting." *The NAFTA Network*. San Francisco: Fraser Institute, 1993.

Christian, Shirley. "Don't Let Mexico's Woes Spoil Our Commitments to Chile." *Wall Street Journal*, February 3, 1995.

Christman, John H. "Border Industries Foster New Jobs, More Exports." *Mexican-American Review*, February 1968.

Claessen, Stijn. "The Optimal Currency Composition of External Debt: Theory and Applications to Mexico and Brazil." *World Bank Economic Review*, Vol. 6, No. 3, September 1992.

Clark, John. "Debt Reduction and Market Reentry under the Brady Plan." (Federal Reserve Bank of New York) *Quarterly Review*, Winter 1993–94.

Cline, William R. "Mexico Too Leveraged to Set Up Monetary Board." *Financial Times*, February 28, 1995.

Cohen, Joshua. "The Rise of the Maquiladoras." *Business Mexico*, 1994.

Conger, Lucy. "Mexico: The Failed Fiesta." *Current History*, March 1995.

———. "Power to the Plutocrats." *Institutional Investor*, February 1995.

Cordery, Adam. "Staying the Course." *Business Latin America*, October 13, 1994.

Corradi, Juan E. "Menem's Argentina, Act II," *Current History*, February 1995.

Crewdson, John M. "Border Region Is Almost a Country unto Itself, Neither Mexican nor American." *New York Times*, February 14, 1979.

Cuauhtemoc, Cardenas. "Misunderstanding Mexico." *Foreign Policy*, Spring 1990.

Danini, Carmina. "Salinas Unveils Five Nominees to Head Bank." *San Antonio Express-News*, March 11, 1994.

Davila, Alberto E., Ronald H. Schmidt, and Gary M. Ziegler. "Industrial Diversification, Exchange Rate Shock, and the Texas-Mexico Border." *Economic Review*, May 1984.

Davis, Bob et al. "One America: The North American Free-Trade Pact May Be Just the First Step toward Hemispheric Bloc." Special World Business Report. *Wall Street Journal*, September 24, 1992.

de la Madrid H., Miguel. "Mexico: The New Challenges." *Foreign Affairs*, Fall 1984.

De Long, Bradford, Christopher De Long, and Sherman Robinson. "The Case for Mexico's Rescue." *Foreign Affairs*, May/June 1996.

De Palma, Anthony. "After the Fall: 2 Faces of Mexico's Economy." *New York Times*, July 16, 1995.

―――. "Fortunes and Fear in Mexican Stocks." *New York Times*, April 12, 1993.

―――. "Mexico Facing Sternest Test." *San Antonio-Express News*, March 25, 1994.

―――. "Mexico Outlines an Economic Plan of Extended Pain." *New York Times*, March 10, 1995.

―――. "Mexico's Market Rebounds with Help." *San Antonio Express-News*, March 26, 1994.

―――. "Waiting for the Other Peso to Drop." *New York Times*, September 18, 1994.

Deloitte Touche Tohmatsu. *World Banking and Securities*, March 1994.

Dennis, Geoffery. "Grupo Financiero Banamex-Accival (Bannacci)." *Latin America Watch*, April 13, 1994.

Diebold, David K. and Natalie Bej. "Latin America: Trade Objectives Beyond U.S.-Mexico Negotiations." *The International Executive*, Vol. 33, July-August 1991, pp. 25–29.

Diehl, Philip N. "The Effect of the Peso Devaluation on the Texas Border Cities." *Texas Business Review*, May-June 1983.

Dillman, C. Daniel. "Assemble Industries in Mexico." *Journal of Inter-American Studies and World Affairs*, February 1983.

―――. "Maquiladoras in Mexico's Northern Border Communities and the Border Industrialization Program." *Tijdschrift voor Econ. en Soc. Georgrafie*, No. 3, 1976.

―――. "Urban Growth along Mexico's Northern Border and the Mexican National Border Program." *Journal of Developing Areas*, July 1970.

Dornbush, Rudiger, Alejandro Werner, Guillermo Calvo, and Stanley Fischer. "Bailouts Are Bad Medicine—in Mexico or Elsewhere." *Business Week*, March 13, 1995.

―――. "Mexico: Stabilization, Reform, and No Growth." *Brookings Papers on Economic Activity* (Washington, D.C.: 1:1994).

Dow Jones Service. "Mexico Privatized 252 Firms in Past 5 Years." *San Antonio Express-News*, February 9, 1994.

Drucker, Peter F. "Mexico's Ugly Duckling—the Maquiladora." *Wall Street Journal*, October 4, 1990.

―――. "The Rise in Production Sharing." *Wall Street Journal*, March 15, 1977.

―――. "Trade Lessons from the World Economy." *Foreign Affairs*, January-February 1994.

Dunaief, Daniel. "Rumors Roil Bank Stocks, Debt As the Peso Dives to a New Low." *American Banker*, March 10, 1995.

Dunning, John H. and Rajneesh Narula. "Transpacific Foreign Direct Investment and the Investment Development Path: The Record Assessed." *Essays in International Business* (Columbia: May 1994).

Edmonds, H. C. "Mexican Banks Open to Foreign Investors." *Financial Industry Issues* (FRBD), First Quarter 1996.

Egan, Jack. "The Onset of Big-Debt Blues." *U.S. News and World Report*, July 24, 1989.

English, Richard D. "Energy in the NAFTA: Free Trade Confronts Mexico's Constitution." *Tulsa Journal of Comparative & International Law*, Fall 1993.

Ericson, Anna-Stina. "An Analysis of Mexico's Border Industrialization Program." *Monthly Labor Review*, May 1970.

Escanero, Jose Luis. "Triplican bancos de El Peso captacion de Cuidad Juarez." *Diario de Juarez*, February 8, 1993.

Escobar, Gabriel. "Argentine Economic Czar Ousted." *Washington Post*, July 27, 1996.

"Europe in the Next Century." *Washington Post*, March 13, 1994.

"Europe's Horn of Plenty." *The Economist*, June 2, 1990.

"Farmers Take Over Two Banks." *Laredo Morning Times*, February 25, 1994.

Fernandez, Albertina. "Mexico Issues First Maquiladora APA" [advance pricing agreement]. *Tax Notes International*, November 13, 1995.

Fernandez, Claudia. "Canada to the Rescue." *Mexico Business*, May 1996.

———. "Rules to Be Released for Foreign Banks." *El Financiero*, January 10, 1994.

Fickenscher, Lisa. "Credit Bureaus Poised for Leap into Mexico." *American Banker*, March 10, 1995.

Fineman, Mark. "Mexican Currency Plunges in Value." *Austin American Statesman*, December 23, 1994.

"Foreign Banks." *Pratt's Letter*, December 24, 1992.

"Foreign Investment Shows Positive Trend." *Mexico Service*, March 5, 1993.

Fraser, Damian. "Edging Closer to U.S. Standards." *Financial Times* (London), February 7, 1994.

———. "U.S. Pact Unlikely to Dent Mexican Distrust." *Financial Times* (London), May 23, 1991.

Freer, Jim. "Coping with the Crisis." *LatinFinance*, October 1995.

———. "U.S. Banks Look North, South." *United States Banker*, June 1992.

Friedland, Jonathan. "Argentine Finance Chief Faces Dilemma: New Minister Must Boost Growth without Reviving Inflation." *Wall Street Journal*, July 29, 1996.

———. "Foreign Investors Bet on a Bright Future for Argentina Despite Recent Woes." *Wall Street Journal*, May 21, 1995.

Fromson, Derek. "Mushrooming Malls: Developers Search for the Perfect Lure." *Business Mexico*, October 1992, pp. 14–19, 43.

"G-7 Face Time." *Investor's Business Daily*, July 1, 1996.

"GATT Analysis: Trade Round Signed—Tricky Problems Persist." Knight-Ridder press release, April 18, 1994.

"GATT Brief: The American Connection." *The Economist*, April 21, 1990.

Gay, Robert. "Mexican Banks: Coping with Credit Risk." *Perspectives on the Americas*, November 22, 1993.

———. "Mexico: Monetary Targets, Peso Volatility and Inflation." *Bankers Trust Research*, January 10, 1996.

———. "Mexico: The Pacto and the Peso." *Bankers Trust Research*, October 6, 1994.

———. "Mexico Soon Will Be Investment Grade." *Bankers Trust Research*, December 14, 1993.

———. "Mexico's Surprising Growth." *Bankers Trust Research*, August 19, 1994.

———. "Peso Volatility and the Mexican CETE Market." *Bankers Trust Research*, February 1, 1996.

———. "A Rousing Recovery: Will It Last?" *Perpectives on Emerging Markets*, February 1996.

———. "Too Much Pessimism on Mexico?" *Perspectives on the Americas*, July 21, 1994.

Gay, Robert and Patrecia Artigas. "Argentina's Great Gambit." *Bankers Trust Research*, March 29, 1995.

George, Edward Y. and Robert D. Tollen. "The Economic Impact of the Mexican Border Industrialization Program." No. 20, Center for Inter-American and Border Studies. (El Paso), 1985.

George, Kelly A. and Lori L. Taylor. "The Role of Merchandise Exports to Mexico in the Pattern of Texas Employment." *Economic Review* (FRBD), 1, 1995.

Getschow, George. "Foreign Investment in Mexico Swells." *Wall Street Journal*, May 12, 1981.

Giermanski, Jim. "Old Maquilas Don't Die, They Just Fade Away." *Mexico Insight*, March 6, 1994.

Goldman, David. "A Revolution You Can Invest In." *Forbes*, July 1990.

Giermansky, Jim and Evan Kalimtgis. "Risk Analysis of the Cost of Capital in Mexico." *Mexico 2000 Council*, June 10, 1993.

Gonzalez-Baz, Aureliano. "A Survey of Mexican Laws Affecting Foreign Businessmen." *Denver Journal of International Law and Policy*, Spring 1974.

Gould, David M. "Free Trade Agreements and the Credibility of Trade Reform." *Economic Review* (FRBD), 1992.

Gould, David M. and William C Gruben. "GATT and the New Protectionism." *Economic Review* (FRBD), Third Quarter 1994.

Gould, David M., Graeme L. Woodbridge, and Roy J. Ruffin. "The Theory and Practice of Free Trade." *Economic Review* (FRBD), Fourth Quarter 1993.

Grayson, George W. "Jefe Diego Challenges the PRI." *San Diego Union-Tribune*, July 24, 1994.

———. "Mexico May Lead the Way in Breaking Down Trade Barriers." *Wall Street Journal*, September 20, 1985.

Greenspan, Alan. "Statement to the Congress." *Federal Reserve Bulletin*, Washington, D.C.: March 1994.

Griffin, Paul A. and Somoa J. R. Wallach. "Latin American Lending by Major U.S. Banks: The Effects of Disclosures about Nonaccrual Loans and Loan Loss Provisions." *The Accounting Review*, Vol. 66, No. 4, October 1991.

Gruben, William C. "Mexican Maquiladora Growth: Does It Cost U.S. Jobs." *Economic Review* (FRBD), January 1990, pp. 15–29.

———. "Policy Priorities and the Mexican Exchange Rate Crisis." *Economic Review* (FRBD), First Quarter 1996.

Gruben, William C. and John H. Welch. "Is NAFTA Economic Integration?" *Economic Review* (FRBD), 1994.

Grunwald, Joseph. "Restructuring Industry Offshore: The U.S.-Mexico Connection." *The Brookings Review*, Spring 1983.

Guillermoprieto, Alma. "The Unmasking." *The New Yorker*, March 1995.

Gunther, Jeffery W. "Mexico Offers Banking Opportunities." *Financial Industry Issues* (FRDB), Fourth Quarter 1992.

"Hacienda Approves Three New Banks." *El Financiero International*, April 11, 1994.

Haines, Renee. "Wresting NADBank from Bureaucrats Providing an Uphill Battle." *Business Weekly*, March 6, 1994.

Hale, David. "The Price Was Right." *The Washington Post National Weekly*, June 10, 1996.

Hall, David. "How to End Mexico's Meltdown." *Wall Street Journal*, January 19, 1995.

Hall, Kevin. "Foreign Firms Help Mexico Power Up." *Journal of Commerce*, July 5, 1994.

———. "Mexican Officials Tighten Regulation of Banks and Brokerage Houses." *Journal of Commerce*, July 16, 1996.

———. "Study Says Currency Boards Failed To Prevent Latin American Crisis." *Journal of Commerce*, February 13, 1996.

Hanke, Steve H. "The Curse of Central Banking." *Forbes*, September 25, 1995.

———. "The Great Modernizer." *Forbes*, September 11, 1995.

———. "Mexico Still Needs a Currency Board." *Wall Street Journal*, February 22, 1995.

———. "Pegged Out." *Forbes*, January 16, 1995.

———. "Why Argentina Is Solid." *Forbes*, May 8, 1995.

Haraf, William S. "NAFTA Opens Doors to Mexican Markets for U.S. Banks." *Bank Management*, January 1994.

Harrell, Louis and Dale Fischer. "The 1982 Mexican Peso Devaluation and Border Area Employment." *Monthly Labor Review*, October 1985.

Hansen, Niles. "Interdependence along the U.S.-Mexico Border." *Texas Business Review*, November-December 1983.

Harris, Lloyd. "The Spanish Conquest." *Mexico Business*, December 1995.

Haslem, John A., Carl A. Scheraga, and James P. Bedingfield. "An Analysis of the Impact of International Activity on the Domestic Balance Sheet of U.S. Banks." *Management International Review*, Vol. 35, 1995.

Hauge, J. R. "Second-Guessing the Rubin Treasury." *The International Economy*, May-June 1995.

Hayes, Robert H. and Gary P. Pisano. "Beyond World-Class: The New Manufacturing Strategy." *Harvard Business Review*, January-February 1994.

Hendricks, David. "Mexican CETES Yield Soars." *San Antonio Express-News*, April 15, 1994.

Hennessy, John M. "Lessons from Mexico." *New York Times*, November 15, 1993.

Herman, Robert. "Mexico's Tesobonos Market Appeals to Risk-Wary Investors." *Journal of Commerce*, July 27, 1994.

Herzog, Lawrence A. "The U.S.-Mexico Transfrontier Metropolis." *Business Mexico*, March 1992.

Hetzel, Robert. "Currency Boards: A Comment." *Caenegie-Rochester Conference Series on Public Policy*, Vol. 39, December 1993.

Holden, Richard J. "Maquiladoras' Employment and Retail Sales Effects on Four Texas Border Communities, 1978–1983: An Econometric Analysis." *Southwest Journal of Business and Economics*, 1985.

Hoyt, Mont P. "Consider How NAFTA Helps Open Doors to New Markets." *Texas Banking*, April 1994.

———. "The Legal Framework of the Mexican Financial System." *Texas Banking*, May 1993.

Hufbauer, Gary C. and Jeffery Schott. "Prescription for Growth." *Foreign Policy*, No. 93, Winter 1993–94.

Hughes, Sallie. "Hacienda Sets Foreign Bank Rules." *El Financiero*, March 14, 1994.

Humpage, Owen and Jean M. McIntire. "An Introduction to Currency Boards." *Economic Review*, Federal Reserve Bank of Cleveland, Vol. 31, 1995.

Hunt, Albert R. "A Wall Streeter Makes Good in Washington." *Wall Street Journal*, April 11, 1996.

Hunt, Harry. "It Is Time to Get Real about Mexico." *Fortune*, September 4, 1995.

Hunter, Linda. "Europe 1992: Economic Review." *Economic Review* (FRBD), January 1991.

"If You Were President of Mexico, What Would You Do?" *The International Economy*, January-February 1996.

"In the United States' Back Yard . . .". *JEI Report*, No. 31A, August 11, 1989.

In-Bond and Industrial Regional Development Committee. "Mexico's Maquiladora Industry." *Business America*, December 1987.

"The Investment Guide to Mexico." *Leaders* (New York), 1991.

"Japan Ups Ante in Mexico." *JEI Report*, No. 25B, June 30, 1989.

Johannes, Laura. "Cities Fight for Freeway to Mexico." *Wall Street Journal*, March 25, 1995.

Junge, George. "Emerging Market Countries in Global Financial Markets." *Economic and Financial Prospects* (Basel), February 1996.

———. "Towards More Active Management at Developing Country Debt." *Economic and Financial Prospects* (Basel), June 1993.

"Kaifu Announces Aid to Mexico." *JEI Report*, No. 35B, September 15, 1989.

Kail, William. "Analyst: Bank Won't Allow Inflation." *The News* [Mexico City], December 9, 1994.

Kiguel, Miguel and Pablo A. Neumeyer. "Seigniorage and Inflation: The Case of Argentina." *Journal of Money, Credit, and Banking*, Vol. 27, August 1993.

Kootnikoff, Lawrence. "Salinas Stumped Critics by Achieving Major Reforms." *San Antonio Express-News*, December 28, 1993.

———. "The Vision of Carlos Salinas de Gortari." *U.S./Latin Trade*, January 1994.

Kopytoff, Verne G. "NAFTA Ignites a Tijuana Realty Boom." *New York Times*, December 24, 1995.

Koslow, Lawrence E. and Rodney R. Jones. "The Mexican-American Border Industrialization Program." *Public Affairs Bulletin*, Vol. 9, No. 2, 1970.

Kramer, Mark. "U.S.-Mexican Border: Life on the Line." *National Geographic*, June 1985, pp. 720–49.

Kraus, James R. "Citicorp Rules the U.S. Banking Roost in Mexico." *American Banker*, February 27, 1992.

Krugman, Paul. "Dutch Tulips and Emerging Markets." *Foreign Affairs*, Vol. 74, July/August 1995.

Kuczynski, Sherry. "Who Should Get Credit For U.S. Export Boom?" *Investors Business Daily*, May 10, 1996.

LaGesse, David. "HBG Questions Line of Credit to Mexico." *San Antonio Express-News*, April 22, 1994.

Langewiesche, William. "The Border." *Atlantic Monthly*, May 1992.

"Latin America Learns Lessons: Sober Reactions Prevent Hangover from 'Tequila Effect'." *Washington Times*, June 4, 1995.

"Latin America Outlook: 1994." *Latin America Watch*, December 15, 1993.

Lawrence, Richard. "Latin America Nips at Asia's Heels as Growth Picks Up in S. Hemisphere." *Journal of Commerce*, September 20, 1996.

Lawson, L. M. "Mexico and United States Join in Border Flood Control." *Engineering News-Record*, October 4, 1934, pp. 419–23.

Leach, Frank. "The Border: What It Is; What It Isn't." *San Antonio Business Journal*, March 31, 1995.

Leach, J. "Country Going Bankrupt? Call the IMF." *Wall Street Journal*, April 10, 1995.

Levin, Baron F. "Can Private Business Afford Mexican Private Banks?" *Global Production*, January 1993.

Levy, Santiago and Sweder van Wijnberger. "Maize and the Free Trade Agreement between Mexico and the United States." *World Bank Economic Review*, Vol. 6, No. 3, September 1992.

Lomelin, Gustavo. [Interview with Finance Minister Guillermo Ortiz] "Resurrecting the Banking System." *El Financiero International*, April 8, 1996.

Lopez, David T. "Low Wages Lures South of the Border." *AFL-CIO American Federationist*, June 1969.

Lowe, Sandy. "Mexican-owned U.S. Banks Wield Edge in Mexico." *San Antonio Business Journal*, March 4, 1994.

Lowenthal, Abraham F. "Latin America: Ready for Partnership?" *Foreign Affairs*, 1992–93.

Ludwig, Mark A. (ed.) "The Mexican Stock Market: What Next?" *U.S./Latin Trade*, June 1994.

Luhnow, David. "Mexico's Banks Booming, But Borrowers Wary of Rates." *San Antonio Express-News*, March 21, 1993.

Lutz, James M. "Shifting Comparative Advantage, the NICs, and the Developing Countries." *The International Trade Journal*, Vol.1, No.4, Summer 1987, pp. 339–58.

Malkin, Elisabeth. "Here Comes the Foreign Banks—Sort Of." *Mexico Insight*, March 6, 1994.

Malpass, David. "20 Reasons Mexico Won't Devalue." *Latin America Watch*, April 21, 1994.

Mancera, M. "Don't Blame Monetary Policy." *Wall Street Journal*, January 31, 1995.

"Manufacturing in Mexico: On Uncle Sam's Coat Tails." *The Economist*, September 16, 1989.

"Maquila Scoreboard." *Twin Plant News*, June 1993.

"Maquilas Crecen 60% en Frontera." *El Diario*, December 25, 1995.

Maxfield, Sylvia. "The International Political Economy of Bank Nationalization: Mexico in Comparative Perspective." *Latin American Research Review*, Vol. 26, No. 3, 1991.

McFadyen, Deidre. "Mexico on a Wall Street Comeback." *El Financiero International*, May 6, 1996.

McLees, John A., John G. Wilkins, and Ignacio Valdes. "Mexico Moves toward Resolution of Maquiladora Transfer Pricing Issues." *Tax Notes International*, July 24, 1995.

McLeod, Darryl and John Welch. "The Problem with the Peso." *Business Mexico*, November 1991.

Mead, Walter. "The True Consequences of NAFTA." *Worth*, March 1994.

Mears, Rona R. "Joint Ventures in Mexico: A Current Perspective." *St. Mary's Law Journal*, Vol. 23, No. 3, 1992.

Memmott, Mark. "Exports to Mexico Soar after NAFTA." *USA Today*, May 25, 1994.

————. "Mexico Rivals Japan in U.S. Buys." *San Antonio Express-News*, May 27, 1994.

Mendoza, Benito Solis. "The Problem Is the Banking System." *El Financiero International*, April 29, 1996.

"Mexican Economy." *Mexico-U.S. Trade Advisory* (Laredo), 1993.

"Mexico Facing Sternest Test." *San Antonio Express-News*, March 25, 1994.

"Mexico to Open Its Bank Border." *San Antonio Express-News*, August 31, 1992.

"Mexico's Bank Bailout Could Cost 12% of GDP." *Investors Business Daily*, March 1, 1996.

"Mexico's Big Two Fight for Dominance." *Euromoney*, March 1994.

"Mexico: Tuburlent Politics Raise Fresh Concerns about Peso Stability." *Lagniappe Letter*, April 1, 1994.

Millman, Joel. "Mexican Tortilla Firms Stage U.S. Bake-Off." *Wall Street Journal*, May 10, 1996.

"Misunderstood NAFTA." *Investor's Business Daily*, February 13, 1996.

"Moctezuma's Revenge." *The Economist*, April 3, 1993.

Moffet, Matt "Ahead of Itself." *Wall Street Journal*, September 24, 1993.

————. "Argentina Is Seeking More IMF Funding As Fallout from Mexico Crisis Continues." *Wall Street Journal*, March 10, 1995.

————. "For Argentina, a 'Mircle' Has Its Limits." *Wall Street Journal*, October 24, 1994.

————. "Mexico Tries to Please Japanese Investors." *Wall Street Journal*, November 1, 1989.

————. "Oil's Role in Mexico Raises Tricky Issues for a Free-Trade Pact." *Wall Street Journal*, November 26, 1990.

Moore, Robert R. "The Government Budget Deficit and the Banking System: The Case of Mexico." *Financial Industry Studies*, October 1993.

"More New Banks on Horizon." *El Financiero*, February 7, 1994.

Moreno, Lorenzo. "The Linkage between Population and Economic Growth in Mexico: A New Policy Proposal." *Latin American Research Review*, Vol. 26, No. 3, 1991.

Morici, Peter. "Free Trade with Mexico." *Foreign Policy*, No. 87, Summer 1992.

Muehring, Kevin. "The Trader at Treasury." *Institutional Investor*, January 1995.

Myerson, Allen R. "The Booming, Bulging Tex-Mex Border." *New York Times*, August 7, 1994.

"NAFTA: So Far, So Good." Special NAFTA Report. *Wall Street Journal*, October 28, 1994.

Naim, Moises. "Mexico's Larger Story." *Foreign Policy*, Summer 1995.

Nationsbank. *Economic Eclectic*, February 1994.

Naunam, Talli. "Movement Strikes Financial Heart of Mexico." *El Financiero International*, February 28, 1994.

Nehoray, Mark. "Transfer Pricing in Mexico—A Window of Opportunity for Maquiladoras." *Twin Plant News*, November 1995.

"New Frontier? Dynamic Border Economy Defies Recession." [Interview with John A. Adams, Jr.] *Mexico Service*, December 1, 1995.

Newman, Gray "Assessing the Damage in Mexico." *Business Latin America*, April 4, 1994.

———. "A Mexican Tragedy." *Business Latin America*, March 28, 1994.

———. "Turmoil in Mexico." *Business Latin America*, January 17, 1994.

———. "Volatility Remains." *Business Latin America*, January 24, 1994.

New York Times Service. "Banacci, MCI Bid for Service in Mexico." *San Antonio Express-News*, January 26, 1994.

———. "Trade's New World Order; Regional Agreements Proliferate." *San Antonio Express-News*, August 30, 1992.

"1993 Inflation Hits 21 Year Low." *Mexletter*, February 1994, pp. 1–4.

Norvell, Scott. "NAFTA Dollars: Banking Reform and Opening Markets Reshape Mexican Finance." *Mexico Business*, May/June 1994.

O'Brien, Timothy L. "Citicorp Halts Expansion Plan within Mexico." *Wall Street Journal*, March 24, 1995.

Obstfeld, Maurice. "International Currency Experience: New Lessons and Lessons Relearned." *Brookings Papers on Economic Activity*, Vol. 1, 1995.

"Oil Potential of Mexico Barely Tapped." *Journal of Commerce*, September 27, 1976.

"On the Brink." *LatinFinance*, March 1996.

Opdyke, Jeff D. "In Border Towns, the Peso's Plunge Fails to Damp the Bustle of Business." *Wall Street Journal*, March 29, 1995.

———. "On the Border, Banker vs. Banker." *Wall Street Journal*, January 1994.

Ortiz, Guillermo. Undersecretary of Finance. "Mexico's Financial Outlook." *Investing in Mexico*. The Conference Board No. 999 (New York), 1992.

Pardee, Scott. "After the Fall: Why Mexico's Banks Will Rebound." *Mexico Service*, December 15, 1995.

Pastor, Robert A. "The North American Free Trade Agreement: Hemispheric and Geopolitical Implications." *The International Executive*, Vol. 26, January-February 1994, pp. 3–31

Pennington, Audrey. "NAFTA Two Years 'Afta'—Is It Boom Time Yet?" *Site Selection*, April 1996.

Perryman Texas Letter, Vol. 5, No. 4, April 6, 1994.

"Peso Weakens to Record Low." *San Antonio Express-News*, December 16, 1994.

Petruno, Tom. "Global Money—Free Flows, Free Falls." *Los Angeles Times*, March 21, 1995

"Perspective Economics de Mexico, 1993–1998." *El Mercado de Valores*, February 1994.

Pfaff, John F. et al. "Technology Transfer in Mexico: Past Patterns and New Problems Related to the North American Free Trade Agreement." *The International Executive*, Vol. 35, March-April 1993.

Platt, Gordon. "Mexico's Banking Sector May Get Universal Flavor." *Journal of Commerce*, June 27, 1994

Poole, Claire. "Too Late?" *Forbes*, January 22, 1992.

Preece, John. "Government Increases Control over Banking System." *El Financiero International*, May 27, 1996.

"President Salinas Adjusts Policies to Avoid Disappointment and Disaster." *Mexico and NAFTA Report*, September 23, 1993.

"Pressure on Peso Continues." *Mexletter*, July 1994.

"Promovera Nadbanc desarrollo en frontera con EU." *El Manana*, July 21, 1994.

Purcell, Susan K. "Mexican-U.S. Relations: Big Initiatives Can Cause Big Problems." *Foreign Affairs*, Winter 1981–82.

Ramirez, Anthony. "Fears Send Markets Plunging." *New York Times*, March 25, 1994.

Randell, Eric D. "Mexican Stocks Poised for Gains." *USA Today*, March 1, 1994.

Rangel, Enrique. "Economy Is Rebounding in Mexico as Market Soars." *Dallas Morning News*, April 2, 1996.

———. "Mexican Retailers Battle for Attention of Monterrey Shoppers." *Dallas Morning News*, August 24, 1993.

Reding, Andrew A. "It Isn't the Peso—It's the President." *New York Times Magazine*, April 9, 1995.

"Reglas para el Establecimiento de Filiales de Instituciones Financieras del Exterior." *El Mercado de Valores*, June 6, 1994.

Rhodes, William R. "The Latin Tigers Are Ready to Roar." *Wall Street Journal*, December 31, 1993

Rice, Harvey. "U.S. Banks Look South of the Border." *Bank Management*, November 1992.

Riding, Alan. "World Push by Mexican Banks Irks Rivals." *New York Times*, April 18, 1981.

Riner, Debarah L. "For Mexico's Zedillo, Path to Reform Gets Steeper." *Knight-Ridder Financial News* (New York City), May 9, 1996.

Robinson, Alan. "Mexico Urged to Cool Economic Engine." *Journal of Commerce*, April 24, 1981.

Rohter, Larry. "Mexico Feels Squeeze of Years of Austerity." *New York Times*, July 25, 1991.

Rosenfeldt, Martin E. "U.S.-Mexico Borderland Industrialization Policies Revisited: The Need for Binational Strategies." *Akron Business and Economic Review*, Winter 1985.

Ross, Carl W. "Mexico: Inflation Target Is Ambitious but Not Far off the Mark." *Perspective on the Americas* (Bankers Trust Research), March 21, 1994.

Ross, Carl W. and Robert S. Gray. "The GATTization of NAFTA." *Bankers Trust Research*, July 2, 1993.

———. "The Mexican Current Account: Balancing the Books." *Bankers Trust Research*, December 19, 1994.

———. "A New Trading Range for the Argentine-Mexican Par Bond Spread." *Perspectives*, June 2, 1995.

Rowen, Hobart. "Back to Third World Debt." *Washington Post*, December 28, 1987.

Rubio, Luis. "Mexico Once Again at the Brink." *Journal of Commerce*, October 24, 1988.

Russell, Joel. "How Countries Compete." *Business Mexico*, 1993.

Sachs, Jeffery. "Making the Brady Plan Work." *Foreign Affairs*, Summer 1989.

Salgado, Alicia and Al Taranto. "Foreign Banks to the Rescue." *El Financiero International*, February 26, 1996.

Salinas-Leon, Roberto. "The Importance of Money." *Journal of Commerce*, October 16, 1996.
———. "Mexican Economy Will Remain Weak until Peso Is Strong." *Wall Street Journal*, July 21, 1995.
———. "Mexico's Export-Led Economic Decline." *Wall Street Journal*, May 24, 1996.
Salomon Brothers. *Emerging Markets Research: Latin America*. March 30, 1994.
Sandeman, Hugh. "Mexico Becomes an Oil Power: Pemex Comes Out of Its Shell." *Fortune*, April 10, 1978.
Sander, Ernest. "A Boom in Baja." *Austin American-Statesman*, July 31, 1994.
Sarmiento, Sergio. "Central Bank Autonomy May Get Mexico Back on the Growth Track." *Wall Street Journal*, June 4, 1993.
———. "Mexican Assassination at a Political Crossroads," and "Mexico's Tough Test." *Wall Street Journal*, March 25, 1994.
———. "No Magic Solutions." *El Financiero*, January 24, 1994.
———. "Stock Market Takes a Breather." *El Financiero*, March 13, 1994.
Scanlan, David. "Colombian Citizens, Companies Feel Devalued [Mexican] Peso's Sting." *Houston Chronicle*, November 26, 1995.
Schwartz, Anne. "Currency Boards: Their Past, Present, and Possible Future Role." *Carnegie-Rochester Conference Series on Public Policy*, Vol. 39, December 1993.
Schwartz, Scott M. "The Border Industrialization Program of Mexico." *Southwest Journal of Business and Economics*, Summer 1987.
Senzek, Alva. "Whither Industrial Policy." *El Financiero International*, May 20, 1996.
Sesit, Michael R. "U.S. Investors Keep Buying Foreign Issues." *Wall Street Journal*, July 25, 1994.
Shapiro, Harvey D. "Tequila Effect? What Tequila Effect?" *Institutional Investor*, October 1995.
Shuffstall, Donald C. "Economic Crisis and Recovery—The Maquiladora: A True National Priority." *Crisis and Response: A Roundtable on Mexico* (San Diego), 1986.
Shwedel, Kenneth. "A Game of Wait and See." *Business Mexico*, December 1992, pp. 4–7.
Sims, Calvin. "President Ousts Finance Chief in Argentina." *New York Times*, July 27, 1996
Singelmann, Peter. "The Sugar Industry in Postrevolutionary Mexico: State Intervention and Private Capital." *Latin America Research Review*, Vol. 28, 1993.
Slovin, Myron B. and Subbarao V. Jaganti. "Bank Capital Regulations and the Valuation Effects of Latin America Debt Moratoriums." *Journal of Banking and Finance*, Vol. 17, 1993.
Smith, Geri. "Salinas Will Pay for Peace." *Business Week*, January 24, 1994.
Smith, Geri and Stephen Baker. "The Fall of Carlos Salinas." *Business Week*, March 27, 1995.
———. "Mexico: A Rough Road Back." *Business Week*, November 13, 1995.
———. "Staying Afloat Quite Nicely, Thank You." *Business Week*, April 8, 1996.
Solano, Manuel F. and Joseph M. Wolf. "Recent Developments in Mexico: The 1996 Mexican Tax Reform and Supreme Court Decision on Assets Tax." *Tax Notes International*, March 25, 1996.
Solis, Dianna and Mary W. Walsh. "U.S. Business near Mexican Border Move Fast to Cope with Changing Peso." *Wall Street Journal*, January 27, 1986.

"The Specter of Instability." *Mexletter*, October 1994.

Springer, Gary L. and Jorge L. Molina. "The Mexican Financial Crisis: Genesis, Impact, and Implications." *Journal of Interamerican Studies and World Affairs*, Vol. 37, Summer 1995, pp. 57–81.

"Still Not Out of the Woods." *Latin American Economy and Business*, June 1994.

Stockton, William. "Mexico's Grand 'Maquiladora' Plan." *New York Times*, January 19, 1986.

Stolp, Chandler. "Texas under Free Trade: Some Sectoral Regional, and Modeling Considerations." *North American Free Trade: Proceedings*, June 14, 1991.

Street, James H. "Prospects for Mexico's Industrial Development Plan in the 1980's." *Texas Business Review*, May-June 1980.

Tangeman, Michael. "The Once, and Future, Banking Crisis?" *Institutional Investor*, November 1995.

Taranto, Al. "The Year of Trading Dangerously." *El Financiero International*, December 26, 1994

Taube, Paul M. and J. Michael Patrick. "Business Credit Availability in the Rio Grande Valley: An Analysis of Business and Bank Needs." *Journal of Borderlands Studies*, Fall 1990.

Terrell, Henry S. "U.S. Branches and Agencies of Foreign Banks: A New Look." *Federal Reserve Bulletin* (Washington, D.C.), October 1993.

Tetley, Susan. "Foreign Banks Increase Stake in Texas." *Financial Industry Issues* (FRBD), 1994.

Thomson Bank Watch. "Declining Fortunes." *LatinFinance*, November 1994.

Thuermer, Karen E. "U.S. Companies Cash in on Borderless Banking." *Global Production*, January 1994.

Thurow, Lester. "To Whom Will World Belong in 21st Century?" *Houston Chronicle*, April 26, 1992.

"Top 50 [Banks] in Emerging Countries." *Euromoney*, June 1992.

"Top 100 Publicly Traded Companies." *Latin Trade*, August 1996.

Torres, Craig. "Bank of Montreal Deal Raises Questions." *Austin American-Statesman*, March 10, 1996.

———. "The Banking Disaster in Mexico Whipsaws an Ailing Economy." *Wall Street Journal*, January 25, 1996.

———. "GE Capital Corp. to Acquire 13% of Mexico's Serfin." *Wall Street Journal*, March 21, 1995.

———. "Investors Focus on Long Term in Mexico City." *Wall Street Journal*, January 25, 1994.

———. "Mexican Ban Posts Big Loss on Peso's Fall." *Wall Street Journal*, January 17, 1995.

———. "Mexican Banks Hang in 'Delicate Balance'." *Wall Street Journal*, January 31, 1995.

———. "Mexican Finance Aide's Glass Is Half Full." *Wall Street Journal*, October 18, 1996.

———. "Mexico Overhauls Banks amid Turmoil." *Wall Street Journal*, March 6, 1995.

———. "Mexico's Devaluation Stuns Latin America—and U.S. Investors." *Wall Street Journal*, December 22, 1994.

———. "Mexico's Goal for '95 Growth May Be Tough." *Wall Street Journal*, December 16, 1994.

————. "Mexico's Pemex Gets $1.1 Billion Loan from J. P. Morgan, Two Other Banks." *Wall Street Journal*, March 16, 1994.

————. "Opening of Mexico's Financial System Won't Bring Any Immediate Rewards." *Wall Street Journal*, October 24, 1994.

————. "Peso's Stability Unnerves Some Mexicans." *Wall Street Journal*, May 2, 1996.

————. "Two Mexican Executives Expected to Battle for Banking, Phone, Clients." *San Antonio Reserve Bulletin*, October 1993.

True, Philip. "5 Year Drought Shoves Northern Mexico toward Disaster." *San Antonio Express-News*, May 19, 1996,

————. "Peasants Warned of Bank Invasion." *San Antonio Express-News*, February 26, 1994.

Truell, Peter. "Mexico, Creditor Nations Reach Accord on Debt." *Wall Street Journal*, June 1, 1989.

Turner, Roger. "Mexico Turns to Its In-Bond Industry As a Means of Generating Exchange." *Business America*, November 28, 1983.

"Turning Point for Mexico." *Latin American Economy and Business*, June 1994.

Unal, Haluk, Asli Demirguc-kunt, and Kwok-Wai Leung. "The Brady Plan, 1989 Mexican Debt-Reduction Agreement, and Bank Stock Returns in United States and Japan." *Journal of Money, Credit, and Banking*, Vol. 25, No. 3, August 1993, pp. 410–29.

Valdez, Abelardo L. "Expanding the Concept of Co-production Beyond the Maquiladora: Toward a More Effective Partnership between the United States and Mexico, and the Caribbean Basin Countries." *The International Lawyer*, Vol. 22, No. 2, Summer 1988, pp. 393–414.

————. "A Proposal for Establishing a United States-Mexico Co-Production Zone." *Law and Policy in International Business*, Vol. 20, No. 4, 1989, pp. 619–54.

Vargas, Lucinda. "The Changing Dynamics of the Maquiladora Industry." Federal Reserve Bank of Dallas-El Paso Branch, *Business Frontier*, Vol. 1, No. 2, September/October 1994.

Weeks, Scott. "Breach of Faith." *LatinFinance*, September 1995.

Weintraub, Sidney. "The Mexican Economy: Life After Devaluation." *Current History*, March 1995.

————. "NAFTA Benefits Flow Back and Forth Across the Rio Grande." *Wall Street Journal*, May 10. 1996.

Welch, John and William C. Gruben. "A Brief Modern History of the Mexican Financial System." *Financial Industry Studies*, Dallas Federal Reserve Bank (FRBD), October 1993.

Welch, John, William C. Gruben, and Daryl McLeod. "The Cost and Benefits of Fixed Dollar Exchange Rates in Latin America." *Economic Review* (FRBD), First Quarter 1993.

Wessel, David, Paul B. Carroll, and Thomas T. Vogel, Jr. "How Mexico's Crisis Ambushed Top Minds in Officialdom, Finance." *Wall Street Journal*, June 6, 1995.

Wiarda, Howard J. "After Miami: The Summit, the Peso Crisis, and the Future of U.S.-Latin American Relations." *Journal of Interamerican Studies and World Affairs*, Spring 1995.

Winfield, Betty. "El Impacto del TLC en los Bancos del Sur de Texas." *Strategic Links*, Vol. 4, February 1994.

"World Trade: Jousting for Advantage." *The Economist*, September 22, 1990.

Zarazaga, Carlos E. "Argentina, Mexico, and Currency Boards: Another Case of Rules versus Discretion." *Economic Review* (FRBD), Fourth Quarter 1995
"Zedillo's Second Economic Package." *LAEB*, April 1995.
Zinser, Adolfo A. "Mexico: The Presidential Problem." *Foreign Policy*, Winter 1987–88.
Zuniga, J. A. and R. Amador. "En diciembre, gran negocio con tesobonos." *La Jornda*, February 7, 1995.

UNPUBLISHED PAPERS, PRESENTATIONS, AND PRESS CONFERENCES

Adams, John A., Jr. "Cross Border Infrastructure." Presentation to MEXCON '96: Manufacturing in Mexico. San Diego: March 1996.
———. "1992–93 Economics Overview and Analysis of Regional Market Trends." Laredo: 1993.
———. "Overview of Banking and Financial Services in Mexico: Prospects in the NAFTA Environment." Presentation to the American Bar Association. Dallas: June 1993.
Angulo P., Carlos. *The "Mexican Risk" Factor in Credit Transactions.* El Paso: 1996.
Angulo P., Carlos, Edmundo Elias Fernandez, and Carol S. Osmond (Baker and McKenzie). *Maquiladoras in the New Environment.* El Paso: 1996.
Baker and McKenzie. *Investing and Manufacturing in Mexico: Legal Aspects.* Dallas: 1991.
Border Trade Alliance. "BTA: Maquiladora Investment Activity Report: Findings and Conclusions." El Paso: 1994.
———. "BTA: Position Papers on the North American Free Trade Agreement." February 1991 and revised ed., Fall 1993.
———. *Southwest Border Infrastructure Initiative.* February 1992 and February 1993.
———. *Southwest Border Infrastructure Initiative: Final Report.* July 1995.
Chicago Mercantile Exchange. *Mexican Peso: Futures and Options.* Chicago: 1995.
Fishlow, Albert, Sherman Robinson, and Raul Hinojosa-Ojeda. "Proposal for a North American Regional Development Bank and Adjustment Fund." Conference proceedings, North American Free Trade. Dallas: June 14, 1991.
Flores, Santos. *An Industry Analysis of the Mexican Securities Market.* Fort Worth: June 1994.
Garza, Vicente V. "LDF Economic Conference Update: Retailing." Laredo: March 1, 1994.
Giermanski, Jim. "The Potential Effect of a North American Free-Trade Agreement on the United States Maquila Industry in Mexico." Laredo: March 1991.
Gruppo, John S. "Banking in Mexico." Presentation to the American Bar Association. Dallas: June 1993.
Kolari, James W. (ed.). "FTA Negotiations and Banking Services: Texas Consortium on Free Trade Financial Services Subcommittee Banking Area Report." June 28, 1991.
Krueger, Robert B. "Establishing a Mexico Lending Program." Unpublished report to the Border Trade Alliance. Puerto Vallarta: February 21, 1994.
KTSA. "Bill Clinton: Presidential Press Conference." [6:30–7:05] The White House, Washington, D.C.: March 23, 1994.

Leach, Frank. "Laredo Development Foundation: The Charts on Laredo." Laredo: February 1994 and February 1995.
LeMaster, Jane and Jim Giermanski. "Labor Mobility under NAFTA: Its Border Impact." Technical Report. Texas A&M International University. February 1994.
Mark, David. "Hazardous Waste Management along the U.S.-Mexican Border." Greenfield Environmental: July 25, 1994.
McNeece, John B. III, Alfredo Andere-Mendiolea, and Jerome A. Grossman. "Issues in Maquiladora Lending." San Diego: 1991.
Nobutoshi Akao (Embassy of Japan, Washington, D.C.) to John A. Adams, Jr. January 11, 1989.
Purcell, John and Dirk W. Damrau. "Mexico: A World Class Economy in the 1990s." Salomon Brothers. New York: 1990.
Taylor, Robert (ed.). "Mexican Financial Reform and Prospects." International Reports, IBC. New York: 1990.
Urquidi, E. Henry. "Latin American Equity Derivatives."*Latin Finance*, February 1996.
Villagomez, Carlos. "The Mexican Financial System and Its Internationalization." Presentation to the ABA. Dallas: June 1993.
Wolff, Nelson. "NAFTA Institutions: The Secretariat and Development Bank." San Antonio: 1994.

THESES AND DISSERTATIONS

Aros, Arnold. *Consumer Lending in Mexico*. Unpublished thesis, March 1967, SWGSB, Dallas.
Barrera, A. B. *A Study of the Economic and Financial Development of Mexico and Its Impact on Laredo, Texas and Its Financial Institutions*. Unpublished thesis, March 1968, SWGSB, Dallas.
Brown, Hollis E. *The Mexican Border Industrial Program: Its Meaning to the El Paso-Juarez Banking Community*. Unpublished thesis, July 1971, SWGSB, Dallas.
Harrison, Donald F. *United States-Mexican Military Collaboration During World War II*. Unpublished dissertation, 1976, Georgetown University.
Land, Cecilia. *The In-Bond Industry in Mexico: Its Impact on the Economy of El Paso*. Unpublished thesis, May 1986, SWGSB, Dallas.
Santoro, Canela. *United States and Mexican Relations during World War II*. Unpublished dissertation, April 1967, Syracuse University.
Saragoza, Alexander. *The Formation of a Mexican Elite: The Industrialization of Monterrey, Nuevo Leon, 1880–1920*. Unpublished dissertation, 1978, University of California, San Diego.
Schuler, K. *Currency Boards*. Unpublished dissertation, 1992, George Mason University.
Zedillo, Ernesto. *External Public Indebtedness in Mexico: Recent History and Future Oil Bounded Optimal Growth*. Unpublished dissertation, 1981, Yale University.

INTERVIEWS

Mike Collins, project manager, Ford Motor Company, March 23, 1994.
Gary Crump, Probursa International Inc., March 7, 1994, Mexico City, April 18, 1994, Laredo, Texas.

Alan Greenspan, Chairman, Federal Reserve, Washington, D.C., April 6, 1995.
William Gruben, Senior Economist, Dallas Federal Reserve Bank, March 3, 1994, Dallas, Texas.
Kevin G. Hall, international business journalist in Mexico, D.F., *Journal of Commerce*, by phone in Laredo, Texas, March 8, 1994.
Ambassador Carla Hills, U.S. Trade Representative, March 11, 1994, Houston, Texas.
Larry Johnson, partner, Baker and McKenzie, international trade expert, March 2, 1994, Dallas, Texas.
John H. Keck, President and CEO, Union National Bank of Texas, February 24, 1994, Laredo, Texas.
R. Blair Krueger, Krueger and Assoc., international banking consultant, February 22, 1994, Puerto Vallarta, Mexico.
Charles Siegman, Senior Associate Director: Division of International Finance, Board of Governors, Federal Reserve, Washington, D.C., March 15, 1994.

BOOKS

Aaronson, Susan A. *Trade and the American Dream*. Lexington, Ky.: 1996.
Acevedo, Carlos Alvear and Alberto Ortega Venzor. *TLC: Marco Historico Para Una Negociacion*. Mexico, D.F.: 1991.
Aguila M., Alfonso and Fernando Carmona et al. *Politica Mexicana Sobre Inversiones Extranjeras*. Mexico, D.F.: 1980.
Andere, Eduardo and Georgina Kessel. *Mexico y el Tratado Trilateral de Libre Comercio: Impacto Sectorial*. Mexico, D.F.: 1992.
Anderson, Terry L. *NAFTA and the Environment*. San Francisco: 1993.
Aspe, Pedro. *Economic Transformation: The Mexican Way*. Cambridge, Mass.: 1993. See also *El Camino Mexicano de la Transformacion Economica*. Mexico, D.F.: 1993.
Aspe, Pedro and Paul E. Sigmund (eds.). *The Political Economy of Income Distribution in Mexico*. New York: 1984.
Baer, M. Dalal. *Mexico and the United States: Leadership Transition and the Unfinished Agenda*. Washington, D.C.: 1988.
Baer, M. Dalal and Sidney Weintraub (eds.). *The NAFTA Debate: Grappling with Unconventional Trade Issues*. Boulder: 1994.
Baerresen, Donald W. *The Border Industrialization Program of Mexico*. Lexington: 1971.
Barnet, Richard J. and John Cavanagh. *Global Dreams: Imperial Corporations and the New Order*. New York: 1994.
Barry, Donald, Mark O. Dickerson, and James D. Gaisford (eds.). *Toward a North American Community*. Boulder: 1995.
Belous, Richard S. and Jonathan Lemco. *NAFTA as a Model of Development*. Albany: 1995.
Bennett, Mark. *Public Policy and Industrial Development: The Case of the Mexican Auto Parts Industry*. Boulder: 1986.
Bennett, Robert L. *The Financial Sector and Economic Development: The Mexican Case*. Baltimore: 1965.
Bernal Sahagun, Victor M. and Bernardo Olmedo Carranza (eds.). *Inversion Extranjera Directa e Industrializacion en Mexico*. Mexico, D.F.: 1986.

Bett, Virgil M. *Central Banking in Mexico: Monetary Policies and Financial Crisis, 1864–1940*. Ann Arbor: 1957.

Biosca, Domenec. *100 Soluciones Para Salir de la Crisis*. Madrid: 1995.

Bovard, James. *The Fair Trade Fraud*. New York: 1991.

Brothers, Dwight S. and Solis M. Leopoldo. *Mexican Financial Development*. Austin: 1966.

Brothers, Dwight S. and Adele E. Wick (eds.). *Mexico's Search for a New Development Strategy*. Boulder: 1990.

Business International Corp. *Succeeding in the New Mexico*. New York: 1991.

Business Monitor International. *Mexico 1994*. London: 1994.

———. *Mexico 1995–97*. London: 1995.

Calvo, Guillermo. *Money, Exchange Rates, and Output*. Cambridge, Mass.: 1996.

Camin, Hector Aguila and Lorenzo Meyer. *In the Shadow of the Mexican Revolution: Contemporary Mexican History, 1910–1989*. Austin: 1993.

Camp, Roderic A. *Intellectuals and the State in Twentieth-Century Mexico*. Austin: 1985.

———. *Mexico's Leaders: Their Education and Recruitment*. Tucson: 1980.

Cardenas, Gilbert and Charles Ellard. *The Economics of the U.S.-Mexico Border: Growth, Problems and Prospects*. Edinburgh, Tex.: 1982.

Cartens, Catherine M. *Las Finanzas Populares en Mexico*. Mexico, D.F.: 1995.

Casanova, Pablo G. *Democracy in Mexico*. Oxford: 1970.

Castaneda, Jorge G. *Los Ultimos Capitalismos*. Mexico, D.F.: 1982.

———. *The Mexican Shock: Its Meaning for the U.S.* New York: 1995.

The Case against Free Trade: GATT, NAFTA, and the Globalization of Corporate Power. San Francisco: 1993.

Chevalier, Francois. *Land and Society in Colonial Mexico: The Great Hacienda*. Berkeley: 1993.

Cline, William R. *Mobilizing Bank Lending to Debtor Countries*. Washington, D.C.: 1987.

Cockcroft, James. *Mexico*. New York: 1982.

Colmenares, David, Luis Angeles, and Carlos Ramirez. *La Nacionalizacion de la Banca*. Mexico, D.F.: 1982.

Conchello, Jose Angel. *El TLC: Un Callejon sin Salida*. Mexico, D.F.: 1992.

Cook, Maria L., Kevin J. Middlebrook, and Juan Molinar Horcasitas (eds.). *The Politics of Economic Restructuring: State-Society Relations and Regime Change in Mexico*. San Diego: 1994.

Cordera, Rolando (ed.). *Desarrollo y Crisis de la Economica Mexicana*. Mexico, D.F.: 1995.

Cornelius, Wayne A. *Mexican Politics in Transition: The Breakdown of a One-Party-Dominant Regime*. San Diego: 1996.

Cumberland, Charles C. *Mexico: The Struggle for Modernity*. New York: 1968.

Dandelin, Jean and Edgar J. Dosman (eds.). *Beyond Mexico: Changing Americas*. Ottawa: 1995.

Davidson, John. *The Long Road North: The Story of a Mexican Worker's Perilous Crossing into the United States*. New York: 1979.

Davila Flores, Alejandro. *La Crisis Financiera en Mexico*. Mexico, D.F.: 1986.

Davis, Diane E. *Urban Leviathan: Mexico in the Twentieth Century*. Philadelphia: 1994.

Dawson, Frank G. *The First Latin American Debt Crisis*. New Haven: 1990.

Deane, Margorie and Robert Pringle. *The Central Banks*. New York: 1994.

Dent, Harry S. *The Great Boom Ahead.* New York: 1993.

DeSoto, H. *The Other Path: The Invisible Revolution in the Third World.* New York: 1989.

Devlin, Robert. *Debt Crisis in Latin America.* Princeton: 1989.

Diebold, William, Jr. (ed.). *Bilateralism, Multilateralism and Canada in U.S. Trade Policy.* Council on Foreign Relations. Washington, D.C.: 1988.

Dillon, K. Burke and Gumersindo Oliveros. *Recent Experience with Multilateral Official Debt Rescheduling.* Washington, D.C.: 1987.

Dominguez, Jorge (ed.). *Mexico's Political Economy: Challenges at Home and Abroad.* Beverly Hills: 1982.

Dominguez, Jorge and James A. McCann. *Democratizing Mexico: Political Opinion and Electoral Choices.* Baltimore: 1996.

Dornbusch, Rudiger. *Exchange Rates and Inflation.* Cambridge, Mass.: 1988.

Eccles, Robert S. *The Transfer Pricing Problem: A Theory for Practice.* Lexington, Mass.: 1985.

Ehrlich, Paul R., Loy Bilderback, and Anne H. Ehrich. *The Golden Door: International Migration, Mexico, and the United States.* New York: 1979.

Espino, Alma and Ana Schwarz. *La Banca Nacionalizada.* Mexico, D.F.: 1983.

Fatemi, Khosrow (ed.). *International Trade and Finance: A North American Perspective.* New York: 1988.

———. *The Maquiladora Industry: Economic Solution or Problem.* New York: 1990.

Falk, Pamela (ed.). *Petroleum and Mexico's Future.* Boulder: 1987.

Fehrenbach, T. R. *Fire and Blood: A Bold and Definitive Modern Chronicle of Mexico.* New York: 1973.

Feinberg, Richard E. and Valeriana Kallab (eds.). *Uncertain Future: Commercial Banks and the Third World.* New Brunswick: 1984.

Fernandez-Kelly, Maria Patricia. *For We Are Sold, I and My People: Women and Industry in Mexico's Frontier.* Albany: 1983.

Galarza, Ernesto. *Merchants of Labor: The Mexican Bracero Story.* Charlotte: 1964.

George, Susan. *A Fate Worse Than Debt: The World Financial Crisis and the Poor.* New York: 1988.

Gereffi, Gary and Donald L. Wyman (eds.). *Manufacturing Miracles: Paths of Industrialization in Latin America and East Asia.* Princeton: 1990.

Giron, Alicia, Edgar Ortiz, and Eugenia Correa (eds.). *Integracion Financiera y TLC: Retos y Perspectivas.* Mexico, D.F: 1995.

Glade, William and Charles Anderson. *The Political Economy of Mexico.* Madison: 1963.

Globerman, Steven and Michael Walker (eds.). *Assessing NAFTA: A Trinational Analysis.* Vancouver: 1992.

Graham, Edward M. and Paul R. Frugman. *Foreign Direct Investment in the United States.* Washington, D.C.: 1989.

Greider, William. *Secrets of the Temple: How the Federal Reserve Run the Country.* New York: 1987.

Grayson, George W. *The United States and Mexico: Patterns of Influence.* New York: 1994.

Grayson, George W. (ed). *Prospects for Mexico.* Washington, D.C.: 1988.

Hacia un Tradado de Libre Comercio en America del Norte. Mexico, D.F.: 1991.

Halebsky, Sandor and Richard L. Harris (eds.). *Capital, Power, and Inequality in Latin America.* Boulder: 1995.

Hall, Douglas K. *The Border: Life on the Line*. New York: 1988.

Hanke, Steve H. (ed.). *Privatization and Development*. San Francisco: 1987.

Hansen, Niles. *The Border Economy: Regional Development in the Southwest*. Austin: 1981.

———. *The Role of Mexican Labor in the Economy of the Southwest United States*. Austin: 1979.

Hansen, Roger. *The Politics of Mexican Development*. Baltimore: 1971.

Hellman, Judith A. *Mexico in Crisis*. New York: 1983.

Heymen, Timothy. *Investing in Mexico*. Mexico City: 1989.

Heymen, Timothy and Arturo Leon y Ponce de Leon. *La Inversion en Mexico*. Mexico, D.F.: 1981.

Hinojosa, Gilberto M. *A Borderland Town in Transition: Laredo 1755–1870*. College Station: 1983.

Holder, Richard J. *Maquiladoras along the Texas/Mexico Border: An Economic Evolution of Employment and Retail Sales Effects on Our Texas Border Cities*. Austin: 1984.

Horgan, Paul. *Great River: The Rio Grande*. New York: 1954.

Huchim, Eduardo. *TLV: Hacia un Pais Distinto*. Mexico, D.F.: 1992.

Huerta, Arturo. *La Politica Neoliberal de Estabilizacion Economica en Mexico: Limites y Alternativas*. Mexico, D.F.: 1994.

Hufbauer, Gary C. and Jeffrey J. Schott. *NAFTA: An Assessment*. Washington, D.C.: 1993.

———. *NAFTA: Issues and Recommendations*. Washington, D.C.: 1992.

Hundley, Norris. *Dividing the Water: A Century of Controversy between the United States and Mexico*. Berkeley: 1966.

James, Harold. *International Monetary Cooperation Since Bretton Woods*. New York: 1996.

Kandell, Jonathan. *La Capital: The Biography of Mexico City*. New York: 1988.

Kennedy, Paul. *Preparing for the Twenty-First Century*. New York: 1993.

———. *The Rise and Fall of the Great Powers*. New York: 1987.

Killick, Tony (ed.). *The IMF and Stabilization: Developing Country Experience*. London: 1984.

Korner, Peter et al. *The IMF and the Debt Crisis*. New York: 1986.

Kraft, Joseph. *The Mexican Rescue*. New York: 1984.

Krugman, Paul R. *Geography and Trade*. Cambridge, Mass.: 1991.

Ladman, Jerry R. (ed.). *Mexico: A Country in Crisis*. El Paso: 1986.

Langewiesche, William. *Cutting the Sign*. New York: 1993.

Latell, Brain. *Mexico at the Crossroads: The Many Crises of the Political System*. Stanford: 1986.

Levy, Daniel and Gabriel Szekely. *Mexico: Paradoxes of Stability and Change*. Boulder: 1987.

Lissakers, Karen. *Banks, Borrowers, and the Establishment*. New York: 1981.

Lustig, Nora. *Mexico: The Remaking of an Economy*. Washington, D.C.: 1992.

Lustig, Nora (ed.). *Coping with Austerity: Poverty and Inequality in Latin America*. Washington, D.C.: 1995.

Lustig, Nora, Barry Bosworth, and Robert Z. Lawrence (eds.). *North American Free Trade Agreement: Assessing the Impact*. Washington, D.C.: 1992.

McGuaghey, William. *U.S.-Mexico-Canada Free-Trade Agreement: Do We Just Say No?* Minneapolis: 1992.

Martinez, Oscar (ed.). *Across Boundaries: Transborder Interaction in Comparative Perspectives.* El Paso: 1986.

———. *Troublesome Border.* Tucson: 1988.

Magaziner, Ira and Mark Patinkin. *The Silent War: Inside the Global Business Battle Shaping American's Future.* New York: 1990.

Meyer, Lorenzo. *Mexico and the United States in the Oil Controversy, 1917–1942.* Austin: 1972.

Miller, Richard B. *Citicorp: Story of a Bank in Crisis.* New York: 1993.

Montgomery, Tommie Sue (ed.). *Mexico Today.* Philadelphia: 1982.

Moore, O. Ernest. *Evolucion de las Instituciones Financieras en Mexico.* Mexico, D.F.: 1963.

Morris, John (ed.). *Japan and the Global Economy: Issues and Trends in the 1990s.* London: 1991.

Morris, Stephen D. *Political Reformism in Mexico: An Overview of Contemporary Mexican Politics.* Boulder: 1995.

Naisbitt, John. *Global Paradox.* New York: 1994.

Nelson, Todd C. and Ronald Cuming. *Harmonization of the Secured Financing Laws of the NAFTA Partners: Focus on Mexico.* Tuscon: 1995.

Newell, G. Roberto and Luis Rubio F. *Mexico's Dilemma: The Political Origins of Economic Crisis.* Boulder: 1984.

Ohnae, Kenichi (ed.). *The Evolving Global Economy.* Boston: 1995.

Oliveri, E. J. *Latin American Debt and the Politics of International Finance.* Westport, Conn.: 1992.

Oppenheimer, Andres. *Bordering on Chaos: Guerrillas, Stockbrokers, Politicians, and Mexico's Road to Prosperity.* New York: 1996.

Orme, William A., Jr. *Continental Shift: Free Trade and the New North America.* Washington, D.C.: 1993.

Padden, R. C. *The Hummingbird and the Hawk: Conquest and Sovereignty in the Valley of Mexico, 1503–1541.* New York: 1994.

Parkes, Henry B. *A History of Mexico.* Boston: 1960.

Paz, Octavio. *The Labyrinth of Solitude and Other Writings.* New York: 1985.

Poniatowska, Elena. *Massacre in Mexico* (translated from *La Noche de Tlatelolco*). New York: 1975.

Potash, Robert A. *Mexican Government and Industrial Development in the Early Republic.* Amherst: 1983.

Porter, Michael E. *The Competitive Advantage of Nations.* New York: 1990.

Prestowitz, Clyde V. *Trading Places: How We Allowed Japan to Take the Lead.* New York: 1988.

Raat, Dirk W. *Mexico and the United States: Ambivalent Visitors.* Athens: 1992.

Raat, Dirk W. and William H. Beezley (eds.). *Twentieth Century Mexico.* Lincoln: 1988.

Ramirez, Miguel D. *Development Banking in Mexico: The Case of the National Financiera, S.A.* New York: 1986.

Randall, Laura (ed.). *Reforming Mexico's Agrarian Reform.* New York: 1996.

Reavis, Dick J. *Conversations with Moctezuma: The Soul of Modern Mexico.* New York: 1990.

Reynolds, Clark W. *The Mexican Economy: Twentieth Century Structure and Growth.* New Haven: 1970.

Reynolds, Clark W. and Carlos Tello (eds.). *U.S.-Mexico Relations: Economic and Social Aspects.* Stanford: 1983.

Riding, Alan. *Distant Neighbors: A Portrait of the Mexican.* New York: 1985.

———. *Mexico: Inside the Volcano.* London: 1985.

Robert Morris Associates (RMA). *A Guide to the Spreading and Analysis of Mexican Bank Statements.* Philadelphia: 1987.

Roberts, Russell D. *The Choice: The Fable of Free Trade and Protectionism.* Englewood Cliffs: 1994.

Robinson, Harry J. and Timothy G. Smith. *The Impact of Foreign Private Investment on the Mexican Economy.* Stanford Research Institute Project 4110. Menlo Park: January 1976.

Rugman, Alan M. (ed.). *Foreign Investment and NAFTA.* Columbia, S.C.: 1994.

Russell, Philip L. *Mexico under Salinas.* Austin: 1994.

Sanders, Sol. *Mexico: Chaos on Our Doorstep.* Landon, Md.: 1986.

Saragoza, Alex M. *The Monterrey Elite and the Mexican State, 1800–1940.* Austin: 1988.

Schettino, Macario. *El Costo del Miedo: La Devaluacio de 1994–1995.* Mexico, D.F.: 1995.

———. *Tratado de Libre Comercio: Que Es y Como Nos Afecta?* Mexico, D.F.: 1994.

Schmidt, Arthur. *The Social and Economic Effect of the Railroad in Puebla and Veracruz, Mexico, 1867–1911.* New York: 1987.

Seligson, Mitchell A. and Edward J. Williams. *Maquiladoras and Migration: Workers in the Mexico–United States Border Industrial Program.* Austin: 1981.

Sepulveda, Cesar and Albert E. Utton (eds.). *U.S.-Mexico Border Region: Anticipating Resource Needs and Issues to the Year 2000.* El Paso: 1982.

Sepulveda Amor, Bernardo, Olga Pellicer de Brody, and Lorenzo Meyer. *Las Empresas Transnacionales en Mexico.* Mexico, D.F.: 1974.

Simpson, Eyler N. *The Ejido: Mexico's Way Out.* Chapel Hill: 1941.

Smart, Charles Allen. *Viva Juarez! The Founder of Modern Mexico.* New York: 1963.

Stoddard, Ellwyn R. *Maquila: Assembly Plants in Northern Mexico.* El Paso: 1987.

Suchlicki, Jaime. *Mexico from Montezuma to NAFTA, Chiapas and Beyond.* Washington, D.C.: 1996.

Szekely, Gabriel (ed.). *Manufacturing Across Borders and Oceans: Japan, the United States, and Mexico.* Center for U.S.-Mexican Studies. San Diego: 1991.

Tannenbaum, Frank. *The Mexican Agrarian Revolution.* New York: 1929.

Tello, Carlos. *La Nacionalizacion de la Banca en Mexico.* Mexico City: 1984.

———. *La Politica Economica en Mexico, 1970–1976.* Mexico, D.F.: 1979.

Thurow, Lester C. *The Future of Capitalism: How Today's Economic Forces Shape Tomorrow's World.* New York: 1996.

Timmons, W. H. *El Paso: A Borderlands History.* El Paso: 1990.

Twomey, Michael J. *Multinational Corporations and the North American Free Trade Agreement.* Westport, Conn.: 1993.

Tyson, Laura D. *Who's Bashing Whom? Trade Conflict in High-Technology Industries.* Washington, D.C.: 1992.

Valdes, Dennis N. *Al Norte: Agricultural Workers in the Great lakes Region, 1917–1970.* Austin: 1991.

van Ginneken, Wouter. *Socio-economic Groups and Income Distribution*. New York: 1980.

Vernon, Raymond. *The Dilemma of Mexico's Development*. Cambridge, Mass.: 1963.

Vernon, Raymond (ed.). *How Latin America Views the U.S. Investor*. New York: 1966.

Weeks, John R. and Roberto Ham-Chande (eds.). *Demographic Dynamics of the U.S.-Mexico Border*. El Paso: 1992.

Weintraub, Sidney. *Industrial Strategy and Planning in Mexico and the United States*. Boulder: 1986.

————. *A Marriage of Convenience: Relations between Mexico and the United States*. New York: 1990.

————. *Mexican Trade Policy and North American Community*. Washington, D.C.: 1988.

Weintraub, Sidney (ed.). *Free Trade between Mexico and the United States?* Washington, D.C.: 1984.

Whitaker, Daniel. *Mexico 1993: Annual Report with Forecasts through End-1994*. London: 1993.

White, Russell N. *State, Class, and the Nationalization of the Mexican Banks*. New York: 1992.

Whiting, Van R., Jr. *The Political Economy of Foreign Investment in Mexico: Nationalism, Liberalism, and Constraints on Choice*. Baltimore: 1992.

Williams, Edward J. and John T. Passe-Smith. *The Unionization of the Maquiladora Industry: The Tamaulipan Case in National Context*. San Diego: 1992.

Wilson, Patricia A. *Exports and Local Development: Mexico's New Maquiladoras*. Austin: 1992.

Wionczek, Miguel S. and Luciano Tomassini (eds.). *Politics and Economics of External Debt Crisis: The Latin American Experience*. Boulder: 1988.

Womack, John, Jr. *Zapata and the Mexican Revolution*. New York: 1968.

Wyeth, Sally. *Site Selection Handbook*. 1985.

Wyman, Donald L. *The United States Congress and the Making of U.S. Policy toward Mexico*. San Diego: 1981.

Index

ADE (Apoyo Inmediato a los Deudores de la Banca), 126–128
AETNA, 167
American Depository Receipts (ADRs), 73
Argentina: banking system, 138, 141–142, 143–146; capital flight, 141–142, 145; Convertibility Plan, 138, 141–142, 144; comparison with Mexico, 136–138, 140–141, 145, 168; Currency Board, 142, 144; economy, 137–142; exchange controls, 138–139, 143; foreign debt restructuring, 6; foreign investment, 138; impact of the 1994–95 Mexico crisis, 135–147; inflation, 144, 146; member of Mercosur, 136, 168; presidential election (1995), 142; taxation, 143; unemployment, 141
Asia Pacific Economic Cooperation (APEC), 89
Aspe, Pedro, 8, 91, 96, 97, 103, 163
AT&T, 103
Aztec Bonds, 5

Baker, James, 5, 7
Banamex, 23, 69, 81, 92, 94, 98, 123, 125, 127, 164
Banca Cremi, 128

Banca Serfin, 98, 123, 126–128, 164
Banco Atlantico, 126
Banco Bilbao Vizcaya, 128, 166–167
Banco Central de la Republica Argentina, 138
Banco de Mexico, 2, 14, 15, 20, 60, 73; intervention to support the peso, 93, 95–96, 98, 103, 116–117, 125; reaction to peso decline, 92, 95, 97, 112, 122, 140; reserve requirements, 15–16, 124
Banco International (BITAL), 98, 123, 126–128, 166
Banco Mexicano, 98, 123, 127
Banco Obrero, 127
Banco Oriente, 128
Banco Santander, 166
Bancomer, 23, 98, 123, 125, 127, 164, 166, 167
Bancomext, 123
Bancrecer, 126
Bank of America, 168
Bank of Boston, 128, 167
Bank of Canada, 95
Bank of International Settlements (BIS), 102, 115, 117–118, 140
Bank of Montreal, 167
Bank of Nova Scotia, 128, 167
Banks, foreign: debt repayment, 6–7, 9;

direct foreign investment, 19–20, 59–
   61, 128, 167; lending to Mexico, 5, 7,
   19
Banks, Mexico: bad loans, 15, 88, 94, 97,
   98–99, 115, 124–128, 163–167;
   capitalization, 19, 22, 54–55, 59–60,
   62, 125; consolidation, 3, 17, 19, 23,
   92, 164; GAAP introduced, 166–167;
   mark-to-market, 166–167; nationalization, 1, 4–5, 9, 19–21, 70, 123;
   nonbank competition, 15, 21–22, 79;
   privatization, 8–9, 23–26, 55, 67, 73,
   98, 124, 165; underbanked, 25–26
Banks, U.S., 1, 5, 17, 21, 41, 43; application to enter Mexican market, 60–61;
   debt repayment, 5, 7, 20–21; direct
   foreign investment, 128, 167; NAFTA
   capitalization guidelines, 61
Banoro, 126
Banorte, 126
Bentsen, Lloyd, 43, 91, 93, 96–97, 113
Blinder, Alan S., 99
Bolivia, 136
Bolsa Mexicana de Valores, 17, 54, 67–
   68, 73–74; capitalization and invest-
   ment, 68, 72, 81, 90, 92–93, 96, 100,
   123, 127, 155–156; impact of 1994
   devaluation, 113, 116; impact on U.S.
   pension funds, 99, 105, 113–114
Borden, Jose Octavio, 142
Border Environmental Cooperation
   Commission (BECC), 44–45
Border Industrialization Program (BIP),
   34–36
Border Trade Alliance (BTA), 44
Bracero Program, 33–34
Brady, Nicholas, 5
Brady Bonds, 117
Brady Plan, 5–7, 22–23, 56, 143
Brazil, 6, 88, 135, 136, 138, 149, 168
Bufete Industrial, 73, 97, 123
Bulgaria, 6
Bush, George, 58, 136

Calvo Clause, 69
Canada, 52, 56–57, 58, 95, 117, 136, 156
Capital flight, 3–4, 16, 43, 93, 103, 113,
   116, 140

Cardenas, Cuauhtemoc, 57
Castaneda, Jorge G., 13, 33, 118
Cavallo, Domingo, 141–147
Cementos de Mexico (CEMEX), 73, 74,
   97, 123
Certificates of Claim on Net Worth
   (CAPS), 22
CETES (Certificados de la Tesoreria), 3,
   18, 73, 75, 98, 156
Chase Manhattan, 168
Chiapas, 90–91, 98, 103, 169
Chicago Mercantile Exchange, 117, 163
Chile, 135–137, 138, 157, 168
chiveros, 42
Cifra, 73
Citibank, 5, 19, 60, 138, 168
Clinton, Bill, 104; response to 1994
   devaluation, 115–128, 140, 144, 171;
   U.S. Congressional response, 115–118,
   171
CNBC, 96
Colombia, 135–138
Colosio, Luis Donaldo, 53–54, 60; assas-
   sination, 53, 54, 92–93, 95, 102, 113,
   125, 170
Comermex, 123, 126, 128
Confia, 127
Corporacion Industrial San Luis, 123
Costa Rica, 6, 157
Credit Institutions Law, 23–24
Continental Shift (Orme), 82
Cuba, 159
Currency Board, 142, 144; British
   influence, 144–145

Dai-Ichi Kangyo Bank, 40
de la Madrid, Miguel, 21, 22, 36, 70
Debt, Mexico: burden, 6, 9, 19, 22; debt-
   for-equity swaps, 70, 95, 102, 118–119;
   efforts to pay, 9; foreign debt crisis, 5,
   18, 20, 51; foreign reserves, 87, 90;
   LIBOR used, 6; percentage GDP, 22;
   rescheduled, 5–7, 22, 128; Wall Street
   reaction, 112, 115, 169
Diaz, Porfirio, 68–69
Diaz Ordaz, Gustavo, 34
Dina, 73
Distant Neighbors (Riding), 16

Dominican Republic, 6
Dornbusch, Rudiger, 87, 90, 97, 99

Eastern Europe, 82, 157
Echeverria A., Luis, 1, 2, 16, 18
Economist, 112
Economy (Mexico): currency board
  concept, 146; current account deficit,
  88, 90, 93–94, 96, 98, 103, 114, 169–
  171; direct foreign investment, 6–8, 13,
  16, 20, 24, 54, 67–83, 88, 90, 99, 102,
  122, 128, 155–156, 164–165, 169; domestic savings, 90–91; "ejido" land
  system, 13–14, 53, 69; exchange
  controls, 4, 14, 34, 36, 73, 91, 93, 99,
  100, 102, 104–105, 115–117, 138, 160;
  foreign investors, 5–7, 113, 128, 167;
  inflation, 2–4, 6, 9, 14, 16–17, 20–22,
  26, 56, 70, 74, 87–88, 123; impact of
  U.S. interest rates, 90–95, 97, 99, 101,
  121, 170; national debt, 4; nationalism,
  2, 160, 164; neoliberal economic policy, 70, 87, 160; peso devaluations, 3,
  4, 18–20, 22–23, 40, 42–43, 59, 80, 87–
  106, 113–114, 159–161; protection-
  ist/closed economy, 1–2, 13, 19, 51,
  74. *See also* Mexico
Ecuador, 6
El Barzon, 98, 125, 128
El Paso Energy, 78
El Salvador, 157
Emerging Mexico Fund, 74
Enterprise of the Americas, 136
European Community (EC), 55, 57, 61,
  89, 94
Exchange Stabilization Fund (ESF), 117–
  119
Exim Bank, 78
Expropriation Law (1936), 69

Farell, Arsenio, 103
Federal Power Commission of Mexico,
  78
Femsa (Coca-Cola), 97
Fernandez, Eduardo, 124
Fernandez, Roque, 141, 146
Fernandez de Cevallos, Diego, 97
Ferrocarriles Nacionales de Mexico

(FMM), 137
FICORCA (Fideicomiso para la
  Cobertura de Riesgos Cambiarios), 7
Financieras, 2, 15–16
Financial Groups Law (1990), 22
First Mexico Income Fund, 74
First National Bank of Chicago, 167
FOBAPROA (Fondo Bancario de Pro-
  teccion al Ahorro), 125–126, 167
Ford, 38, 72
Foreign Investment Law (1973), 16, 70,
  75–77, 81
Foreign Investment Law (1993), 40, 61–
  62, 71, 74–81; text of law, 181–197
France, 68–69

GAAP (Generally Accepted Accounting
  Principles), 166
GE Capital, 128
Gemex, 73, 123
General Agreement on Tariffs and Trade
  (GATT): background to NAFTA, 8;
  Mexico membership, 7–8, 19, 22, 25–
  26, 41, 44, 55, 89, 136; reduction of
  duties, 7–8; Uruguay Round, 40, 61
General Agreement on Trade in Services
  (GATS), 61
General Electric, 78
General Motors, 38, 72
Generalized System of Preferences (GSP),
  35, 39
Germany, 115, 121
GMAC, 167
Gold Reserve Act (1934), 117
Goldman Sachs, 103
Gould, Jay, 69
Grant, U. S., 69
Great Britain, 68, 69, 115; currency
  boards, 144; Mexican debt restructur-
  ing in 1880's, 69
Greenspan, Alan, 2, 93, 99, 115–116,
  122, 140
Gross Domestic Product (GDP), Mexico,
  88, 91, 128, 164; decline, 7, 9, 22, 114;
  growth, 3, 13, 15, 52, 123; projected,
  100
Groupo Alfa, 103
Groupo Financiero Abaco, 167

Groupo Financiero Cremi-Union, 125
Groupo ICA, 78
Groupo Posadas, 123

Hale, David, 146
Hanke, Steve, 139
Harp Helu, Alfredo, 92
Helms-Burton Act (1996), 159

Import substitution, 13, 18, 34, 51. *See also* Latin America
Institutional Investor, 113
Inter-American Development Bank, 78
International Bank of Commerce, 43
International Monetary Fund (IMF), 87–88, 104, 143; debt restructure, 5–6, 23, 115, 125, 128; as lender of last resort, 144–145, 154, 162–163; Mexican response to, 20–21, 90–91, 95, 115, 116–117, 140, 154, 171; response to assassination of Colosio, 93, 105
Inverlat, 127, 128, 167
Italy, 6, 69

J. P. Morgan, 5, 143, 168
Japan, 6, 39–40, 44, 72, 115, 156, 163
Japanese Economic Institute, 39
Japanese Export-Import Bank, 6
Japanese External Bank, 115
Jones, James, 97
Jordan, 6
Juarez, Benito, 68

Korea, 6, 55

Laredo, Texas, 33, 37–38, 42–43, 52
Laredo National Bank, 43
Latin America: capital flight, 4, 53, 138, 140, 170; domestic savings, 91; import substitution, 14, 136; inflation profile (1990–1996), 137; investment and growth, 54, 70, 73, 82, 113, 123, 135–138, 153, 155, 157, 160, 168–169
Law of Credit Institutions (1974), 3, 17
Law of Invention and Trademarks (1976), 70
Lopez Portillo, Jose, 2, 4–5, 17–18, 20–21

Mancera, Miguel, 103
Maquiladora (twin plants), 33; Asian competition, 38–40; Border Industrialization Program (BIP), 34–36; customs considerations, 35, 40–41; defined, 46 n.12; employment, 35–37, 40–41, 123, 157; growth, 34–37, 40–41, 43–45, 57, 123, 156–157; industrial development, 33, 36–39, 43–44, 76; Japanese investment, 39–40; just-in-time manufacturing, 38; technology transfer, 34, 36, 38, 40, 44, 57, 77, 157; transfer pricing, 157–159; U.S. public response to, 35, 159
Marshall Plan (1948), 171
Menem, Carlos Raul, 137, 138, 142–143, 145–146
Mercantile Bank, 43
Mercosur, 136, 168
Mexican Investment Board (MIB), 79
Mexican Investment Company, 74
Mexico: Constitution of 1917, 23, 69, 76, 77, 120; domestic savings rate, 90–91, 153; exports, 87, 90, 122, 144, 154, 156, 162; foreign exclusion regulations, 70; immigration, 33–34, 38–39; population, 9, 13, 37–38, 42, 52–53; railroads, 68–69, 77, 78, 79, 81, 159, 169; silver production, 69; taxation, 14, 16, 41, 156–159, 163; toll roads, 80; tourism, 36, 77, 80, 122, 123, 157; unemployment, 83, 98. *See also* Economy (Mexico)
Mexico City, 52, 76, 128
Mexico Equity and Income Fund, 74
Mexico Fund, 74
Mexico Shock (Castaneda), 33
Mexico 2000 Council, 67
Ministry of Finance and Public Credit (SHCP), 73
Moody's, 56, 125
Monterrey, Mexico, 52, 76
Mulroney, Brian, 58
Multibanco Comermex, 98

NAFINSA (Nacional Financiera), 15, 16, 18, 81, 123
Nasdaq, 74

National Banking and Securities Commission, 62, 73, 124, 165
National Commission on Foreign Investment (CNIE), 76, 79
National Foreign Investment Registry, 81
New York Stock Exchange, 74
New Zealand, 55–56
Nigeria, 6
North American Development Bank (NADbank), 44
North American Financial Group (NAFG), 95–96
North American Free Trade Agreement (NAFTA), 2, 32, 124; anti-NAFTA groups, 40, 90; Chile, membership, 168–169; implementation, 9, 40, 92, 104, 115; Japanese opposition to, 40; market access, 59–62, 127; Mexico and GATT, 7–8, 25–26; national treatment, 58–59; rules of origin, 39
Norwest Bank, 43

Obregon, Alvaro, 93
Olympics (1968), 14
On the Border (Miller), 32
Organization for Economic Cooperation and Development (OECD), 8, 169; Mexico membership, 22, 55, 89, 141; response to peso crisis, 93–94; transfer pricing guidelines, 158–159
Organization of Petroleum Exporting Countries (OPEC), 1973 oil shock, 3, 19
Ortiz, Guillermo, 97, 104, 116–117, 119, 156, 160, 165

Pact for Stability, Competitiveness and Employment (PECE), 54
Pacto, 100, 102, 105, 139, 163
PAN (National Action Party), 57, 97; electoral victories, 97
Paraguay, 168
Peru, 136, 138, 140
Petrobonds, 18
petrodollars, 5, 115
Petroleos Mexicanos (PEMEX), 18, 77, 137
Petroleum, Mexico: exploration, 68, 76–

77, 79, 120; exports, 36, 42, 83, 121, 156–157, 162; expropriation and nationalization, 69; Mexican oil reserves, 2–3, 18, 120–121; petrochemical sector, 77; pricing, 3, 19; swaps, 21, 119. *See also* OPEC
Philippines, 6
Phillips Curve, 144
Poland, 6
PRI (Partido Revolucionario Institucional), 9, 14, 18, 52, 97; government policy, 6, 53, 159–160
Probursa, 126, 128, 166
PROCAPTE (Programa Emergente de Capitalizacion Temporanea), 127–128
Promex, 126

Regan, Donald, 21
Reich, Robert B., 32
Rubin, Robert, 112, 115, 119, 122
Ruiz Massieu, Jose Francisco, 100

Sachs, Jeffrey, 144
Salinas de Gortari, Carlos, 97; devaluation of 1994, 87–106, 112, 139, 170; Director of Planning (1982–88), 7; presidency, 8, 22–23, 51, 53–55, 58, 75, 87, 96–97, 137; suspends financial operations, 93; World Trade Organization (WTO) directorship, 100, 141; Zapatista uprising, 90
Salinas-Leon, Roberto, 163
Samalayuaca II, 78
Secretariat of Commerce and Industrial Development (SECOFI), 74, 76, 79, 158, 166
Securities Market Law (1975), 3, 17
SEDESOL, 81
Serra-Puche, Jaime, 55, 67, 103, 105, 162; resignation, 140
Shafer, Jeffrey, 104
Silva Herzog, Jesus, 21
Spain, 68–69
Standard & Poor's (S&P), 56, 98, 164
Sumitomo Bank, 40
Summers, Lawrence H., 96–97, 104, 106, 135, 164

Summit of the Americas, 104, 168
Swiss Bank Corporation, 104

Technocrats, 7–9, 88, 160–162
Technology Transfer Law (1973), 70
Telefonos de Mexico (Telmex), 73, 74, 103
Televisa, 73
Tellez, Luis, 103
Tello, Carlos, 20
"Tequila effect," 89, 113, 135, 140–141,
    143, 144, 157
Tesobonos, 73, 75, 88, 91, 95, 98–99,
    104–105, 114, 117, 122, 141, 156
Thailand, 90
Tribasa, 73, 97

UDI (Unidades de Inversiones), 127
United Nations, 40
Uruguay, 6, 142, 168
Uruguay Round (GATT), 61
U.S.-Canadian Free Trade Agreement, 57–
    59
U.S. Federal Reserve, 5, 15, 18, 21, 60,
    90–91; concern about Mexico default-
    ing on debt, 99; currency swaps
    (bridge loans), 21, 118–119; Federal
    Open Market Committee (FOMA), 95;
    oil reserve account at New York Fed,
    128; response to peso crisis, 2, 95–99,
    100, 102, 104, 140

U.S. International Trade Commission,
    41
U.S. Treasury, 5, 18, 90; response to
    peso crisis, 93–102, 115, 117–122,
    140

Value-added tax (VAT), 122, 143, 163
Venezuela, 6, 135–136, 138, 157, 168
Veracruz, 113
Vitro, 73, 97
Volcker, Paul, 21

World Bank, 5–6, 23, 115, 117, 125,
    140, 143, 162, 168, 171

Yacimientos Petroliferos Fiscales (YPF),
    143

Zabludovsky, Jaime, 162
Zapata National Liberation Army
    (EZLN), 90
Zapatista uprising, 90. See also Chiapas
Zedillo Ponce de Leon, Ernesto:
    FICORCA director (1983), 7; fiscal
    policies, 123; on 1994 devaluation,
    112, 116–117, 118, 120, 123; presi-
    dency, 56, 93, 96–96, 99, 163, 169;
    response to peso crisis, 99–106, 139–
    140, 146, 153–154, 164

About the Author

JOHN A. ADAMS, JR., is First Vice President and Manager of Private Banking at the Norwest Bank in Laredo. He holds a Ph.D. from Texas A & M University, is a graduate of the American-Nicaraguan School in Managua, and completed the Southwestern Graduate School of Banking at Southern Methodist University with honors. Dr. Adams was named National Exporter of the Year by the U.S. Small Business Administration, and is Vice Chairman of the Industry Sector Advisory Council for trade and policy review at the U.S. Department of Commerce. He is the author of three books and speaks regularly at international trade conferences worldwide.